A Student Grammar of Spanish

A Student Grammar of Spanish is a concise introduction to Spanish grammar, designed for English-speaking undergraduates. Assuming no prior knowledge of grammatical terminology, it explains each aspect of Spanish grammar in clear and simple terms, provides a wealth of glossed examples to illustrate them, and helps students to put their learning into practice through a range of fun and engaging exercises.

Clearly organized into thirty units, each covering a different aspect of the grammar, the book functions both as an essential reference guide and as a comprehensive workbook. Individual topics can be looked up via a user-friendly cross-referencing system, and concise definitions are provided in a useful glossary of grammatical terms. The exercises, which include paired and group activities, are suitable for both classroom use and self-study. Each unit is split into two levels, basic and intermediate, making this grammar the perfect accompaniment to any first- or second-year undergraduate course.

Ronald E. Batchelor has now retired from the University of Nottingham, where he taught French and Spanish for forty years. He has also held teaching posts at the universities of Besançon, France, and Valencia, Spain. He has published ten books, including *Using Spanish: A Guide to Contemporary Usage* (with Chris Pountain), *Using Spanish Synonyms*, *Using Spanish Vocabulary*, *Using French* and *Using French Synonyms* (all published by Cambridge University Press).

A Student Grammar of
Spanish

RONALD E. BATCHELOR

CAMBRIDGE
UNIVERSITY PRESS

CAMBRIDGE UNIVERSITY PRESS
Cambridge, New York, Melbourne, Madrid, Cape Town, Singapore, São Paulo

Cambridge University Press
The Edinburgh Building, Cambridge CB2 2RU, UK

Published in the United States of America by Cambridge University Press, New York

www.cambridge.org
Information on this title: www.cambridge.org/9780521670777

First published 2006

Printed in the United Kingdom at the University Press, Cambridge

A catalogue record for this book is available from the British Library

Library of Congress Cataloguing in Publication data
Batchelor, R. E. (Ronald Ernest)
A student grammar of Spanish / Ronald E. Batchelor.
    p.   cm.
Includes bibliographical references and index.
ISBN-10: 0-521-67077-2 (paperback)
ISBN-13: 978-0-521-67077-7 (paperback)
1. Spanish language – Grammar.   2. Spanish language – Textbooks for foreign speakers – English.   I. Title.
PC4112.B385   2006
468.2′421 – dc22   2005012927

ISBN-13   978-0-521-67077-7 paperback
ISBN-10   0-521-67077-2 paperback

Contents (*Índice de materias*)

Preface   *page* vii

Acknowledgments   x

Glossary of grammatical terms   xi

Note on the text   xix

Short bibliography   xx

1   Alphabet, spelling and pronunciation
    (*Alfabeto, ortografía y pronunciación*)   1

2   Definite and indefinite articles and gender
    of nouns (*Artículos definidos e indefinidos y género de
    sustantivos*)   10

3   Number (*El plural*)   32

4   Verbs (*Los verbos*)   40

5   Perfect tense and pluperfect tense (*El [pretérito]
    perfecto y el pluscuamperfecto / antecopretérito* [**M**])   46

6   Future tense and future perfect tense (*El tiempo futuro y el
    futuro perfecto*)   53

7   Imperfect tense (*El tiempo imperfecto/copretérito* [**M**])   58

8   Preterit tense or past definite (*El pretérito
    indefinido / pretérito perfecto simple*)   63

9   Conditional tense (*El tiempo condicional*)   71

10 Progressive tense or gerund (*El tiempo progresivo
    o el gerundio*)   75

11 The imperative mood (*El modo imperativo*)   81

12 Irregular verbs (*Los verbos irregulares*)   89

13 *Ser* and *estar* (*Ser y estar*)   97

Contents

14 Transitive and intransitive verbs, and
reflexive verbs (*Los verbos transitivos e intransitivos, y los verbos
reflexivos*)   107

15 Impersonal verbs (*Los verbos impersonales*)   119

16 Subjunctive (*El subjuntivo*)   129

17 Personal pronouns (*Los pronombres personales*)   154

18 Possessive adjectives and pronouns, relative
and interrogative pronouns (*Los adjetivos y pronombres
posesivos, los pronombres relativos e interrogativos*)   166

19 Indefinite pronouns (*Los pronombres indefinidos*)   176

20 Demonstrative adjectives and pronouns (*Los
adjetivos y pronombres demostrativos*)   183

21 Adjectives (*Los adjetivos*)   189

22 Personal or distinctive *a* (*La preposición a con
el complemento directo*)   198

23 Prepositions (*Las preposiciones*)   205

24 Prepositions *por* and *para* (*Las preposiciones por y
para*)   220

25 Adverbs (*Los adverbios*)   227

26 Interrogative and negative sentences (*Las frases
interrogativas y negativas*)   238

27 Numbers and measurements. Time and
dimensions (*Los números y las medidas. El tiempo [duración = la
hora] y las dimensiones*)   246

28 Comparatives and superlatives (*Los comparativos y
superlativos*)   261

29 Word order (*El orden de las palabras*)   269

30 Augmentatives and diminutives (*Los aumentativos
y diminutivos*)   278

Model answers / Soluciones y modelos   285

Index of grammar and vocabulary   319

Subjunctive index   329

Preface

According to the very latest estimates (2004), Spanish is the native tongue of well over 350 million people, 100 million of whom live in Mexico and 24 million in the USA. It is therefore a major world language, the fourth largest in terms of speakers. Its study thus offers all students a meaningful and attractive prospect of establishing contact with a very wide range of Spanish speakers coming from numerous countries. Any student of Spanish will benefit, both personally and culturally, from communication with such a vast array of people bound together by a common language. Spanish as a mother tongue unites countries as far apart as New York or London are from Pekin, but distance does not necessarily entail intractable difference. Surprising as it may seem, it is often as easy for an English-speaking student of Spanish to understand the Spanish of Mexico, Argentina, Colombia, Peru or Ecuador as it is for an English or American person to understand the language of some parts of Scotland, for instance, or for a Spanish speaker to understand the language of some regions of Andalucía.

Any learner of Spanish will need, certainly in the early stages of contact with the language, a grammar book which assists her/him through the initial maze. Such a volume needs to appeal both to the beginner and to the student who has acquired some basic knowledge. The present book is designed precisely to cater for these differing needs, while bearing in mind the North American reader and his/her British counterpart. Furthermore, it must aim to include both Iberian Spanish and the Spanish of the Americas. This balancing act is not as delicate as it may first appear. Long experience has taught the present author that there is much more in the field of Spanish grammar that brings Spanish speakers together than separates them, while the differences between the English of the United Kingdom and of the United States need not be exaggerated.

This book on Spanish grammar has therefore a general appeal which deals with most aspects of the grammar in a straightforward and uncomplicated way. It treats the grammatical structures of Spanish as expressed in Spain and Mexico. Mexico is taken as a model for the whole of Spanish America, since to attempt a comprehensive coverage of all Spanish America would serve little purpose, especially since the grammar, as apart from vocabulary, of Spanish differs little from one country to another. Mexican Spanish is one of the standard variants, partly due to the exportation of movies and *telenovelas* (soap operas), while it is unquestionably the most prevalent variety found in the South West of the United States. **M** indicates that the word or structure is specifically Mexican while it may be confidently assumed that, where **M** does not appear, usage is Iberian but will be understood and even used in Mexico, as well as in most of the other Spanish-speaking countries in the Americas. A simple illustration of a Mexican alternative may be seen in some of the headings to exercises where *to fill in blank spaces* is translated as **rellenar los blancos** for Iberian Spanish and **llenar los espacios** for Mexican Spanish.

This volume covers all major grammatical points of Spanish in a user-friendly and direct way, and recognizes that humor is part of the learning process. You'll learn much more if you study with a smile, while Mexicans lead the way in the field of humor. The present author learnt a lot from Cantinflas, the Mexican comedian.

All the points are presented in an easily accessible way, and are reinforced, at every phase and after each level, by exercises, while suggested solutions to these exercises can be found at the end of the book. Some exercises are short, some much longer, and some involve the student in role play, a well-tried method for developing linguistic skills, and in games such as puzzles. A fun element is central to the concept and genesis of the book.

There are paired or group exercises in both levels of nearly every unit. They encourage you to use and speak Spanish. You'll be surprised how much progress you make by insisting on speaking the language. It is difficult to suggest the amount of time needed for these particular exercises since the author does not want to be prescriptive. Often, a time of five minutes is suggested for preparing yourself for the exercise but teachers/instructors have their constraints.

All the exercises in level 1 have instructions in English. To reflect the more advanced work in level 2, the instructions are in Spanish.

Naturally enough, the exercises are more demanding and challenging in the second level than in the first. But the key is there to help you out. Of course, use the key wisely. Don't take a peek at the answers until you have really tried to deal with the exercise in question.

Examples are often presented in the feminine form. The text avoids sexist bias and reaches out to females and males alike. The treatment of each grammatical area follows a very clear pattern. Basic points are covered, logically, at the beginning, and are separated off from the more advanced grammatical features. The book is thus divided into two levels by an image where the climbing of stairs representing letters suggests more progressive work.

It should be emphasized that the present work is a self-help book, and does not require the constant presence of, or reference to, a teacher. Furthermore, constant cross-referencing should help the student to gain a clear and more rounded picture of all the grammatical points.

American English takes precedence over British English. American spelling is preferred to its English counterpart but this should present no problem whatever to the non-American learner. Where there could be lexical misinterpretation, both American and British terms appear side by side.

The book contains a "Glossary of grammatical terms" which will help you understand any semi-technical grammatical expressions you may have difficulty with. Use this glossary regularly to familiarize yourself with the terms used in the text. It is so much easier to come to grips with the grammar of a foreign language if you gain some insight into the way that even the English language functions.

The text also has a comprehensive index designed to direct you to any particular point of grammar or vocabulary you wish to consult.

The book is up-to-date. For instance, you will come across a section on the problems of gender now that females are working in fields once inaccessible to them. Compound nouns, once unusual in Spanish, except for just a few, are springing up like mushrooms, and the text pays serious attention to them.

The word "grammar" often has a daunting resonance, but it is by making your way through the intricate web of grammatical structures and conquering the foreign way in which Spanish speakers express themselves, that you will not only derive intellectual satisfaction from your achievements but also emotional enjoyment from what is, in the final analysis, the desire to establish a permanent and worthwhile association with a dominant world culture.

Acknowledgments

I am deeply indebted to Dr. J. Pérez Larracilla, Mexican colleague and friend, for his sure and indigenous knowledge of Mexican Spanish and his permanent willingness to offer me advice and information whenever needed.

The book has also greatly benefited from the myriad comments and suggestions of my colleague Dr. Tim McGovern.

Let us not forget all the Spanish speakers who have patiently and accurately responded over the years to a continual bombardment of questions.

However hard I try, and I have tried numerous times, I cannot produce a perfect text. But help is always at hand in the form of my copy-editor, Leigh Mueller, who has performed her customary and exemplary trick of ironing out all my inconsistencies and improving on the presentation of the work.

Glossary of grammatical terms

ACCENT	Sign written over a letter, often a VOWEL, at least in Spanish, e.g. *café*, *corrió* (ran), *España* (here over a consonant, see TILDE), *averigüe* (may check) (see DIERESIS). ACCENT is often confused with STRESS. See STRESS
ADJECTIVE	A word that describes a NOUN. It agrees with the noun it qualifies, e.g. *una casa hermosa, nubes grises, un chico alto* (a lovely house, grey clouds, a tall boy)
ADJECTIVE, DEMONSTRATIVE	An ADJECTIVE that points to something, e.g. *este hombre, **esa** mujer, **aquella** casa, **aquellas** calles* (this man, that woman, that house, those streets)
ADVERB	A word or group of words that modify a VERB, ADJECTIVE or another ADVERB, e.g. *Puedo hacerlo **fácilmente*** (I can do it easily), *Este pan es **muy** bueno* (This bread is very good)
AGENT	The person or thing performing the action indicated by the VERB, e.g. *El **gato** atacó al perro* (The cat attacked the dog). Here the agent is the cat, as in the following example: *El perro fue atacado por el **gato*** (The dog was attacked by the cat)
AGREEMENT	**There are three kinds of AGREEMENT in Spanish. 1. AGREEMENT in number.** ADJECTIVES, VERBS and ARTICLES agree with the NOUNS and PRONOUNS they relate to, e.g. *La chica lista **hace** sus **deberes**.* 2. **Gender AGREEMENT.** ADJECTIVES agree with the NOUN they qualify, e.g. *un chico alto, una chica guapa* 3. **AGREEMENT of TENSE.** A correspondence of TENSES is often, but not always, required in Spanish, e.g. *Yo **quería** que mi hermano me **ayudara** (I wanted my brother to help me), Le **he dicho** que iré (I have told him/her that I will go), Le **dije** que iría (I told her/him I would go)* (see "GUIDANCE ON VERBS")
ANTECEDENT	A word or PHRASE to which a PRONOUN refers. The word or PHRASE always precedes the PRONOUN, e.g. *The boy who lives down the road is a genius.* **Boy** is the ANTECEDENT of **who**. When the ANTECEDENT is unclear or indeterminate, the following VERB is very often in the SUBJUNCTIVE MOOD

APOCOPATION	Shortening of some ADJECTIVES when they immediately precede a NOUN, e.g. *un* **buen** (from **bueno**) *café* (good coffee), *un* **mal** (from **malo**) *vino* (bad wine)
APPOSITION	Two words placed side by side, so that the second word modifies the first, e.g. *Madrid,* **capital** *de España.* It may be said that **capital** is in APPOSITION to **Madrid**
ARTICLE, DEFINITE	Word which, when placed in front of a NOUN, determines it by giving it GENDER and NUMBER, e.g. **el** *padre,* **la** *madre,* **los** *padres,* **las** *madres.* English equivalent is the easier, all-purpose **the**
ARTICLE, INDEFINITE	Determines a NOUN when placed in front of it, but less precise than the DEFINITE ARTICLE, e.g. **un** *coche,* **una** *mesa,* **unos** *coches,* **unas** *mesas.* The English equivalent is **a** and **some**
AUGMENTATIVE	Letters added to the end of a word to indicate an increase in size, or an unpleasant or frightening appearance, e.g. *cas**ona*** (large, stately house), *pic**acho*** (large, towering peak), *cas**ucha*** (ugly, unpleasant house, hovel)
CLAUSE	Words forming part of a sentence, containing a FINITE VERB
CLAUSE, MAIN	A CLAUSE that can stand alone as a sentence, e.g. *Bajé las escaleras* (I went down the stairs)
CLAUSE, SUBORDINATE	A CLAUSE in a sentence that depends on a MAIN CLAUSE to make sense, e.g. *Fui al mercado antes de que llegara mi hermano* (I went to the market before my brother arrived). **Fui al mercado** is the MAIN CLAUSE while **antes de que llegara mi hermano** is the SUBORDINATE CLAUSE
COMPARISON	Applies to ADJECTIVES and ADVERBS that are modified to convey greater or lesser intensity, e.g. **mejor**, **peor**, **menos/más** *listo* (better, worse, less/more intelligent)
COMPLEMENT	Word, PHRASE, or CLAUSE that completes the meaning of a sentence: **a genius** is the complement of *She is* **a genius**. **He would be early** is the complement of *I hoped* **he would be early**
CONJUGATION	Model followed by VERB forms. There are three regular CONJUGATIONS in Spanish: *habl**ar***, *com**er***, *viv**ir***. Unfortunately, for us foreigners, there are numerous IRREGULAR VERBS which include RADICAL/STEM CHANGING VERBS. IRREGULAR VERBS can confuse Spanish speakers, especially children, so we are not alone

CONJUNCTION	Any word or group of words, but not a RELATIVE PRONOUN, that connects words or PHRASES, e.g. *Tomé el primer plato y el segundo, pero no el postre* (I had the first course **and** the second **but** not the dessert)
CONSONANT	A speech sound or letter other than a VOWEL, e.g. *b, c, d*
DIERESIS	Orthographical sign placed above *u* > *ü* in the SYLLABLES *gui* and *gue*. This produces a pronunciation of two SYLLABLES of two distinct VOWEL sounds where normally you have a DIPHTHONG, e.g. *cigüeña*
DIMINUTIVE	Letters added to the end of a word to indicate the meaning of "small." It often conveys an affectionate tone. The Mexicans are fond of DIMINUTIVES, even more than the Spaniards, e.g. *golpecito* (tap, small blow), *mesilla* (small, bed-side table)
DIPHTHONG	A VOWEL sound, occupying a single SYLLABLE, and containing up to two VOWELS, e.g. *aire, caigo*
GENDER	What distinguishes NOUNS as well as PRONOUNS. All NOUNS and PRONOUNS have a GENDER, not just male and female human beings and animals, e.g. *el chico* (the boy), *la chica* (the girl), *el sol* (the sun), *la luna* (the moon), *lo/le* veo (I see him), *la* veo (I see her). AGREEMENT must be made between the NOUN and ADJECTIVE or PAST PARTICIPLE, except when used to form the PERFECT TENSES, with *haber*)
INTERJECTION	Words that express an exclamation and denote any strong emotion, e.g. *¡Dios mío!, ¡Híjole!* (**M**) (Jeez!, Wow!, Gee!)
LANGUAGE, FIGURATIVE	Language that uses a figure of speech, e.g. *Luchó como un león* (She fought like a lion), *izar la bandera de la libertad* (to raise the standard of freedom)
NOUN	A word used to name a person, thing or concept. NOUNS can be concrete (*hombre* [man], *coche* [car]) or abstract (*alegría* [joy], *malestar* [uneasiness])
NUMBER, CARDINAL	A NUMBER which enables us to count *Uno, dos, tres . . .*
NUMBER, ORDINAL	A NUMBER indicating order in which things appear. *Primero, segundo, tercero . . .* (First, second, third . . .)
PERSONAL "A"	Used before a direct object that is a well-known person or pet animal, e.g. *Vi a Juana / a tu perro* (I saw Juana / your dog). Causes great awkwardness

	to Spanish speakers for they frequently think that it involves an indirect object as in *(Le) Doy el libro a Juan* (I give the book to Juan)
PHRASE	A meaningful group of words in a sentence, that does not contain a finite VERB, e.g. *en el jardín* (in the yard/garden), *por la calle* (down the street). Don't be confused by the Spanish *frase* which means both sentence and PHRASE
PREFIX	SYLLABLE or SYLLABLES attached to the front of a word, e.g. *antirracista, anticonstitucional*
PREPOSITION	A word that usually comes before a NOUN. It expresses the relation of things to each other in respect of time and place, e.g. *con mi amigo, Voy a México, a las seis, en la mesa, sobre la silla, bajo el árbol, Viene de Arizona*
PRONOUN, DEMONSTRATIVE	PRONOUN that indicates something. *Éste es bueno, aquélla es mala* (This one is good, that one is bad). The written ACCENT is not necessary but careful writers prefer it
PRONOUN, INTERROGATIVE	PRONOUN involving a QUESTION, e.g. *¿Quién ha ganado el premio?* (Who has won the prize?). Other INTERROGATIVE PRONOUNS are *¿cuál?* (which?), *¿qué?* (*what?*), *¿cuyo?* (whose?), *¿cuánto?* (how much?)
PRONOUN, PERSONAL	A word that replaces a NOUN. There are two kinds of PERSONAL PRONOUNS, subject, and direct and indirect object PRONOUNS, e.g. *Yo, tú, él, ella, Ud., nosotros/as, vosotros/as, Uds.* (I, you, he, etc.) are subject PRONOUNS. *Me, te, lo/le, la, nos, os, los/les* and *las* (me, you, him, her, it, us, you, them) are direct object PRONOUNS while, *me, te, le, nos, os, les* (*to* me, you, him, her, it, us, you, them) are indirect object PRONOUNS. E.g. *Yo la veo* (I see her/it), *yo os/los* (**M**) *veo* (I see you), *Yo le doy el coche* (I give him/her/you the car)
PRONOUN, POSSESSIVE	A PRONOUN indicating possession, e.g. *el mío / la mía, el tuyo / la tuya, el suyo / la suya, el nuestro / la nuestra, el vuestro / la vuestra, el suyo / la suya* (mine, yours, etc.). *¿Dónde está la mía?* (Where's mine?)

PRONOUN, RELATIVE	Links a relative CLAUSE to what precedes it, e.g. *Vi al chico* **que** *vino ayer* (I saw the boy **who** came yesterday). Other relative pronouns are **el que**, **quien**, **el cual**
QUESTION, DIRECT	A sentence asking a straight QUESTION, e.g. *¿Adónde vas?* (Where are you going?)
QUESTION, INDIRECT	QUESTION included in a SUBORDINATE CLAUSE, e.g. *Me preguntó* **adónde iba** (She asked me where I was going)
SESEO	Pronunciation of the Spanish *z* and *c* before *e/i* as if they were an *s* as in *soft*. The *c* is pronounced as the *th* in *thick* is pronounced, but only by a relatively small number of people, in central and northern Spain. The whole of Spanish America and Andalucía are characterized by the ***SESEO***
SINGULAR/PLURAL	A SINGULAR NOUN refers to one object while a PLURAL NOUN refers to more than one, e.g. *el árbol / los árboles* (the tree / the trees)
STEM	Root form of a word, e.g. **compr** is the stem of the VERB **comprar** or the NOUNS **compra** and **comprador**
STRESS/STRESSED SYLLABLE	The SYLLABLE of a word spoken most loudly or most forcibly. STRESS is crucial to meaning in both Spanish and English. Compare **hablo** (I speak) with **habló** (he spoke), and both *invalids* in *The invalid had an invalid ticket*. Not to be confused with ACCENT
SUFFIX	SYLLABLE or SYLLABLES attached to the end of a word. These are often AUGMENTATIVES and DIMINUTIVES, e.g. *hombr***ón**, *jardin***cito**, *mes***illa**
SUPERLATIVE	Applies to ADJECTIVES and ADVERBS that are modified to the greatest or least intensity, e.g. *Es la* **mejor/peor** *estudiante* (She is the best/worst student)
SYLLABLE	A combination or set of units of sound. It always contains a VOWEL. **Voy** contains one SYLLABLE. **Iba** contains two SYLLABLES and **íbamos** contains three SYLLABLES
TILDE	The orthographic sign over the ***n*** > ***ñ*** that changes the sound. The ***n*** of **pino** has the English sound ***n*** as in **pine**, while the ***ñ*** of **niño** has the English sound ***ni*** as in **pinion**. Most Spanish speakers refer to the *ñ* as a TILDE, although, strictly speaking, the TILDE is the sign over the ***n***. TILDE also refers to any written ACCENT over a VOWEL, e.g. *rompí* (I broke), *ganó* (she/he/you won)
TRIPHTHONG	Three VOWELS forming a single SYLLABLE. Contains two weak VOWELS (*i*, *u*) and one strong (*a*, *e*, *o*), e.g. *camb***iái***s*, *aprec***iéi***s*
VOWEL	The sounds of a language that are not classified as CONSONANTS, and which, in the case of Spanish, can form a SYLLABLE. Spanish has five VOWELS: ***a***, ***e***, ***i***, ***o***, ***u***

Guidance on verbs

AGREEMENT	Correspondence between masculine and feminine NOUNS and part of the VERB, and between the PLURAL of NOUNS and correct form of the VERB, e.g. *Está sentada* (She is sitting down), *Los chicos* jugan *en la calle* (The boys are playing in the street)
AUXILIARY	An AUXILIARY VERB which helps to form a COMPOUND TENSE or precedes an INFINITIVE. In the sentence *He leído el libro*, *He* is the AUXILIARY VERB. In the sentence *Voy a ver una película*, *Voy* is the AUXILIARY VERB
COMPOUND TENSE	TENSE made up of the verb *haber* and a PAST PARTICIPLE, e.g. *He/ había/ habría* [etc.] *andado/ hablado/ escrito*
CONDITIONAL	Includes a condition and a result, e.g. *Si me das* el dinero, *compraré* el pan (If you give me the money, I'll buy the bread), *Si me hubieras dado* el dinero, (yo) *hubiera/ habría comprado* el pan (If you had given me the money, I would have bought the bread)
CONTINUOUS/ PROGRESSIVE	A compound VERB made up of the VERB *estar* (to be) and a PRESENT PARTICIPLE, e.g. *Estoy leyendo* el libro (I am reading the book), *Estaba preparando* la comida (I was preparing the meal). *Ir* is sometimes used in this way, e.g. *Va amaneciendo* (It's starting to get light), *El camino* **iba bajando** (The path kept going down)
FINITE VERB	The form of a VERB which is not the INFINITIVE, e.g. *corre/ corriendo* (he runs/running), *leo/ leyendo* (I read/reading), *hablamos/ hablando* (we speak/ speaking)
FUTURE PERFECT	TENSE that refers to a future event that will have happened before a given moment, e.g. *Habremos llegado* antes de que salga (We will have arrived before she leaves)
FUTURE TENSE	TENSE referring to the future, e.g. *Iré* (I'll go)
GERUND	Spanish VERB form ending in *-ando, -iendo, -yendo*, like *-ing* in English, e.g. *andando* (walking), *corriendo* (running), *yendo* (going), *leyendo* (reading)
HISTORIC PRESENT	Present TENSE used to invest a description or narration with a greater vividness: *Yo caminaba tranquilamente en el bosque, y ¡fíjate! veo a mi gran amigo que me dice que* . . . (I was wandering through the wood when – imagine it! – I see/saw my great friend who tells/told me that . . .)
IMPERATIVE	Part of the VERB which conveys a command, e.g. *¡habla!* (speak!), *¡vete!* (go away!), *¡come!* (eat!)
IMPERFECT	TENSE indicating a continuous or repeated action in the past, e.g. *Yo jugaba (al) fútbol* (I used to play / was playing / would play / played football)

INFINITIVE	Part of a VERB which does not change, and which you always find in dictionaries, e.g. *vivir* (to live), **andar** (to walk), **ver** (to see)
INTRANSITIVE	A VERB that does not have a direct object or COMPLEMENT. *Ir* (to go) and **venir** (to come) are INTRANSITIVE VERBS. See TRANSITIVE
IRREGULAR VERB	A VERB that does not conform to a pattern. Very troublesome for foreign learners and Spanish-speaking children. *Ir* and **ser** are such VERBS. Interestingly and understandably enough, small Spanish children try to "regularize" IRREGULAR VERBS, as often happens in English. No examples given here!
MOOD, INDICATIVE	Part of a VERB which makes a clear statement, e.g. **Está** *listo* (He's ready), *Me* **gusta** *el chocolate* (I like chocolate)
MOOD, SUBJUNCTIVE	Part of a VERB which indicates emotion, pleasure, fear, uncertainty, doubt. It is usually used in a SUBORDINATE CLAUSE, but not always. Has nearly disappeared in English (e.g., *It is possible he* **be** *right*), but very common in all TENSES in Spanish and Italian, becoming less common in French where the imperfect SUBJUNCTIVE is very infrequent. E.g. *Es posible que* **tenga** *razón* (It's possible she is/be right), *Era imposible que* **tuviera** *razón* (It was impossible that she was right)
PAST ANTERIOR	TENSE made up of the PRETERIT of *haber* and a PAST PARTICIPLE, e.g. *Cuando* **hubo llegado**, *fuimos juntos al* . . . (When she had arrived, we went . . . together). This TENSE is only used in elevated language, novels, etc. The TENSE in common discourse is the PLUPERFECT
PAST PARTICIPLE	Part of the VERB which, in conjunction with the VERB *haber*, makes up the PERFECT TENSE, e.g. **he andado / hablado** (I have walked/spoken)
PERFECT TENSE	COMPOUND TENSE made up of **haber** and PAST PARTICIPLE, e.g. *He visto* (I have seen). Much less used in Spanish America, where it is replaced by the PRETERIT. See "Verbs," Unit 5
PLUPERFECT	TENSE formed by IMPERFECT of **haber** (**había**) and the PAST PARTICIPLE, e.g. *cuando* **habíamos hablado** (when we had spoken)
PRESENT PARTICIPLE	Name given to the part of the VERB ending in **-ing** in English and in **-ando** and **-iendo** in Spanish, e.g. *habl***ando** (speaking), *com***iendo** (eating)
PRETERIT	Simple past TENSE. Refers to a specific or completed action in the past. Almost entirely replaces the past perfect in Spanish America (see "Verbs," Unit 5),

e.g. ***fui*** (I went/was), ***hablé*** (I spoke), ***llegaron*** (*they arrived*). British English spelling PRETERITE

PRONOMINAL VERB
A VERB that is conjugated in all its forms with the PRONOUNS ***me***, ***te***, ***se***, ***nos***, ***os***. This means that the subject and the reflexive PRONOUN are the same person, e.g. *Yo **me veo** en el espejo* (I see myself in the mirror), ***Me rasuro*** (***M***) **/ *me afeito*** *con la máquina* (I shave with the electric razor)

RADICAL/STEM CHANGING VERB
A VERB that is REGULAR in its endings but does not fit an obvious pattern so that Spaniards call them IRREGULAR. These verbs are "irregular" because the stressed VOWEL changes in certain parts of the VERB, e.g. *querer – qui**e**ro, qui**e**res, qui**e**re, queremos, queréis, qui**e**ren / contar – c**ue**nto, c**ue**ntas, c**ue**nta, contamos, contáis, c**ue**ntan*. Can cause difficulty, especially in the imperfect SUBJUNCTIVE. It could be legitimately argued that these VERBS are not IRREGULAR since they do conform to a specific pattern. The English description RADICAL / STEM CHANGING is much more helpful than IRREGULAR. See "Irregular verbs," Unit 12

REFLEXIVE
A VERB conveying an action done by a person or thing to himself/itself, e.g. ***Me lavo*** (I wash (myself)), *El sol **se esconde** detrás de las nubes* (The sun hides behind the clouds). The English does not have a REFLEXIVE form in the second case but it is necessary in Spanish. Otherwise, you would be wondering what the sun was hiding. There are many VERBS that behave both non-reflexively and reflexively in Spanish

REGULAR VERB
A VERB that conforms to a pattern. Very reassuring for foreign learners, and Spanish-speaking children. ***Hablar***, ***comer*** and ***vivir*** are REGULAR VERBS.

TENSE
Part of the VERB which indicates the moment when an action or thought takes place, e.g. ***nado*** is the present TENSE of the VERB ***nadar***. ***Nadaba*** is the IMPERFECT TENSE of the VERB ***nadar***

TRANSITIVE
A VERB that takes a direct object, e.g. ***Veo*** *la puerta* (I see the door). See INTRANSITIVE

VOICE, ACTIVE/PASSIVE
The ACTIVE VOICE relates to the subject of the sentence performing the action. The sentence *The boy broke the window* is in the ACTIVE VOICE, whereas *The window was broken by the boy* is in the PASSIVE VOICE. A VERB in the ACTIVE VOICE can be TRANSITIVE or INTRANSITIVE but a VERB in the PASSIVE VOICE can only be TRANSITIVE

Note on the text

Most translations of either whole sentences, phrases or individual words are given when it is felt that they are necessary for an accurate understanding of the grammar under consideration. However, in quite a few cases, for example, *inteligencia*, a translation is not given, whereas *celo* (**zeal**) would be.

Abbreviations

JPR Jorge Pérez Larracilla
M Mexican (Spanish)

Short bibliography

If you wish to progress beyond the confines of this basic volume, you will find the following useful.

Grammars

Alarcos Llorach, Emilio, *Gramática de la lengua española*, Real Academia Española, Madrid: Espasa, 2003 (Very comprehensive but for Spanish speakers, and not presented in tabular form so finding what you want can be time consuming.)
Butt, J., *Spanish Grammar*, Oxford: Oxford University Press, 2000
Butt and Benjamin, *A New Reference Grammar of Modern Spanish*, London: Arnold, 2001 (Very comprehensive and for the most advanced students among you.)
Kattán-Ibarra and Pountain, *Modern Spanish Grammar*, London: Routledge, 1997
Maqueo, Ana María, *Español para extranjeros* (3 volumes), México: Limusa, Noriega Editores, 2002 (Excellent work but very diffuse, presented from a Mexican point of view, and in this sense very useful, notably for North American speakers of English.)

Verb forms

Kendris, *501 Spanish Verbs*, New York: Barron's Educational Series, 2000
Rosario Hollis, María, *Spanish Verbs*, Teach Yourself Books, London: Hodder and Stoughton, 1994

Note. The present book does not include all the verb tables, for reasons of space. It is recommended that you acquire one of these two above.

Usage

Batchelor, R. and Pountain, C., *Using Spanish*, Cambridge: Cambridge University Press, 1994; 2nd edition, 2005 (This book has a concise section on Spanish grammar but also includes numerous chapters on vocabulary and the way the language is used. This includes register, or levels of language.)

Dictionaries

The Oxford Spanish Dictionary, Oxford / New York: Oxford University Press, 2000 (Excellent coverage of Spanish American, but you need to be a little wary since Spanish American is so diffuse.)

Spanish English English Spanish Dictionary, Glasgow: Harper Collins, 2001 (Every bit as good as the dictionary above.)

Simon and Schuster Spanish–English English–Spanish Dictionary, New York: Simon and Schuster, 1998 (Again, as good as the two above.)

Larousse Gran Diccionario, Español–Francés Français–Espagnol, Barcelona: Larousse, 2002 (Very good dictionary but not so comprehensive as the three above. However, it is extremely helpful for those of you who are aspiring to two languages or more.)

Of all the monolingual dictionaries, the author has found the following particularly useful:

Diccionario Salamanca de la Lengua Española, Salamanca: Santillana, 1996.

This limited bibliographical section would not be complete without reference to a truly splendid work by Manuel Seco, *Diccionario de DUDAS y dificultades de la lengua española* (10th edition), Madrid: Espasa, 2002 (1st edition, 1961). This volume carries you well beyond dictionary information, and has served the present author for almost forty years, who refers to it frequently, even and often to assist Spanish speakers in clarifying uncertainties in their own language. Furthermore, it is not an indigestible book, and is therefore accessible to many of you who will have worked through this current volume.

Unit 1 *(Unidad 1)*

Alphabet, spelling and pronunciation (*Alfabeto, ortografía y pronunciación*)

The Royal Spanish Academy, founded in 1713, by the Duque d'Escalona, aims to preserve and improve the Spanish language. The Grammar (see bibliography) and Dictionary (*Diccionario de la Lengua Española*, 2 vols., 22nd edn., Madrid: Espasa Calpe) published by it are the standards of the language, but this only applies to Spain. It can no longer legislate for the Spanish of the Americas which has a lexical richness and diversity which can be initially confusing and certainly challenging. But fear not, for compensation is at hand, the grammar of the various countries concerned is comfortingly uniform and we must be grateful for this – and this includes the author. We must also be grateful to the Real Academia for helping to keep the language relatively stable.

Level **1**
1.1 **Alphabet, spelling and pronunciation** (*Alfabeto, ortografía y pronunciación*)
1.2 **Stress** (*El acento tónico*)

1.1 Alphabet, spelling and pronunciation

As with the grammar, Spanish pronunciation is happily uniform, with the consequence that once you have conquered the sounds, you are not enmeshed in the mire associated with, for example, the innumerable and irreducible irregularities of English pronunciation. Furthermore, the spelling system of the Spanish language is really quite easy compared to English. Aim for a perfect accent and real fluency. This will not only help you immeasurably in your communication with Spanish speakers but also allow you to appreciate more the written word, especially literature which is its highest expression.

Letters with pronunciation indicators (Letras con indicadores de pronunciación)
(See level 2, where all the comments below, notably on consonants, are considerably developed.)
la a (English *ah*), la b(e)(English *bay*), la b(e) grande (**M**), la c(e), ch(e), d(e) (English *th* as in *either, those*), e (like English *a* in *take*), (e)f(e), g(e) (when before *e* and *i*, as in English *horse* but more guttural; when before *a, o* and *u*, hard as in *gate* or *goat*), h (hache), i (like English *ee* as in *seek*), j (jota) (as in English *horse* but more guttural), k(a), (e)l(e), (e)ll(e), (e)m(e), (e)n(e), (e)ñ(e), o (like English *o* as in *hope*), p(e), q (cu), r (e)r(e), (e)rr(e) doble, doble r (e)rr(e) (**M**), (e)s(e), t(e), u (like English *oo* as in *food*), (u)v(e), la b(e) chica (**M**), w (uve doble), doble uve (**M**), x (equis) (*qui* sounds like the English *ki*), y (i griega) (when a vowel is equivalent to *i*), z (zeta/zeda)

NB
   i All letters are feminine
  ii *Mayúscula* f. capital letter
 iii *Minúscula* f. small letter
 iv *La hache = h*
  v As isolated letters, *r* and *rr* are the same sound, which explains the use of *doble* for *rr*
 vi Before *e* and *i* the Iberian *c* sounds like the English *th* as in *thick*, while before *a*, *o* and *u* it sounds like the English *c* in *cut*. In all Spanish America and much of southern Spain, the *c* before *i* and *e* sounds like the English *ss*.
 vii The Iberian *z* sounds like the English *th* as in *thick* but in all Spanish America and much of Southern Spain it sounds like the English *ss*
viii The *x* in México is pronounced as a *jota*
 ix The *n* with the tilde is nearly always referred to as la *eñe*
  x Great importance is attached to the vowels in Spanish. Their sounds are full and clear, while those of the consonants can be obscure and even be suppressed.

1.2 Stress

In Spanish, as in English, in words of two or more syllables, one is pronounced more forcibly than the others. This forcible utterance is called stress. In writing, it appears thus: *á, é, í, ó, ú*. As it would be laborious, unnecessary and even confusing to place an accent-mark over every written word, words are grouped into classes. Words coming into these classes do not need the written accent, and only the exceptions require it. Here are some of the basic rules governing the use of stress and the written accent. The rest will appear in level 2.

   i The greater part of words ending in a vowel are stressed (but not in writing) on the penultimate (next to last) syllable: *pero* (but), *perro* (dog), *lleva* (he/she takes), *carro* (**M**)/*coche* (car), *casa* (house), *bomba* (bomb/pump), *libro* (book)
  ii The greater part of words ending in *n* or *s* are stressed (but not in writing) on the penultimate: *toman* (they take, you take), *margen* (margin/edge), *imagen* (image/picture), *volumen*, *martes* (Tuesday), *crisis*
 iii The greater part of words ending in other consonants than *n* or *s* (including all infinitives) are stressed (but not in writing) on the last syllable: *esperar* (to hope / wait for), *decir* (to say), *alfiler* (pin), *peral* (pear tree), *perejil* (parsley, and extraordinarily the name of a rock, a Spanish possession a few hundred yards off the Moroccan coast), *altivez* (haughtiness), *majestad* (majesty), *magnitud*
 iv All exceptions to these rules require a written accent over the accented syllable: *café* (coffee/café), *pedís* (you ask), *revés* (setback), *encontró* (she/he met/found), *césped* (lawn), *mármol* (marble), *ángel*, *difícil* (difficult), *fácil* (easy)
  v All words stressed on a syllable previous to the penultimate require an accent mark: *músico* (musician), *héroe* (hero), *régimen* (regime), *línea* (line), *dábamos* (we used to give), *crepúsculo* (twilight), *atmósfera, gramática* (grammar)
 vi There is a clear choice on two words: *oceano/océano, periodo/período*

Exercises Level 1

i Pronunciation drill (*ejercicio de pronunciación*)
Read aloud all the letters of the following sentences which are very common proverbs or expressions. It is best if you can find a Spanish speaker or a teacher of Spanish to

help you with these sounds, at least initially. The proverbs are uncomplicated so you can easily work out their meaning and find a proper English equivalent from the rough translation:

> *Empezar la casa por el tejado* – To begin (building) the house with the roof
> *Quien mala cama hace, en ella yace* – He who makes a bad bed lies on it
> *Poderoso caballero es Don Dinero* – Powerful gentleman is Mr. Cash
> *Más vale pájaro en mano que cien volando* – Better a bird in your hand than a hundred flying
> nadar como un pez – *to swim like a fish*
> dormir como un tronco – *to sleep like a log*

ii Put in, where necessary, all the accents in the following passage. Also answer the questions on the passage:

Viajando a traves de la ciudad de Mexico
La ciudad de Mexico es una de las mas grandes del mundo, y como en toda gran ciudad, el transporte es muy diverso, y ofrece muchas opciones para viajar de un lugar a otro. Se puede viajar en automovil, taxi, colectivo, camion, bicicleta, y trolebus. La mayoria de la poblacion hace uso del transporte publico. Los vehiculos mas utilizados de manera privada son los automoviles y los taxis.

a Is there a written accent if you put *opciones* in the singular?
b Is there a written accent on *ciudad* if you put it in the plural?
c Is there a written accent on *lugar* (correctly spelt here?), *camion* (correctly spelt here?), *trolebus* (correctly spelt here?) and *poblacion* (correctly spelt here?) if you put them in the plural?

Level **2**

2.1 **Diphthongs and triphthongs** (*Diptongos y triptongos*)
2.2 **Consonants** (*Consonantes*)
2.3 **Elision in speech** (*Elisión/Sinalefa*)
2.4 **Rules governing the use of written accents** (*Reglas que determinan los acentos escritos*)
2.5 **Spelling traps** (*Trampas de ortografía*)
2.6 **Orthographical changes with *y* and *o*** (*Cambios ortográficos con **y** y **o***)

2.1   Diphthongs and triphthongs

(Spelling these two words is just one example of how much easier Spanish spelling is than its English counterpart.)

We should pay particular attention to this subject, as its understanding is necessary for a grasp of the laws of the written accent.

   i Spanish diphthongs and triphthongs are indivisible combinations of vowels pronounced as single syllables, laying the stress on the more sonorous syllables, and passing rapidly over the weaker or less sonorous. If both vowels are weak (*i* and *u*), the stress falls on the last of the two, as: *ruido* (noise), *viuda* (widow)

  ii The gradual scale of the sonority or strength of the vowels is as follows: *a, o, e, i, u, A, o, e* are called strong vowels, while *i* and *u* are weak vowels

iii Diphthongs cannot be formed from the strong vowels alone, but are a combination of a strong and weak vowel, or of *i* and *u* combined. When two strong vowels combine, each is considered as a separate vowel: *real* (real/royal), *aéreo, héroe, oasis*

iv Triphthongs are composed of one strong vowel between two weak ones

v In brief, a Spanish diphthong consists of a vowel preceded or followed by either *i* or *u*. In a triphthong, one of the latter two is on each side of the strong vowel

vi Examples of diphthongs – **ia**: *Asia, Santiago;* **ai**: *aire, caigo* (I fall), *fraile* (monk); **ie**: *miente* ((s)he lies), *piedra* (stone), *tiempo;* **ei**: *reina* (queen), *veinte, pleito* (lawsuit), *treinta;* **io**: *maniobra* (maneuver), *patriota, piocha* (pickax), *violento;* **oi**: *oigo* (I hear), *boina* (beret); **ua**: *cuanto, guante* (glove), *fragua* (forge); **au**: *pausa, cautela* (prudence); **ue**: *fuego* (fire), *puente* (bridge), *muestra* (sample); **eu**: *feudo* (fiefdom), *Europa, neutro;* **uo**: *cuota* (quota), *continuo;* **iu**: *triunfo* (triumph), *oriundo* (originating); **ui**: *buitre* (vulture), *ruido* (noise), *fuiste* (you were/went), *Luisa*

vii Examples of triphthongs – **iai**: *cambiáis* (you change), *variáis* (you vary); **iei**: *apreciéis* (that you should appreciate), *irradiéis* (that you should radiate), *contagiéis* (that you should infect); **uai**: *menguáis* (you diminish), *averiguáis* (you check out); **uei**: *amortigüéis* (that you should deaden), *santigüéis* (that you should bless)

viii Since a diphthong or triphthong is, in pronunciation, treated as a single syllable, it requires a written accent as with a single vowel.

ix In diphthongs containing a strong vowel, and in triphthongs, the accent mark belongs over the strong vowel; when placed over the weak one, the diphthong or triphthong disappears to become two syllables. Thus in *causa* and *Cáucasa, au* is a diphthong, but not in *saúco* (willow tree); *iai* in *variáis* is a triphthong but not in *temíais*. As we shall see later, in Spanish America, e.g. Mexico, triphthongs hardly exist, since the second person plural (*vosotros/os/vosotras/as*) is replaced by *Uds.* A lot easier, and certainly for Mexicans who find triphthongs quaint, rebarbative or just plain difficult to pronounce, with the result that the present author can become a figure of fun.

x If a syllable requiring a written accent contains a diphthong or a triphthong, the accent must be placed over the strong vowel; *huésped* (guest), *después, estudiáis, óiganos* (listen to us). In the case of a diphthong, if both vowels are weak, the spoken accent falls on the second vowel. No written accent occurs here: *circuito, ruido, he huido* (I have fled).

xi Whenever the weak vowel of a triphthong or diphthong is stressed, or the first vowel when both are weak, the written accent is placed over the said vowel, to show that there is no diphthong or triphthong: *ataúd* (casket, coffin), *país* (country), *increíble, raíz* (root), *poesía, día, leía* ((s)he was reading), *baúl* (trunk), *paraíso* (paradise)

xii A mute *h* between two vowels does not prevent a diphthong. The written accent is accordingly placed: *barahúnda* (ruckus, bedlam), *ahínco* (earnestness), *ahíto* (full, stuffed), *búho* (owl), *prohíben* (they forbid), *rehúso* (I refuse), *retahíla* (string, series), *vahído* (dizzy spell)

2.2 Consonants

i *F, k, l, m, n* and *p* have at all times the same value in Spanish as in English: *fama, kilo, comer, madre, entre, padre*

ii *B* and *v* have the same sound as in English, depending on where they are in the word. When they are in an initial position, the *b* of *burro* is the same as the *b* of *but*, and the same goes for the *v* in *vaca*. However, when *b* and *v* are within a word and especially between two vowels, the lips are pressed lightly together, creating a kind of lisp: *haber, saber, lavar, cavar* (to dig)

iii *C* has two sounds. Before *e* and *i*, it is pronounced like *th* in *thin*: *centro, encima, cielo*. In all other cases, it has the sound of *k*: *encanto* (charm), *cura* (priest), *cruz* (cross), *esclavo* (slave)

iv However, in nearly all southern Spain and the whole of Spanish America, the pronunciation of *c* before *e* and *i*, as with *z* in all cases, is that of *c* as in *city* or *center*. *Centro = sentro, encima = ensima, cielo = sielo, caza = casa* (room for confusion here!), *zapato = sapato, durazno = durasno* (**M**). For Spanish American speakers of Spanish, the *th* sound of *c* and *z* is generally regarded as pedantic, affected and even archaic, harking back to colonial times

v *Ch* is pronounced like *ch* in **church**: *muchacha, chica, chava* (**M**) (girl), *chévere* (**M**) (fantastic)

vi *D* never has the decided English sound of *d*, but has a tinge of the sound of *th* in *then*: *ciudad, dar, desde, doler, hablado, pegado*. In many parts of Spain, when *d* occurs between two vowels, and especially in past participles of the *-ado* type, the *d* can disappear completely in the spoken language. Thus, *hablado* (spoken) ends up as *hablao, pasmado* (amazed) as *pasmao, pegado* (hit) as *pegao*. The practice is frowned upon by purists, and is not characteristic of Spanish America where, as we shall see in the section on verbs, the perfect tense *he hablado* (I have spoken) is largely replaced by the preterite *hablé* (I spoke). Mexicans, for instance, find it odd and even illiterate.

vii *G* has two sounds. Before *e* and *i*, it has the sound of a strongly aspirated *h*. In all other cases it sounds like *g* in *go*: *gestión* (procedure), *gente, giro* (turn), *gimnasio, garage* (**M**) (second *g* as in American English), *gusto* (pleasure)

viii In order to obtain the hard *g* of *gusto* before *e* and *i*, a *u* is inserted. In this case, the *u* is silent: *guiar* (to guide), *guisar* (to cook), *enseguida, pegue* (that he hits), *agregue* (that she should add). But if the *u* is retained as an independent sound, a diaresis is placed over it (i.e. *ü*) – *lingüista, agüero* (omen), *desagüe* (drain, wastepipe) – but here it has a swallowed sound as in *agua*

ix *H* has a slight trace of aspiration before *ue*: *hueco* (hollow), *huevo* (egg)

x *J* has in all cases the same sound as *g* has before *e* and *i*: *juicio* (judgment), *jerga* (slang), *jugar* (play), *enjambre* (swarm)

xi *Ll* **had** until recently the sound of the letters *lli* as in the English *million*. But such a sound is considered pedantic by most Spanish speakers, and this includes all Spanish America, so that we end up with a double *y*, rather like the *y* in *your* but slightly elongated: *gallego* (Galician [in northern Spain]), *llamar, llorar, lluvia, pollo*

xii *N* presents no problem for an English speaker

xiii *Ñ* has the sound of the letters *ni*, as in *pinion*: *niño, señor, otoño*

xiv *Q* occurs only before *ue* and *ui*, and sounds like *k*, the following *u* being always silent: *tanque* (**M** = gas tank in car), *quebrar* (to break), *parroquia* (parish)

xv *R* has a roll, and a more marked roll (like a double *rr*) at the beginning of words: *regla, parar, mirar, enredar* (to confuse), *cortar*. If you have a Scottish accent, you will have no problem at all. When an initial *r* is preceded by an *s*, as in *los rayos* (rays) /

los rollos (rolls), the *s* often disappears so that we end up with *lo- rayos/rollos*, and this is not only restricted to the untutored classes

xvi *S* sounds like *ss* as in *hiss*. No real problem here, except for the immediately preceding comment

xvii *T* is softer than the English *t*, and is pronounced with the tongue touching the palate more gently: *tratar* (to treat), *pato* (duck), *total*

xviii *V*. See *b*

xix *W*. An import found in, for example, *Wágner = Vágner*, *Wáshington = Váshington*

xx *X* requires considerable comment, notably for Mexico. In Spain, the sound is of *x* as in *axle*; *exacto*, *exigir* (to demand). However, when it precedes a *c* it frequently ends up as an *s*: *excelente = escelente*, *exceso = esceso*. Condemned by purists, it is in general practice, although formal speech would require *excelente*. In Mexico, the *x* has three pronunciations. The first is as in Spain, i.e. between two vowels: *taxi*, *máximo*, *laxitud*. The second is like a *jota*, as in *México*, *Oaxaca* (city and state). The *jota* sound of the *x* overflows onto words like *xenofobia*. There is confusion whether the *x* of this word should be pronounced as an English *x* or a *jota*. One for the quiz program. Informed opinion is that this initial *x* should be pronounced as the English *x*. The third pronunciation is like an *s*. This pronunciation occurs not infrequently, especially with names of Aztec origin. Thus we have: *Xochitl*, *Xochimilco* (district in the south of Mexico City). Finally, the *x* of words like *excelente* and *explicar*, preceding a consonant, is like the English *x*, and not like an *s*, as in Spain.

xxi *Y* has the same value as in English and, for *z*, see point iv above

2.3 Elision in speech

i When a vowel at the end of one word immediately precedes a vowel at the beginning of the next word, the two vowels run together in speech. A mute *h* does not change this feature: *si‿es así*, *cuesta‿un peso*, *otro‿año*, *su‿hacienda/hilo*

ii This also applies to three words: *Fue‿ a‿ Europa*, *salió‿ a‿ España*

iii When the two vowels are the same, one is always lost in rapid speech: *la ayuda = l'ayuda*, *para agradecerle = par'agradecerle*. Note the very common, colloquial Mexican expression for **many**: *hasta pa'aventar pa'arriba (hasta para aventar para arriba)*

2.4 Rules governing the use of written accents

When one or more pronouns are added to any part of a verb so as to shift the accented syllable to the antepenultimate (two before the last one), or still farther from the end, the accent is marked: *para comérmelo* (for me to eat it all up), *para conseguírtelo* (to get it for you), *dándoselos* (giving them to her/him/them, you).

When two Spanish words are combined, each retains its original accent, whether written or not. This is especially common with adverbs: *cortésmente* (written accent on the first *e* and stress on the first two *e*'s), *naturalmente* (stress on second *a* and first *e* of *mente*), *correctamente* (stress on the first two *e*'s), *ferrocarril* (stress on *e* and *i*).

Where there are two monosyllables of identical form, the more emphatic one is distinguished by a written accent:

dé, give (subjunctive of *dar*)	*de*, of, from	*té*, tea	*te*, you
él, he, him	*el*, the	*tú*, you	*tu*, your
mí, me	*mi*, my	*¡vé!*, go!	*ve*, sees (present of *ver*)
más, more	*mas*, but	(imperative of *ir*)	
sé, I know, be (imperative of *ser*)	*se*, one's self		
sí, yes, one's self	*si*, if		

Note also: ***aun*** (even), ***aún*** (still), and *solo* (alone), *sólo* (only)

Examples

Aun los más torpes lo entienden = Even the dumbest understand it
Aún no ha venido tu papá = Your father still hasn't come
Está solo/a = (S)he's alone
Tiene sólo cinco años = She's only five

To distinguish between the interrogative or exclamatory and the relative use of pronouns and adverbs, a written accent is placed on the first two. Frequently, Spanish speakers, even very literate ones, fail to observe this rule, so you could be in good company if you fail here too:

¿cómo?	how?	*como*	as, if	*¿cuál?*	which?	*cual*	which
¿cuándo?	when?	*cuando*	when	*¿cuánto?*	how much?	*cuanto*	as much
¿dónde?	where?	*donde*	where	*¿qué?*	what?	*que*	which, that
¿quién?	who? whom?	*quien*	who, whom				

Examples

¿Cómo puede hacerlo?	Como no puede hacerlo ahora, será mejor esta tarde
¿Cuándo vienes?	Viene cuando puede
¿Dónde está el chico?	Sé donde está
¿Quién lo ha hecho?	Yo sé quien lo ha hecho
¿Cuál de los dos viene?	Yo sé cual de los dos viene
¿Cuánto cuesta?	Te doy todo cuanto quieras
¿Qué has dicho/dijiste?	Me dice que regresa mañana

A problem can arise, even for Spanish speakers, when the question is indirect, or a question is implied, as in:

Le pregunté cuándo volvería = I asked her/him when (s)he would come back
*¿Por qué me preguntas dónde está la chava (**M**)?* Why do you ask me where the girl is?

Notice also the upside-down question mark at the beginning of the sentence. The same happens with an exclamation mark/point: *¡Híjole!* (**M**), *¡Jolín!* (both = "Jeez! Heavens above!")

2.5   Spelling traps

Here are just a few Spanish words that have a near, and therefore misleading, spelling equivalent in English. There are many more. This small list serves to point out that you should be wary of skating over words without paying detailed attention to them:

*a*tormentar, *cacao*, *centinela* (sentry), *cómplice* (accomplice), *con*memorar, *dign**a**tario* (dignitary), *ejemplo*, *éxtasis*, *femenismo*, *feminino*, *fisonomía*, *hipocresía*, *independiente*, *inmediato*, *inmigrante*, *inmunitario*, *inventorio*, *literario*, *literatura*, *profecía*, *quimioterapia*, *radiactividad*, *responsabilidad*, *sicomoro*, *tarifa*, *tenis*, *vainilla*

2.6 Orthographical changes with *y* and *o*

For the sake of avoiding the concurrence of two like sounds, *y* (and) is changed to *e* when the following word begins with *i* or *hi*. This also happens with *o* (or) which becomes *u* before initial *o* or *ho*.

Examples

*español **e** inglés*	Spanish and English
*padre **e** hijo*	father and son
*María **e** Isabel*	Mary and Elizabeth/Isabel
*plata **u** oro*	silver or gold
*vida **u** honor*	life or honor
*siete **u** ocho*	seven or eight

However, when a diphthong is involved, *y* does not change.

Examples

*madera **y** hierro*	wood and iron
*él **y** yo*	he and I/me
*limón **y** hielo*	lemon and ice

Note: There are almost no double consonants, except ***ll*** and ***rr***.

Exercises Level 2

i Lee el siguiente párrafo en voz alta y en clase, e indica el uso de la sinalefa. Al escribir las palabras, pon un ⌣, o sea subrayando el espacio entre las palabras apropiadas o dentro de una palabra:

A través de su historia, los Estados Unidos se han caracterizado como un gran crisol étnico. Esto quiere decir que, aunque la población está constituida de muchos grupos de personas de distinto origen, existe no obstante un pueblo norteamericano. Tradicionalmente, los inmigrantes se han asimilado a la cultura norteamericana después de una o dos generaciones. Debido a la insistencia de los padres, los hijos han hablado en inglés y, gradualmente, han adoptado las nuevas costumbres de la patria adoptiva.

ii Ejercicio de lectura. Lee las siguientes frases en voz alta y en clase con un acento o mexicano o español:

Hace un aire muy fuerte	Cierra la puerta	Veracruz es un puerto de mar
It's windy	*Close the door*	*Veracruz is a sea port*
El charro cruza el Río Bravo	¿Cuál es la causa del accidente?	Se oye un ruido en la recámara (**M**)

The horseman crosses the Río Grande

Mi vecina es viuda desde hace
dos años

*My neighbor has been a widow for
two years*

Es imposible poner una vaca en
una baca (*confusion here?*)

*It's impossible to put a cow on a roof
rack*

*What is the cause of the
accident?*

Es necesario que cambiéis
de coche (*this 2nd pl form
not in* **M**)

It is necessary you change cars

El charro rasguea la
guitarra

*The horseman strums the
guitar*

*You can hear a noise in the
bedroom*

No creo que apreciéis el
valor de este libro (*this
2nd pl form not in* **M**)

*I don't think you appreciate the
value of this book*

iii Intenta pronunciar estos trabalenguas (*tongue twisters*) que no tienen sentido:

Un tigre, dos tigres, tres tigres triscan trigo en un trigal
A tiger, two tigers, three tigers chew wheat in a wheat field

Tres tristes tigres tragaban trigo en tres tristes trastos sentados en un trigal
Three sad tigers swallowed wheat on three sad pieces of trash sitting in a wheat field

Un tubo tiró un tubo y otro tubo lo detuvo. Hay tubos que tienen tubos pero este tubo
no tuvo tubo
*A tube threw a tube and another tube stopped it. There are tubes which have tubes but this tube did not
have a tube*

Aquí tienes otro trabalenguas que te permite practicar la **doble rr (M) / rr doble**. ¡Y
tiene sentido!

Detrás de un carro corría un burro. (Puedes adivinar el sentido de esta frase)

**iv Aquí tienes un pequeño trozo mexicano. Pon los acentos y la puntuación en su lugar
correcto. Puntos, comas, y mayúsculas han sido insertados para ayudarte.**

Cada vez que me visita mi cuate (*pal*), siempre me pregunta por que no tengo una buena chamba
(*job*). Le pregunto Por que me preguntas siempre lo mismo. Me contesta Como tu cuate, puedo
preguntarte cualquier cosa. Pero contesto a mi vez Quien te crees tu para preguntarme que
chamba tengo. Bueno, si no quieres responderme, Donde trabajas y cual es tu trabajo. Me enoja
(*annoys*) que insistas tanto. Yo se donde trabajo y como es y parale (*that's enough*). Cuando te vas

RB/JPL

Unit 2 *(Unidad 2)*

Definite and indefinite articles and gender of nouns (*Artículos definidos e indefinidos y género de sustantivos*)

Level **1**

1.1 **The definite and indefinite articles** (*Los artículos definidos e indefinidos*)

1.2 **General features of gender – masculine nouns** (*Detalles generales de sustantivos masculinos*)

1.3 **General features of gender – feminine nouns** (*Detalles generales de sustantivos femeninos*)

1.4 **Further features of gender** (*Otros detalles de género*)

1.5 **Nouns of varying gender** (*Nombres de género variable*)

1.1   The definite and indefinite articles

The articles in Spanish, as with all Romance languages, vary in form to indicate gender and number. In this unit we shall deal with gender. There are no available rules for determining the masculine and feminine genders of Spanish nouns. The gender of most Spanish nouns have, unfortunately, to be learnt, just as learners of English have to learn how to spell individual words. It is true that there is usually a reason for the gender assigned, but the origin is frequently obscure or untraceable. Nevertheless, there are some general considerations of great help to the learner. What is certain is that retaining the gender of nouns will help to prevent cerebral decay.

i First we must look at how the definite and indefinite article are used before the noun:

	Masculine	**Feminine**
Definite article	*el* the	*la* the
Indefinite article	*un* a/an	*una* a/an

These articles are always placed before the noun:

el hombre	the man	*la mujer*	the woman
un hombre	a man	*una mujer*	a woman

ii Feminine nouns beginning with a stressed *a* or *ha* are preceded by *el* and not *la*:

el agua	the water	*el hacha*	the ax	*el (h)arpa*	the harp	*el asma*	asthma
el hambre	the hunger	*el alma*	the soul	*el ama de la casa*		housewife	

Other feminine nouns preceded by *el*:

el alza	rise, increase		*el habla*	speech
el ancla	anchor		*el hada*	fairy
el aula	lecture room		*el haya*	beech tree
el haba	bean			

But remember that if the article precedes an unstressed *(h)a*, *la* is used:

la ambición, *la alhaja* – the jewel, *la Alhambra / hamaca* – hammock

The change does not occur before adjectives of like form:

la alta torre – the tall tower, *la alta estimación* – the high esteem

iii When the masculine singular form of the definite article, *el*, comes immediately after the prepositions *a* or *de*, there is a contraction: *al*, *del*

al niño / al profesor / al bosque	to the child / teacher / wood
del chico / del hombre / del coche	of the boy / man / car

iv If the noun is feminine, *a la / de la* are used, as you would expect:

a la / de la casa	to / of the house
a la mesa / de la mesa	to / of the table

From now on, *the* for *el* and *la* will not be used in the lists.

1.2 General features of gender – masculine nouns

i Names and designations of males, and the males of large and well-known animals, are masculine, irrespective of endings:

el caballo	horse		*el león*	lion
el cardenal	cardinal		*el príncipe*	prince
el centinela	sentry		*el monarca*	monarch
el cura	priest		*el tigre*	tiger

ii Gender associated with noun ending – in most cases, nouns ending in *o* are masculine:

el barco	boat		*el libro*	book
el caso	case, example		*el ojo*	eye
el cigarro	cigar(ette) (i.e. both)		*el palo*	stick
el hombro	shoulder			

Exceptions are:

la dínamo	dynamo		*la moto*	motorcycle
la foto	photo		*la radio*	radio
la mano	hand			

Foto and *moto* are shortened forms of *fotografía* and *motocicleta* while *radio* is masculine in Mexico. *Radio* meaning "radius" is masculine in Spain and Mexico.

iii Some masculine nouns ending in *o* do not change their ending when denoting females:

la miembro	member	*la soprano*	soprano
la modelo	model	*la testigo*	witness

iv Nouns ending in *or* are mainly masculine:

el amor	love	*el color*	color
el autor	author	*el conductor*	driver
el calor	heat	*el valor*	courage, valor

Exception:

la labor work

When a feminine noun is implied or understood: *la Gestapo, la UNESCO*.

v Nouns ending in *aje*:

el andamiaje	scaffolding	*el paisaje*	landscape
el equipaje	baggage	*el viaje*	journey

vi Nouns ending in *men*:

el certamen	contest	*el volumen*	volume
el régimen	régime		

vii Nouns ending in *gen*:

el origen but *imagen* is feminine

viii The proper names of countries or territories are masculine, except when they end in unstressed *a*.

(el) Brasil, (el) Canadá, (el) Chile, (los) Estados Unidos (United States), *(el) Japón, (el) México, (los) Países Bajos* (Netherlands), *(el) Panamá, (el) Perú*

The following countries are therefore feminine.

Argentina, Australia, Bolivia, China, Colombia, España, Francia, Grecia, Guatemala, Holanda, India, Italia, Nueva Zelanda, Rusia, Venezuela

ix The following types of noun are all masculine.

Rivers	*el Amazonas* (Amazon), *el Río Bravo* (**M**) (Rio Grande) but *el* **Río Grande** in Spain, *el Paraná, el Sena* (Seine), *el Támesis* (Thames), *el Colorado, el Nilo, el Rin* (Rhine)
Seas/Oceans	*El Atlántico / el Pacífico / el Mediterráneo*
Months	*enero* (January), *mayo*
Mountains	*El Himalaya, el Acongagua, los Andes, el Popocatepetl, los Alpes;* and volcanos: *el*

	Vesubio (Vesuvius) (but *las* (*Montañas*) *Rocosas* = Rockies)
Cars	*el Chrysler, el Ford, el Toyota, el Mercedes, el Porsche, el Maserati*
Watches	*el Seiko, el Longines*
Ships and aircraft carriers	*el Reina Mary, el Nimitz, el Enterprise*
Airplanes	*el Boeing, el Concorde*
Languages	*el español, el francés, el inglés británico / americano, el ruso, el chino*
Metals	*el hierro* (iron), *el cobre* (copper), *el acero* (steel), *el bronce* (bronze)
Many trees	*el olmo* (elm), *el roble* (oak), *el fresno* (ash), *el álamo* (poplar) **but** *el* (i.e. feminine) *haya* (beech), *la encina* (holm oak), *la higuera* (fig tree)

1.3 Feminine nouns

i The designations of females are feminine:

la dama	lady	*la princesa*	princess
la gallina	hen	*la reina*	queen
la muchacha	girl	*la vaca*	cow

ii Most nouns ending in *a* are feminine:

la casa	house	*la puerta*	door
la caza	hunting	*la ventana*	window
la comida	meal, food		

Exceptions – nouns denoting males:

| *el artista* | artist | *el guardia* | guard |
| *el cura* | priest | *el jesuita* | jesuit |

Note also that *centinela* is a masculine noun = sentry

iii The majority of nouns ending in *o* change it to *a* to form the feminine:

el alumno / la alumna	pupil
el amigo / la amiga	friend
el cocinero / la cocinera	cook
el conocido / la conocida	acquaintance
el criado / la criada	male / female servant
el huérfano / la huérfana	orphan
el muchacho / la muchacha	boy / girl

iv Nouns ending in: *–ma*, *-dad* (many of these), *-tad* (just a few of these), *-tud*, *-ión* (many of these), *-umbre*, *-ie* and *-sis* are feminine:

-ma

(el) asma	asthma	*la gema*	gem
la cama	bed	*la lima*	file
la crema (***M***)	cream	*la trama*	plot
la estratagema	stratagem	*la yema*	yolk, fingertip
la forma	form		

-dad

la agilidad	agility	*la severidad*	severity
la ansiedad	anxiety	*la sociedad*	society
la enfermedad	sickness, illness	*la verdad*	truth
la eternidad	eternity		

-tad

la libertad (freedom)

-tud

la longitud, virtud (virtue)

-ión

la ambición, intuición, nación, pasión, región, sensación

-umbre

la certidumbre (certainty), *costumbre* (custom), *cumbre* (peak), *muchedumbre* (crowd)

-ie

intemperie (bad weather), *planicie* (plain), *serie* (series)

-is

crisis, metamorfosis, síntesis, tesis

But the following are masculine:

el carisma, cisma (schism), *clima, cometa* (comet), *delta, día* (day), *emblema, mapa, planeta, problema, tranvía* (streetcar / tram).

In all these cases, save *día, mapa*, and *tranvía*, the fact that these nouns end in *a* but are masculine is explained by their Greek origin. Etymology can be fascinating.

Note also: *pijama* which is masculine in Spain and feminine in Mexico. Matters are not improved with this word since it is even spelt differently in Mexico: *piyama*. The same goes for American and British English (*Pajamas* [*AE*] / *pyjamas* [*BE*]), so it is difficult to win here.

v The following are also masculine:

el avión	airplane	*el sarampión*	measles
el gorrión	sparrow	*el camión*	truck but commonly *bus* in **M**
and			

el análisis	analysis	*el éxtasis*	ecstasy
el apocalipsis	apocalypse	*el paréntesis*	parenthesis
el énfasis	emphasis		

vi The following types of nouns are feminine:

Islands	*las Filipinas, las Marianas, las Malvinas, Córcega* (Corsica), *Cerdeña* (Sardinia), *Sicilia* (last three in the Mediterranean). **But** *las Islas de los Galápagos* (Galapagos Islands)
Letters of the alphabet	*la a, la b, la c, la h* (*hache*), etc.
Firms	*la Ford, la British (Airways), la General Motors*

These are all the rules of any value. Much could be said about remembering the gender of Spanish nouns. However, suffice it to say that the simplest and easiest way to learn the gender is, when you come across a new noun, put the article in front of it every time, and you will learn by association, following the pattern of a Spanish-speaking child.

1.4 Further features of gender

i Where the names of animals do not have distinct masculine and feminine forms, *macho* and *hembra* (invariable) are used to make the distinction, but the gender does not change:

el rinoceronte / los rinocerontes / la ardilla (squirrel) / *las ardillas macho* (for all four nouns)
el ratón (mouse) / *los ratones / la ardilla / las ardillas hembra* (for all four nouns)

ii Family relations and titles
With nouns denoting titles and family relations, a masculine plural in Spanish may correspond to a masculine and feminine pair:

Tengo tres hijos	I have three children
los Reyes Católicos	the Catholic Monarchs (Queen Isabel and King Fernando)
los chicos	the boys (and girls)
los niños	the children / the boys
los duques de Alba	the Duke and Duchess of Alba
los Presidentes	the President and First Lady
los Señores García	Mr. and Mrs. Garcia
los novios	the engaged couple

iii It could sometimes be unclear what certain plurals mean with respect to gender.
Niños, chicos, hijos and *reyes* are good cases in point. *Hijos*, for instance, could signify three sons, or two sons and one daughter, or one son and two daughters. Unfortunately, for females, even when the male is in a minority, as in the last case, the plural is still masculine. Clarification comes with, for example: *dos hijos y una hija, dos hijas y un hijo*. And if this still does not clear up the ambiguity, and you had three sons, you could say *tres varones* after *tres hijos*: *Tiene tres hijos, o sea* (that is) *tres varones*.

1.5 Words of varying gender

i

arte When masculine singular = individual art: *el arte azteca/clásico/precolombiano*
      When collective = the Arts: *las bellas artes/artes decorativas/plásticas*

mar   Masculine in general: *Me gusta nadar en el mar, el Mar Mediterráneo*
      Sometimes feminine in formal, poetic style, and frequently in set phrases:
      *Lo/La (**M**) pasé la mar de bien* (I had a great time), *en alta mar* (on the high seas),
      mar gruesa (heavy sea), *mar picada* (choppy sea), *hacerse a la mar* (to put to sea)

margen When = river bank it is feminine and usually found in literary texts
        When masculine = margin (of page/maneuver), edge (of society)

ii There are nouns that are both masculine and feminine and with the same meaning:

casete	cassette	*linde*	boundary (usually feminine)
interrogante	question	*maratón*	marathon (usually feminine)
armazón	(frame of a structure)	*lente* (= lens but ***los lentes*** in **M** = glasses, i.e. for seeing)	

iii Names of towns
Usually towns are feminine but practice is not always clear, and there is no true guide:

en la Roma antigua, Guanajuato es bella, la atractiva París

On the other hand it is perfectly acceptable to say:

todo Chihuahua/Acapulco/Valencia

There seems to be no rigid rule on this point. It would even appear that in Mexico towns are usually masculine, even when they end in *a*, like *Chihuahua*.

iv Soccer teams are referred to as masculine:

El Puebla, el Guadalajara, el Toluca, el Barcelona (more usually *el Barça*), *el Real (Madrid)*

Exercises Level 1

i Find the gender and meaning of the following nouns, and put *el/la/un/una* before them:

casa, silla, plato, mesa, foco (**M**), bombilla, libro, botella, cuaderno, habitación, costa, fuente, reina, amigo, burro, caballo, jardín, mapa (*careful!*), rey, víctima (*careful!*), área, arma

ii Put *del / de la / al / a la* before the following nouns and find their meaning:

casa, mesa, caballo, habitación, mapa, víctima, área, arma, árbol, calle, pared, taza, pájaro, escuela, departamento (**M** = *apartment*), apartamento, ángel, águila, anchoa, alga

iii Complete with the correct article indicating gender (choose which is more appropriate between the definite and indefinite article but either will do in some cases):

a (_) chica trabaja todo (_) día
b En (_) suelo hay (_) gato
c (_) padre está sentado en (_) sillón
d ¿Ves (_) reloj en (_) mesa?

e (_) flor está en (_) jardín

f (_) mujer está en (_) calle

g Veo (_) árbol en (_) parque

h (_) estudiante habla con (_) profesora / (_) profesor

i (_) pájaro canta en (_) cielo

j (_) casa está detrás de (_) jardín

iv Paired activity

Objective – Learn the gender of nouns

Method – Ask each other, in turn, the gender of a noun.

Both participants spend two minutes collecting a list of ten nouns, from level 1.

Example

The first person asks: *¿Cuál es el género del nombre "carro?"* (What is the gender of the noun *carro?*) Answer: *"Carro" es masculino.*

The partner asks: *¿Cuál es el género del nombre "casa?"* Answer: *"Casa" es femenino.*

When all ten questions have been asked, the teacher/instructor brings the class together and asks, in simple Spanish, if there are any difficult genders.

Level 2

2.1 More on the definite and indefinite articles (*Más detalles sobre los artículos definidos e indefinidos*)

2.2 The neuter gender (*El género neutro*)

2.3 Same noun but different meaning according to the gender (*El mismo sustantivo pero otro sentido según el género*)

2.4 Problem genders (*Géneros problemáticos*)

2.5 Gender of compound nouns (*Género de nombres compuestos*)

2.6 Words distinguished by the ending a/o (*Voces con terminación a/o*)

2.7 Misleading similarities (*Falsos amigos*)

2.1 More on the definite and indefinite articles

i A few nouns with endings other than *a* have a common form for both genders:

el/la cómplice, el/la criminal, el/la hereje (heretic), *joven* (young man or girl), *mártir, miembro, reo* (accused person / convicted offender), *testigo* (witness), *vocal* (committee member)

ii Names of some cities are preceded by the definite article:

El Cairo, El Cabo (Cape Town), *La Coruña* (in Spain), *El Cuzco* (in Peru), *El Ferrol* (in Spain), *La Habana*

Hence *Voy a El Cabo, a El Cairo, a La Coruña*, but in speech, in Spain, you frequently hear *Voy al Ferrol*, and most Mexicans would say *Voy a Cuzco*.

iii The names of several countries have traditionally been preceded by the definite article, especially when the country is masculine, but this usage is fast disappearing. These include *el Brasil, el Canadá, el Chile, el Ecuador, el Japón, el Paraguay, el Uruguay*, but nearly all Spanish speakers say nowadays *Voy a Brasil, Canadá, Japón*, etc. At the same time, there are three countries where the definite article is still used: *Los Estados Unidos, El Reino Unido* (United Kingdom), *La India*. It should be added that when the plural *Los* precedes *Estados Unidos* when it is the subject of a verb, the verb is in the plural. When *Estados Unidos* stands alone, i.e. without *Los*, as the subject of the sentence, the verb is in the singular: *Los Estados Unidos forman un bloque económico muy importante / Estados Unidos se opone a la sugerencia* (. . . is opposed to the suggestion).

iv The definite article is required if the name of the country is qualified by an adjective or a phrase:

el Asia rusa, el Asia Menor, el México contemporáneo, la fecunda Italia (fertile Italy), *la Argentina de los años sesenta* ((. . .) of the sixties)

v Technically, each noun is preceded by the article but this usage is also slipping away, and not only in speech. When the nouns are closely associated with each other, this is especially true. It also applies to nouns of different gender:

la energía y celo (m) que muestra	the energy and zeal he shows
El descuido y negligencia (f) del soldado	the soldier's carelessness and negligence
El interés, inteligencia (f), honradez (f) del empleado	the clerk's interest, intelligence and honesty

vi The article is not repeated after *o* = or, before a noun that is merely a synonym or explanation of the preceding noun:

el vestíbulo o entrada de la casa	the hall or entrance to the house
Edimburgo es la capital o ciudad principal de Escocia	Edinburgh is the capital or main city of Scotland

vii Both definite and indefinite articles are omitted before a noun in apposition (i.e. when it explains a preceding noun):

Veracruz, principal puerto en la costa oriental de México	Veracruz, main city . . .
Quito, capital de Ecuador, posee un clima delicioso	Quito, Ecuador's capital, possesses . . .
Unamuno, autor de la Generación del '98	Unamuno, author of . . .

viii The article is used to express any of the elements or features of nature, animals and plants of which only one can be supposed to be under consideration:

El cielo es azul	The sky is blue
El sol puede ser peligroso	The sun can be dangerous
El lirio es una flor vistosa	The lily is a bright and colorful flower
El zorro tiene fama por su astucia	The fox is well known for its cunning
La tierra es redonda	The earth is round
La cigüeña es un ave pasajera	The stork is a migratory bird

ix The article is used of representatives of a race, or parts or faculties of man, taken in a general sense:

El panameño	Panamanian
*los estadounidenses / estadunidenses (**M**)*	North Americans
el blanco	white person
el negro	black person
los chinos	(the) Chinese
los comunistas	(the) Communists

el hígado	(the) liver
el corazón	(the) heart
la memoria	(the) memory
el alma	(the) soul

x It is used of epithets or nicknames following a proper name of a person:

Pedro el Cruel	Peter the Cruel
Isabel la Católica	the Catholic Isabel
Alejandro el Grande	Alexander the Great (but also *Alejandro Magno*)

xi A striking difference between Spanish and English is the use of the definite article in Spanish before any noun that is representative of the entire class or species:

El hombre es mortal	Man is mortal
El pan es nutritivo	Bread is nutritious
Las flores son el adorno de la tierra	Flowers are the adornment of the earth

xii The Spanish article is used when nouns represent abstract qualities or ideas:

los estragos del tiempo	the ravages of time
El orgullo es un defecto	Pride is a defect
La envidia es un pecado capital	Envy is a capital sin
El destino del hombre no se puede evitar	Man's destiny cannot be avoided

xiii The article is often used before a verb in the infinitive:

El hablar tanto es su falta principal	Speaking so much is his main fault
El comer y el beber son necesarios a la vida	Eating and drinking are necessary to life
El leer alto es una buena práctica	Reading aloud is a good practice
El nadar es muy sano	Swimming is very healthy

xiv The article is omitted when reference is made to professions:

Es médico / doctor(a) / profesor(a) / ingeniero(a) / enfermero(a), contable = (S)he is a doctor/ teacher/engineer/nurse/accountant

But if the noun is qualified the article (usually indefinite) is used:

Es una doctora muy hábil	She is a very skillful physician/doctor
Es una contable muy competente	He is a very competent accountant

xv The article is also omitted when a noun and adjective occur so frequently that they become a set expression:

Es buena persona	(S)he is a very nice person
Es buen católico	He's a good Catholic
Es gran orador	He's a great speaker

xvi In elegant style, the article is frequently omitted in enumerations:

Asistieron al partido hombres, mujeres, niños, ancianos, y hasta burros Men, women, children, old people and even donkeys went to the match

xvii Formation of masculine/feminine pairs:

The most common masculine/feminine pairs are:

-o/-a	el tío / la tía	(uncle/aunt)
-e/-a	el monje / la monja	(monk/nun)
-or/-ora	el autor / la autora	(author)

Note also the following less common distinctive feminine endings:

-esa	el abad / la abadesa	abbott/abbess
-isa	el profeta / la profetisa	prophet/prophetess
-riz	el actor / la actriz	actor/actress

Note also nouns ending in **-ista**, e.g. *el/la corista* (chorister) / *pianista* (pianist), *violinista* (violinist).

Note that the feminine form of *corista* has the meaning of "chorus girl."

xviii However, complications are not far away as illustrated by the two following categories:

a When the feminine form **already has** a distinct meaning:

el físico	physicist		*la física*	physics
el alcalde	mayor		*la alcaldesa*	mayor's wife
el policía	police officer		*la policía*	police (force)

b When there **was** no feminine form in existence, and few females in the job:

ministro (was masculine and feminine) and now *ministra* for feminine form
presidente (was M and F) and now *presidenta* for feminine form
cónsul (*el* was used for both genders) but now *la cónsul*
agente (formerly *el* for both genders) but now *la agente*

As women take on new roles in Western society, Spanish has, like French and Italian, had to find new feminines, and feminists are doing their best to establish new forms. The feminine form of professional nouns is now used regularly and applies to women in these professions. For example, *médica* signifies "female doctor" and not "doctor's wife" but *médico* is still by far the preferred term; *alcaldesa* means "female mayor" and can mean "mayor's wife"; *abogada* only means "female lawyer"; *policía* is now the accepted term for "policewoman" as well as "policeman" and "police force" (room for dangerous confusion here?); *primera ministra* has now supplanted *primer ministro* for a female "prime minister." This change to a markedly feminine form still does not encourage dictionaries to put an equal number of examples in the feminine, as is the case in the present work, so there is a residual resistance somewhere.

The following are now acceptable feminine forms, in addition to those quoted above: *árbitra* (referee), *candidata, clienta, concejala* (city / town hall councilor), *diputada* (member of parliament), *edila* (member of town hall council), *jefa* (head of an establishment), *reportera, senadora, sirvienta* but, even here, *concejal* and *edil* can be feminine.

There is some limited comfort for females with a feminist tendency in the following: the feminine form *modista* can mean "male fashion designer" but *modisto* is in current use. However, strange as it may seem, *un desnudo* has to be masculine, as in French and Italian. Does this say anything about the Latin psyche? Or does the noun simply refer to the painting or sculpture? Perhaps it is the latter. On the other hand, a male film star has to be feminine: *una estrella.*

2.2   The neuter gender

i The neuter form of the article, *lo*, is not applicable to nouns since all nouns are masculine or feminine. It is used before adjectives, participles, adjectival pronouns and occasionally adverbs. The effect of placing *lo* before such words is to form a phrase which often has an abstract idea:

lo agradable	what is pleasant, pleasantness
lo mexicano	what is Mexican
lo hecho / dicho / mencionado	what is/was done/said/mentioned
Lo ocurrido me impactó	What (had) happened affected me deeply
Hice lo posible / lo necesario	I did what I could / what was necessary
Prefiero lo práctico a lo decorativo	I prefer what's practical to the decorative

ii The substantive or "noun" nature of the adjective or participle preceded by *lo* is very clear when it is followed by *de* and a noun. This construction is not always easy to put into English:

lo claro de la frase	the clarity of the phrase/sentence
lo extraño del asunto	the curious thing about the business
lo tonto de sus palabras	the dumb thing in what he said
sin pensar en lo complicado de la tarea	without thinking about how complicated the job would be
Lo más difícil fue entenderlo	The most difficult thing was to understand him

2.3   Same noun but different meaning according to the gender

A number of Spanish nouns are both masculine and feminine, but have different meanings which are sometimes related. This phenomenon, common to all Romance languages, really does test our memory.

i The feminine noun is collective while the masculine is individual:

	F	M
batería	battery (of guns), (car) battery, footlights, percussion section of orchestra, set of kitchen utensils	drummer (in band)
defensa	defense (in most senses)	defender (in soccer)
escolta	escort (group)	escort (individual)
guardia	guard (group), custody	guard (individual), policeman
policía	police, policewoman	policeman

ii The feminine noun is literal, while the masculine noun is a person or thing associated with a metaphoric function:

	F	M
bestia	beast, uncouth woman	uncouth man, brute
cabeza	head	head of an organization

calavera	skull	reckless/rakish man
cámara	camera	cameraman
caza	hunt	fighter (airplane)
cura	cure	priest (Catholic)
espada	sword	swordsman, matador
facha	appearance, look	fascist (term of abuse)
génesis	origin	Book of Genesis
guía	guidebook, female guide	guide (person)
mañana	morning	future
meta	objective, goal	goalkeeper
pareja	couple (of people), female partner	male partner
recluta	recruitment	rookie, recruit
vigía	watchtower	watchman

NB *Cabeza* is always feminine in Mexico, whether referring to a part of the anatomy or to the head of an organization or the family: *El padre es la cabeza de la familia* = The father is the head of the family

iii Others

	F	**M**
capital	capital city (national or provincial)	capital (i.e. money)
central	head office, telephone exchange; *central nuclear/ hidroeléctrica* = nuclear/ hydroelectric power station	center forward, central defender (soccer)
cólera	anger	cholera
coma	comma	coma
cometa	kite	comet
corriente	flow, current (of water, electricity)	current month
corte	(royal) court, *Las Cortes* = Spanish Parliament	cut (general), outage, power cut
editorial	publishing house	lead article
final	final (match)	end (of street, show, game)
frente	forehead	front (part) (battle, political front)
hincha	grudge, ill will	supporter (in sport)
moral	ethics, morale	blackberry bush
orden	order, command, military or religious order as in *la Orden de Calatrava*	order, arrangement as in *orden alfabético*, civil order as in *las fuerzas del orden*
ordenanza	decree, ordinance	office boy, orderly (in armed forces)
panda	gang	panda
parte	part (of something)	report as in *parte meteorológico* = weather forecast
pendiente	slope (on hill)	earring

pez	pitch, tar	fish (alive in water)	
radio	radio (but in **M** = masculine)	radius, spoke (in wheel), radium	
terminal	bus/airplane terminal (but both are feminine in Mexico)	(electrical) terminal	
vocal	vowel, female committee member	male committee member	

2.4 Problem genders

The gender of the following words is especially liable to confusion, particularly if you have studied, or are studying, French and/or Italian. Please have sympathy with the present author.

i Words ending in *e*:

	M		**F**
auge	boom, highest point	*base*	base
avance	advance	*catástrofe*	catastrophe
cauce	(river) bed/course	*gripe*	flu, bad cold
declive	slope, incline	*higiene*	hygiene
enchufe	electrical plug, influence	*índole*	nature, character
fraude	fraud	*mole*	mass, bulk
peine	comb	*pirámide*	pyramid
síndrome	syndrome	*sede*	see, seat (of government)
timbre	bell, postage stamp (in **M**)		

ii Words ending in *al*:

	M		**F**
cereal	cereal	*cal*	lime
zarzal	bramble, thicket	*central*	power station, telephone exchange, head office
		espiral	spiral
		multinacional	multinational
		postal	postcard
		sal	salt
		señal	sign
		sucursal	branch (office)

iii Words ending in *ante* and *ente*:

	M		**F**
ante	suede, elk	*constante*	constant
componente	component	*mente*	mind
paciente	patient (but can be feminine)	*patente*	patent
		pendiente	slope
		simiente	seed

iv Words ending in *z*:

M		**F**	
aprendiz	apprentice, learner	*faz*	surface, face
avestruz	ostrich	*hoz*	sickle, gorge
cáliz	chalice	*lombriz*	worm
matiz	hue, shade (of meaning)	*perdiz*	partridge
pez (alive)	fish	*tez*	complexion
regaliz	licorice		

v A number of feminine words:

armazón	frame (work)	*metrópoli*	metropolis
bilis	bile	*miel*	honey
cárcel	prison	*sangre*	blood
circular	circular	*sien*	temple (on head)
crin	horse's mane	*tos*	cough
flor	flower	*tribu*	tribe
líbido	libido	*víctima*	victim

NB *Armazón* can be masculine. ***Sartén*** (fry/frying pan) is feminine in Spain but masculine in Mexico. This is also true of ***radio*** when it means "radio."

There is much variation in Spanish in the naming of new gadgets:

el aspirador / la aspiradora	vacuum cleaner
el batidor / la batidora	whisk
la freidora	deep-fat fryer
la lavadora	washing machine
el secador	hair dryer
el tostador / la tostadora	toaster

These modern gadgets become a gender minefield when we consider them in Mexico, and it serves no great purpose to dwell lengthily on them. However, as an illustration, and no more than this, of the other possibilities, the following genders are standard in Mexico:

la aspiradora / la batidora / la secadora (hair dryer)

And now for a piece of information that baffles the author as much as it will you.

Azúcar (sugar) is masculine in Spain and other countries like Colombia, but feminine in Mexico. That's the easy bit. Since ***azúcar*** is feminine in Mexico, you would expect the definite article preceding it to be ***la***. But no. All Mexicans whom I have consulted make it clear that they say ***el azúcar***. Furthermore, they say and write: *El azúcar es blanca / refinada / morena* (brown). How you reconcile ***el*** in this case with the feminine form of the adjective, i.e. *blanca*, etc., is anyone's guess. Here is an attempt at an explanation. The author suspects that most Mexicans confuse the initial ***a*** of ***azúcar*** with that of ***agua***, for example, where ***el*** is required (see 1.1. ii above), to deal with the spoken stress on the first ***a***. But, there is no spoken stress on the initial ***a*** of ***azúcar***. It falls on the ***u***. Of course, Iberian Spanish requires: *El azúcar es blanco / refinado / moreno*. At the same time, most dictionaries cover themselves by saying that ***azúcar*** is masculine and feminine (***ambos*** = both)!

2.5 Gender of compound nouns

Another possible minefield, since many of these terms are fairly modern and therefore have unestablished forms, and, in keeping with the ease with which English lends itself to placing two or more nouns side by side, compound nouns are starting to burgeon in Spanish. However, the gender of compound nouns follows a certain logic.

i Two masculine nouns are obviously masculine:

café concierto	café (with live music)	*retrato robot*	photo fit
café teatro	dinner theater	*tiempo récord*	record time
piso piloto	show apartment, flat	*vehículo todo terreno*	land rover, 4x4, off-road vehicle

ii Two feminine nouns are naturally feminine:

bomba trampa	booby trap (bomb)	*palabra clave*	key word
etapa reina	star part (of cycle race)	*prueba reina*	key event (in sports race)
hora punta	commute hour, rush hour		
lengua madre	mother tongue		
madre patria	mother country		

NB *bocacalle* (street turning) and *madreselva* (honeysuckle) now constitute single words and follow the above rule

iii When two nouns are of different gender, the first determines the gender of the compound noun. Masculine nouns include:

camión cisterna	tanker (vehicle)	*factor sorpresa*	surprise factor
coche bomba	car bomb	*gas ciudad*	town gas
coche cama	sleeper (train)	*papel moneda*	paper money
coche patrulla	patrol car		

But this is not true of **radiorreceptor** (radio receiver), which is masculine, since **radio** is feminine.

iv Similarly, if the first noun is feminine, the compound noun is feminine:

cama nido	trundle bed, bunk bed	*fecha tope*	final/closing date
cárcel modelo	prison in Barcelona	*hora pico* (**M**)	commute hour
célula madre	mother cell (organism)	*luz piloto*	pilot light
ciudad dormitorio	dormitory town	*zona euro*	euro zone

v Compound nouns formed with other parts of speech are usually masculine and form one word:

abrelatas	can opener	*pasatiempo*	hobby, pastime
altavoz	loudspeaker	*portavoz*	spokesperson
espantapájaros	scarecrow	*quedirán*	public opinion
hazmerreír	laughing stock	*quehaceres*	domestic chores
paraguas	umbrella	*rompecabezas*	puzzle
pararrayos	lightning conductor	*terremoto*	earthquake

Finally three other compound nouns: *el/la purasangre* (thoroughbred horse), *la sinrazón* (injustice), *la enhorabuena* (congratulations).

2.6   Words distinguished by the ending *a/o*

Because of its distinctive gender endings, Spanish does not have many words with the same form but different meanings. However, as in Italian, there are numerous pairs of words distinguished only by *a* and *o* endings which are easily confused, and are a splendid test of your memory. The Mexicans do not make it any easier as with **bolso/bolsa** below. These are known as gender paronyms, or doublets (**dobletes** in Spanish). Below is a small selection of such testing words, so put your memory cap on now:

Feminine	**Masculine**
acera	**acero**
sidewalk, pavement	steel
acta	**acto**
minutes, record of a meeting	action, deed, act (in play)
arca	**arco**
chest, box	arch(way), bow (violin, archery)
banca	**banco**
banking (as system)	bank (as individual establishment), bench
bolsa	**bolso**
(any) bag, lady's purse / handbag (**M**), Stock Exchange (**Bolsa**)	lady's purse / handbag
bomba	**bombo**
bomb, pump	bass drum
caña	**caño**
reed, stalk, (sugar) cane, (fishing) rod, beer glass	pipe, jet
carga	**cargo**
load to be carried, charge (military and explosive)	burden, responsibility
casa	**caso**
house	case, instance
copa	**copo**
wine glass, trophy, top of tree	snowflake / cornflake
cuenta	**cuento**
account, bill	story, tale
fonda	**fondo**
tavern, small restaurant	bottom, background, fund
fosa	**foso**
grave, sea / land depression	pit, hole, ditch
fruta	**fruto**
fruit (as on the table) Note that **frutos secos** = nuts	fruit (as on a tree)
helada	**helado**
frost	ice-cream

libra	***libro***
pound (weight, money)	book
manga	***mango***
sleeve (coat, shirt)	handle
marca	***marco***
brand, trademark, record (sport), stain	frame (of picture)
moda	***modo***
fashion, style	way (of doing something), method
muñeca	***muñeco***
wrist, female doll	male doll (***muñeco de nieve*** = snowman)
pala	***palo***
shovel, spade	stick, post, mast
papelera	***papelero***
waste (paper) basket, paper mill	paper manufacturer
partida	***partido***
departure, register, certificate (of birth/marriage/death), game (chess)	(political) party, game (football)
pata	***pato***
leg (of animal)	duck
pimienta	***pimiento***
pepper (for seasoning)	pepper (vegetable)
****plata***	***plato***
silver, money (**M**)	plate, dish, course of meal
puerta	***puerto***
door	port, pass (in mountains)
punta	***punto***
point, sharp end	dot, speck, point (in scoring)
rata	***rato***
rat	short time
seta	***seto***
mushroom	hedge
tormenta	***tormento***
storm (usually violent)	torment, anguish
trama	***tramo***
plot, intrigue	section, stretch (of road)
vela	***velo***
sail, candle	veil

* At the risk of emphasizing the generation gap between reader and author, **Plata** is also the name of the Lone Ranger's horse = *Silver*. If, like the author as a child, you followed the western series entitled *The Lone Ranger* (*El Llanero solitario*), you would know what I mean.

2.7 Misleading similarities

This section is less to do with grammar than with semantics or fields of meaning. However, it seems useful to introduce you to the problem of "misleading similarities" or ***falsos amigos*** which include not only nouns but also verbs and adjectives. By "misleading similarities," we mean a word which has a similar form in two languages but which has different meanings in both languages. The expression *falso amigo* is less common in Spanish than in French (*faux ami*) where the phenomenon is very frequent (French > English and vice versa – and Italian > English and vice versa for that matter), although among the well-informed it is well known. Interference from one language to another is likely in these cases, so it is worthwhile giving special attention to them. Mexican importations from the USA can also produce considerable confusion. (See * after the list below.) So, when you consult a Spanish-speaking physician / doctor, you don't want to be treated for a cold when you are constipated, and you don't want to consult a psychotherapist for embarrassment when you are pregnant (see *constipado* and *embarazada* below). And never treat your *carpeta* like a carpet or your company will soon be plunged into bankruptcy, or you will fail your examinations. Also be careful with the use of *lujuria* and *lujo*, listed below. In order then to avoid these pitfalls, give some attention to this small list of the most common *falsos amigos* (there are many more):

Falso amigo	English equivalent	English cognate	Spanish equivalent
actual	present, i.e. now	actual	verdadero, real
la barraca	hut, shed	barracks	el cuartel
la carpeta	file, folder	carpet	la alfombra
la confidencia	confidential remark	confidence	la confianza
*constipado	cold	constipated	estreñido
la decepción	disappointment	deception	el engaño
la desgracia	misfortune	disgrace	la vergüenza, el escándalo
el disgusto	displeasure	disgust	el asco, la aversión
embarazada	pregnant	embarrassed	confuso, **violento
el éxito	success	exit	la salida
fastidioso	annoying	fastidious	quisquilloso, puntilloso
gracioso	witty, funny (person)	gracious	afable, cortés
la ingenuidad	frankness	ingenuity	el ingenio, la ingeniosidad
largo	long	large	extenso, amplio, ancho
la lectura	reading	lecture	la conferencia, la clase
la librería	bookstore/shop	library	la biblioteca
la lujuria	lust	luxury	el lujo
la miseria	poverty, squalor	misery	la pena, el sufrimiento
el muslo	thigh	muscle	el músculo
notorio	famous	notorious	de mala fama
la pinta	appearance, look	pint	= medio litro
quitar	to remove / take away	to quit	dejar, salir de
sensible	sensitive	sensible	sensato, prudente
simpático	nice	sympathetic	compasivo, comprensivo
el suceso	event	success	el éxito
la tabla	board	table	la mesa

* You can understand the confusion here if you consider the etymology of these two words. *Constipado* and "constipated" come from the Latin *stipor* = "to compress" / "fill" / "block up." It should be added that Mexican Spanish can be ambiguous here. *Constipado* can mean "constipated" in Mexico, so that if you went to a Mexican physician/doctor, and said you were *constipado*, you would need to add, for example: *Tengo la nariz tapada* (My nose is blocked up) or: *Estoy constipado de la panza / del estómago*.

** Yes, strange as it may seem, ***violento*** can certainly have the meaning of "embarrassed," as in: *Si te sientes violenta, volveremos a casa* = If you feel embarrassed, we'll go home. Mexico does not use ***violento*** with this meaning, and would offer ***apenado***, for example. Of course, ***violento*** has the meaning of "violent" in both countries.

Ejemplos

Es un chiste muy gracioso	It's a very funny/witty joke
Es el gracioso de todas las reuniones	He's the funny man at all the parties
¡Niño! eres un poco fastidioso, no paras de molestar	Hey, there, you really are a bit troublesome, you don't stop playing around
Su novia es hermana de una novelista notoria	His girl friend is the sister of a famous novelist

Exercises Level **2**

i **Rellena el blanco / Llena el espacio (M) con la palabra correcta, o sea el artículo definido o indefinido, donde sea necesario. En algunas casos hay que añadir tambien *a* o *de*.**

Ejemplo España es (_) gran país agrícola > España es *un* gran país agrícola
  a México es (_) gran nación
  b (_) muchedumbre está en (_) plaza
  c (_) estudiante prepara (_) tesis
  d (_) ambición (_) hombre no tiene límites
  e (_) alma es eterna
  f (_) avión imita (_) gorrión
  g (_) cocinera prepara (_) comida
  h Es (_) médico y muy listo
  i (_) padres tienen cuatro hijos, (_) hijas y (_) hijos
  j (_) físico estudia (_) física
  k (_) ministro llega con (_) ministra
  l (_) abogada habla con (_) alcalde
  m Voy (_) Cairo/(_) Cabo
  n (_) policía forma parte (_) policía
  o (_) bueno es que hable muy bien (_) español
  p Me impresionó mucho (_) ocurrido

ii **Pon las siguientes palabras según su orden correcto para crear frases coherentes. En algunos casos, hay que añadir también *a* o *de*.**

  a comedor chica el come la en
  b a escuela la el va muchacho
  c reina viaja la el Isabel Reina en
  d autor de largo libro el es
  e trama lo es una tiene interesante que complicada
  f extraño que no es lo venga
  g cónsul habla presidenta con la la
  h probable haga mañana lo lo que es
  i el Coruña Cairo nació la vive pero en en
  j apagón estropeó un se central la y se produjo

k arreglar para hice posible asunto lo el

l lo carta fácil es más escribir la

iii **¿Cuál es cuál? Pon el género correcto en las frases siguientes. En algunos casos, hay que añadir también *a* o *de*.**

a (_) batería se encontró (_) batería estropeada

b (_) defensa de hoy no suele jugar en (_) defensa

c (_) guardia formaba parte de (_) guardia

d (_) cabeza se hizo daño en (_) cabeza

e (_) cámara tomó (_) cámara

f (_) cura se interesa por (_) cura de las almas

g (_) Génesis se refiere (_) génesis del hombre

h Entiendo (_) cólera del médico cuando contempla (_) cólera

i Es imposible poner (_) coma cuando has sido afectado por (_) coma

j Hubo (_) corte eléctrico durante una sesión de (_) Cortes

k (_) fin (_) final fue emocionante

l El sargento dio (_) orden para imponer (_) orden

m (_) panda fue al zoológico para ver (_) panda

n Se me cayó (_) pendiente y rodó por (_) pendiente

o No funcionaba (_) terminal en el circuito eléctrico y hubo un apagón en (_) terminal de autobuses

p (_) vocal no sabía pronunciar todas (_) vocales

q (_) facha (_) facha parecía amenazante

iv **Aquí tienes catorce frases incompletas. Se trata de completarlas. Cada frase contiene dos palabras (dobletes) a las cuales les falta la *a* o la *o*, y posiblemente una *s* que indica el plural. Tienes que poner la *a* o la *o* en su lugar correcto para que la frase tenga un sentido lógico. Busca también el artículo definido o indefinido, o posiblemente el adjetivo demostrativo/posesivo que convenga.**

Ejemplos

Anda con cuent(_) cuando habla de(_) cuent(_) corriente > Anda con cuent**os** cuando habla de su cuent**a** corriente

Comer helad(_) cuando ha caído un(_) helad(_) tan fuerte me parece una bobada >

Comer helad**os** cuando ha caído un**a** helad**a** tan fuerte me parece una bobada

a Usa es(_) pal(_) para sacar es(_) pal(_) del camino porque no nos deja pasar

b To lo advierto por última vez, si tú no me haces cas(_), entonces saldré corriendo hacia tu cas(_) y te acusaré con tu mamá

c Cuando llueve mucho, y hace frío, nuestr(_) set(_) se llena de hongos y set(_)

d En invierno, cuando esté nevando, saldré a llenar mi cop(_) con cop(_) de nieve

e Vivo cerca de(_) puert(_) que es muy famoso por sus casitas con puert(_) de color rojo

f Un(_) plat(_) de plat(_) es mucho más costoso que un(_) plat (_) de loza

g Un(_) pat(_) usualmente tiene dos pat(_), y si no, entonces es(_) pat(_) que no tiene dos pat(_) es cojo

h Mi libr(_) pesa menos que medio kilo pero más que un(_) libr(_)

i Hace un rat(_) que no veo un(_) rat(_) en el parque. ¿Será que se fueron de vacaciones?

j El accidente dejó un(_) marc(_) en la pintura; ahora tendremos que cambiar su marc(_)

k Yo te aseguro que, aunque no sepa de música, un(_) bomb(_) no puede hacer tanto ruido como un(_) bomb(_)

l Las chicas de un harem podrían fabricar much(_) vel(_) con un(_) vel(_)

m El lugar donde comemos todos los días, que es un(_) fond(_), tiene un pasillo tan largo que es imposible ver que hay a(_) fond(_)

n Me gusta ver la cara de mi amada a través de su vel(_), alumbrada sólo con un(_) vel(_)

v Rellena los blancos / Llena los espacios (M) con la palabra que convenga. En cada caso, intenta encontrar una palabra española que pueda ser engañosa o malinterpretada cuando se traduce literalmente al inglés. La lista de arriba concerniente a falsos amigos te ayudará. Al final de la frase, escribe una traducción inglesa de la palabra que elijas.

Ejemplos

Este carro (**M**) / coche tiene un diseño(_) > Este carro tiene un diseño muy **actual** (*up-to-date*)

En el momento (_) hay mucho paro > En el momento **actual** hay mucho paro (*present*)

No creo yo en la (_) de la gente> No creo yo en la **ingenuidad** de la gente (*openness, sincerity*)

a Da gusto tratar con él por su (_)

b Ese niño necesita hacer algunos ejercicios de (_). No lee bien.

c ¿En qué (_) compraste el libro aquel?

d Aquellas familias viven en la más absoluta (_), no tienen nada para comer

e En los (_) se le está acumulando mucha grasa

f Manuel tiene (_) de enfermo. Ha perdido mucho peso

g Soy mucho más (_) al frío que al calor

h Eva es una chamaca (**M**) muy (_). Me cae muy bien

i Una (_) de windsurf no tiene nada que ver con una mesa de cocina

j Esos (_) inquietantes alarman a todos los ciudadanos

k Me llegó la (_) de que te casaste en Acapulco

l El médico / doctor (**M**) americano se confundió cuando le dije que estaba (_). Me dio pastillas para el estreñimiento

m Tuvo la (_) de perder a su hijo en un accidente

n Creo que está (_) de cinco meses

o Finalizó sus estudios con (_)

vi Actividad a realizar en parejas

Objetivo – aprender el sentido del nombre según el género

Método – Cada uno elige diez nombres con género variable. A le hace a B (y viceversa) preguntas sobre los sentidos del nombre cuando es masculino y cuando es femenino.

Ejemplos

PREGUNTA: ¿Cuál es el sentido de *cometa* cuando es femenino?
RESPUESTA: El sentido es *kite*
PREGUNTA: ¿Cuál es el sentido de *orden* cuando es masculino?
RESPUESTA: El sentido es *order* como en *arrangement*

Después, el / la profesor/a reúne a toda la clase para comentar el problema de los géneros variables.

Unit 3 *(Unidad 3)*
Number *(El plural)*

Level **1**
1.1 **Plural of nouns** (*El plural de los sustantivos/nombres*)
1.2 **Anglicisms** (*Anglicismos*)
1.3 **More on the formation of plurals** (*Más detalles sobre la formación de nombres en plural*)

1.1   Plural of nouns

i In the plural, the definite article has the following forms, agreeing with the nouns they accompany:

Masculine	**Feminine**
los the	*las* the
los hombres / chicos / libros	*las mujeres / chicas / mesas*
men/boys/books	women/girls/tables

ii The plurals of all Spanish nouns end in *s*. Nouns ending in an unstressed vowel or diphthong merely add an *s*:

la casa / las casas	house/houses
el mexicano / los mexicanos	Mexican/Mexicans
la tribu / las tribus	tribe/tribes
el agua / las aguas	water/waters

Monosyllables are treated in the same way:

el pie / los pies (foot/feet), *la fe / las fes* (faith/faiths)

iii Nouns ending in a consonant insert *e* as a connecting vowel:

el jardín / los jardines (yard/yards / garden/gardens), *el mártir / los mártires, el autor / los autores, el canal / los canales*

iv Final *z* is changed to *ces*:

el cáliz / los cálices	chalice/chalices
la cruz / las cruces	cross/crosses
el juez / los jueces	judge/judges
el matiz / los matices	shade of meaning / nuance / shades of meaning / nuances
la raíz / las raíces	root/roots

la voz / las voces	voice/voices
el desliz / los deslices	error/slip-up / errors/slip-ups

v The nouns ending in a stressed vowel also add *es*:

el bambú / los bambúes	bamboo/bamboos
el esquí / los esquíes	ski/skis
el rubí / los rubíes	ruby/rubies
el tabú / los tabúes	taboo/taboos
el marroquí / los marroquíes (frequently in speech = los marroquís)	Moroccan/Moroccans
el magrebí / los magrebíes	person(s) from the Maghreb (North Africa)
el yemení / los yemeníes	Yemeni/Yemenis
*el hindú / los hindúes	Hindu/Hindus
el israelí / los israelíes	Israeli/Israelis

* Also, although incorrectly but very common = Indian (from India).

However:

mi papá = my pop/dad	*mis papás* (***M***) = my mom and dad / parents

vi Unstressed endings in *is*, *es* and *us* in words of more than one syllable, pure Latin terms, and family names ending in *z* not stressed on the last syllable do not change:

el/los análisis	analysis/analyses
la/las crisis	crisis/crises
el/los lunes	Monday, Mondays
el/los déficit	deficit/deficits
el/los ultimátum	ultimatum/ultimatums
el/los superávit	surplus
Martínez (name) / *los Martínez*	Martinez / (the) Martinez
el virus / los virus	virus/viruses

vii Final diphthongs ending in *y* require *es* for their plural:

el rey / los reyes	king/kings
el convoy / los convoyes	convoy/convoys

1.2 Anglicisms

i Some Anglicisms have the English plural form though usage is uncertain here:

el gángster / los gángsters	gangster/gangsters
el récord / los récords	record/records
el club / los club(e)s	club/clubs
el líder / los líders / los líderes	the leader/leaders
el míster / los místers	soccer coach (Who would guess *míster?*)/ soccer coaches

Understandably, from the point of view of pronunciation, the plural of *el lord* is *los lores*.

ii Some nouns have stress on different syllables in singular and plural:

el carácter / los caracteres	character/characters
el régimen / los regímenes	régime/régimes
el espécimen / los especímenes	specimen/specimens

1.3 More on the formation of plurals

i In the formation of plurals, the place of the stress and the sound of the final consonant of the singular remain the same, and the spelling reflects this:

el almacén / los almacenes	warehouse/warehouses
el cañón / los cañones	canyon/canyons
la imagen / las imágenes	image/images
el jardín / los jardines	yard/yards /garden/gardens
el/la joven / los/las jóvenes	youth/youths
el lápiz / los lápices	pencil/pencils
el margen / los márgenes	margin/margins
el origen / los orígenes	origin/origins
la virgen / las vírgenes	virgin/virgins

ii Some plurals in Spanish do not have a concise equivalent in English:

los tíos	the uncle and aunt
los padres	the father and mother / parents
*los papás (**M**)*	the father and mother / parents

Exercises Level **1**

i Put the following nouns in the plural with the definite and indefinite article:

Example

muchacho > los/unos muchachos, muchacha > las/unas muchachas
padre, madre, libro, estudiante, pared, árbol, inglés, francés, martes, primavera, otoño,
pie, tribu, matiz, voz, atlas, caries, ratón, cárcel, buey, jersey, alemán, reloj

ii Fill in the nouns in their plural form. Note that *está* means "is" and *están* means "are." These two forms are from the verb *estar* = to be

Example

El vaso está en el salón	Los vasos están en los salones
El niño está en la casa	El jardín está detrás *(behind)* del edificio
El árbol está en el parque	La hoz está en la montaña
El gato está cerca de *(near)* la puerta	La nación está contenta
El lápiz está en la mesa	La niña está feliz
La flor está en el florero	La tribu está en la selva

iii Put in the singular. See note on the verb *estar* immediately above.

Example

Los alumnos están en los jardines – El alumno está en el jardín

Hay árboles en los jardines

Los estudiantes están en las aulas
Los cuadros están cerca de las ventanas
Los ingleses están en los hoteles
Los alemanes están en los salones
Los reyes están en los palacios
Los convoyes están en las carreteras
Las bicicletas están en las banquetas (**M** = *sidewalks/pavements*)

iv Paired activity
Objective – learn the plural of nouns
Method – Two people collect ten nouns each from the various lists above. Each person asks the other what the plural of a given noun is.

Example

PREGUNTA: ¿Cuál es el plural de *inglés* (What is the plural of *inglés*)?
RESPUESTA: El plural de inglés es *ingleses*

When all twenty nouns have been dealt with, the teacher/instructor will call the class together to discuss findings.

Level 2
2.1 Compound nouns (*Nombres compuestos*)
2.2 Spanish plural = English singular (*Plural español = singular inglés*)
2.3 Spanish singular = English plural (*Singular español = plural inglés*)
2.4 Agreement in number and verb (*Concordancia entre plural y verbo*)
2.5 Noun + *ser* + noun (*Nombre + ser + nombre*)

2.1 Compound nouns

Usually, the first noun is put in the plural but the second noun may also take a plural *s*, although this is less frequent, and would even sound strange if, for example, the last word of the following expression had an *s*: *un vehículo todo terreno, vehículos todo terreno*. It should be added that, since compound nouns and their pluralization are a comparatively recent linguistic phenomenon, hard and fast rules are still difficult to come by, and Spanish speakers hesitate themselves, so we are in good company. The following is just a small selection of the ever-increasing number of compound nouns as they are used in the plural:

las bocacalles	street entrances
las ciudades dormitorio	dormitory towns
las ciudades modelo	model cities
las fechas tope	final/closing dates
las ideas clave	key ideas
los coches bomba	car bombs
los coches patrulla	patrol cars
los factores sorpresa	surprise factors
los sectores clave	key sectors
los límites tope	final/closing dates
las células madre	mother cells
los retratos robot	photofits

las carreras reina	main races
las horas punta	commute/rush hours
*las horas pico (**M**)*	commute/rush hours

Note: **Clave** is certainly one of the nouns often used in the plural.

los elementos claves	key elements
las ideas claves	key ideas
las actividades claves	key activities

2.2 Spanish plural = English singular

There is often a plural noun in Spanish corresponding to an English singular noun:

las agujetas	stiffness (in limbs) (but shoelaces in **M**!)
*por los aires	through the air
las andas	portable platform (for religious processions)
*los aplausos	applause
*las barbas	beard
*las bodas	wedding
los cascotes/escombros	rubble
*los celos	jealousy
*los conocimientos	knowledge
*(los) Correos	Post Office
las cosquillas	tickling
con creces	with interest (financially), abundantly
los cubiertos	cutlery
los datos	information/data
los deberes	homework
¡Buenos Días!	Good morning!
los efectivos	personnel
las enaguas	petticoat
a mis expensas	at my expense
*las fuerzas	strength
*los funerales	funeral
*los honorarios	fees (professional)
las investigaciones	research
las lluvias	rain(s)
las municiones	ammunition
¡Felices Pascuas/Navidades!	Merry Christmas!
*las nieves	snow
los pertrechos	gear
hacer progresos	to make progress
*los remordimientos	remorse
las tinieblas	darkness
los transportes (públicos)	public transportation
en vísperas de	on the eve of

*It has to be added that this list is only a rough guide, since many of these nouns (*) may be used in the singular, but in a different way. However, the following three nouns are also used in the singular with no real change of meaning:

aplauso, funeral, remordimiento:

El aplauso duró varios minutos	The applause lasted for minutes
Al funeral asistió mucha gente	Many people attended the funeral
No siente el menor remordimiento	She feels not the slightest remorse

> *El aire* means "the air" as in *Necesitamos aire para respirar* (We need air to breathe) or *Hay mucho aire hoy* (It's breezy today) while the plural would be used in *saltar por los aires* (to explode into the air)
>
> *Las bodas* is used in *las bodas de plata/oro* (silver/golden wedding) but in the singular it means specifically "wedding" as in *Ayer asistí a una boda* (Yesterday I attended a wedding)
>
> *El celo* means *zeal* (el celo religioso) and *heat* (of animals = *en época de celo*)
>
> *Cosquillas* is used in the expressions *hacer/tener cosquillas* (to tickle / to be ticklish) and is rarely used in a singular form
>
> *Dato* may be used in the singular as: a piece of data = datum
>
> *Deber* means *duty*
>
> *Las lluvias* is frequently used in *las lluvias abundantes/torrenciales* (heavy/torrential rain) but *No me gusta la lluvia* (I don't like rain)
>
> *Las nieves* has a poetic touch, as in *Escasean las nieves este año* (There has not been much snow this year). But *Me gusta jugar en la nieve* (I like playing in the snow)
>
> Many more examples could be cited but we are now moving into the area of usage, which is not the intention of the book

2.3 Spanish singular = English plural

This is the reverse of 2.2:

*el alicate	pliers
*la braga	panties, knickers
*la escalera	stairs
la estadística	statistics
*la gente	people
*la malla	tights
*el pantalón	pants, trousers
*el pijama / la piyama (**M**)*	pajamas
*la pinza	pincers
la táctica	tactics
*la tropa	troops

The words asterisked also have a plural form. In fact, *alicates, bragas, escaleras, mallas* and *pinzas* are used more than their singular counterparts. *Los pantalones* is used as frequently as its singular equivalent. The same is true of *las tropas*.

As with *estadística* and *táctica, la física* and *la política* seem to suggest a plural but are singular.

2.4 Agreement in number and verb

Difficulties can occur, even for Spanish speakers, when a collective noun is followed by *de* + plural noun, just as in English we may hesitate over: "The government states/state that . . ." or "The police has/have released a statement." In the following cases, logic requires a plural, but purists would argue for the singular:

> *Un número de profesores se reúne esta tarde* (A number of teachers meets this afternoon) but *se reúnen* is acceptable
>
> *Un grupo de chicos jugaba en el patio* (A group of boys were playing in the yard) but *jugaban* is acceptable
>
> *La mayor parte / La mayoría de los carros fue estropeada* (Most of the cars were damaged) but *fueron estropeados* is acceptable
>
> *El noventa por ciento de los estudiantes saca una buena nota* (90% of the students get a good mark). *Sacan* is acceptable
>
> *Similarly: la mitad / un tercio de las chicas . . .* (half / a third of the girls . . .), *una docena / un centenar de coches . . .* (a dozen/hundred-odd cars . . .), *Buena parte de los edificios . . .* (A good part of the buildings . . .), *medio millón de jóvenes . . .* (half a million young people . . .)

Los Estados Unidos is usually followed by a plural verb while *Estados Unidos* (i.e. no definite article) is followed by a singular verb:

Los Estados Unidos proponen un pacto	The United States propose a pact
Estados Unidos sugiere una mesa redonda	The United States suggests a round table

2.5 Noun + *ser* + noun

Ser agrees in number with the following noun:

El problema son los estudiantes	The problem is the students
La manifestación eran unos gamberros que rompían cristales	The demonstration was hooligans breaking windows

Exercises Level **2**

i Pon en singular donde sea necesario

Ejemplo (las primeras palabras del ejercicio) Los gobiernos pasan . . . > El gobierno pasa por una crisis económica, sobre todo el lunes . . .

Los gobiernos pasan por crisis económicas, sobre todo los lunes. Yo creo que las crisis tienen sus orígenes en los virus de las computadoras. Es casi cierto que los déficits de los gobiernos superan los diez billones de dólares y que rompen todos los récords. Los déficits no tienen nada que ver con los regímenes políticos. Esperan que los superávits vuelvan en los próximos meses. Los elementos claves de esta situación residen en las fechas límite en que los gobiernos, los lores y sobre todo los gángsters, tendrán que devolver todos los billones prestados o robados. La alternativa es ingresar a todos los granujas que son culpables en cárceles modelo.

RB/JPL

ii Pon en plural donde sea necesario

Ejemplo (las primeras palabras del ejercicio) El joven, con un amigo israelí . . . > Los jóvenes, con amigos israelíes . . .

El joven, con un amigo israelí y una amiga hindú, entró en el almacén con papel moneda. Quería comprar una luz piloto pero no estaba en la zona euro y no hablaba español. Sólo sabía una palabra clave, nada más, porque su lengua madre era el árabe. El dueño le ofreció una luz piloto de gran calidad. Salió del almacén y, con su amigo israelí y su amiga hindú, entró en una bocacalle oscura. Se encontró en un café donde tomó un té árabe de menta, y regresó a la estación para ver a su amigo yemení.

iii Rellena los blancos / Llena los espacios (M) en las siguientes frases con palabras en plural

Ejemplo Avanzó (_) en las tinieblas > Avanzó a ciegas en las tinieblas

a Tengo (_) por haber hecho demasiado ejercicio
b El coche bomba saltó por los (_)
c Una salva de (_) acompañaba al líder de la carrera
d Los obreros rellenaron el hoyo con los (_) de la obra
e Dame tus (_) personales para rellenar la ficha
f El estudiante hace muchos (_) en la universidad
g Me dan miedo las (_) cuando llega la noche
h Falta poco para que festejemos las (_) de plata
i Pon los (_) en la mesa, por favor
j Ganaron el Premio Nobel con sus (_) sobre el cáncer

iv Actividad en parejas
Objetivo – estudiar el plural de nombres compuestos
Método – dos personas eligen diez nombres compuestos (ver 2.1). A le hace a B preguntas (y viceversa) sobre la formación del plural de nombres compuestos. Aquí, se trata de un partido

Ejemplo

PREGUNTA: ¿Cuál es el plural de *idea clave*?
RESPUESTA: El plural de *idea clave* es *ideas clave(s)*
　　　　　　　(Hay dos posibilidades)

Lógicamente, la persona que consiga más respuestas gana el partido.

Unit 4 *(Unidad 4)*

Verbs *(Los verbos)*

Level **1**

1.1 **Present indicative of the three model verbs** *(Indicativo del presente de los tres verbos modelos)*

1.1 Present indicative of the three model verbs

All Spanish verbs in the infinitive end in **-ar**, **-er** or **-ir**. They are divided into three classes or conjugations according to these endings:

1st conjugation	*compr**ar***	to buy
2nd conjugation	*vend**er***	to sell
3rd conjugation	*viv**ir***	to live

The vowels **a**, **e** and **i** are characteristic of these three conjugations. The first conjugation includes approximately 90 percent of all the verbs in the language, so we have no justification in complaining here. There are about 300 verbs which deviate from these patterns, but this figure includes some uncommon verbs little used except in quizzes, for instance.

If we cut off the endings **ar**, **er**, **ir** from the infinitive, we have the stem of the verb to which endings of various moods and tenses are to be added. This excludes the future and conditional. Spanish verbs therefore reflect the pattern of Romance languages like French, Italian and Portuguese. Here, then, is the conjugation of the three model verbs in the present indicative:

	1st person	*yo*	*compr**o***	*vend**o***	*viv**o***
	2nd person	*tú*	*compr**as***	*vend**es***	*viv**es***
Sing.	3rd person	*él*			
		ella ⎫	*compr**a***	*vend**e***	*viv**e***
		Ud. ⎭			
	1st person	*nosotros/as*	*compr**amos***	*vend**emos***	*viv**imos***
	2nd person	*vosotros/as*	*compr**áis***	*vend**éis***	*viv**ís***
Plur.	3rd person	*ellos* ⎫			
		ellas ⎬	*compr**an***	*vend**en***	*viv**en***
		Uds. ⎭			

(See Unit 17.1.1. for the use of the *vosotros / as* forms.)
The present indicative corresponds to three English forms:

yo compro / tú compras, etc.	I buy / do buy / am buying / you buy, etc.
yo vendo / tú vendes, etc.	I sell / do sell / am selling / you sell, etc.
yo vivo / tú vives, etc.	I live / do live / am living / you live, etc.

Since the endings of Spanish verbs, like those of Italian verbs and, to a lesser extent, French verbs, have a distinctive sound characteristic, the subject pronouns **yo**, **tú**, **él**, etc. are much less used than in English. They are only used to avoid ambiguity or to stress the reference to a particular person. If you wanted to say "I am buying a house," you would probably say in Spanish "***Compro una casa***." However, if you wanted to highlight the fact that you are buying the house and not someone else, your brother, a friend, etc., you would probably say "***Yo*** *compro la casa (y no él)*." Furthermore, if reference has already been made to, say, *él*, *ella* or *Ud*. and their corresponding plurals, although the verb ending is the same, it is likely that the subject pronoun would not be repeated.

Exercises Level **1**

i Put in the correct form of the present indicative of the verb shown in parentheses so that it fits the subject pronoun. You need not put in the pronoun in your sentence:

Example

(Yo / estudiar) el italiano > Estudio el italiano

(Yo/comprar) un carro, (Tú/buscar) una flor, (Él/Ella/Ud./necesitar) dinero, (Ella/tocar) el piano, (Nosotros/as/platicar [**M**]) con un amigo, (Vosotros/as/hablar) español, (Ellos/Ellas/Uds./rentar (**M**) / alquilar) una casa

ii Put the infinitive into the correct form so that it corresponds to all the subject pronouns indicated:

yo/tú/él/ella/Ud./nosotros/as/vosotros/as/ellos/ellas/Uds.   estudiar el portugués
beber vino
comer pan
viajar mucho
correr los cien metros
aprender la natación
limpiar la cocina
escribir una carta
abrir la puerta

iii The following phrases are not in the right order and need to be placed in a logical sequence, which then produces a small narrative in the present tense. Also, put the infinitives in their corresponding forms. There is not just one fixed order of sentences. So, feel free to use your imagination.

Colocar un sello / timbre (**M**) en el sobre
Meter la carta en el buzón
Platicar (**M**) / **hablar** con el cartero
Mandar la carta a Estados Unidos
Los amigos **recibir** la carta al día siguiente
Caminar (**M**) / **andar** hasta Correos
No **manejar** un carro (**M**) / **conducir** un coche
(Yo) **entrar** en la cocina y **abrir** la ventana
Regresar a casa
Escribir una carta en la mesa
Los amigos **vivir** en Estados Unidos

Beber tequila juntos en un café
Respirar el aire

iv Find the appropriate form of a verb to be placed in the following sentences

Example

Yo (_) en la Ciudad de México > Yo vivo en . . .

Yo (_) tequila, Tú (_) tacos (**M**) / tapas, Él (_) una casa, Nosotros (_) un carro, Vosotros (_) una carta, Ellas (_) una tarjeta, Uds. (_) mañana

v Paired activity
Objective – To use the present tense
Method – Ask each other five questions in the present tense, using the three verbs **comprar**, **vender** and **vivir**

Example

PREGUNTA: ¿Qué compras?
RESPUESTA: Compro una casa
PREGUNTA: ¿En dónde vive Juan?
RESPUESTA: (Juan) vive en Monterrey

Afterwards, the teacher/instructor will bring you together to discuss your findings.

Level **2**
2.1 Rules and agreement of verbs (*Reglas y concordancia de verbos*)

2.1   Rules and agreement of verbs

i The greater number of verbs which govern an infinitive do so directly without any connecting preposition:

Deseo leer el periódico	I want to read the newspaper
Temo ofenderla	I am frightened of offending her
Necesito beber agua	I need to drink water

Aprender and **enseñar**, two basic verbs, require **a** before an infinitive:

*Aprendo **a** hablar chino*	I am learning to speak Chinese
*Enseño a los alumnos **a** tocar el arpa*	I am teaching the pupils to play the harp

ii A number of phrasal verbs, consisting of **tener** (to have) followed by a noun, usually require **de** before an infinitive. The following are among the most usual:

Tener ganas de . . .	To be inclined to / keen on . . .
Tener miedo de . . .	To be frightened to . . .
Tener medios de/para . . .	To have the means to . . .
Tener tiempo de . . .	To have the time to . . .
Tener intención de . . . (also with **la**)	To intend to . . .

Ejemplos

*Tengo ganas de ir a la alberca (**M**)*	I feel like going to the swimming pool
Tiene (la) intención de regresar	She intends to come/go back

iii In some cases the verb is followed by a definite article and then a noun + *de* +
infinitive:

Tener la bondad de . . .	To have the kindness to . . .
Tener la costumbre de . . .	To be accustomed to . . .
Tener la desgracia de . . .	To have the misfortune of/to . . .
Tener el gusto de . . .	To have the pleasure of . . .
Tener el honor de . . .	To have the honor of . . .
Tener la intención de . . .	To intend to . . .
Tener la ocasión/oportunidad de . . .	To have the opportunity to . . .
Tener el privilegio de . . .	To have the privilege of . . .
Tener la suerte de . . .	To be lucky to . . . / to have the good fortune to . . .

Ejemplos

Ten la bondad de acompañarme	Kindly accompany me
Tengo el gusto de presentarles . . .	I have the pleasure of introducing to you . . .

iv When the verb has two or more joint subjects of either number, it is regularly put in
the plural:

Ejemplos

Mi padre y yo nadamos cada día	My father and I swim each day
Tú y tu hermana* jugáis cada día	You and your sister play each day
La niña y la madre leen un libro	The child and the mother read a book

* But *juegan* in Mexico

v The subject is frequently placed after the verb. It does not affect the meaning, but
gives variety and balance to the sentence:

Ejemplos

Llega mi padre a las tres	My father arrives at three
Viajan mis hermanos en primera	My brothers (and sisters) travel first class
Almorzamos nosotros a las dos	We have lunch at two

vi Some verbs do not always have a strict equivalent of tense in English. This applies to
their use both in the present tense and in the imperfect. (See also unit 7 on the
imperfect tense.) It can also apply to the preterit but discussing this is not necessary
for our purposes here. Such verbs are: ***soler***, ***llevar***, ***hacer***.

Ejemplos

Suelo ir al cine los viernes	I usually go to the movies on Fridays
*Suele rentar un carro (**M**) el domingo*	He usually rents a car on Sundays
Solemos pasar la Semana Santa en el campo	We usually spend Easter week in the countryside
Llevo más de un mes estudiando mucho	I've been studying a lot for more than a month
*¡Lleva dos años intentando manejar el carro (**M**)/conducir el coche!*	He's been trying to drive the car for two years!

Empecé a trabajar hace dos semanas   I began working two weeks ago
Trabajo desde hace dos semanas   I have been working for two weeks

Notice the use of the present tense (**llevo** and **trabajo**) in these constructions.

Exercises Level **2**

i **Pon en su orden correcto las siguientes palabras. Al mismo tiempo, pon el infinitivo en la forma correcta del indicativo. No hay obligación de usar los pronombres personales si el sentido está claro**

Ejemplo miedo entrar casa en tener oscura la de >Tengo miedo de entrar en la casa oscura
piano tocar yo el a aprender, tomar ganas agua tener vaso de de un yo, aprobar suerte examen tener de el la, tener no cuenta pagar la medios de los ellos, ella intención la castellano tener estudiar de, la boletos (**M**) de los bondad comprar él tener, costumbre trabajar mañana la la por de tener nosotros, el presentar de a novia gusto a tener yo mi te, ¿abrir querer Ud. ventana la?, ¿vino querer tú copa una de nosotros con tomar?

ii **Escribe frases con los siguientes grupos de palabras. Puedes usar cualquier tiempo (tense)**

Ejemplo querer subir > Quiero subir a la cumbre de la montaña
querer enseñar leer, desear invitar cenar, necesitar leer escribir, mandar llamar al plomero (**M**) / fontanero, aconsejar escribir, decidir mandar apagar

iii **Planeas ir de vacaciones. Escribes una carta sencilla en primera persona y en indicativo del presente, usando todos los verbos que quieras para mostrar lo que quieres hacer. Intenta usar sobre todo verbos seguidos de una preposición / o sin una preposición, y un infinitivo. Aprovecha sobre todo las expresiones en 2. 1. i, ii, iii.**

Ejemplo Tengo la oportunidad **de visitar** los Estados Unidos

iv **Cambia los verbos *soler*, *llevar* y *hacer* al presente de indicativo**

Ejemplo Ella (soler) ir al teatro cada semana > Suele ir al teatro . . .
     Yo (soler) acostarme a las once
     Ellos (soler) cenar muy tarde
     Nosotros (soler) ir al cine cada sábado
     (Ellos) (llevar) un mes en Madrid
     Ella (llevar) un mes aprendiendo a manejar (**M**) / conducir
     Llegué aquí (hacer) cinco minutos
     Estoy aquí desde (hacer) diez minutos

v **Actividad en parejas**
Objetivo – Usar *tener* + nombre + *de*
Método – Cada persona encuentra seis expresiones y le hace preguntas a la persona de enfrente

Ejemplos

PREGUNTA: ¿Tienes ganas de nadar?
RESPUESTA: Sí, tengo (ganas de nadar)

PREGUNTA: ¿El chamaco (**M**) / chico tiene miedo de entrar en aquella casa?
RESPUESTA: Sí, tiene miedo (de entrar en aquella casa)

In these answers, a Spanish speaker would probably not repeat the full sentence. However, it would be good for you to repeat it for practice.

Unit 5 *(Unidad 5)*

Perfect tense and pluperfect tense (*El [pretérito] perfecto y el pluscuamperfecto / antecopretérito* [**M**])

Level **1**
1.1 **Perfect tense** (*El [pretérito] perfecto*)

1.1 Perfect tense

Haber and the perfect tense (with some reference to *tener*)

There are two equivalents in Spanish of the English verb *to have*: **haber** and **tener**. They are not interchangeable. They are both used for the creation of the perfect tense, but for the moment, in level 1, we shall concentrate on **haber**. (See also "Irregular Verbs," 12.1.1.)

The perfect tense in Spanish is made up of the present tense of **haber** (*to have*) and the past participle of the verb in question. This is similar to the English equivalent construction. The perfect tense in Spanish for verbs ending in **-ar** is as follows:

	1st person	*He compr**ado***	I have	bought
Sing.	2nd person	*Has compr**ado***	You have	bought
	3rd person	*Ha compr**ado***	(S)He has / You have	bought
	1st person	*Hemos compr**ado***	We have	bought
Plur.	2nd person	*Habéis compr**ado***	You have	bought
	3rd person	*Han compr**ado***	They/You have	bought

-Er and **-ir** verbs follow a similar, but not identical, pattern:
***Comer*:**

*He/has/ha/hemos/habéis/han com**ido***   I/you/(s)he/you/we/you/they have/has
                                                  eaten

***Vivir*:**

*He/has, etc., viv**ido***   I/you, etc., have/has eaten

Unfortunately, there are a large number of irregular verbs the past participles of which do not respect this simple pattern. They will be dealt with in level 2.

To a large extent, the use of the perfect tense in Spanish corresponds to the use of the perfect tense in English. However, there is one important reservation here. In all Spanish

America, the perfect tense is used much less frequently than in Iberian Spanish. Three simple examples will illustrate this feature. When you get up in the morning, you would say in Spain "*¿Has dormido bien?*" ("Have you slept well?"), but in Mexico the question would almost certainly be "*¿Dormiste bien?*" ("Did you sleep well?"). Again, during the morning, say at eleven o'clock, if a Spaniard asked you what you had done that morning, (s)he would doubtless say "*¿Qué has hecho esta mañana?*" but in Mexico that question would be "*¿Qué hiciste esta mañana?*" A third and final example: after having just eaten a meal, a Spaniard would probably say "*¿Has comido bien?*" but a Mexican would doubtless ask "*¿Comiste bien?*" In other words, in Mexico a different tense is used. This tense is called the past definite or preterit tense, and will be treated in a later chapter (unit 8), so we shall not concern ourselves any more with it here. It should be pointed out, in consequence, that the illustrations in this unit will **not** involve Mexican Spanish, since it would not be logical or authentic to provide examples with a Mexican flavor.

It may be more helpful, and certainly more logical, to call the perfect tense the **past indefinite tense** for one simple reason, and that is the meaning of **indefinite**. Although the perfect tense refers to the past, it is really the recent past which can often overflow onto the present moment. In this sense, it is not perfect, or complete, at all. For instance, it is as though there is business left undone in the sentence: "*He hablado con Juan*" ("I have spoken to Juan"). This sentence suggests that there remains something to add, like "*¿Y qué ha dicho?*" ("What has he said / did he say?"), hence the appropriateness of **indefinite**. However, the perfect tense in Iberian Spanish stretches further back in time than in English, which is why you may legitimately and logically say "*He perdido el conocimiento*," but the equivalent English "I have lost consciousness" has no meaning at all, unless you have a spectacular imagination. Mexican Spanish is much more like English in this last example, for it too would require a great leap of the imagination.

The perfect tense is therefore used in the following cases:

i Where an action has begun in the past and continues until the present moment:

He vivido aquí varios años   I have lived here for a number of years

ii Where an action has been repeated several times and can continue to be repeated:

Lo he leído cuatro veces   I have read it four times

iii Where an expected action has still not taken place:

El médico no ha llegado   The doctor has not arrived

iv Where an action has taken place in the very recent past:

Han adivinado la verdad   They have guessed the truth

The following further examples will illustrate the usage of the perfect tense in Spanish:

He hablado con mi amiga	I have spoken with my (female) friend
Han llegado tus hermanos	Your brothers (and sisters) have arrived
He terminado la lectura del libro	I have finished reading the book
¿Has aprendido italiano?	Have you learnt Italian?
Hemos comido unos pasteles muy ricos	We have eaten some very nice cakes

Exercises Level **1**

i **Write in the perfect tense of the verb indicated and use the appropriate form of the verb *haber*:**

Example

Yo/perder mis llaves   >   He perdido mis llaves

a (Yo) aprender español   f (Ella) pasar un año en Nuevo México
b ¿(Tú) copiar el informe?   g No (él) llegar todavía
c (Ellos) comer una enorme paella   h ¿Qué (tú) comprar hoy?
d (Ellos) jugar al fútbol esta tarde   i (Nosotros) vivir en Puebla
e Llover todo el día   j (Vosotros) meter la carta en el buzón

ii **Answer the following questions. If you are adventurous, you could use the negative (see unit 26):**

a ¿Han llegado tus amigos?   f ¿Has encontrado tu cartera?
b ¿Quién ha preparado la cena?   g ¿Mamá ha planchado las camisas?
c ¿Has entendido la pregunta?   h ¿Habéis comido bien?
d ¿Han vivido en Tejas / Texas (**M**)? i ¿Ha llovido hoy?
e ¿Has seguido todo el curso?   j ¿Has podido terminar tu trabajo?

iii **Following the example below, write out the full perfect tense conjugation for each sentence:**

Example

He trabajado todo el día – has trabajado todo el día, ha trabajado todo el día, hemos trabajado todo el día, habéis trabajado todo el día, han trabajado todo el día

a He empezado el libro hoy   d He comido unas tapas
b No he vivido en San Francisco   e No he aprendido la lección
c He corrido en la maratón   f He ido al colegio hoy

iv **Paired activity but involving the whole class. Bear in mind that this exercise would not easily apply to Mexico where the perfect tense is not used very much. This explains why the *vosotros*, and not *Uds.* form is used here (see 17.1.1.).**

Objective – To use the perfect tense with different subject pronouns

Method – Two class members ask each other ten questions, and afterwards the class is free to ask them both questions

Use words like *¿Cuándo?*/When?, *¿A qué hora?*/At what time?, *¿Por qué?*/Why?, *¿Cómo?*/How? to introduce your questions. Use verbs like *comer, correr, comprar, aprender, andar, vender, vivir, preparar, seguir, hablar.*

Example

PREGUNTA: ¿Qué has hecho esta mañana?
RESPUESTA: He trabajado dos horas

Pregunta hecha por la clase (Question asked by the class): ¿Qué habéis hecho esta mañana?

Respuesta dada por los otros dos (Answer given by the other two): Hemos trabajado dos horas

Level **2**
2.1 **Passive perfect tense** (*El pasivo del pretérito perfecto*)
2.2 **Pluperfect tense** (*Pluscuamperfecto / antecopretérito* (**M**))
2.3 **Note on the past anterior** (*Nota sobre el pretérito anterior*)

2.1 Passive perfect tense

i The perfect tense of the passive is formed, as in English, in the following way:

Haber + past participle of ***ser*** + past participle of the verb in question

*La venta ha sido aplazad**a***	The sale has been postponed
*Los coches han sido reparad**os***	The cars have been repaired
*La comida ha sido preparad**a***	The meal has been prepared
*El dinero ha sido devuelt**o***	The money has been returned

Note that, in these cases, the past participle of the main verb agrees in gender and number with the subject, as highlighted. If you think about it, the past participle functions like an adjective which agrees in gender and number. It should be added here that there is a natural tendency to use the reflexive form of the verb, and not the passive form as above. (See unit 14 on the reflexive which takes us into deeper water.)

ii The auxiliary verb *haber* is not separated by another word from the past participle, as is often the case in French and Italian:

He estudiado muy mal la lección	I have studied the lesson very badly
Todavía no han llegado	They still haven't arrived
Siempre han sacado buenas notas	They have always gotten good marks
Has hecho muy bien tu trabajo	You've done your work very well

iii When a past participle is used with a verb other than *haber*, agreement in number and gender occurs, since it operates like an adjective:

*Deja la(s) ventana(s) abiert**a(s)***	Leave the window(s) open
*He encontrado la caja cerrad**a***	I found the box locked
*Encontré a la chica escondid**a***	I found the girl hidden
*Dejé la televisión rot**a***	I left the television broken

iv When conjugated with *haber*, the past participle never agrees with its object:

He escrito la carta	I have written the letter
Han abandonado la casa	They have left/abandoned the house
Hemos alquilado dos coches	We've rented two cars

v However, when the verb *tener* is used with a participle, agreement does occur since the meaning is not quite the same. Compare these two sentences with *haber* and *tener*:

*He escrit**o** la cart**a***	I have written the letter
*Tengo escrit**a** la carta*	I've gotten the letter written

Similarly:

*Han abandonad**o** la casa*   *Hemos alquilad**o** dos coches*
*Tienen abandonad**a** la casa*   *Tenemos alquilad**os** dos coches*

When ***tener*** is used, the past participle operates like an adjective, agreeing with the noun.

vi Past participle used as a noun. This is a very common practice, not only in Spanish but also in French and Italian. English has few equivalents to this phenomenon. The nouns in these cases may often be found in the plural. Below is a short list:

accidentado(s)	the injured (in an accident)
acusado(s)	the accused
consultado(s)	those who were / have been consulted
convocado(s)	those who were / have been called
encuestado(s)	those questioned (for a survey)
entrevistado(s)	those who were / have been interviewed
excluido(s)	those excluded
herido(s)	the wounded
inscrito(s)	those who were / have been registered
jubilado(s)	the retired
marginado(s)	those who were / have been excluded
privilegiado(s)	the privileged
rescatado(s)	those rescued

It goes without saying that, if these past participles / nouns were in the singular, the translation might be "the one who was / had been / has been," etc. What is certain is that English cannot very easily accommodate this phenomenon.

2.2 Pluperfect tense

The imperfect of ***haber*** with the past participle forms the pluperfect tense. It is equivalent to the English *had done / spoken / walked*, etc. It represents an action or event not only past but occurring before another past event. The usage is thus the same in both languages:

Me dijo que Armando se había ido   She told me that Armando had gone away
Pensábamos que el niño se había acostado   We thought the child had gone to bed
Me di cuenta de que habían cambiado el dinero   I realized they had changed the money

2.3 Note on the past anterior

This is a literary tense, little used in current speech and general writing or newspapers, for instance, although it does appear in narrative writing, novels and so on. You will probably not need to use it but it is useful to recognize it. It has the same use and meaning as the pluperfect.

It is preceded by such conjunctions as

apenas hardly   *no bien* no sooner
cuando when   *tan pronto como* as soon as

después de que after   *al momento que* as soon as
en cuanto as soon as   *luego que* as soon as

and is formed with the preterit of **_haber_** and a past participle:

Apenas hubo pronunciado estas palabras cuando se oyó un ruido ensordecedor
Hardly had she pronounced these words when we heard a deafening noise

Cuando los catedráticos hubieron otorgado el premio el público empezó a aplaudir
When the professors had bestowed the prize, the audience began to clap

Exercises   Level **2**

i **Escribe un pequeño párrafo conteniendo todos los siguientes verbos. Ponlos en pretérito perfecto como si escribieras (*as if you were writing*) un diario que se refiriera (*referred*) a todo lo que acaba de ocurrir (*has just happened*). Te ayudamos con los sustantivos (*nouns*).**

Llegar estación. Encontrar a (*see unit 22 for the personal* "a") un amigo. Hablar política y fútbol. Comer restaurante. (Él) regresar su pueblecito. (Yo) permanecer plaza. Encontrar a una amiga. Tomar café. Vivir momentos agradables. Despedir (*See off*) a mi amiga estación. Regresar casa.

ii **Tienes que crear un formulario que contenga (*contains*) preguntas sobre perfiles (*profiles*) de personas que hacen solicitudes en lo que a un empleo se refiere. Pon todos los verbos en pretérito perfecto y en tercera persona, o sea *Ud.*:**

Ejemplo Viajar mucho – ¿Ha viajado mucho Ud.?

Deportes: Jugar al fútbol. Nadar en el mar. Correr los diez mil metros. Estudiar la esgrima. Hacer esquí. Estar en el Polo Norte. Subir al Himalayo a las Montañas Rocosas. Ver la Copa del Mundo. Querer batir el récord del mundo de cinco mil metros. Cazar rinocerontes. Meter cinco goles un un partido de fútbol

Finanzas: Invertir veinte mil dólares. Perder una gran cantidad de dinero. Ahorrar el cincuenta por ciento de su sueldo. Preferir una cuenta corriente (*checking/current*) a las otras cuentas. Saber distinguir entre varios tipos de acciones

Capacidad imaginativa: Pintar cuadros. Tocar un instrumento de música. Cocer pan al horno. Soñar con / realizar hazañas heroicas. Remendar camisas

Sensibilidad: Oír mucha música clásica. Ver películas de Luis Buñuel. Leer *Los Hermanos Karamazov*. Traducir una novela al inglés. Escribir poesía. Componer sinfonías

Personalidad y sentido práctico: Convertirse al budismo. Temer grandes tentaciones. Reñir a sus niños. Reírse de un pobre desgraciado (*poor unfortunate person*). Poner la mesa todos los días. Huir de un peligro. Fregar platos. Sufrir problemas psicológicos

iii **Un niño / una niña vuelve del colegio y le hace su mamá varias preguntas sobre la tarde pasada en presencia de su maestra. Imagínate las preguntas y las contestaciones entre la mamá y el niño / la niña.**

iv **Acabas de visitar (*You have just visited*) un rancho. Di lo que has hecho (*Say what you have done*), usando el pretérito perfecto, y la primera persona singular y plural. Puedes aprovechar las siguientes palabras:**

Llegar rancho de un amigo. Abrir barrera. Entrar casa. Platicar ranchero. Presentar familia. Introducir salón. Visitar corral. Ver los burros, otros animales. Subir a caballo.

Recorrer hacienda. Ir pesca. Despedirse. Prometer regresar un día a verlos otra vez. Volver a casa muy feliz

v Usa los dos verbos *haber* y *tener* en las siguientes frases. Distingue claramente entre estos verbos empleados en pretérito perfecto.

Ejemplo

(Yo) Haber/tener copiado todos los documentos – He copiado todos los documentos / Tengo copiado**s** todos los documentos

a (Yo) Haber/Tener alquilar / rentar (**M**) una casa

b (Ella) Haber/Tener escribir cuatro cartas

c (Ellos) Haber/Tener preparar la cena

d (Nosotros/as) Haber/Tener organizar la visita

e ¿(Vosotros/as) Haber/Tener planear la táctica?

vi Forma una sola frase con las dos siguientes frases. Se trata de usar el pretérito (ver la unidad 8) y el pluscuamperfecto / antecopretérito (M) y en este orden.

Ejemplo

Adriana compró un huipil (traditional Indian dress). Ella lo dijo.

Adriana dijo que había comprado un huipil

a El bebé estuvo enfermo. La mamá nos contó.

b Ha habido muchos problemas. Adriana lo admitió

c Vinieron unos científicos franceses. Avisaron en el departamento

d Llegaron ayer. Me lo dijo

e El chico comió cinco helados. Lo supe esta mañana

f Las estudiantes se fueron de vacaciones. Me enteré esta tarde

g Las chicas aprobaron todos sus exámenes. Me lo dijeron sus madres

h El carro se descompuso (**M**). Me avisó mi cuate (**M**)

i Subieron ochenta viajeros al camión (**M**) (= *bus*). Me lo dijo mi padre

j Hubo un accidente. Me informó una policía

k El coche se averió. Me lo dijo mi padre

Unit 6 *(Unidad 6)*

Future tense and future perfect tense (*El tiempo futuro y el futuro perfecto*)

1.1 The future

i The future tense, which in English is made up of the use of *will* and *shall*, is formed in Spanish by adding the following endings to the full infinitive of the verb:

			comprar	*vender*	*vivir*
	é	e.g	*comprar**é***	*vender**é***	*vivir**é***
Sing.	*ás*		*comprar**ás***	*vender**ás***	*vivir**ás***
	á		*comprar**á***	*vender**á***	*vivir**á***
	emos		*comprar**emos***	*vender**emos***	*vivir**emos***
Plur.	*éis*		*comprar**éis***	*vender**éis***	*vivir**éis***
	án		*comprar**án***	*vender**án***	*vivir**án***

A point of interest: these endings are related to the present tense of the verb **haber**. Once the Latin inflexion system had died out, it was replaced by the infinitive of the verb and **haber**, so that **compraré** originally meant *I have / am to buy*. These comments also apply to the future tense in French, Italian and Portuguese.

ii In this manner are formed the futures of all regular verbs, and, we must be grateful for this, nearly all irregular verbs. Rather than deal with the future of irregular verbs in the section on the latter, it seems helpful to treat them here, since they are so few in number.

caber	*cabré*	*cabrás*	*cabrá*	*cabremos*	*cabréis*	*cabrán*
decir	*diré*	*dirás*	*dirá*	*diremos*	*diréis*	*dirán*
haber	*habré*	*habrás*	*habrá*	*habremos*	*habréis*	*habrán*
hacer	*haré*	*harás*	*hará*	*haremos*	*haréis*	*harán*
poder	*podré*	*podrás*	*podrá*	*podremos*	*podréis*	*podrán*
poner	*pondré*	*pondrás*	*pondrá*	*pondremos*	*pondréis*	*pondrán*
querer	*querré*	*querrás*	*querrá*	*querremos*	*querréis*	*querrán*
saber	*sabré*	*sabrás*	*sabrá*	*sabremos*	*sabréis*	*sabrán*
salir	*saldré*	*saldrás*	*saldrá*	*saldremos*	*saldréis*	*saldrán*

tener	*tendré*	*tendrás*	*tendrá*	*tendremos*	*tendréis*	*tendrán*
valer	*valdré*	*valdrás*	*valdrá*	*valdremos*	*valdréis*	*valdrá*
venir	*vendré*	*vendrás*	*vendrá*	*vendremos*	*vendréis*	*vendrán*

iii The use of the future is practically the same as in English. It refers logically to a future event that has not taken place.

Examples

Le diré a mi madre que . . .	I'll tell my mother that . . .
Será necesario ir mañana	It'll be necessary to go tomorrow
Pasaremos un mes en México	We'll spend a month in Mexico
¿Cuándo iremos al parque?	When will we go to the park?
Saldremos la semana próxima	We'll leave next week

iv It is interesting to note that the future tense is increasingly less used in Spanish, a phenomenon reflected in both French and Italian. It is frequently replaced by the construction *ir* + **infinitive**, which is similar to the English:

*Voy a tomar el camión (**M**)*	I'm going to / I'll catch the bus
Vamos a ver la película mañana	We're going to / We'll see the movie tomorrow
¿Vas a ver a tu hermana mañana?	Are you going to / Will you see your sister tomorrow?

Exercises Level **1**

i **Change the verbs in the following sentences from the present tense to the future tense. Change the adverbs of time if necessary. (See unit 25.2.6 for help on adverbs, if you need it.)**

Example

Te doy ahora la lección	>	Te daré la lección más tarde

Les leo el cuentito (**M**) / cuentecito ahorita
Recogemos las manzanas inmediatamente
El jefe está ahora en la oficina
Busco el video (**M**) / vídeo dentro de dos minutos
La chica viene en seguida
Te llamo después
Pago la factura en este banco
Hago el trabajo hoy

ii **Change to the future the verbs in italics**

Example

Le *doy* el libro al chico	>	Le daré el libro al chico

Me *dan* una botella de vino	*Sale* con sus amigos
¿*Dice* la verdad?	¿*Vienes* con tu papá?
Hace sus deberes	*Compramos* un carro
Pone las flores en la mesa	*Vendemos* la casa

Viven en Venezuela	*Abro* la puerta
El programa *dura* cinco minutos	*Reciben* los regalos

iii Change the subject and verb according to the new subject indicated

Example

Saldremos a las diez (Yo) > Saldré a las diez

En México cenaremos a las diez (Tú)
¿Llegaréis mañana? (Ella)
Iremos de vacaciones a Acapulco (Ellos)
Mandaré la carta esta tarde (Nosotros)
Aprenderé a manejar el carro (**M**) (Ellas)
Sabré pronto leer el ruso (Ud.)
Pondremos los huevos en el frigorífico (Yo)
Abrirán la puerta del cine a las diez (Él)

iv Paired activity but with class participation
Objective – To use the future tense
Method – Two members of the class ask each other ten questions and give the answers. These questions and answers are followed by class participation which involves other pronouns which are not necessarily used since the verb endings are usually sufficient

Example

	PREGUNTA:	¿Qué harás mañana?
	RESPUESTA:	Iré al cine
Class intervention	PREGUNTA:	¿Qué harán Uds. (**M**) / haréis mañana?
	RESPUESTA:	Iremos al cine

Use questions involving words like: *¿Cuándo?* (When?) / *¿A qué hora?* (At what time?) / *¿Dónde?* (Where?), as well as *¿Qué?*
Use verbs like *comprar, vender, vivir, hacer, salir, venir, ir, ser, estar, poner*

Level **2**
2.1 **Future perfect tense** (*El futuro perfecto*)
2.2 **Further remarks on the future** (*Más comentarios al futuro*)

2.1 Future perfect tense

i The future perfect suggests a degree of conjecture or possibility. This is a relatively easy concept since it corresponds well to the English equivalent. It refers to an action regarded as completed at the time of speaking:

Habrán llegado a la estación	They will have arrived at the station
Habré perdido mi cartera en la calle	I probably lost / will have lost my wallet in the street

Antes de la semana próxima habrás terminado la faena	Before next week you will have finished the job
¿Qué habrá pasado?	What has / could have happened?

2.2 Further remarks on the future

The future is frequently used to replace the present tense to convey the idea of conjecture or probability:

Tendrá treinta años	She's probably thirty years old
Estarán dormidos los niños	The children are probably / must be asleep
Conoceréis este cuento	You may know this story

i In short, emphatic declarations, and in brief requests for instructions, the present indicative often replaces the future in colloquial language. This is a very common practice and corresponds to what is happening in French and Italian. Are we becoming lazy? Certainly, it is easier to use the present tense than the future. Here are some examples:

Voy a su casa luego	I'll go to her house later
Salen mañana	They('ll) leave tomorrow
No pago la cuenta	I'll not pay the bill
Si insistes, te parto la cara	If you insist, I'll punch you
Pero ¿qué hago?	But, what will I do?

Exercises Level **2**

i **Cambia al futuro perfecto las siguientes frases:**

Ejemplo Trabajarán todo el día > Habrán trabajado todo el día
a Llegarán a las tres
b Serán estudiantes ejemplares
c ¿Cuánto ganará?
d Tendrán un tren de vida fantástico
e ¿Qué hará la chica?
f ¿Cuántos años tendrá?
g Sabrá al menos tres idiomas
h La gallina pondrá dos huevos al día

ii **Imagínate que seas (*you are*) un adivino / una adivina (*fortune teller*). Usando el futuro de probabilidad, te encuentras a una persona (mujer u hombre) en un lugar público y especulas sobre su vida, sus actividades, su profesión, su familia, su capacidad intelectual, su afición a los deportes, su ropa, su casa. Aprovecha los vocablos de abajo como guía:**

ser, tocar música, ejercer abogado(a)/contable, trabajar con una empresa internacional, viajar mucho piloto, tener mujer/hombre y dos hijos, tener mucho cariño, estar casado(a), estar dotado(a) de inteligencia, disponer de mucho dinero, estar capaz de correr, comprar una casona / un departamento (**M**), crear una vida

iii **La semana próxima, la clase se divide en parejas. Un/a participante desempeña el papel (*carries out the role*) de adivino/a, y el otro / la otra desempeña el papel de la persona cuyo futuro está en manos del adivino / de la adivina. Imaginen la conversación que habrán preparado durante esta semana. Aquí tienen el inicio de la conversación:**

ADIVINO (estudiando su bola de cristal): Será Ud. un hombre muy rico
CLIENTE: Pero soy muy pobre
A.: Le tocará la lotería
Cl: ¿Cuánto ganaré?
A.: Ganará millones de pesos

Unit 7 *(Unidad 7)*

Imperfect tense (*El tiempo imperfecto/copretérito* [**M**])

Level **1**

1.1 **The imperfect tense** (*El tiempo imperfecto/copretérito* [**M**])

1.1 The imperfect tense

The imperfect tense is to be studied in conjunction with the preterit or past definite in the next unit (unit 8), since they are frequently linked to each other.

In addition to the perfect tense (a compound tense) treated in Unit 5, Spanish has two past tenses of simple form: the imperfect (***pretérito imperfecto*** or ***copretérito*** as it is known in Mexico) and the preterit. In regular verbs, the imperfect tense is obtained by adding the following endings to the stem:

1st conjugation	2nd and 3rd conjugation
-aba	*-ía*
-abas	*-ías*
–aba	*-ía*
–ábamos	*-íamos*
–abais	*-íais*
–aban	*-ían*

Imperfect tense of the model verbs:

Sing.	*compr**aba***	*vend**ía***	*viv**ía***
	*compr**abas***	*vend**ías***	*viv**ías***
	*compr**aba***	*vend**ía***	*viv**ía***
Plur.	*compr**ábamos***	*vend**íamos***	*viv**íamos***
	*compr**abais***	*vend**íais***	*viv**íais***
	*compr**aban***	*vend**ían***	*viv**ían***

NB   You will note that the first and third person singular of these conjugations are the same so sometimes, to avoid ambiguity, it may be necessary to use the pronouns ***yo***, ***Ud.***, ***él*** and ***ella***, although context would usually make this clear.

The formation of the imperfect tense is different in only three irregular verbs. This makes the learning of the imperfect quite easy. The three awkward verbs are:

ser:	*era*	*eras*	*era*	*éramos*	*erais*	*eran*
ir:	*iba*	*ibas*	*iba*	*íbamos*	*ibais*	*iban*
ver:	*veía*	*veías*	*veía*	*veíamos*	*veíais*	*veían*

The fundamental value of the imperfect tense is to express continuance, as of an action prolonged either in itself or by successive repetition. It conveys what was habitual, customary, and describes qualities of persons or things, and the place or condition in which they were, in the past. **Yo compraba** corresponds to the English *I was buying, used to buy, would buy* and *bought*. In this sense, it is much simpler than the several English equivalents, which makes life difficult for Spanish speakers learning English: and for English speakers this compensates for the subjunctive, for instance, to be studied in unit 16.

Various ways in which the imperfect is used:

i To convey repeated and habitual past actions:

Yo iba siempre al mismo supermercado	I always went to the same superstore
*Los cuates (**M**) se divertían cada día en la alberca (**M**)*	The friends had fun every day in the swimming pool
Fumaba una cajetilla diaria	She smoked a packet a day

ii To describe an action that was in progress:

Leía el periódico	She was reading the newspaper . . .
Salía del colegio cuando . . .	I was coming out of school when . . .
Estábamos en la playa cuando . . .	We were on the beach when . . .
Planeaban visitar España	They planned (were planning) to visit Spain

iii To describe physical, mental or emotional states in the past:

Estaba agotada	She was exhausted
Los mellizos tenían once años	The twins were eleven years old
Adorábamos la ópera	We adored opera
Hacía sol todos los días	It was sunny every day
Sabían resolver todos los problemas	They could solve all the problems

iv To refer to the time in the past:

Era la una	It was one o'clock
Eran las cuatro y media	It was half-past four

Exercises Level **1**

  i Change the subject of the verb to the subject in brackets:

Example

Yo comía carne una vez a la semana (Él) > Él comía carne una vez a la semana

  a Yo guardaba el dinero en una bolsa (Nosotras)
  b Hablaban todos los días en el patio (Nosotras)
  c Salíamos muy temprano por la mañana (Yo)
  d Veía la televisión todas las noches (Ellos)
  e Íbamos de compras el viernes (Ella)
  f Yo corregía los ejercicios por la tarde (Nosotros)
  g Comíamos a la una (Yo)
  h Tenía que tomar el tren en Guanajuato (Ellas)
  i Lavaban los platos después de la cena (Yo)

ii **Fill out the spaces with the imperfect tense of the verb indicated. Choose your own subject.**

Example

(_) comer el pescado (preferir) > Preferían comer el pescado

a (_) comprar el libro (querer)
b (_) leer este libro (pensar)
c (_) que salir (tener)
d (_) a ver la tele (ir)
e (_) invitar a todo el mundo (querer)
f (_) ganas de nadar (tener)
g (_) ir al mercado (necesitar)
h (_) jugar golf (**M**) (pensar) (not *jugar al golf* as in Spain)

iii **Paired activity**
Objective – Use of the imperfect tense
Method – The two participants ask each other ten questions in the imperfect tense. Answers are also given in the imperfect tense.

Examples

PREGUNTA: ¿En dónde vivías en México?
RESPUESTA: (Yo) Vivía en Monterrey
PREGUNTA: ¿Qué vendía el comerciante en el mercado?
RESPUESTA: Vendía fruta y verduras

The teacher will then bring the whole class together to discuss the findings

Level **2**
2.1 Certain verbs with no English equivalent (*Ciertos verbos sin equivalente inglés*)

2.1 Certain verbs with no English equivalent

There are a number of verbs which are used in the imperfect tense, and in the present tense (see relevant section on the present tense in unit 4), and do not have a proper English equivalent. Among these are: *acostumbrar, soler, llevar, hacer*. They are used in the following way:

acostumbrar hacer algo	to be accustomed to doing something
soler hacer algo (less used in **M**)	to be accustomed to doing something
llevar tanto tiempo haciendo algo / hacer tanto tiempo	(to) have been doing something for so much time / to take so much time to do . . . / so much time ago

Ejemplos

Acostumbraba desayunar huevos con jamón	I usually had ham and eggs for breakfast
Solía estudiar sobre todo por la mañana	I usually studied mainly in the morning
Estos melones solían ser muy ricos	These melons used to be very good

Solían venir aquí los martes	They used to / would come on Tuesdays
Yo llevaba diez años en Veracruz cuando . . .	I had been in Veracruz for ten years when . . .
Llevaban tres días trabajando cuando . . .	They had been working for three days when . . .
Llevaba dos días sin fumar	I had not smoked for two days
Hacía seis meses que había llegado	He had arrived six months before
Habían salido para Brasil hacía un mes	They had left for Brazil a month before
Hacía seis meses que habían sido capturados	They had been captured six months before

Exercises Level 2

i Elije un verbo adecuado después de *pero* y ponlo (*put it*) en pretérito imperfecto

Ejemplo

Yo quería ir al teatro pero (_) > Yo quería ir al teatro pero no tenía tiempo

a Intentaba hallar (**M**) / encontrar trabajo pero (_)
b Procuraban resolver el enigma pero (_)
c Parecían ingleses pero (_)
d Siempre lograban programar el viaje pero (_)
e Cada día evitábamos las faenas de la casa pero (_)
f Siempre prometías recogerme en tu carro pero (_)
g Preveíamos salir cada fin de semana pero (_)
h De vez en cuando insistía en devolver el dinero pero (_)

ii Ibas a la sierra con frecuencia (solo o con amigos/as). Usando los verbos de abajo, escribe una pequeña redacción que relata las actividades que realizabas. Huelga añadir que el pretérito imperfecto es el tiempo dominante

ir, llamar, tener rentado/alquilado, salir, estar, ser, llegar, conducir, bajar, subir, aumentar, sudar, hacer, cultivar, poder, querer, advertir, planear, prohibir.

iii Llena los espacios (M) / Rellena los blancos con *soler*, *llevar* o *(desde) hacer*, según el sentido. Se trata de usar el pretérito imperfecto.

Ejemplo

Yo (_) diez años trabajando en la empresa cuando gané la lotería > Yo llevaba . . .

a Nosotros (_) dos años en la casa cuando decidimos comprarla
b Ella (_) escritas dos cartas cuando tuvo que salir
c Ellos (_) mucho rato esperando en la estación
d Yo (_) media hora en el hospital
e Yo (_) leer toda la tarde
f Estos melones (_) ser muy ricos pero ahora no son tan buenos
g Tú (_) venir aquí cada fin de semana pero no vienes nunca ahora
h Él (_) manejar un carro (**M**) pero después del accidente lo vendió
i Yo leía un libro (_) mucho tiempo cuando sonó el teléfono
j Él estudiaba (_) tres años cuando se licenció

iv Actividad en parejas
Objetivo – El uso de los verbos *acostumbrar*, *soler*, *llevar* and *hacer* in the imperfect tense, y según su uso en 2.1.

Método – Cada uno de la pareja le hace al otro cinco preguntas en imperfecto. El otro contesta y hace cinco preguntas a su vez

Ejemplos

PREGUNTA: ¿Qué solías hacer en Santa Mónica?
RESPUESTA: Solía nadar todos los días
PREGUNTA: ¿Adónde acostumbrabas ir de vacaciones?
RESPUESTA: Acostumbraba ir a Acapulco

Después, el profesor reúne a todo el mundo para recabar (*collect together*) todas las preguntas y respuestas.

Unit 8 *(Unidad 8)*

Preterit tense or past definite *(El pretérito indefinido / pretérito perfecto simple)*

1.1   Preterit tense

The preterit tense, or past definite, in Spanish, as in English, is used to described single, completed actions in the past. These actions may be single or multiple. It corresponds therefore to the English *I spoke / ran / did / went*, etc. = *hablé, corrí, hice, fui*. It needs to be distinguished from the imperfect and perfect tenses, a distinction which will be dealt with in level 2.

Formation: to the stem are added the following

1st conjugation	2nd and 3rd conjugations (2 and 3 are the same)
-é	*-í*
-aste	*-iste*
-ó	*-ió*
-amos	*-imos*
-asteis	*-isteis*
-aron	*-ieron*

Preterit tense of the three model verbs

Sing.	*compré*	*vendí*	*viví*
	compraste	*vendiste*	*viviste*
	compró	*vendió*	*vivió*
	compramos	*vendimos*	*vivimos*
Plur.	*comprasteis*	*vendisteis*	*vivisteis*
	compraron	*vendieron*	*vivieron*

This has been easy up to now. However, there are a number of irregular verbs the stems of which are entirely different from the stems of the infinitive. The one compensation is that the preterits of **ser** and **ir** are the same, so you save a few minutes here. Now, let's look at the main irregular verbs:

dar (**d**)	di	diste	dio	dimos	disteis	dieron
decir (**dij**)	dije	dijiste	dijo	dijimos	dijisteis	dijeron
estar (**estuv**)	estuve	estuviste	estuvo	estuvimos	estuvisteis	estuvieron
haber (**hub**)	hube	hubiste	hubo	hubimos	hubisteis	hubieron
hacer (**hic**)	hice	hiciste	*hizo	hicimos	hicisteis	hicieron
ir (**fu**)	fui	fuiste	fue	fuinos	fuisteis	fueron
ser (**fu**)	fui	fuiste	fue	fuinos	fuisteis	fueron
poder (**pud**)	pude	pudiste	pudo	pudimos	pudisteis	pudieron
querer (**quis**)	quise	quisiste	quiso	quisimos	quisisteis	quisieron
saber (**sup**)	supe	supiste	supo	supimos	supisteis	supieron
tener (**tuv**)	tuve	tuviste	tuvo	tuvimos	tuvisteis	tuvieron
venir (**vin**)	vine	viniste	**vino	vinimos	vinisteis	vinieron

Note *hizo where the **c** is logically changed into a **z** to preserve the sound. Otherwise a retained **c** would produce a **k** sound. And don't become inebriated with ***vino*! (What's the joke here?)

As stated above, the preterit refers to completed actions, no matter how long these actions last. They could have lasted for hundreds of years, but if they have ended, the preterit is used.

Examples

Fui a Nueva York la semana pasada	I went to New York last week
Regresaron de Inglaterra en junio	They came back from England in June
¿Cuándo aprendiste a nadar?	When did you learn to swim?
Julio César vivió cincuenta y siete años y murió en el año 44 antes de Cristo	Julius Caesar lived for fifty-seven years and died in 44 BC
Cervantes, como Shakespeare, nació en el siglo dieciséis, y murieron el mismo año	Cervantes, like Shakespeare, was born in the sixteenth century, and they died in the same year

A series of sequential actions is also conveyed by the preterit:

Regresé a las diez, me acosté en seguida y me levanté muy temprano	I returned at ten o'clock, went to bed straight away and got up very early

Exercises Level 1

i In the following sentences, change the subject for the new one in brackets

Example

Metí el dinero en el bolsillo (Ella) >   (Ella) metió el dinero en el bolsillo

a Salí después de desayunar   (nosotros)
b Abrió la puerta   (la chica)
c Cerraron la ventana   (yo)
d ¿Qué comisteis en el restaurante?   (tú)
e Perdió su bolso en la playa   (yo)
f Fui a Madrid la semana pasada   (ellas)
g ¿A qué hora volvieron anoche?   (tú)
h Los turistas pasaron un mes en el hotel (mi hermano)
i ¿Por qué bebiste tanta coca cola?   (ellos)

j Estuve en Málaga ayer   (nosotras)
k ¿Por qué hiciste tus deberes anoche?   (el chico)
l No viniste a verme el domingo pasado   (él)

ii In the following sentences change the verb in italics into the preterit:

Example

José *bebe* mucha agua > Antonio bebió mucha agua

a Juan *compra* dos panecillos
b *Voy* al colegio
c *Cumplo* dos años
d Los chicos *regresan* tarde
e Los políticos no *están* de acuerdo
f Las mujeres *preparan* una comida rica
g A las diez *salen* a pasearse por el parque
h ¿Por qué no me *invitáis* a cenar?
i ¿*Vives* lejos de Los Ángeles?
j *Hace* un poco de natación

iii Answer the following questions, using the preterit

Example

¿Dónde dormiste anoche? > Dormí en mi cama, ¡claro!

a ¿A dónde fuiste ayer?
b ¿Cuánto tiempo pasaste allí?
c ¿Estuviste con amigos?
d ¿Disfrutó mucho todo el mundo?
e ¿Se quedaron contigo todos tus amigos?
f ¿Comisteis / comieron (**M**) en un café?
g ¿Qué comieron (**M**) / comisteis?
h ¿Qué bebisteis / bebieron (**M**)?
i ¿Volvisteis / Regresaron (**M**) muy tarde?
j ¿Dormiste bien?

iv Paired activity

Objective – To use the preterit or past definite tense

Method – Ask each other ten questions. After all the pairs have completed their question and answer session, you all come together. You choose one pair and ask them questions in the plural, using *Uds*. If you were in Spain you would use the *vosotros* form. You should end up practicing the *yo, tú, nosotros/as, vosotros/as* and *Uds*. forms of the verb

Examples

PREGUNTA: ¿Dónde fuiste ayer?
RESPUESTA: Fui a la alberca (**M**)/piscina
PREGUNTA: ¿Dónde encontraste tu libro?
RESPUESTA: Encontré mi libro en mi casa *or preferably* Lo encontré en mi casa

Examples with whole class

PREGUNTA: ¿Por qué fueron/fuisteis a la alberca (**M**) / piscina ayer?
RESPUESTA: Fuimos a la alberca (**M**) / piscina por que hacía calor
PREGUNTA: ¿Dónde vivieron/vivisteis el año pasado?
RESPUESTA: Vivimos en Veracruz

You need to be smart here because you could need the imperfect tense at times. See unit 7.

Here are some verbs you could use:

encontrar, caminar, correr, llegar, recibir, venir, comprar, dar, decir, estudiar, trabajar, arreglar, esperar, perder

Level **2**

2.1 **Differences between the preterit and the imperfect** (*Diferencias entre el pretérito y el imperfecto*)

2.2 **Differences between the preterit and the perfect** (*Diferencias entre el pretérito y el pretérito perfecto*)

2.3 **The preterit and perfect in Mexico** (*El pretérito y el pretérito perfecto en México*)

2.1 Differences between the preterit and the imperfect

i Whereas the imperfect tense relates to events that have no clear ending, or take place over an unspecified period of time, the preterit refers to a very sharply defined action or event. The Spanish equivalent of the English *I was reading the paper when my sister walked in* is: *Leía el periódico cuando entró mi hermana*. The imperfect is continuous time while the preterit cuts across this continuum. Put another way, when we express two past actions, occurring at the same time, the shorter action is conveyed by the preterit while the longer one is in the imperfect. This explanation is better understood by a simple diagram:

Past	Present

Leía el periódico (longer action)

cuando entró mi hermana (shorter or single action)

Otros ejemplos

Mientras escribía la carta dieron las once	While I was writing the letter, it struck eleven o'clock
*Mientras se abría la puerta dejé caer / se me cayó la pluma (**M**) / el bolígrafo*	While the door was opening I dropped the pen

ii Words associated with the preterit: *ayer, la semana pasada, el año pasado, anoche, una vez, de repente, de súbito, súbitamente* (in other words, specific points in time). Words associated with the imperfect: *mientras, todos los días, cada año, con frecuencia, frecuentemente, a menudo, de niño, de joven* (in other words, habitual or general features in the past).

iii Of course, these words do not automatically trigger the imperfect or the preterit; witness the following cases:

*Ayer jugué béisbol (**M**) / al béisbol*	Yesterday I played baseball
Ayer jugaba fútbol cuando llovió	Yesterday I was playing football when it rained
De niño tocaba la guitarra	As a child I used to play the guitar
De niño empecé a tocar la guitarra	As a child I began to play the guitar

iv In historical narration, the distinction is not always so clear. The preterit can apply to actions or events of some duration, but it still evokes something accidental or temporary.

Ejemplos

César escribió la historia de sus conquistas	Caesar wrote the history of his conquests
Los aztecas conquistaron toda Mesoamérica	The Aztecs conquered all Meso-America

If the preterit tenses in the above were changed to the imperfect, their sentences and meaning would be incomplete without some complementary clause such as:

César escribía . . . cuando estalló una guerra	Caesar was writing . . . when a war broke out
Los aztecas conquistaban . . . cuando llegaron los españoles	The Aztecs were conquering . . . when the Spaniards arrived

v In narrations the preterit tells the occurrences which provide the thread of the story while the imperfect describes the scenes in which they occurred; witness the following narrative:

El sol **brillaba** en un cielo sin nubes. **Soplaba** una brisa muy agradable y las olas **chapoteaban** dulcemente sobre el agua. El barco **deslizaba** silenciosamente por entre las rocas, el gorjeo de las gaviotas nos **embelesaba** y **disfrutábamos** de la tranquilidad del ambiente. De súbito, se **oyó** una explosión ensordecedora, y **apareció** en el cielo un cohete que **creó** un destello azul. Nos **quedamos** atónitas. Nos **entró** una sensación de asombro. RB

(There is quite a lot of new vocabulary here. But you can guess the meaning in most cases.)

2.2 Differences between the preterit and the perfect

The following comments are complicated by different usage in Spanish America and Iberian Spanish. Remarks are limited initially to Spain but Spanish American and, notably, Mexican usage will subsequently be treated. If the occurrence took place within a space of time not yet expired, as this day, month, year, etc., or if it is in any way connected with the present, the perfect tense is employed. But if distance in time intervenes, the preterit may well be used. Compare the two examples:

He escrito dos cartas esta mañana	I wrote two letters this morning
Escribí dos cartas ayer	I wrote two letters yesterday

He escrito could not be easily be used in the second case. However, ***escribí*** could be used in the first case if the point at which the person speaks is the evening, and not, say, mid-day or two o'clock in the afternoon. It is all a question of relation between the time of speech and the time referred to.

Compare two further examples related to getting up in the morning.

¿Has dormido bien?	Have you slept well? / Did you sleep well?

would be used first thing in the morning but in the evening one would probably ask:

¿Dormiste bien anoche?	Did you sleep well last night?

Further examples illustrating the differences

No he ido a España este año (includes the present time)	I haven't been to Spain this year
No fui a España este año (excludes the present time)	I didn't go to Spain this year
Le escribí a mi padre el Martes (excludes the present time)	I wrote to my father on Tuesday
Le he escrito a mi padre varias veces (includes the present time)	I've written to my father a few times
México ha producido muchos autores eminentes (includes the present time)	Mexico has produced many eminent writers
México no produjo muchos autores eminentes en el siglo dieciocho (excludes the present time)	Mexico did not produce many eminent writers in the eighteenth century

The perfect and the preterit are used with no distinction in such statements as:

Lo hice / lo he hecho hace cinco minutos	I did it five minutes ago

Interestingly enough, the English perfect could not be used here.

2.3 The preterit and perfect in Mexico

(See also the perfect, unit 5, level 1.)

As in most other South American countries, in Mexico the perfect is used much less than in Spain. For instance, in two examples quoted above, only the preterit would be used:

¿Dormiste bien? (after just getting up)	Did you sleep well?
Lo hice hace cinco minutos	I did it five minutes ago

Further examples

Me lavé los dientes (just now)	I've cleaned my teeth
¿Viste la película?	Have you seen / Did you see the movie?
Votaron al presidente (today)	They've voted for the president
Subió el precio	The price has gone up

Of course the last example could mean: *the price went up* (i.e weeks ago)

Level 2

i Completa:

Ejemplo

Admiraba la bahía cuando (_) > oí un ruido ensordecedor

a Bebía tranquilamente mi tequila cuando (_)
b Carlos tocaba el piano cuando (_)
c Regresaban de la playa cuando (_)
d Pensábamos en ti cuando (_)
e Comíamos mariscos cuando (_)
f Veíamos la televisión cuando (_)
g Jugábamos al béisbol cuando (_) (Jugábamos béisbol . . . in **M**)
h Dormíamos cuando (_)
i Manejaba el carro (**M**) cuando (_)
j Planchaba los pantalones cuando (_)
k Hablaba por teléfono cuando (_)

ii Cambia el infinitivo entre paréntesis al pretérito simple o al pretérito imperfecto, según el sentido

El verano pasado (ir) de campamento a la sierra. Me (acompañar) varios amigos que (estudiar) en la misma universidad. Cada uno (llevar) una mochila, y (tener) bastante dinero para una semana. (Tener) un carro que (ser) muy viejo pero que (funcionar) muy bien. Antes de llegar al campamento, (llenar) el tanque de gasolina. Cuando (estar) en el campamento (montar) las dos tiendas. Los chicos (preparar) la cena y las chicas, ¿por qué no? (dar) un paseo. Al día siguiente, (subir) a la alta sierra. (Haber) muchas plantas y animales y el sol (verse) resplandeciente. (Asolearse [**M**] / (Tomar) el sol. (Disfrutar) mucho de la naturaleza. Nos (gustar) mucho estar en contacto con el mundo natural. Es porque (estar) allí. (Regresar / Volver) a casa después de una semana que (estar) llena de recuerdos agradables.

iii Contesta las preguntas, usando el pretérito perfecto, indicando "varias veces"

Ejemplo

¿Fuiste a Cuernavaca? > Sí, he ido tres veces

a ¿Oíste el ruido en la calle?
b ¿Leíste la novela que te había prestado?
c ¿Vio Ud. esa película?
d ¿Perdiste tus llaves?
e ¿Fueron Uds. al Museo de Antropología?
f ¿Visitaron Uds. Palenque?
g ¿Te caíste en el colegio?

iv Actividad en parejas

Objetivo – Empezar una frase con el imperfecto / copretérito (**M**) y terminarla con el pretérito

Método – La primera persona (A) de la pareja empieza una frase con el imperfecto y la segunda (B) la termina con el pretérito. Intenten crear seis frases

Ejemplos

A: (Yo) cantaba en el salón cuando (_)
B: entró mi hermana
A: Mi padre andaba en bicicleta cuando (_)
B: vió al cartero

Después, el profesor recoge varias frases de la clase entera y las escribe en el pizarrón (**M**) / la pizarra

Unit 9 *(Unidad 9)*

Conditional tense (*El tiempo condicional*)

Level **1**

1.1 **The conditional** (*El condicional*)

i This tense corresponds to the English *would*, so it has a future idea, both in form and usage. Its endings are added to the full infinitive, just as with the future tense. You should not find the formation of the conditional difficult if you have no trouble with the future. Here are the forms of the conditional:

	-ía	*compraría*	*vendería*	*viviría*
Sing.	**-ías**	*comprarías*	*venderías*	*vivirías*
	-ía	*compraría*	*vendería*	*viviría*
	-íamos	*compraríamos*	*venderíamos*	*viviríamos*
Plur.	**-íais**	*compraríais*	*venderíais*	*viviríais*
	-ían	*comprarían*	*venderían*	*vivirían*

ii Here are the conditionals of twelve irregular verbs. These follow the pattern of the future of these irregular verbs:

	Future	**Conditional**	
caber:	*cabré*	*cabría>*	*cabrías,* etc.
decir:	*diré*	*diría>*	*dirías,* etc.
haber:	*habré*	*habría>*	*habrías,* etc.
hacer:	*haré*	*haría>*	*harías,* etc.
poder:	*podré*	*podría>*	*podrías,* etc.
poner:	*pondré*	*pondría>*	*pondrías,* etc.
querer:	*querré*	*querría>*	*querrías,* etc.
saber:	*sabré*	*sabría>*	*sabrías,* etc.
salir:	*saldré*	*saldría>*	*saldrías,* etc.
tener:	*tendré*	*tendría>*	*tendrías,* etc.
valer:	*valdré*	*valdría>*	*valdrías,* etc.
venir:	*vendré*	*vendría>*	*vendrías,* etc.

The conditional always depends upon a past tense, expressed or understood. Its primary value is to convey a future idea or event from a past time. It bears the same relationship to a past tense as the future does to the present tense. It is helpful to see the future alongside the conditional. Compare the sentences in the sets below:

Te aseguro que lo haré	I assure you that I'll do it
Te aseguraba que lo haría	I assured you that I would do it
Voy a preguntarle si llegará pronto	I'll ask her if she'll arrive soon
Iba a preguntarle si llegaría pronto	I was going to ask her if she would arrive soon
Te digo que regresaré mañana	I tell you I'll return tomorrow
Te dije que regresaría mañana	I told you I would return tomorrow

iii In this manner the conditional is extended to apply as a future after any past tense, whether indicative or subjunctive (see unit 16, level 2 on the subjunctive, for examples).

Era seguro que tendría razón	It was certain that he would be right
Pensé que tal vez la encontraría por aquí	I thought that perhaps I'd find her here

Exercises Level **1**

i Change the infinitive to the conditional in the following sentences:

Example

Le dije que (venir) mañana > Le dije que vendría mañana

a Te expliqué que (llegar) mis parientes antes
b Nos avisaron que la boda (ser) a las doce
c Luisa dijo que (ir) a la modista
d Me comentó que (aprender) a conducir
e Pensamos que era tarde y que no (servir) comidas
f Le platiqué que no (poder) regresar mis hermanos
g Contestamos que el precio de la casa (ser) demasiado alto
h Le prometí que mis abuelos (cuidar) a los niños
i Les dije que nosotros (coincidir) en Barcelona
j Supuse que tú (comprar) las flores

ii Change as in the example, i.e. present + future > preterit/imperfect + conditional

Example

Creo que (él) tendrá bastante dinero > Creía que tendría bastante dinero

a Dice que saldrá a las nueve
b Opinamos que no vendrán sus papás
c Dicen que no habrá luz mañana
d Luis cree que Ana no hará nada
e Pedro me avisa que el cartero no vendrá más tarde
f ¿Por qué me comentas que rentarás un carro (**M**)?
g Supongo que hará frío mañana
h Creo que aprobará el examen
i Piensa que pondrán la película *Casablanca* esta noche
j Estoy seguro de que nevará esta tarde

iii Paired activity

Objective – To practice the conditional used after the imperfect or preterit
Method – The first person (A) starts a sentence with either the imperfect tense (see unit 7 for a reminder) or the preterit (see unit 8 for a reminder). The second person (B) completes the sentence with a conditional. Try to complete six sentences

Examples

A: Le dije que (_)
B: (yo) iría esta tarde
A: Les prometía cada día que (_)
B: regresaríamos el año que viene

See further examples in 9.1.1. ii and iii

iv **Activity for one brave person to face the whole class and explain how the Spanish conditional is formed and how it is used in Spanish. Is the formation of the Spanish conditional easier than in English? Is it useful to know the formation of the future in Spanish in this context? The adventurous person could obtain cooperation and her/his answers from the class. This could be an activity to be prepared for next week.**

Level **2**
2.1 **Conditional perfect** (*Pretérito condicional*)

2.1 Conditional perfect

This tense conveys an idea or an event related to the future in the past. It corresponds to the English *would have done / spoken / walked*, etc. = *habría hecho / hablado / caminado (**M**) / andado*. It has a complication in that it often involves the use of the subjunctive, and you are referred to the subjunctive (see unit 16, especially level 2). As in the example above, the conditional perfect is formed by the conditional of the verb ***haber*** followed by the past participle of the main verb. In other words, its formation is the auxiliary or helping verb ***haber*** + past participle.

Ejemplos

habría / habrías / habría / habríamos / habríais / habrían comprado = I would have bought, etc.
habría . . . . vendido = I would have sold, etc.
habría . . . . vivido = I would have lived, etc.

Besides this temporal function, the conditional perfect is also used to suggest supposition and hypothesis, with the idea of *must have* or *probably**

Examples

Ya habría llegado cuando salimos	She must have arrived when we left
Habría escrito la carta antes	He must have written the letter before
*Según la policía cuatro pandilleros (**M**) habrían cometido el delito*	According to the police, four delinquents must have committed the offense

*The conditional perfect corresponds to the preterite use of ***deber de*** as in:

Debió de acabar el trabajo ayer	She must have finished the work yesterday
Debí de perder el conocimiento	I must have lost consciousness
Debió de hacer frío	It must have been cold

There is some uncertainty among many Spanish speakers whether ***deber*** should be followed by ***de*** in this construction. However, the consensus among grammarians is that the construction should be ***deber de***.

Exercises Level **2**

i Cambia como en el ejemplo – presente + futuro > pretérito/imperfecto + condicional:

Creo que los plomeros (**M**) / fontaneros habrán terminado el trabajo para las seis > Creí/Creía que los plomeros/fontaneros habrían terminado . . .

a Su padre dice que habrá acabado el examen

b Estamos seguras de que habrán arreglado el carro (**M**)

c Es casi cierto que se habrá descompuesto (**M**) / averiado la lavadora

d Nos advierte que habrá llovido antes de la noche

e Nos promete que habrán cargado los camiones a las seis

f Sugiere que el conflicto se habrá resuelto a finales de mes

g Contesta que habrán construido el edificio dentro de un año

h Me informa que habrán corregido en breve los errores del horario

i Te garantizo que el abogado nos habrá entregado el documento a las dos

j El comandante insiste en que la guerra habrá terminado en enero

k Estoy convencida de que los policías habrán hallado (**M**) / encontrado al chico perdido

ii Actividad en parejas

Objetivo – estudiar la concordancia entre el pretérito y el condicional

Método – la pareja colabora para crear seis frases que incluyan un verbo en pretérito y un verbo en condicional. Después, varias parejas le presentan sus frases a la clase entera. Abajo, encuentran una serie de verbos en pretérito que pueden ayudarlos a empezar la frase:

Estuve, fue, sugerimos, advertí, contestaron, dijimos, avisamos, comentó, aseguraron, preguntó

Ejemplos

La policía nos advirtió que los ladrones regresarían

Supuse que nos darían el dinero

Unit 10 *(Unidad 10)*

Progressive tense or gerund
(El tiempo progresivo o el gerundio)

Level **1**

1.1 **The present participle of the verb** (*El participio activo del verbo*)

1.1 The present participle of the verb

i The place of the present participle, as part of the verb, has been taken by a form adopted almost unchanged from the Latin and called the *gerund*. In regular **-ar** verbs this is formed by adding **-ando** to the stem; in regular **-er** and **-ir** verbs by the addition of **-iendo**:

comprar > comprando	to buy > buying
vender > vendiendo	to sell > selling
vivir > viviendo	to live > living

This is also the case in most of the irregular verbs:

dar > dando	*hacer > haciendo*	*ser > siendo*
estar > estando	*querer > queriendo*	*tener > teniendo*
haber > habiendo	*salir > saliendo*	*ver > viendo*

Some irregular verbs are slightly different:

caer > cayendo	*construir > construyendo*	*dormir > durmiendo*
ir > yendo	*oír > oyendo*	*traer > trayendo*

ii The distinctive feature of the gerund is that it can be combined with different tenses, as in the examples below:

¿Qué está haciendo Papá? Está leyendo el periódico	What's Pa/dad doing? He's reading the newspaper
Está tocando el violín	She's playing the violin
¿De qué están/estáis hablando?	What are you talking about?
¿Qué has estado haciendo hoy?	What have you been doing today?
Estaba yo escribiendo cuando entró	I was writing when she came in
Mañana a estas horas estaremos viajando	At this time tomorrow we'll be traveling

The preterit of ***estar*** (***estuve***, etc.) is also used in the same way but this will be treated in level 2.

iii There is also a perfect of the gerund made up of the past participle and the gerund of the auxiliary verb **haber**:

habiendo comprado	having bought	*habiendo ido*	having gone
habiendo vivido	having lived	*habiendo visto*	having seen

Examples

Habiendo comprado la fruta, regresé a casa	Having bought the fruit, I returned home
Habiendo vivido en Phoenix diez años, decidimos . . .	Having lived in Phoenix ten years, we decided . . .
Habiendo ido al mercadillo cuatro veces, estaba cansado	Having been to the market four times, I was tired

iv When the gerund governs one or more personal pronouns (see unit 17) they are added to it to form one word. This entails the placing of a written accent over the correct vowel to keep the stress in the same place.

Examples

encontrándola	meeting her
dándomelo	giving it to me
encontrándose fuera sin llave	being outside without a key
volviéndome para ver mejor	turning round to see better
pidiéndome libros que . . .	asking me for books that . . .

v However, if the gerund is governed by *estar*, *ir*, *andar* or *venir*, the pronouns may either precede the verb or be joined to the gerund. Compare the sentences in the pairs:

*Le estoy escribiendo ahorita (**M**)* *Estoy escribiéndole ahorita*	I'm writing to him/her now
*Me estaba rasurando (**M**) cuando . . .* *Estaba rasurándome cuando . . .*	I was shaving when . . .
Ella se va americanizando *Ella va americanizándose*	She's becoming Americanized

vi But with **haber**, the pronoun is always attached to **haber**:

Habiéndome dado cuenta de que . . .	Having realized that . . .

Exercises Level **1**

i Put the written accent in the correct place

Examples

viendolos > vié**ndolos**   pidiendomelas > pidié**ndomelas**

a encontrandolos	d prestandolas	g dandoselos	j entendiendome
b afeitandose	e rasurandome (**M**)	h describiendomelo	k llenandose
c apoyandolos	f vaciandolo	i trayendolo	l reconociendome

ii Answer as in the examples:

¿Qué estás haciendo? > Estoy viendo televisión

¿Por qué están limpiando la recámara (**M**)? > Están limpiando la recámara por que está sucia

a ¿Qué estás mirando?

b ¿Qué están pintando? (**M**)

c ¿Por qué están lavando los platos? (**M**)

d ¿Por qué estáis fregando los platos?

e ¿Dónde estás comiendo en este momento?

f ¿Dónde estás durmiendo? (*Does this sentence makes sense?*)

g ¿Quién está contestando al teléfono?

h ¿Quién está preparando la comida?

i ¿Dónde estáis recogiendo los papeles?

j ¿Qué estás pidiendo?

iii Change as in the example, i.e. simple present > progressive + *ahorita*:
Cocino de vez en cuando / a veces > Estoy cocinando ahorita

a Trabajo de vez en cuando / a veces

b Leo de vez en cuando / a veces

c Ve la televisión de vez en cuando / . . .

d Pide dinero de vez en cuando / . . .

e Vendo fruta de vez en cuando / . . .

f Enseño la física de vez en cuando / . . .

g Oye el radio (**M**) / la radio de vez en cuando / . . .

h Trae cartas de vez en cuando / . . .

i Escriben tarjetas de vez en cuando / . . .

j Corremos de vez en cuando / . . .

k Abren (**M**) botellas de vino de vez en cuando / . . .

l Abrís la ventana de vez en cuando / . . .

iv Change as in the example (two ways):
Estás arreglando el carro   >   Lo estás arreglando / Estás arreglándolo

a Estoy comprando sardinas

b Está vendiendo periódicos

c Estamos corrigiendo exámenes

d Están tirando piedras

e ¿Por qué estás pidiendo ayuda?

f ¿Por qué estás pidiendo dinero?

g ¿Dónde estás sirviendo la cena?

h Está trayendo los libros

i Están escribiendo los ejercicios

j Estoy aprendiendo el vocabulario

v Paired activity
Objective – to practice the progressive tense

Method – the first person (A) asks the second person (B) (and vice versa) what (s)he is doing, and what every one else is doing/writing/saying, etc.

This involves the whole range of pronouns, except *vosotros*, if you are in Mexico

Examples
A: ¿Qué estás haciendo?

B: Estoy escribiendo una carta

A: ¿Qué están haciendo?

B: Estamos viendo la televisión

A: Pero, ¿qué están haciendo ellos, no Uds.?

B: Perdón, están jugando al ajedrez

Feel free to use your imagination. I/You/he/she/we/they (*Yo/tú/él/ella/nosotros/as/ ellos/as*) could be swimming (*nadando*), running (*corriendo*), speaking (*platicando (**M**)/ hablando*), walking (*caminando/andando*), smashing bottles (*¡rompiendo botellas!*), climbing a mountain (*escalando una montaña*), getting drunk (*emborrachándome/te/se/nos* – hope not), robbing a bank (*robando un banco* – hope not), or sleeping (*durmiendo* – could you answer here?)

Level 2

2.1 More features of the use of the gerund (*Más detalles sobre el uso del gerundio*)

2.1 More features of the use of the gerund

i In clauses where it could be difficult to ascertain which of several pronouns is the subject of the gerund, the appropriate personal pronoun is inserted immediately after the gerund. Compare the two following sentences:

Me la encontré regresando yo del teatro	I met her coming back (when I came back) from the theater
Me la encontré regresando del teatro	I met her coming back (when she came back) . . .

Further examples

Tenía miedo de que mi hermano, no estando yo presente, cometiera un disparate	I was frightened that my brother, if I were not present, would do something stupid
Veo a los niños jugando en el jardín	I see the children playing in the yard/garden
*Hallé (**M**) a mi hermana escribiendo una carta*	I found my sister writing a letter
Aquí tengo su tarjeta anunciando su boda	I've gotten their card announcing the wedding

ii The gerund also serves to describe the action of a verb it accompanies:

Los chicos venían/vinieron corriendo	The children came running up
El camino iba bajando al mar	The path went (on) down to the sea
Continuó/Siguió hablando	He went on talking
Pasé la noche trabajando	I spent the night working

Note. In many cases, Spanish uses the infinitive which is governed by a preposition, and not the gerund as in English:

No soy capaz de distinguir entre estos colores	I am not capable of distinguishing between these colors
No tardará en venir	She'll not be long in coming
La dificultad consiste en encontrarlo en casa	The difficulty consists in finding him at home
Después de comer, salimos a la terraza	After eating, we went out onto the terrace
Antes de ir a la estación . . .	Before going to the station . . .

iii After verbs of seeing and hearing, the infinitive is more usual than the gerund:

La vimos bailar	We saw her dance (dancing)
Los vi venir	I saw them come (coming)
La oímos tocar el piano	We heard her play(ing) the piano

iv Note the difference below between the gerund when preceded by the preterit and the gerund when preceded by the imperfect. In the first case, the event is terminated, while continuity is suggested in the second.

Ejemplos

María estuvo trabajando allí dos años	Mary was working there for two years
Estaba trabajando allí cuando la conocí	She was working there when I met her
Estuvimos lavando la ropa todo el día	We were washing clothes all day
Estábamos lavando la ropa cuando llegó . . .	We were washing clothes when . . . arrived
Federico estuvo viajando tres meses	Frederic was traveling for three months
Estaba viajando un mes cuando . . .	He had been traveling a month when . . .

Exercises Level **2**

i Escribe frases completas como en el ejemplo, usando el tiempo progresivo y el pretérito

Ejemplo

Muchacho limpiar casa cuando entrar hermana > El muchacho estaba limpiando la casa cuando entró su hermana

a Músico tocar guitarra cuando resbalar sobre un plátano
b Mi padre dormir cuando empezar llorar bebé
c Familia cenar cuando sonar teléfono
d Carmen telefonear al momento que yo querer mandar un e-mail
e Carlos limpiar su recámara (**M**) / habitación mientras yo jugar jardín
f Todo el grupo bailar cuando la violinista empezar toser
g El mesero servir desayuno cuando romper copa
h El chofer (**M**) / chófer preguntar dirección cuando llegar la policía

ii Ordena los vocablos de las siguientes frases con un poco de lógica y cambia los infinitivos al indicativo o gerundio donde sea necesario.

Ejemplo

colina subir la muchacho correr el > El muchacho subió la colina corriendo

a correr venir estudiantes tarde ser porque las
b cantar calles las tunas ir por las
c salón llorar prima mi el entrar en
d la comentar amigos seguir política los
e pasar alumno día todo estudiar el el
f cocina a volver cojear ella la
g río cruzar nadar el el poeta Byron
h atravesar la correr calle el perro

iii Elige el imperfecto progresivo o el pretérito progresivo como en los ejemplos. Cambia el infinitivo al indicativo donde sea necesario.

Ejemplos

Ana (estar) estudiando toda la tarde	>	Ana estuvo estudiando . . .	
Pedro (estar) cortando leña cuando (hacerse) daño en el dedo	>	Pedro estaba cortando leña cuando se hizo daño en el dedo	

a La madre (estar) lavando los platos hasta la una

b Los jóvenes (estar) bailando hasta las doce

c El financiero (estar) vendiendo acciones cuatro meses

d Yo (estar) manejando (**M**) tranquilamente cuando se me reventó una rueda

e Rosa (estar) guisando cuando entró su hija

f Nosotros (estar) comiendo cuando sonó el timbre

g Los pandilleros (**M**) / gamberros (estar) rompiendo los cristales cuando llegó la policía

h Ellas (estar) dando un paseo cuando empezó a llover

i Yo (estar) leyendo toda la tarde sin interrupción

j El vecino (estar) cavando toda la semana en el jardín

iv Actividad para toda la clase

La clase elige a uno de sus miembros. Esta persona se pone delante de la clase y hace la mímica (*mimes*), haciendo gestos que pueden ser exagerados. Hace gestos con las manos, los pies y el cuerpo entero. Hace hasta muecas (*grimaces*). Al hacer estos gestos, la persona, ya convertida en actor/actriz, le pregunta a la clase:

¿Qué estoy haciendo?

La clase contesta según el gesto / los gestos. Por ejemplo:

Estás golpeando la pared **o**

Estás tirando de la nariz **o**

Estás doblando los dedos **o**

Estás mirando por la ventana

Si no es correcta la respuesta, el actor / la actriz puede decir, por ejemplo:

No, estoy peinándome (*I'm combing my hair*)

Si no ríen (**M**) / reís durante esta escena, no reirán (**M**) / reiréis nunca

Unit 11 *(Unidad 11)*

The imperative mood (*El modo imperativo*)

Level **1**

1.1 **Forms of the imperative** (*El imperativo*)

1.2 **How to soften the possible aggressive nature of the imperative**
(*Como suavizar la posible agresividad del imperativo*)

1.1 Forms of the imperative

The imperative in Spanish conveys the idea of direct orders or commands: *¡Habla!* = Speak!, *¡Come!* = Eat!, *¡Abre!* = Open! are the imperative forms of the verbs *hablar, comer* and *abrir*. This form corresponds to the second person singular form of the verb (*tú*). There also exists a second person plural. The imperative forms of the three model verbs are as follows:

	Singular		**Plural**	
comprar	*¡Compra!*	Buy!	*¡Comprad!*	Buy!
vender	*¡Vende!*	Sell!	*¡Vended!*	Sell!
abrir	*¡Abre!*	Open!	*¡Abrid!*	Open!

Examples

¡Compra pan! = Buy bread! *¡Vende la casa!* = Sell the house!

¡Abre la puerta! = Open the door!

¡Corred! = Run! *¡Leed!* = Read!

Four essential remarks must be made here.

i The first is that the second person plural imperative form corresponding to *vosotros* is rarely used, and it could be argued from the author's long experience that it is rapidly disappearing. It sounds odd, awkward and associated with very formal language. One has the suspicion that young Spanish speakers no longer learn it at school. The present author has only ever heard *¡Salid!* on one occasion in countless years of living in Spain. Furthermore, in Spanish America, it does not exist. Mexicans regard it as archaic, and an object of fun or even derision. They replace it completely by the *Uds.* form. (See level 2.)

ii The second remark is that the negative forms of the imperative, both singular and plural, are really taken from the subjunctive. These negative or subjunctive forms will be treated in level 2.

iii Thirdly, the imperative forms may seem too sharp or aggressive to many Spanish speakers, with the result that other forms of order or request are often resorted to. (See below, level 1.2.)

iv Fourthly, the polite *Ud.* and *Uds.* forms are also derived from the subjunctive (see the subjunctive, unit 16). Hence:

	Singular	**Plural**
comprar	*¡Compre pan!* Buy bread!	*¡Compren pan!* Buy bread!
vender	*¡Venda la casa!* Sell the house!	*¡Vendan la casa!* Sell the house!
abrir	*¡Abra la puerta!* Open the door!	*¡Abran la puerta!* Open the door!

The question of whether you would use the *Ud.* form of the imperative could lead to much debate. You would need to know a person quite well to issue orders, and knowing a person well would doubtless exclude the use of the *Ud.* form. The singular form *Ud.* has no exercises for this very reason. You should merely be able to recognize it. The plural form *Uds.* has exercises because, as seen below, it replaces the *vosotros* form in Mexico.

A number of irregular verbs have only an abbreviated form for the imperative corresponding to *tú.* Their second person plural form is regular, and, of course, becoming archaic:

	Singular	**Plural**	
decir	*¡Di!*	*¡Decid!*	Say!
hacer	*¡Haz!*	*¡Haced!*	Do/make!
ir	*¡Ve!*	*¡Id!*	Go!
poner	*¡Pon!*	*¡Poned!*	Put!
salir	*¡Sal!*	*¡Salid!*	Go out!
tener	*¡Ten!*	*¡Tened!*	Have!
venir	*¡Ven!*	*¡Venid!*	Come!

The plural forms above need merely to be recognized, for they are not used these days. But, how does a person addressing a group of children, students or pupils to whom (s)he would normally use the *vosotros* form, give an order? Certainly not, for example, *¡Salid!* or *¡Hablad!* The teacher would resort to a subterfuge like *Salimos* or *¡Salgamos!*

The *Ud.* and *Uds.* forms of the irregular verbs above are as follows:

¡Diga!/¡Digan! – ¡Haga!/¡Hagan! – ¡Vaya!/¡Vayan! – ¡Ponga!/¡Pongan! – ¡Salga!/¡Salgan! – ¡Tenga!/¡Tengan! – ¡Venga!/¡Vengan!

1.2 How to soften the possible aggressive nature of the imperative

As mentioned above, the possible aggressive character of the imperative is often mitigated by a gentler form of speech. The infinitive is often used in speech and, sometimes, in commercial labelling:

Llamarme esta tarde (instead of **Llámame** . . .)   Call me this afternoon
Escribirme cuando puedas (instead of   Write to me when you can
   Escríbeme . . .)

Mandarnos la factura ahora (instead of **Mándenos** . . .)	Send us the bill now
No decírselo (instead of **No se lo digas**)	Don't tell her/him
Mantenerse fuera del alcance de los niños (on a medicine bottle)	Keep out of the reach of children
No fumar (instead of **No fumen** – in a lift, for instance)	Don't smoke; No smoking
Empujar (instead of **Empuje(n)** – on a door)	Push
Tirar (instead of **Tire(n)** – on a door)	Pull

Other ways of avoiding the imperative in common use:

Me lo envías hoy	Send it to me today (i.e. the indicative with a slight rising intonation)
Me pone otra copa	Please give me another wine glass (to a waiter and with rising intonation)

Exercises Level **1**

i Change the infinitive to the imperative, using *tú*, as in the example

Example

Mirar por la ventana > Mira por la ventana

a Vender estas flores
b Ir ahora
c Comprar dos panes
d Abrir la puerta
e Preparar la comida
f Hacer tus deberes ahora
g Salir antes de las cinco
h Comer estos caramelos
i Decir "Adiós" a tu hermano
j Leer el periódico
k Venir esta tarde
l Hablar con la profesora
m Poner tus libros en la mesa
n Darle una silla a esta señora

ii Change the indicative to the imperative, using *tú*, as in the example

Discutes el precio > Discute el precio

a Compras la verdura
b Rompes la caja
c Estacionas el carro (**M**)
d Aparcas el coche
e Mandas la carta
f Vendes tu camioneta
g Coges* estos papeles
h Tomas estos papeles
i Aguantas esta maleta
j Abres este sobre
k Bebes este vino
l Haces el planchado

* Not used this way in many Spanish American countries, including Mexico. It is considered indecent. It has the meaning of "to screw." Oddly enough, the standard term in Mexico and Spain, *tirar* = to throw/pull, also means "to screw" in Colombia. How to replace in Mexico and Colombia? *Tomar un camión / estos papeles* = to catch a bus / these papers. *Echar una pelota* = to throw a ball

iii Find a more courteous way of giving the following orders, as in the example

Poner la mesa > pones la mesa (por favor) (Spaniards do not seem to worry too much about *por favor* whereas the use of *please* in England borders on the squeamish, at least for Spanish speakers)

a Escribir la carta	f Darle la llave a tu madre
b Conducir el coche	g Meter los cuchillos en el cajón
c Hablar con el cartero	h Pagar la cuenta
d Echar la tarjeta al buzón	i Leer en alta voz
e Poner las servilletas	j Reservar boletos (**M**) de avión

iv Class activity
Objective – to practice the imperative mood
Method – a class member is chosen to stand in front of the class and give orders in the imperative. The class has to respond with actions.

Examples

Levanten los brazos (*Everyone raises their arms – at least we hope so!*)
Cierren los ojos (*Everyone closes their eyes*)
Abran la boca (*Open your mouth*)

These are standard orders but someone among you must have more imagination than the author. However, here are some verbs that can help you:

Quitar, amarrar las agujetas (**M**) / atar los cordones, poner un libro en el suelo, tocar, empujar, tirar de, gritar, platicar (**M**) / hablar, leer, escribir, esconder un libro, salir de la clase (only two or three, please), regresar, escuchar al profesor

 Level **2**

2.1 **The Mexican use of the *Uds.* form of the imperative** (*El uso mexicano de la forma **Uds.** del imperativo*)

2.2 **The first person plural of the imperative** (*La forma **nosotros** del imperativo*)

2.3 **The negative form of the imperative** (*La forma negativa del imperativo*)

2.4 **The imperative with pronouns** (*El imperativo con pronombres*)

2.5 **The negative imperative with pronouns** (*El imperativo negativo con pronombres*)

2.1 The Mexican use of the *Uds.* form of the imperative

As noted above, the plural form **vosotros** does not exist in Mexico, as in other Spanish American countries. **Uds.** replaces it. Thus, both to people unknown or to friends a Mexican would say:

Escriban una carta – Write a letter   *Manejen el carro* – Drive the car
Abran la ventana – Open the window   *Hablen español* – Speak Spanish

Such usage sounds disconcerting to a Spaniard when it is regularly observed by a Mexican towards a Spaniard whom the Mexican would know well. For a Spaniard, **Uds.** implies persons you do not know, or hold in great respect or esteem. But, there you are. It is a feature the present author has great difficulty in accommodating, at least from the emotional point of view.

2.2 The first person plural of the imperative

The imperative is also used, as in English, in the first person plural:

¡Hablemos francés!	Let us speak French!
¡Corramos hasta la barrera!	Let's run to the gate!
¡Vivamos hasta los cien años!	Let's live till we are a hundred!

The subjunctive form is used here.

2.3 The negative form of the imperative

The negative form of the imperative, the negative subjunctive, requires particular attention. Here are the forms:

No hables	Do not speak
No hable (Ud.)	Do not speak
No hablemos	Let us not speak
No habléis ("Have fun" in Mexico)	Do not speak
No hablen ("Have fun" in Spain)	Do not speak

Similarly: *-er No comas/coma/comamos/comáis/coman* = Don't, eat, etc.

-ir No abras/abra/abramos/abráis/abran = Don't open, etc.

The importance of the knowledge of the subjunctive forms is highlighted here. As far as this unit is concerned, it is useful to learn the negative forms of the subjunctive of some irregular verbs:

decir:	*No digas/diga/digamos/digáis/digan* = Don't say, etc.
hacer:	*No hagas/haga/hagamos/hagáis/hagan* = Don't do, etc.
∗ir:	*No vayas/vaya/vayamos/vayáis/vayan* = Don't go, etc.
poner:	*No pongas/ponga/pongamos/pongáis/pongan* = Don't put, etc.
salir:	*No salgas/salga/salgamos/salgáis/salgan* = Do not go out, etc.
tener:	*No tengas/tenga/tengamos/tengáis/tengan* = Do not have, etc.
venir:	*No vengas/venga/vengamos/vengáis/vengan* = Do not come, etc.

∗ ***Vayamos*** is much less used than the straightforward indicative ***Vamos***, as Mexicans, or copycat cowboys, would say in Western films: ***¡Vamos, muchachos!*** These are the first foreign words the present author learnt as a young child watching westerns. You are never too young to start a foreign language.

2.4 The imperative with pronouns

i Pronouns are added to the imperative when the imperative is affirmative:

Págame mañana = Pay me tomorrow
Ábrela en seguida = Open it straight away
Dímelo = Tell me (it)

Déjame trabajar = Let me work
Cuídate = Take care (of yourself)
Dámelas = Give them to me
Escríbela = Write it
Escríbanles = Write to them

ii When the *nos* of the first person plural is added, the *s* of the imperative is dropped:

Sentémonos = Let's sit down
Vámonos = Let's go

In the above examples, note the written accent over the appropriate vowel to keep the correct stress in the sound.

iii Similarly, when the pronoun *os* is added to a *vosotros* imperative the *d* is lost:

¡Sentaos y callaos!   Sit down and keep quiet!
¡Lavaos!   Wash yourselves!

Exceptionally, this is not the case with *irse* > *idos* (Go away).
    Furthermore, in Mexico, as in all Spanish American countries, the question does not arise: *¡Siéntense y cállense!*, *¡Lávense!* Speaking to small children, this would never be the case in Spain.
    However, in Spain, here also the infinitive is starting to creep in:

¡Sentaros y callaros! ¡Lavaros!

iv The negative infinitive which has the value of the negative imperative is commonly used on notices, in commercials/adverts:

No pisar el césped   Do not walk on the grass
No fumar en el ascensor   Do not smoke in the elevator/lift
No derrochar energía   Do not waste energy

2.5 The negative imperative with pronouns

i When pronouns are used with the subjunctive in its negative form, they precede the verb:

¡No lo estropees! Don't damage it!   *¡No me digas!* You don't say!
¡No lo hagáis! Don't do it!   *¡No la vendas!* Don't sell it!
¡No la abras! Don't open it!   *¡No me hables!* Don't speak to me!
¡No la escriban! Don't write it!   *¡No lo pongas allí!* Don't put it there!
¡No se lo dé! Don't give it to him!

ii Frequently, the straightforward subjunctive occurs as in the following cases:

¡Qué te diviertas!   Have a good time!
*¡Qué lo / la (**M**) pases bien!* Have a good time
¡Qué se alivie! (sickness)   May it get better!
¡Qué tengas suerte!   Good luck!

iii In speech, and this is easy, it is also common to hear an infinitive preceded by *a*:

¡A pasarla (M) bien!	Have a good time!
¡A pasarlo bien!	Have a good time!
¡A dormir bien!	Sleep well!
¡A comer!	Food's/meal's ready! It's on the table!
¡A comer bien!	Have a good meal!
¡A disfrutar!	Enjoy yourselves!

Exercises Level **2**

i Cambia el infinitivo al imperativo con *Uds.* como si estuvieras en México y no en España:

Ejemplo

Escribir un e-mail a la familia > Escriban un e-mail a la familia

a Hallar la dirección ahora
b Manejar con prudencia
c Platicar con todos los cuates
d Lavar la ropa / los platos
e Jalar la cuerda
f Poner el auto en el garage

g Tomar el camión mañana
h Hacer la reservación ahora
i Empacar las maletas
j Subir al árbol
k Prender el radio (**la** *in Spain*)
l Limpiar el sartén (**la** *in Spain*)

ii Cambia al negativo como en el ejemplo:

Prepara la comida > No prepares la comida

a Agrega (**M**) (*careful*) un poco de sal
b Escribe la tarjeta ahora
c Corre hasta la verja (*railings*)
d Abre la lata
e Dale el coche a tu papá
f Dile la verdad a tu mamá
g Pon la mesa
h Haz la tarea

i Ven ahora
j Coge (*careful*) / Toma (**M**) esta pelota
k Cuida la casa
l Prepara la comida
m Platica (**M**) (*careful*) en la cocina
n Lava (**M**) los platos
o Duerme una siesta
p Aprende a manejar (**M**)

iii Cambia al negativo como en el ejemplo

Dale la revista > No le des la revista

a Espérame
b Invítalos a cenar
c Ponlo en mi cama
d Levántate
e Acuéstate
f Hazlo más tarde
g Ayúdala
h Apágala
i Llámalos

j Escúchalas
k Pídele diez dólares
l Ciérrala
m Siéntate
n Búscalas
o Pruébala
p Visítalos hoy
q Despiértate
r Explícamelo

iv Eres un muchacho muy respondón / una muchacha muy respondona (*full of nerve / cheeky*) y no quieres hacer lo que te pide tu hermano/a mayor. El/la hermano/a es bastante agresivo/a pero tú pisas muy fuerte (*stick to your guns*). El hermano te da órdenes (a menudo con la forma afirmativa del imperativo) y tú las rechazas (con la forma negativa). Escribe un pequeño diálogo que exprese este enfrentamiento. Lo puedes escribir como si estuvieras en México o en España:

Inicio del diálogo (en México):

Hermano mayor:	Oye, ¡Dame la pelota!
Hermano pequeño:	¡No me hables así!

v Actividad en grupos de cinco

Objetivo – Aprender a dar órdenes tanto con la forma *Uds.* como con la forma del infinitivo. Se usa también el imperativo en negativo con el reflexivo

Método – Un miembro de cada grupo de cinco da órdenes a los otros cuatro. Ellos obedecen estas órdenes

Ejemplos

¡Pónganse la chamarra (**M**) / la chaqueta!
¡No cierren los ojos! (eso, sí, es pan comido – *what's this?*)
¡Abrir la boca!
¡No se levanten!

Se pueden aprovechar los siguientes verbos:
Ponerse, hablar, platicar, sentarse, pararse (**M**), levantarse, volverse, caminar, detenerse, respirar, dejar de respirar (¡Tengan cuidado!), inclinarse, enderezarse, tirar de las orejas, soltar las orejas, quitarse, cubrir la cara, peinarse, estrecharle la mano a tu vecino/a, darle un besito a tu vecina (los mexicanos y los españoles lo hacen sin problema, y esto incluye al autor)

Unit 12 *(Unidad 12)*

Irregular verbs (*Los verbos irregulares*)

Level **1**

1.1 **Irregular verbs** (*Los verbos irregulares*)

1.2 **Radical changing verbs** (*Los verbos con diptongación*)

1.1   Irregular verbs

Irregular verbs have the habit of worrying people, for they seem to herald a long list of tiresome tenses to be learnt, when it would have been so much kinder if these verbs or their users had made an effort towards conformity to the types we already know. Certainly, Spanish irregular verbs are more complicated than English verbs, and there do seem to be a lot of them. However, many of them are quite rare, so that perhaps fifty irregular verbs need to be learnt, and others are compounds from shorter irregular verbs conjugated like them. *Suponer* comes from *poner*, *devolver* comes from *volver*, *detener* comes from *tener*, and so on. So, numerous Spanish irregular verbs are not unique.

Space does not allow a full tabulation of all Spanish irregular verbs. Good-quality dictionaries such as the Collins, the Oxford, or the Simon and Schuster contain all the necessary information. The *Spanish Verbs* by María Rosario Hollis (Teach Yourself Books) and *501 Spanish Verbs* by Kendris (Barron's Educational Series) are also very helpful.

This unit is an introduction to Spanish irregular verbs, while it is suggested you refer to other units for irregularities in verbs when they are used in the future tense (unit 6), conditional (unit 9), imperfect (unit 7), perfect (unit 5), preterit (unit 8), and the subjunctive (unit 16) and imperative moods (unit 11). See also unit 13 for the irregular verbs **ser** and **estar**. To avoid over-complication at this stage, we shall limit ourselves to the present tense of irregular verbs. A certain number have to be learnt because they have a habit of recurring in the language. In other words, they comprise some of the most useful and necessary verbs. Among the most common irregular verbs are:

caer (to fall), *haber* (to have), *hacer* (to do/make), *ir* (to go), *poner* (to put), *tener* (to have), *ver* (to see), and two verbs to be treated separately in the following unit, i.e. *ser* (to be) and *estar* (to be)

They are conjugated in the following way:

	caer	**haber**	**hacer**	**ir**	**poner**	**ver**
yo	caigo	he	hago	voy	pongo	veo
tú	caes	has	haces	vas	pones	ves
él(la / Ud.)	cae	ha	hace	va	pone	ve
nosotros / as	caemos	hemos	hacemos	vamos	ponemos	vemos
vosotros / as	caéis	habéis	hacéis	vais	ponéis	veis
ellos(as / Uds.)	caen	han	hacen	van	ponen	ven

It is important to bear in mind, and this is occasionally pointed out throughout the book, that in Spanish America the *vosotros / as* form is not used and is replaced by *Uds*.

1.2 Radical changing verbs

There is another large group of verbs which Spanish speakers call "irregular," but which English speakers refer to as "radical/stem changing." This latter designation seems to be much more helpful than the blanket "irregular," for most of the verbs in question follow a set pattern, and once you have learnt the pattern you have easy and accurate access to a whole range of verbs. However, within these sets of radical changing verbs, some do not follow the pattern everywhere. The special feature of these radical changing verbs is that the root vowel of the infinitive changes to a diphthong, in the indicative for instance. This explains why well-informed Spanish speakers refer to this phenomenon as *diptongación* = diphthongization. In the following tables, you will see that in the first, second, third person singular and third personal plural the root vowel **u** changes to **ue**, the root vowel **e** changes to **ie**, the root vowel **e** changes to **i**, and the root vowel **o** changes to **ue**

jugar (to play)	**cerrar** (to shut)	**pedir** (to ask for)	**soltar** (to release / let go)
juego	cierro	pido	suelto
juegas	cierras	pides	sueltas
juega	cierra	pide	suelta
jugamos	cerramos	pedimos	soltamos
jugáis	cerráis	pedís	soltáis
juegan	cierran	piden	sueltan

Other common verbs where this change takes place are as follows:

o–ue	**e–ie**	**e–i**
contar (to count/relate/tell)	*defender* (to defend)	*corregir* (to correct)
costar (to cost)	*empezar* (to begin)	*despedir* (to dismiss)
devolver (to give back)	**fregar* (to wash up)	*impedir* (to prevent)
dormir (to sleep)	*mentir* (to [tell a] lie)	*investir* (to invest)
encontrar (to meet/find)	*pensar* (to think)	*seguir* (to follow)
llover (to rain)	*perder* (to lose)	
poder (to be able)	*querer* (to want/wish)	
recordar (to remember)	*recomendar* (to recommend)	
resolver (to [re]solve)	*regar* (to water/irrigate)	

tostar (to toast)
volar (to fly)
*volver (to go/come back)

sentir (to feel/regret)
tener (to have)
tentar (to touch/try/tempt)
venir (to come)
verter (to pour/spill)

* little used in **M** with this meaning

Another common verb in the *-ue* classification is **soler** (to be in the habit of). See examples below.

Examples

o > ue

Cuenta del uno al diez	Count from one to ten
Contamos contigo	We count on you
Puedo hacerlo	I can do it
Podemos ir hoy	We can go today
Suelo leer por la mañana	I usually read in the morning
Solemos tomar el tren	We usually take the train

e > ie

Defiendo mi punto de vista	I defend my position
Defendemos la democracia	We defend democracy
El chocolate me tienta	Chocolate tempts me
Tentamos a los niños con caramelos	We tempt the children with candies/sweets
Riego el césped	I water the lawn
Regamos el césped	We water the lawn

e > i

Corrige los ejercicios	He corrects the exercises
Corregimos el error	We correct the error
Me impiden ir	They prevent me from going
Los impedimos trabajar	We prevent them from working

Exercises **Level 1**

i Change the infinitive to the present indicative

Example

Yo (poner) la taza en la mesa > (Yo) Pongo la taza en la mesa

a La maceta (caer) por el balcón
b Yo (hacer) mis deberes
c Ella (hacer) su trabajo
d Yo (ir) al cine
e Ellos/as (ir) al parque
f Uds. (ir) a casa de sus papás (**M**)
g Yo no (poder) ir al pueblo
h ¿Qué (querer) Uds. hacer? (**M**)

i Yo (tener) quince años
j ¿(Venir) vosotros esta tarde? (*not in* **M**)
k ¿(Venir) Uds. esta noche? (**M**)
l Yo no (ver) el pájaro
m ¿(Decir) tú la verdad?
n Yo le (dar) un regalo a mi papá
o Ella (querer) estudiar
p No (querer) nosotros leer

ii Change as in the example

Juego fútbol (**M**) (nosotros) > Jugamos fútbol (**jugar al fútbol** *in Spain*)

a No tengo prisa (él)
b Vuelves a casa (nosotros)
c Cierras la puerta (yo)
d Quiero ir a la alberca (ellos) (**piscina =** *Spain*)
e ¿Preferís leer? (Uds.)
f Duermes poco (nosotros)
g Devuelve el dinero (ellos)
h Resolvemos el ejercicio (yo)

i Pienso comprarlo (nosotros)
j ¿Cuándo empiezas el trabajo? (ellos)
k Pierdo el conocimiento (is this possible?) (ellos)
l No encuentro la bolsa (ellas)
m Pido dinero (nosotros)
n Encienden la chimenea (yo)
o Recordamos su nombre (yo)
p Jorge cuenta las naranjas (yo)

iii Answer the questions as in the examples:

¿Cierras la puerta? > Sí, cierro la puerta
¿Encontráis la solución? > Sí, encontramos la solución

a ¿Sigues en tu carro? (**M**)
b ¿Repiten Uds. la frase? (**M**)
c ¿Sirves la cena ahora?
d ¿Seguimos en nuestro coche?
e ¿Quién corrige los ejercicios?
f ¿Me pides un favor?
g ¿Duermen Uds. bien? (**M**)

h ¿Vuelan mucho Uds.? (**M**)
i ¿En qué piensan Uds.? (**M**)
j ¿En qué piensan ellas?
k ¿Quién lava (**M**) / friega los platos?
l ¿Invierten Uds. todo el dinero?
m ¿Nos impedís (not in **M**) salir?
n ¿Recomiendas este restaurante?

iv Paired activity

Objective – using irregular verbs in the present tense
Method – each of the pair asks the other to conjugate the present tense of an irregular verb. This can include stem changing verbs. The more you practice these irregular verbs the easier it will become. The author is proof of this.

Examples

Conjuga el verbo *hacer* en tiempo presente
(Yo) hago / (tú) haces / (él/ella/Ud.) hace (*see 1.1 above for the rest*)
Conjuga el verbo *preferir* en tiempo presente
(Yo) prefiero / (tú) prefieres / (él/ella/Ud.) prefiere / preferimos / preferís (*not* **M**) / ellos/ (ellas/Uds.) prefieren
Remember that you rarely need the subject pronoun as the ending of the verb is good enough. And it's quicker. It may call for thinking time but try to lose the habit!

Level **2**
2.1 **Further common irregular verbs** (*Más verbos irregulares comunes*)
2.2 **Spelling (orthographical) changes** (*Cambios ortográficos*)

2.1 Further common irregular verbs

Listed below is another group of irregular verbs, the forms of which have to be learnt. The present tense is given, sometimes alongside the present subjunctive, merely to illustrate the irregularities. It is suggested you consult a list of verb tables for a full list of irregularities for these verbs, and in their different tenses. This will be especially helpful for the exercises. The preterit can be particularly deceptive. *Erguir* and *caber*, for example, look impossible. Ask Spanish-speaking children! As for their preterits, a fiend in the Middle Ages must have been hard at work.

erguir (to straighten up/raise) – *yergo, yergues, yergue, erguimos, erguís, yerguen*
Present subjunctive: *yerga, yergas, yerga, irgamos, irgáis, irgan*
caber (to be contained in, to be room for) – *quepo, cabes, cabe, cabemos, cabéis, caben*
Present subjunctive: *quepa, quepas, quepa, quepamos, quepáis, quepan*
Preterit (erguí/erguiste/irguió/erguimos/erguisteis/irguieron –
    cupe/cupiste/cupo/cupimos/cupisteis/cupieron)
***freír** (to fry) – *frío, fríes, fríe, freímos, freís, fríen*
Present subjunctive: *fría, frías, fría, friamos, friáis, frían*
oír (to hear) – *oigo, oyes, oye, oímos, oís, oyen*
Present subjunctive: *oiga, oigas, oiga, oigamos, oigáis, oigan*
oler (to smell) – *huelo, hueles, huele, olemos, oléis, huelen*
Present subjunctive: *huela, huelas, huela, olamos, oláis, huelan*
saber (to know) – *sé, sabes, sabe, sabemos, sabéis, saben*
Present subjunctive: *sepa, sepas, sepa, sepamos, sepáis, sepan*
* **Reír(se)** (to laugh) and **sonreír** (to smile) are the same as **freír**

2.2 Spelling (orthographical) changes

An irregular verb is, strictly speaking, one which, in its inflections, varies in any way from that of the model verb of its conjugation. If this definition were rigorously adhered to, the number of irregular verbs would rise in a spectacular manner; but in the greater number, the deviations are so uniform as to constitute a kind of secondary regularity, and may be grouped into several classes. The majority of the deviations are purely related to spelling, and spelling changes merely preserve the sound of the stem as presented in the infinitive. The following changes according to tense, mood or subject of the verb are necessary to observe uniformity of pronunciation. They appear notably in the first person singular of the present indicative (**corrijo** = I correct), the first person singular of the preterit (**busqué** = I looked for), and the present subjunctive (**busque** = that I should look for). However, this comment is only for general guidance. Here are the main spelling changes:

i *-car:* > **-c** before *e* > **que**

buscar   **Preterit**: *busqué, buscaste, buscó*, etc.
(to look for)   **Present subjunctive**: *busque, busques, busque*, etc.

Other common similarly affected verbs:

acercar (to bring closer), *achacar* (to impute / accuse), *arrancar* (to pull / set going), *atracar* (to lock/jam), *comunicar* (to communicate), *educar* (to educate), *falsificar* (to falsify), *intoxicar* (to poison), *invocar* (to invoke), *justificar* (to justify), *marcar* (to mark/score), *notificar* (to notify), *pacificar* (to pacify), *volcar* (to overturn)

ii *-gar:* > *-g* before *e* > *gue*

apagar	**Preterit**: *apagué, apagaste, apagó,* etc
(to extinguish)	**Present subjunctive**: *apague, apagues, apague,* etc

Other common similarly affected verbs:

agregar (to add), *ahogar* (to drown), *castigar* (to punish), *cegar* (to blind/block up), *colgar* (to hang [things]), *desahogar* (to relieve), *desplegar* (to unfold), *fregar* (to wash up* / scrub), *halagar* (to flatter), *indagar* (to investigate), *llegar* (to arrive), *naufragar* (to be shipwrecked), *negar* (to deny), *pagar* (to pay), *plegar* (to fold), *rogar* (to request), *segar* (to mow/cut)

* Not in **M**. The Mexicans use *lavar los platos* in this context

iii *-gua:* *-gu* before *e* > *güe*

averiguar	**Preterit**: *averigüé, averiguaste, averiguó,* etc
(to find out)	**Present subjunctive**: *averigüe, averigües, averigüe,* etc

Similarly: *apaciguar* (to appease)

iv *-eger:* *-g* before *o* or *a* > *j*

escoger	**Present indicative**: *escojo, escoges, escoge,* etc
(to choose)	**Present subjunctive**: *escoja, escojas, escoja,* etc

Similarly: **coger* (to catch/take)

*Not in **M** which means "to screw": what the dictionaries call a taboo word. It is interesting to note here how language and meaning vary from one country to another. This is a digression but it is worth saying for your future studies.

Tirar means "to throw" in Spain or "throw down" (onto the ground) / "away" (if trash) but in Colombia we come back to the taboo meaning of *coger*. *Concha* is a shell in Spain and Mexico but in Argentina it is again a most offensive taboo word (look it up!).

v *-gir:* *g* before *o* or *a* > *j*

corregir	**Present indicative:** *corrijo, corriges, corrige,* etc
(to correct)	**Present subjunctive:** *corrija, corrijas, corrija,* etc

Similarly: *elegir* (to choose/elect), *sumergir* (to submerge)

vi *-cer:* *c* before *o* or *a* > *zc*

conocer	**Present indicative**: *conozco, conoces, conoce,* etc
(to know)	**Present subjunctive**: *conozca, conozcas, conozca,* etc

Similarly: *agradecer* (to thank), *amanecer* (to dawn), *anochecer* (to fall [of night]), *atardecer* (to get dark), *cocer* (to cook/bake), *crecer* (to grow), *esclarecer* (to clarify), *escocer* (to sting/smart), *obedecer* (to obey), *parecer* (to appear/seem), *perecer* (to perish), *reconocer* (to recognize), *vencer* (to conquer/expire)

vii *-cir*: *c* before *o* or *a* > *zc*

traducir   **Present indicative**: *traduzco, traduces, traduce*, etc
(to translate)   **Present subjunctive**: *traduzca, traduzcas, traduzca*, etc

Similarly: *esparcir* (to scatter), *lucir* (to shine)

viii *-zar*: *z* before *e* > *c*

almorzar   **Preterit**: *almorcé, almorzaste, almorzó*, etc
(to have lunch) **Present subjunctive**: *almuerce, almuerces, almuerce, almorcemos*, etc

Similarly: *cazar* (to hunt), *comenzar* (to commence), *empezar* (to begin), *esforzarse* (to strive), *forzar* (to force), *localizar* (to locate)

Exercises Level **2**

i Cambia al pretérito como en el ejemplo:

Me río todo el día > Me reí todo el día

a Oye el ruido
b No quepo aquí
c No sé la respuesta
d Sonríe como La Gioconda
e La casa huele a pino
f Fríe papas
g El caballo yergue las orejas
h Dice que no
i No puedo correr
j Hago todos mis deberes
k Va al teatro
l Quiere comer ahora

ii Pon el infinitivo en subjuntivo como en el ejemplo:

Ejemplo
Hace falta que (apagar/tú) la luz > Hace falta que apagues la luz

a Hace falta que (colgar/ella) el sombrero
b Hace falta que (fregar/yo) los platos
c Es importante que (plegar/nosotros) las sillas
d Me dice que (permanecer/yo) en este lugar
e El director insiste en que (establecer/ellos) un sucursal aquí
f Es esencial que (merecer/nosotros) el trofeo
g El capitán ordena que (desplegarse/ellos)
h Le pido al chico que (obedecer) al maestro
i Es esencial que le (agradecer) el regalo a tu padre
j No creo que (escoger/ellos) al mejor jugador

iii Cambia al pretérito como en el ejemplo:

Ejemplo
Busco mi cartera > Busqué mi cartera

a Le comunico el mensaje al hermano
b Educo a mi hijo
c Cazo conejos
d Me esfuerzo en terminar el trabajo
e Empiezo a jugar al ajedrez
f Castigo al niño travieso
g Marco un gol antológico en la Copa Mundial

h Pago todas mis deudas
i Acerco la mesa a la pared
j Reconozco a mi amigo

iv Perdiste cien dólares. Describe, en pretérito y en primera persona, tu experiencia a partir de la pérdida hasta encontrarlos. Usa los siguientes verbos con cambios ortográficos (*spelling changes*), ¡y mucha imaginación!: Comunicar, acercar, esforzar, empezar, desplegar, plegar, colgar, halagar, volcar, marcar, tocar, explicar, practicar

Ejemplo

Perdí cien dólares . . . Se lo comuniqué a mi hermano . . .

v **Actividad en grupos de cinco**

Objetivo – practicar la conjugación de verbos irregulares

Método – un(a) representante del grupo elige un verbo. Empieza a conjugarlo, pero sólo en primera persona (yo). Los otros cuatro siguen conjugando a su vez, cada uno escogiendo una persona (tú, él/ella/Ud., nosotros/as, Uds.). Pueden elegir el pretérito si quieren.

Ejemplo

Oír El representante dice: (Yo) oigo
    Su amigo sigue con: (tú) oyes
    El amigo siguiente dice: (él/ella/Ud.) oye
    Otro amigo dice: (nosotros) oímos
    El último dice: (ellos/ellas/Uds.) oyen

Pero, no olvidar que, en España, se usa la forma correspondiente a *vosotros* (*oís*) y pueden recitarla si quieren.

Se puede hacer igual con, por ejemplo, el pretérito de *oír*
Oí, oíste, oyó, oímos, oísteis, oyeron.

Otras sugerencias de verbos que, salvo *sonreír* and *freír*, hasta ahora no han aparecido en el texto: oler, teñir, sonreír, freír, errar, dormir, reñir. Cuando hayas aprendido bien el uso de estos verbos, experimentarás una gran satisfacción.

Unit 13 (Unidad 13)

Ser and *estar* (*Ser y estar*)

Level **1**
1.1 **Basic distinctions between *ser* and *estar*** (*Distinciones básicas entre **ser** y **estar***)
1.2 ***Ser* and *estar*** + **adjective** (*Ser y estar* + *adjetivo*)
1.3 **Further differences between *ser* and *estar*** (*Más diferencias entre ser y estar*)
1.4 ***Ser* and *estar* with prepositions, and *hay*** (*Ser y estar* con preposiciones, y **hay**)

1.1 Basic distinctions between *ser* and *estar*

As in Italian, there are in Spanish two verbs, ***ser*** and ***estar***, corresponding to the English verb *to be*. They are not used interchangeably and can lend themselves to confusion. However, each one has distinct provinces. In form, they are quite irregular:

	ser	*estar*	
Yo	*soy*	*estoy*	I am
tú	*eres*	*estás*	you are
él			he is
ella	*es*	*está*	she is
Ud.			you are
nosotros/as	*somos*	*estamos*	we are
vosotros/as	*sois*	*estáis*	you are
ellos			they are
ellas	*son*	*están*	they are
Uds.			you are

The fundamental distinction is that ***ser*** expresses an inherent or essential quality. Indeed, its Latin etymology (***esse***) suggests essence; ***estar***, on the other hand, suggests an external or accidental quality or condition. The following contrasted examples will help to illustrate this feature:

a *La caja es redonda* The box is round **b** *La sopa es rica* The soup is nice
La caja está vacía The box is empty *La sopa está fría* The soup is cold
c *Son inteligentes* They are intelligent **d** *Es terca* She's stubborn
Están bien educados They are well educated *Está indecisa* She's undecided

In (**a**), an essential characteristic of the box is that it is round, hence the use of ***ser***. That the box is empty entails the use of ***estar*** because, at some later time, it could be full. In (**b**), the soup is nice, and the suggestion is that it is a type of soup that is always nice, hence the use of ***ser***, whereas the fact that the soup is cold is a temporary state of affairs, which leads to the use of ***estar***. After all, it could be hot. In (**c**), the people are innately intelligent, always have been and always will be, unless, unpredictably, they become unbalanced. **Ser** is the appropriate verb here. The well-educated people could have been poorly educated, but may have been born awash with money so are well educated. The contingent nature of their education is characterized by **estar**. Finally, in (**d**), one of the girl's permanent features is that she is stubborn, as implied by **ser**. Notwithstanding her stubbornness, she could be undecided at a particular moment, which explains the use of **estar**.

1.2   *Ser* and *estar* + adjective

It can happen, unfortunately, that the same adjective may be used with both verbs, according to the idea in the mind of the speaker or the writer. Here, the distinction is usually clearly marked but not always. It is comforting to note that many Spanish speakers do sometimes hesitate over **ser** or **estar**, which explains why a good all-Spanish dictionary will offer guidance on frequent occasions. The following examples illustrate difference of meaning of an adjective, according to the use of **ser** or **estar**:

a *Es pálida*   She's pale   (Her complexion is naturally pale)
    Está pálida   She's pale   (because of sickness or fear)
b *Estas manzanas son agrias*   These apples are sharp   (That's their characteristic)
    Estas manzanas están agrias These apples are sharp   (They aren't usually sharp)
c *La mujer es amable*   The woman is pleasant   (She always is)
    La mujer está amable   The woman is pleasant   (i.e. today)
d *El hombre es loco*   The man is mad   (needs medical attention)
    El hombre está loco   The man is mad   (furious or has some crazy idea)
e *Tu hermano es bueno*   Your brother is good   (agreeable person)
    Tu hermano está bueno   Your brother is in good
                           health
f *Mi hijo es malo*   My son is bad   (i.e. naughty and always is)
    Mi hijo está malo   My son is unwell

For all the above uses of these adjectives with **ser** and **estar**, it is quite clear that **ser** suggests permanency or essence, while **estar** relates to a passing state.

1.3   Further differences between *ser* and *estar*

There are some examples of contrast between **ser** and **estar** which are difficult to appreciate. However, if you look behind the implications of the use of each verb in the following pairs of examples, you will understand the differences:

ser	*estar*
Somos todos libres en este país	*¿Estás libre para salir hoy?*
We are all free in this country	Are you free to go out today?
Todos mis estudiantes son listos	*¿Están (**M**) / estáis listos?*
All my students are intelligent	Are you ready?
Esta muchacha es muy viva	*Esta costumbre está todavía viva*
This girl is very lively	This custom is still alive

No es seguro que puedan hacerlo	*Estoy segura de que vendrán hoy*
It's not certain they can do it	I'm sure they'll come today
Desde que le tocó la lotería, es feliz	*Estoy feliz con mi nuevo trabajo*
Since winning the lottery he's been happy	I'm happy with my new job

Note. Although **feliz** may be used with both **ser** and **estar**, depending on the meaning, it would be unusual for **contento** to be used with **ser**. It is almost always used with **estar**:

Está muy contenta con el nuevo empleado / con su nuevo coche
She's very happy with the new worker / with her new car

In isolation:

ser	estar
Implies existence or identity	Implies location or state of health
todo lo que es all that is	*¿Está Pedro?* Is Peter there?
¿Quién es? Who's that/there?	*¿Cómo estás?* How are you?

1.4   Ser *and* estar with prepositions, and *hay*

i   **Estar** is used in the following prepositional phrases where it can be seen that the circumstances are temporary:

Está con (la) gripe	*Estoy sin dinero*	*El cuarto está a oscuras*
She's got the flu	I'm without money	The room is in darkness
Hoy está de mal/buen humor	*Mi abuela está de luto*	
Today he's in a bad/good mood	My grandmother is in mourning	

ii   Idioms with prepositions

Ser
When denoting origin, or referring to substance, or belonging: **ser de**

Somos de Chihuahua	*Esta mesa es de madera*
We're from Chihuahua	This table is of wood
La perfección no es de este mundo	
Perfection is not of this world	

To become of:

¿Qué ha sido de ella?	*¿Qué será de mí?*
What's happened to her?	What'll happen to me?

Estar
estar para / a punto de to be about to / on the point of	*estar para* to be in the mood for
Yo estaba para / a punto de salir I was about to go out	*No estoy para bromas* I'm not in the mood for joking

estar por to be inclined to
Estoy por llamarlo I'm inclined to phone him
estar por (impersonal) (remains to be)
Su mejor novela está por escribir
Her best novel remains to be written

estar por to be in favor of
Estoy por la paz I'm in favor of peace
estar en que to believe
Estoy en que no se da cuenta
I believe he doesn't realize

iii When used as nouns, **ser** and **estar**, the distinction becomes even clearer:

el ser humano = human being

el bienestar del hombre = man's wellbeing

iv Note the invariable expression **hay** = there is/are. (See also unit 15, level 1.2, for more information on **hay**, and its various tenses.) You might expect **ser** and **estar** here but this is not the case.

Examples

Hay un árbol cerca del río
Hay muchos autos en la calle
Hay un estudiante en el aula
Hay centenares de espectadores
Hay sólo un invitado
Hay unos veinte muchachos

There is a tree near the river
There are many cars in the street
There is a student in the lecture hall
There are hundreds of spectators
There is only one guest
There are about twenty boys

Exercises Level **1**

i Fill in the spaces with *ser* or *estar*. Bear in mind that you may often leave out the personal pronouns when they are subjects of the sentence

a (Yo) (_) alto
b (Ella) (_) morena
c ¿(_) segura?
d El hijo (_) contento
e (_) siempre feliz
f (Nosotros) (_) libres hoy
g ¿Dónde (_) Tijuana?
h (Ella) (_) enferma
i El niño (_) chico (**M**)
j ¿Quién (_) ese autor?
k Uds. (_) bien educados (**M**)

l Uds. (_) muy listas (**M**)
m La casa (_) cuadrada
n Estas papas (**M**) / patatas (_) demasiado calientes
o La muchacha (_) amable hoy
p Estos jitomates (**M**) (_) jugosos
q El bosque (_) hermoso
r El bebé (_) desnudo
s Estas calles (_) estrechas
t Este carro (**M**) (_) largo

ii Write sentences, or a small dialogue, with *ser* and *estar*, using the following words which are adjectives, nouns or expressions:

Pálido, enfermo, de mí, gripe, médico, acatarrado/constipado, seguro, claro, simpático, listo, dispuesto, chistoso, malo, descontento, vivo, feliz, normal, cuarto oscuro, por recomendar fruta, entretenido, de buen humor, a punto de

iii Paired activity
Objective – Distinguish between *ser* and *estar*
Method – Each person asks her/his partner a series of ten questions based on *ser* and *estar*.

Examples

PREGUNTA: ¿Eres alto/a o pequeño/a?
RESPUESTA: Soy alto/a
PREGUNTA: ¿Dónde estás?
RESPUESTA: Estoy en el salón (**M**) / la sala de clase
PREGUNTA: ¿Dónde están tus cuates (**M**) / amigos?
RESPUESTA: Están en el pasillo

Don't forget the agreement with *ser* and *estar* if it is accompanied by an adjective. Afterwards, the teacher can call the class together to discuss the findings

Level **2**

2.1 **Various tenses of *ser* and *estar*** (*Varios tiempos de **ser** y **estar***)

2.2 ***Ser* and *estar* with nouns, pronouns, infinitives and clauses** (***Ser** y **estar** con nombres, pronombres, infinitivos y oraciones*)

2.3 ***Ser* and *estar* with the gerund** (***Ser** y **estar** con el gerundio*)

2.4 ***Ser* and *estar* in the passive voice with a past participle** (***Ser** y **estar** en voz pasiva con participio de rasado*)

2.5 ***Ser* and *estar* + adjective** (***Ser** y **estar** + adjetivo*)

2.1 Various tenses of *ser* and *estar*

Some of the tenses of ***ser*** and ***estar*** reappear in the treatment of tenses in different units, for example in the unit on the preterit (unit 8). However, it seems useful to list them all together here. The present tense appears in level 1 of this unit. Here are the others, and this includes the subjunctive forms as well:

Ser

Past participle: *sido* > *he/había/habré/habría sido . . . has/habías/habrás/habrías sido . . .*

Preterit: *fui fuiste fue fuimos fuisteis fueron*

Imperfect: *era eras era éramos erais eran*

Future: *seré serás será seremos seréis serán*

Imperative: *sé sea (Ud.) seamos sed sean (Uds.)*

Present subjunctive: *sea seas sea seamos seáis sean*

Imperfect subjunctive: *fuera fueras fuera fuéramos fuerais fueran + fuese fueses fuese fuésemos fueseis fuesen*

Estar

Past participle: *estado* > *he/había/habré/habría estado . . . has/habías/habrás/habrías estado . . .*

Preterit: *estuve estuviste estuvo estuvimos estuvisteis estuvieron*

Imperfect: *estaba estabas estaba estábamos estabais estaban*

Future: *estaré estarás estará estaremos estaréis estarán*

Imperative: *está esté (Ud.) estemos estad estén (Uds.)*

Present subjunctive: *esté estés esté estemos estéis estén*

Imperfect subjunctive: *estuviera estuvieras estuviera estuviéramos estuvierais estuvieran + estuviese estuvieses estuviese estuviésemos estuvieseis estuviesen*

Now we shall illustrate refinements of the distinctions and contrasts presented in level 1.

2.2 *Ser* and *estar* with nouns, pronouns, infinitives and clauses

ser	estar
Always used:	Idiomatic usages:
*Soy doctor (**M**) / médico*	*Estás hecho un hombre*
I'm a physician/doctor	You've turned into a man (big fellow)
¿Quién es el jefe?	*Estoy hecha una sopa*
Who's the boss?	I'm soaked to the skin
No es nada	*Están hechos polvo*
It's nothing	They're exhausted
Ver es creer	*Estoy hecha añicos*
Seeing is believing	I'm exhausted
Durante la guerra mi padre fue capitán	
During the war my father was a captain	
(and not the imperfect either = *era*)	

With adverbs of place

ser	estar
With subjects representing an event:	Designating place: (very common use)
La charla es en la otra aula	*El Museo de Arqueología está en la*
The talk is in the other lecture theater	*Ciudad de México*
(***Estar*** is not possible here)	The . . . is in Mexico City
Reorganization of a sentence for stress:	*¿Dónde estás?*
Donde te vi fue en la Calle Mayor	Where are you?
It was in the Main/High Street that I saw	*El libro está en el estante*
you	The book is on the shelf
Fue en Denver donde (not ***que***!) *nos*	*La misma idea está en su novela*
conocimos	The same idea is in her novel (Although
It was in Denver that we met (i.e. for the	the idea is used metaphorically here,
first time)	it is still ***estar***)

Note the difference between **ser** and **estar** when the adverbs **lejos / cerca** and adjectives **cercano / lejano** are used:

Mi país es lejano / distante	My country is far away
Mi ciudad está lejos	My town is far away
*Mi departamento (**M**) es cercano a la plaza*	My apartment is near the square
El Zócalo está cerca del Ayuntamiento	The main square (in Mexico City) is near the City/Town Hall

Note that **estar** is always used with **bien** and **mal**:

No está mal   It's not bad   *Está bien*   It's OK

(in both cases, when speaking of the appreciation of something)

2.3 *Ser* and *estar* with the gerund

ser	estar
Note: **fui llegando, fue llegando** (I was / you were arriving, etc.) are forms of **ir llegando**	Always used in the formation of progressive tenses: *Estaba leyendo el periódico cuando . . .* I was reading the newspaper when . . . *Aquella tarde estuve leyendo un libro* That afternoon I was reading a book

2.4 *Ser* and *estar* in the passive voice with a past participle

Ser, in the first example, suggests an action while **estar** suggests a state as a result of an action:

ser	estar
El carro fue arreglado por el mecánico The car was repaired by the mechanic	*El carro estaba arreglado* The car was repaired (in state of repair)
Many past participles used as adjectives: *La película era muy aburrida* The movie was very boring *El joven es muy atrevido* The youth is very daring Also in this category: *callado* – quiet, reserved *cansado* – tiring, tiresome *confiado* – trusting *desconfiado* – distrustful *descreído* – disbelieving *disimulado* – cunning *divertido/entretenido* – entertaining *osado* – daring *pesado* – boring, dull *sufrido* – long-suffering	*Este pan está vendido* This bread is sold (has been sold) *El vaso está roto* The glass is broken *La ventana estaba abierta/cerrada* The window was open/closed **When associated with a reflexive or transitive verb** *Está levantada* She's up *Estamos aburridos* We're bored *Está muerta* She's dead *Está callado* He's quiet (now, but he could be noisy)

Note that many past participles with **estar** are the equivalent of English present participles:

acostado	lying down	*dormido*	sleeping
acurrucado	huddling (together)	*echado*	lying down
agachado	bending over (of body)	*inclinado*	leaning
agachapado	crouching	*repantigado*	lolling
agarrado (a)	clinging (to)	*sentado*	sitting
arrimado (a)	leaning (on)	*tendido*	lying down
arrodillado	kneeling	*tumbado*	lying down
colgado	hanging		

Ejemplos

Estaba acostada / dormida cuando entré She was lying down / sleeping when I walked in
Pasa todo su tiempo acostado / dormido / repantigado / sentado / tumbado He spends all his time lying down / sleeping / lolling about / sitting / lying down

Further examples illustrating the difference between an action (***ser***) and a state which is the result of an action (***estar***). Contrast the following:

Esta novela fue escrita por Unamuno	*Aquí está escrito que . . .*
This novel was written by Unamuno	It is written here that . . .
Los chicos fueron divididos en cuatro grupos	*El libro estaba dividido en diez capítulos*
The children were divided into four groups	The book was divided into ten chapters
Esa niña fue muy distraída	*Estaba distraído, no podía aplicarme*
That girl was absent-minded	I was distracted, I couldn't concentrate
¿Es Ud. casado o soltero?	*No estoy casado todavía*
Are you married or single? (implies legal or social status)	I'm not married yet (but may be one day)

2.5 *Ser* and *estar* + adjective

ser	estar
With adjectives classifying the subject into a category as in nationality/religion	When referring to sickness, even when it is permanent
Mi esposa es venezolana My wife is Venezuelan *Aquel señor es argentino* That gentleman is Argentinian *El león es carnívoro* The lion is a carnivore	*Está enferma desde niña* She's been sick since childhood *Estos árboles están enfermos* These trees are damaged **But** when **enfermo** is a noun, **ser** is used *Los drogadictos son enfermos* Drug addicts are sick people
When the adjective is an inherent property of the subject *El carbón es negro* Coal is black (i.e. all) *El hielo es frío* Ice is cold (i.e. all)	When suddenness or irony are implied *¡Qué alta estás!* How tall you are! (Are you wearing very high heels?) *Hoy la nieve está blanquísima* The snow is very white today (more than usual)
	(cont.)

ser	estar
When the adjective is a possible physical or moral property of the subject, even though this may not be "inherent" or "permanent," and is liable to change *Juanito es alto* Johnny is tall *El vecino es rico* The neighbor is rich *La mujer es joven* The woman is young *El cuento es triste* The tale is sad	An appreciation of clothes, well-fitting or otherwise *El abrigo te está corto* Your coat is short on you *Estos pantalones no me están bien* These pants don't fit me
Where the adjective expresses a measurement, quantity or comparison *Los jitomates (M) son caros* Tomatoes are expensive **but:** *Los jitomates están caros;* i.e. at the moment *La calle es estrecha* The street is narrow *Juana es distinta de su hermana* Juana is different from her sister	When referring to a profession or job *Estuvo de maestra en el pueblo* She was an elementary/primary school teacher . . . *Está de párroco* He's a parish priest Note the use of *de* in the above two examples When referring to temperature *Hoy estamos a cero grados* Today it's zero degrees
Where the subject is a proposition or its equivalent *Este problema es difícil* This problem is difficult *Mandar la carta es fácil* Sending the letter is easy	When referring to the price of things *El jamón está a cincuenta pesos* The price of ham is fifty pesos When referring to time *Hoy estamos a quince* Today is the fifteenth

Exercises Level 2

i Rellena los blancos / Llena (*M*) los espacios con *ser* o *estar*. Hay varias posibilidades

a ¿(_) fácil la novela?

b Sí, y ahora (_) hecho polvo

c ¿(_) lloviendo?

d Sí, y ahora (_) hecho una sopa

e El bosque (_) muy lejos

f El bosque (_) cercano al castillo

g Y (_) cerca del río, también

h ¿(_) nadando en el río?

i (_) nadando toda la mañana

j (_) muy atrevido nadando allí

k No pasa nada. El río (_) tranquilo hoy

l Y había otros chicos que (_) nadando en el río

m ¿Pero el agua (_) fría?

n No, (_) templada

o ¿Tus amigos (_) muy revoltosos?

p No, (_) muy tranquilos y no se meten con nadie

ii ¿Cuál es la diferencia entre los dos usos de los siguientes adjetivos/nombres? ¿Se usa *ser* o *estar*?

Ejemplo

Una persona **aburrida** y una película **aburrida**

Una persona **aburrida** es una persona que no es capaz de divertirse. Se usa con **estar**

Una película **aburrida** produce aburrimiento y genera poco interés. Se usa con **ser**

a Una subida **cansada** y un caminante **cansado**
b Un chico **callado** y una plaza **callada**
c Un dolor **molesto** y una persona **molesta**
d Un **enfermo** y una persona **enferma**
e Una persona **confiada** (**ser**) y una persona **confiada** (**estar**)

iii Actividad en parejas

Objetivo – Aplicar el uso de *ser y estar*

Método – uno (A) de la pareja elige diez adjetivos y nombres y el otro (B) tiene que usarlos con *ser* o *estar*. Hay que usar todos los pronombres o nombres

Ejemplos

A: triste
B: (No) estoy triste
A: mercado
B: Están en el mercado
A: calle
B: Los vecinos están en la calle
A: rubio
B: Es una chica rubia

Después de esta actividad, un representante de la clase escribe su trabajo en el pizarrón (**M**) / la pizarra, y los otros miembros de la clase ofrecen otras posibilidades.

Unit 14 *(Unidad 14)*

Transitive and intransitive verbs, and reflexive verbs (*Los verbos transitivos e intransitivos, y los verbos reflexivos*)

This unit should be read in conjunction with the unit on pronouns (unit 17).

Level **1**

1.1 **Transitive verbs** (*Verbos transitivos*)

1.2 **Intransitive verbs** (*Verbos intransitivos*)

1.3 **More differences between transitive and intransitive verbs** (*Más diferencias entre verbos transitivos e intransitivos*)

1.4 **Reflexive verbs** (*Verbos reflexivos*)

1.5 **Use of the pronoun** (*Uso del pronombre*)

1.6 **Reflexive verbs as reciprocal verbs** (*Verbos reflexivos como verbos recíprocos*)

1.7 **Reflexive verbs with parts of the body** (*Verbos reflexivos con partes del cuerpo*)

1.8 **Variations on the place of the reflexive pronoun** (*Variaciones sobre la posición / ubicación (**M**) del pronombre reflexivo*)

1.1 Transitive verbs

A transitive verb has a subject – an actor who or which acts directly upon some person or thing and an object. This object must be expressed or the verb ceases to be transitive. This comment applies to both Spanish and English. Thus in **Veo la casa** (I see the house), **veo** is a transitive verb because it has an object, i.e. **casa**. Examples of other verbs used transitively, and there are innumerable verbs that may be used in this way, are:

Lee el periódico	She reads the newspaper	*Veo la película*	I see the movie
Conduce el coche	She drives the car	*Visito la ciudad*	I visit the town
Prepara la cena	He prepares the meal	*Toman el avión*	They catch the airplane

1.2 Intransitive verbs

If the verb does not have a direct object it is used intransitively. Here are some examples:

Corro / ando todos los días	I run / walk every day
Vamos a Roma	We are going to Rome

107

Venimos aquí con frecuencia	We come here frequently
Los niños nadan en el río	The children swim in the river
El sol brilla	The sun shines
El pasto (M) / la hierba crece	The grass grows

1.3 More differences between transitive and intransitive verbs

In English, most verbs may be used transitively or intransitively. This is not the case in Spanish. If we take the use of a transitive verb in English, *The man opens the door*, we discover that the verb *to open* may be used intransitively: *The door opens*. The Spanish equivalent *abrir* may only be used transitively: *El hombre abre la puerta*. It cannot be used in an intransitive way unless it becomes reflexive (i.e. *La puerta se abre*; see "Reflexive verbs" below: 1.4). **But**, before passing on to reflexive verbs, we would do well to consider how the two Spanish verbs *bajar* and *subir* may be used transitively and intransitively. By comparing the transitive and intransitive uses of *bajar* and *subir*, you will see the differences more clearly:

Transitive use	**Intransitive use**
Baja las escaleras	*Bajan de la montaña*
She goes down the stairs	They go down the mountain
Baja los libros, por favor	*Los precios bajan / suben*
Bring down the books, please	Prices are going down/up
El niño sube las escaleras de dos en dos	*Sube al primer piso*
The child goes up the stairs two by two	She goes up to the first floor
Sube los sillones con una polea	*La temperatura sube*
She takes up the armchairs with a pulley	The temperature's going up

1.4 Reflexive verbs

i A transitive verb is called *reflexive* when its action returns upon the actor – in other words, when the subject and object are identical. A reflexive verb is a kind of transitive verb because it does have a direct object. Although reflexive verbs exist in English, it is possible in most cases not to use them. For example, we would much more easily say *I washed this morning* than *I washed myself this morning*. However, in Spanish, this is not the case. If we said **Lavé esta mañana** a Spanish speaker would wonder what you were washing, the car, your clothes, sheets, etc. If you wanted to say that you were actually washing yourself, you would need to use a reflexive pronoun with the verb *lavar*. So, the *me* of *me lavo* is most necessary if you want to be clear about what is being washed – in this case, you. Whatever the form of the subject, and whether expressed or not, the object is always a pronoun, always expressed, and agreeing in person and number with the verb (see unit 17 for pronouns).

The usual position of the pronominal object or pronoun object is immediately before the verb or the auxiliary verb. The following pattern of the verb *bañarse* (to have a swim but in **M** to have a shower) will serve for all tenses and combinations:

yo me baño
tú te bañas
él / ella / Ud. se baña
nosotros / as nos bañamos
vosotros / as os bañáis
ellos / ellas / Uds. se bañan

ii Bear in mind again that the **Uds**. in Mexico, as in all Spanish America, is used to cover **vosotros / as** as well as the **Uds**. of Spain.

Of course, **bañar** is also used non-reflexively to mean *to give a bath to* or *to give a shower to* (**M**).

Here are just a few very common verbs used reflexively and non-reflexively:

acercar	to bring closer	*acercarse*	to get closer
acostar	to put to bed	*acostarse*	to go to bed
*afeitar (not in **M**)*	to shave (someone)	*afeitarse*	to shave (yourself)
alegrar	to make happy	*alegrarse*	to cheer up
arreglar	to arrange, to fix	*arreglarse*	to get ready
avergonzar	to put to shame	*avergonzarse*	to be ashamed
cansar	to tire	*cansarse*	to get tired
despertar	to wake (someone) up	*despertarse*	to wake up
enfadar	to make angry	*enfadarse*	to get angry
*enojar (**M**)*	to make angry	*enojarse*	to get angry
levantar	to lift up	*levantarse*	to get up
mojar	to wet	*mojarse*	to get wet
pasear	to take for a walk	*pasearse*	to go for a walk
*rasurar (**M**)*	to shave (someone)	*rasurarse*	to shave (yourself)

iii A great number of verbs may be used reflexively in this way.

Examples of verbs used reflexively and non-reflexively

Acerca la silla, por favor	Bring the chair closer, please
Me acerco a la ventana	I get closer to the window
Voy a pasear al perrito	I'm going to take the dog for a walk
Se están paseando	They're out for a walk
*Su actitud enoja (**M**) a todo el mundo*	Her attitude makes everyone angry
Se enoja al enterarse de lo ocurrido	She gets angry when she learns what has happened

1.5 Use of the pronoun

i When the subject is a pronoun, it is often omitted unless emphasis is required. The reflexive pronoun usually tells you what the subject is. As with all pronouns (see unit 17 on pronouns), the reflexive object can be attached to the infinitive or precede an auxiliary verb coming before the infinitive. The meaning is the same. It may be added in passing that these two usages are equally common in Italian, and in Old French.

Me quiero lavar / Quiero lavarme	I want to wash
¿Te quieres acostar? / ¿Quieres acostarte?	Do you want to go to bed?
*Nos vamos a rasurar / Vamos a rasurarnos (**M**)*	We are going to have a shave

ii One of the most common and idiomatic uses of Spanish reflexive verbs, as with many idiomatic uses, does not have a direct equivalent in English. The reflexive may be used in the singular or plural form. The reflexive can only be rendered in a passive way in English, unless you choose to change the English construction completely:

Se venden periódicos aquí	Newspapers are sold here / They sell newspapers here
*Se compran carros (**M**) en un supermercado*	Cars are sold in a supermarket / They sell . . .
Se alquila un piso	Apartment for rent
*Se renta un departamento (**M**)*	Apartment for rent
Se busca una secretaria	We are looking for a secretary (to work)
Se plantea el siguiente problema	The following problem arises
Se reduce la deuda a mil dólares	The debt is reduced to a thousand dollars

iii Complications arise when the reflexive pronouns (see unit 17 on pronouns) are no longer the direct object but the indirect object. Take the following two cases:

Me lavo	I wash (myself)	*Me lavo las manos*	I wash my hands
Me corto	I cut myself	*Me corto el dedo*	I cut my finger

In these cases, **Me** in **Me lavo** is a direct object but in **Me lavo las manos** it is an indirect object, since the direct object is **las manos**. Similarly, in the second example, **el dedo** is the direct object and **Me** is the indirect object. Note also that, in this type of construction, a possessive adjective is not used – rather the definite article. This is not the case in English. Fortunately, pronouns preceding verbs in the perfect tense have no repercussions on the past participle, as they do in French and Italian, largely because the perfect tense in Spanish is only conjugated with **haber**, and not **ser** or **estar**.

Examples

Se ha vendido la casa	The house has been sold
*Se han comprado los boletos (**M**) / las entradas*	The tickets have been bought

1.6 Reflexive verbs as reciprocal verbs

i Reflexive verbs can often be referred to as reciprocal verbs when several actors or subjects act upon each other. In these cases, the subject is always plural:

Se engañan	They deceive themselves / They deceive one another
Nos felicitamos	We congratulate ourselves / each other
Se miran	They look at themselves / at each other
Se ven en el espejo	They see themselves / each other in the mirror
Se ayudan los siniestrados	The victims help themselves / each other

ii Sometimes, a reinforcing expression is used to make the meaning clear:

Se detestan mutuamente	They loathe each other
Los políticos no se entienden entre sí	Politicians don't understand each other

Los soldados se ayudan unos a otros	The soldiers help each other
Se odian una a otra	They hate each other

iii There are some Spanish verbs which may only be used in the reflexive form, or are rarely used in a non-reflexive form, and have no genuine reflexive interpretation:

abstenerse de	to abstain from
arrepentirse de	to repent of
atreverse a	to dare to
ausentarse	to absent yourself
dignarse	to deign to
jactarse de	to boast of
quejarse de	to complain of

Examples

Se arrepienten de su error	They repent over their error
Se atreve a subir a la cumbre	She dares to climb up to the top
Se digna concedernos una entrevista	She deigns to give us an interview
Nos quejamos de nuestra mala suerte	We complain of our bad luck

1.7 Reflexive verbs with parts of the body

Where parts of the human body are concerned, the reflexive pronoun is very common. It has repercussions in other parts of the sentence as well. Consider the following sentences:

Me pongo la chaqueta	I put on my jacket
Te quitas los zapatos	You take your shoes off
Se rompió el brazo	He broke his arm
Se hace daño en el tobillo	She hurts her ankle
*Se lastimaron la cabeza (**M**)*	They hurt their heads

Note two features here. One is the use of the reflexive and the second is the use of the definite article before the direct object: **la chaqueta**, **los zapatos**, etc. The possessive adjectives corresponding to *my, your . . .* (**mi**, **tu**, **su**, etc.) are not possible here. The reflexive does the work of the possessive adjective.

1.8 Variations on the place of the reflexive pronoun

As seen above, and with all other personal pronouns, the reflexive is regularly attached to the infinitive or may precede an auxiliary verb which comes before the infinitive.

Quiero lavarme / Me quiero lavar	I want to wash (myself)
Vamos a acostarnos / Nos vamos a acostar	We are going to bed
Debo hacerlo / Lo debo hacer	I have to do it

Similarly, the reflexive is either attached to the gerund or placed before the verb **estar**. Bear in mind that a written accent needs to be placed over the appropriate vowel when the reflexive is added to the gerund:

Estoy lavándome / Me estoy lavando   I am washing (myself)
Está rasurándose / Se está rasurando   He's shaving (himself)
Están paseándose / Se están paseando   They are out for a walk

Exercises Level **1**

i Mark the following verbs as transitive or intransitive, i.e. *T* or *I*:

a Escribo la carta
b Tira la pelota
c Miran la montaña
d Subo al camión (**M**)
e Nadan en el lago
f Beben agua
g El sol brilla

h Salen del edificio
i Duermo como un lirón
j El autobús para cada cinco minutos
k Nunca vacilo
l No como nada
m Los conduzco a la estación
n Le da el libro a su hermana

ii Replace the subject pronouns as in the example:
Me lavo a las ocho (tú/nosotros/ellos) > te lavas / nos lavamos / se lavan

a Me levanto (él/ella/vosotros/Uds.)
b Te peinas bien (él/ella/vosotros)
c Se (**M**) desayuna a las ocho (yo/ella/Uds.)
d Me arreglo en diez minutos (nosotros/Uds.)
e ¿A qué hora te *duchas? (vosotros/Uds.)
f ¿Dónde te **bañas? (él/ella/Uds.)
g Me disfrazo de pirata (ellos/Uds.)
h Te presentas a las nueve (yo/nosotros/vosotros)
i Me quejo en recepción (tú/nosotras/ellas)
j Se alegra con su éxito (ellos/Uds.)

ducharse is rarely used in **M**
****bañarse** in **M** means *to take a shower/bath*. In Spain, it usually means *to go for a swim*

iii Make a sentence as in the example, using a reflexive:
El perro no quiere al gato + El gato no quiere al perro > El gato y el perro no **se** quieren
a Rosa no entiende a Luis + Luis no entiende a Rosa
b Sara me escribe + Yo le escribo a Sara
c Conozco al doctor + Él me conoce
d Juana se despide de nosotros + Nos despedimos de Juana
e Le ayudo a María + Ella me ayuda a mí
f Carlos quiere a Teresa + Teresa quiere a Carlos
g Adriana no conoce a Jorge + Jorge no conoce a Adriana
h No le hablo a Roberto + Roberto no me habla

iv Paired activity
Objective – To distinguish between transitive and intransitive verbs
Method – The two persons find a series of ten Spanish verbs each. Then, *A* asks *B* and vice versa whether each verb in question is transitive or intransitive. If the verb is

transitive, then *A* and *B* must find an object to complete the sentence. Remember that an intransitive verb does not have an object, and if you end up with an object, you can be sure it is used as a transitive verb. Of course, there are some verbs which can be used transitively and intransitively, as with *comer* below, or *correr* (*Corre los cien metros* or *Corre*). So, try to find some verbs which may be used in a transitive and intransitive way (see *bajar* and *subir*, 1.3, to start with).

Example

A: *andar*
B: *andar* es un verbo intransitivo
B: *tocar*
A: *tocar* es un verbo transitivo (Toco la guitarra)
A: *comer*
B: *comer* es un verbo transitivo (Como carne / Estoy comiendo carne). Pero es también un verbo intransitivo (Como / Estoy comiendo)

The teacher then calls you all back to discuss your findings. You may need her / his insight to distinguish between the two uses of some verbs.

Level 2

2.1 **Impersonal uses of the reflexive** (*Usos impersonales del verbo reflexivo*)

2.2 **Different meaning (sometimes) when the verb is used reflexively** (*Sentido diferente [algunas veces] cuando el verbo se usa de forma reflexiva*)

2.3 **The reflexive used as an intensifier** (*El verbo reflexivo usado para poner énfasis*)

2.1 Impersonal uses of the reflexive

i An important characteristic of the Spanish reflexive *se* is its impersonal use. It has no equivalent in English, or in French or Italian for that matter. Neither is it easy to explain or translate. The closest we can get is by stating that *se* used in this way is an "independent speech element of impersonal character." Furthermore, the *se* here is not the subject of the sentence, even though it appears at the beginning of, or near to the beginning of, the sentence. Sorry about such a complicated explanation but there seems no simple way of dealing with this question. This use of *se* is quite unique, which is why many examples will be the most helpful method of illustrating the feature:

Se les ayudó a las víctimas	The injured were helped
Se le vio al hombre	The man was seen
No se le ve	He/She is nowhere to be seen
Se le detuvo a la mujer	The woman was stopped/arrested
Se les aconsejó comprarlo	They were advised to buy it
Se les pidió ayuda	They were asked for help
Se nos reclamó una compensación	They claimed compensation from us
Se les puso una multa	They were fined

Se nos entregó una carta   A letter was delivered to us
Se le ve guapa   She is good-looking
Se les avisará a los accionistas   The shareholders will be informed

An explanation, now that we have the examples, may be clearer. If we take the second example, if we had said **Se vio el hombre (en el espejo)** we would mean that the man saw himself in the mirror. To suggest that the man was seen by someone else, the reflexive **se** precedes **le** which becomes an indirect object. In all the sentences above, there is an indirect object: **les**, **le**, **os**, **nos**. For a Spanish speaker, it is an elegant way of avoiding what could be a heavy or cumbersome passive.

ii This construction leads to the very common use of **se**, albeit more in written form, in the following way. It is as much a question of word order as anything else:

A todos los miembros se les pidió que contribuyeran más dinero
All the members were asked to contribute more money
A muchas alumnas se les animó a trabajar más duro
Many pupils were encouraged to work harder
Al autor se le alabó por su nueva novela
The author was praised for his new novel

iii The impersonal **se** is also used with intransitive verbs:

Cuando se tiene treinta años   When you are / one is thirty years old
Cuando se es viejo   When you are / one is old
Si se muere   If you die / one dies
Se vive mal aquí   You don't live well here

iv The impersonal **se** is also commonly used with verbs such as **permitir**, **prohibir**, **poder**:

No se permite bañarse aquí   You cannot swim here
No se puede pisar el césped   You cannot walk on the grass (Please do
                                         not . . .)
Se prohíbe fijar carteles   You can't stick posters (here) (i.e. Stick no
                                         bills)

v Referring back to the construction listed in level 1.5: **se compran carros** or **se venden pisos** – you will frequently come across a lack of agreement, i.e. **se vende pisos** or **se repara televisores**. There is some discussion over the grammatical legitimacy of this construction. It is probably best to avoid it, although it is extremely common.

2.2 Different meaning (sometimes) when the verb is used reflexively

Many verbs have a slightly different meaning sometimes, but not always, when used reflexively. Here is a short list:

Non-reflexive	Reflexive
aparecer to appear (used most commonly)	***aparecerse*** to appear as of a ghost
Apareció a la puerta / en el parque She appeared in the door / in the park	*La Virgen se les apareció a los pastorcillos* The Virgin appeared to the shepherds
bajar to go down	***bajarse*** to get off
bajar las escaleras / de la montaña To go down the stairs / the mountain	*Bájate del tren en Zaragoza* Get off the train in Saragossa
casar to marry (someone to another)	***casarse*** to get married
Los casó el alcalde The mayor married them	*Se casó con una colombiana* He married a Colombian
desayunar to have breakfast	***desayunarse*** to have breakfast **(M)**
¿Has desayunado? Have you had breakfast?	*¿Ya te desayunaste?* Have you had breakfast already?
enfermar to fall sick	***enfermarse*** to fall sick **(M)**
Enfermó del corazón She fell sick with heart trouble	*Se enfermó del estomágo* She fell ill with stomach troubles
entrenar to train (used transitively but see opposite)	***entrenarse*** to train (but increasingly used non-reflexively in this meaning)
Este técnico entrena al equipo This manager trains the team	*Esa atleta (se) entrena todos los días* That athlete trains every day (This non-reflexive use is not always accepted)
parar to stop (used transitively and intransitively)	***pararse*** to stop, to stand up **(M)** (used intransitively)
El portero paró el penalti The goalkeeper stopped the penalty	*Se paró a hablar con la vecina* He stopped to speak to the neighbor
El tren para aquí todos los días The train stops here every day (*se* not possible here)	*Se pararon (M) / levantaron los alumnos* The pupils stood up
regresar to return, to give back (more common in **M** and second meaning only in **M**)	***regresarse (M)***
	¿Cuándo se regresaron? When did you come back?
Regresaron a casa They returned home	
Me regresó (M) el paquete She returned the packet to me	
subir to go up, to rise	***subirse*** to get on
Subimos la montaña We went up the mountain	*Se subió al avión* She got on the airplane
	Me subí al windsurf I got on the windsurfer
Los precios suben Prices are going up	

2.3   The reflexive used as an intensifier

The reflexive is also used as an intensifier. Its use in the following examples illustrates how the reflexive pronoun gives a "stronger," though essentially similar, meaning.

Non-reflexive	Reflexive
caer to fall	*caerse* to fall (often used of a person)
La maceta cayó por el balcón The flower pot fell over the balcony (but *caerse* is possible here as in *Se cayó la lámpara* The lamp fell over)	*Se cayó del árbol* She fell from the tree *Se cayó de espaldas* She fell over backwards
comer to eat	*comerse* to eat up
He comido bien I've had a good meal	*Se comió todas las papas (M) / patatas* He ate all the potatoes
dormir to sleep	*dormirse* to go to sleep
¿Dormiste bien? Did you sleep well?	*Me dormí en seguida* I fell asleep immediately
encontrar to find, to meet	*encontrarse* to come across, to meet unexpectedly
No encuentro al chico I can't find the boy *La encontré en la estación* I met her at the station (i.e. I had been planning to meet her)	*Me le encontré sin darme cuenta* I bumped into him/her without realizing *Se encontró un billete de diez dólares en la calle* He found a ten-dollar bill in the street
ir to go	*irse* to go away
Voy a Palenque I'm going to Palenque	*Se fueron a Brasil* They went to Brazil
leer to read	*leerse* to read (can suggest great interest)
Leí el libro I read the book	*Me leí cuatro novelas en una semana* I read four novels in a week
llevar to carry, to wear, to take, to bring	*llevarse* to take away
Llevaba una maleta She was carrying a suitcase *Llevaba una falda escocesa* He was wearing a kilt *Quédate allí y te lo llevo* Wait there and I'll bring it to you	*Me lo llevé a España* I took it to Spain *El ladrón se llevó todas las joyas* The thief went off with all the jewels
marchar to march, to work (of mechanism)	*marcharse* to go away
Los soldados marcharon todo el día The soldiers marched all day *Mi reloj marcha bien* My watch is working well	*Se marcharon* They went off (little used in **M**)
morir to die	*morirse* to be dying
(Se) murió su padre el año pasado His father died last year *El hombre murió a manos de un ladrón* The man died at the hands of a thief	*Se moría cuando llegó el doctor (M)* He was dying when the physician arrived However, you can say *morir* and *morirse de frío/hambre*
ocurrir to happen	*Ocurrirse* to occur (to someone)
Ocurrió el accidente ayer The accident happened yesterday	*Se me ocurrió decirle que . . .* It occurred to me to say to her . . .
	(cont.)

116

Non-reflexive	Reflexive
pasar to pass, to happen *Los años pasaron* The years passed *¿Qué pasó?* What happened?	***pasarse*** to pass, to spend, to pass by (often with the idea of a person doing something) *Me pasé toda la tarde leyendo* I spent all afternoon reading *Se me pasó la oportunidad* I missed the opportunity
quedar to remain, to be left, to agree *Quedan diez minutos / dos bollos* Ten minutes / two buns remain *Hemos quedado el lunes a las siete* We have agreed on Monday at seven *Quedamos en vernos a la una* We agreed to meet at one	***quedarse*** to remain (with this meaning merely a stronger form of ***quedar***) *Se quedó en casa* He remained at home
salir to go out, to turn out (correctly or otherwise) *Salió del edificio a las dos* She left the building at two *Este cálculo no me sale* I can't solve this calculation	***salirse*** to go out (merely a stronger form of ***salir***, and suggesting a determined feeling) *Se enfadó y se salió del café* She got angry and marched out of the café *Se salió a mitad de la película* She went out in the middle of the film (probably in anger or discontentedness)
tomar to take, drink *¿Qué vas a tomar?* What'll you have?	***tomarse*** to drink (probably quickly) *Se tomó cuatro cañas* He drank / knocked back four glasses of beer
venir to come *Vino a California hace dos años* She came to California two years ago	***venirse*** to come (often with a purpose) *Se vino a Guanajuato para montar una empresa* He came to Guanajuato to set up a company

Exercises Level 2

i Cambia la ubicación (*M*) / posición del reflexivo como en el ejemplo:
Se van a quejar con el encargado > Van a quejar**se** con el encargado

a Te debes despedir inmediatamente
b Los muchachos se están asoleando (**M**)
c Te puedes caer por las escaleras
d ¿Se van a casar pronto?
e Me estoy ensuciando el vestido

ii Cambia como en los ejemplos:
Pienso acostar**me** > **Me** pienso acostar
El bebé está riéndo**se** muy contento > El bebé **se** está riendo muy contento

a Pensamos irnos a las dos de la tarde
b Quieren quedarse en el hotel
c Desean levantarse temprano

d Pedro va a enojarse mucho

e Tienes que levantarte ahora

f Sigo divirtiéndome

g Continuamos paseándonos

h Estoy arreglándome

i Están pintándose los ojos

j Estás ensuciándote la ropa

iii Cambia como en el ejemplo, añadiendo una preposición si es necesaria. Hace falta un poco de imaginación:

Abres la puerta > Se está abriendo la puerta

a El profesor aburre a todo el mundo

b Acuestas a los niños

c La fiesta alegra a los niños

d La lectura me cansa

e Paseo a la familia

f Te secas el pelo

g El técnico entrena al equipo

h El cura casa a los novios

iv Rellena los blancos / Llena los espacios (M) con el verbo y el pronombre reflexivo correctos. Tienes el verbo en infinitivo. Puedes ponerlo en presente o en pretérito simple, y de vez en cuando, en imperfecto, y escribir un texto de España o de México. En lo que se refiere al modelo mexicano que se propone, se detectan algunos detalles algo distintos del texto original.

(Yo) (_) levantar a las siete. (Yo) (_) lavar con un poco de jabón. (_) lavar con la manopla, (_) frotar / tallar (**M**) el cuerpo con esponja / zacate (**M**) y (_) limpiar la cara con agua caliente. (_) acercar al espejo. (_) ver en él. (_) afeitar / rasurar (**M**) de mala gana. Veo en el espejo a una persona que (_) arreglar pero que no (_) pintar como mi esposa. (_) mojar la cara con más agua. Esa persona que (_) mostrar en el espejo (_) enojar (**M**) / enfadar por la faena. (_) cansar con tanto trabajo. (_) cortar el dedo con la navaja y (_) enojar/enfadar otra vez. (_) presentar después una mujer y (_) ver ahora dos personas en el espejo. (Nosotros) (_) saludar, pero no (_) reconocer. No (_) hablar / platicar (**M**) porque no (_) conocer. (_) ver ahora dos personas que (_) dar un toque agradable y que (_) preparar para salir a la calle. (_) arreglar bien. La mujer (_) quitar los rulos / tubos (**M**) para poner (_) guapa y para poder poner (_) el sombrero. Los dos (_) endomingar / pulir (**M**) porque querer presentar (_) perfectamente vestidos con sus amigos. Salen sin hablar (_) y sin dirigir (_) la palabra el uno al otro.

v Prepara para la semana próxima un trozo describiendo un pequeño episodio de tu propia vida. Usa verbos reflexivos como los de arriba en el pasaje anterior. Se puede tratar de la primera hora de la mañana cuando te levantas, una visita al cine/teatro, un viaje al centro de la ciudad, un encuentro imprevisto, o cualquier anécdota relacionada con tu vida personal. El profesor pedirá a varios estudiantes que le presenten su tarea a toda la clase. Los que escuchen las presentaciones tomarán apuntes, lo que producirá un debate (en español, ¿por qué no?) sobre el uso de los verbos reflexivos. Y ¡mucha imaginación!

Unit 15 (*Unidad 15*)

Impersonal verbs (*Los verbos impersonales*)

Level **1**

1.1 **Impersonal verbs** (*Verbos impersonales*)

1.2 **Uses of *haber*** (*Usos de **haber***)

1.3 **Impersonal use of *hacer* meaning *ago* and *since*** (*Uso impersonal de **hacer** con el sentido de **desde***)

1.1 Impersonal verbs

Impersonal verbs have neither subject nor object. Whatever they represent as being or as going on, nothing is suggested as taking any active part in it. There is no perfect example of such a verb in English but Spanish, like Italian, has many that are either always or occasionally used. The English pronoun *it* is a mere form of expression due to the habit of our language, but it does not represent the actor. Interestingly enough, the English *it* corresponds to the French *il*. The verbs in question here are frequently associated with weather or natural phenomena:

i *llover* (to rain), *nevar* (to snow), *tronar* (to thunder), *lloviznar* (to drizzle), *granizar* (to hail), *relampaguear* (to be lightning – very difficult to translate! [any suggestions?] and an excellent example of why literal translations are not to be recommended), *hacer* (to be) (especially this last one):

Llueve mucho	It rains a lot	*Relampaguea*	There's lightning
Está nevando	It's snowing	*Hace buen tiempo*	It's nice weather
Está tronando	It's thundering	*¿Qué tiempo hace?*	What's the weather like?
Llovizna	It drizzles	*Hace (mucho) viento*	It's (very) windy

ii With respect to weather, we should point out here the differences between *hacer* and *tener*. Whereas **hacer** is used to refer to the condition of the weather, *tener* is used for a person's reaction to it. Compare the following examples:

Hace calor	It is hot	*Hace frío*	It is cold
Tengo calor	I am hot	*Tengo frío*	I am cold

Estar caliente does not mean to be hot, unless used figuratively about the opposite sex!

iii Furthermore, **estar** is used in this context, but for things:

Esta cama está fría	This bed is cold
La sopa está muy caliente	The soup is very hot

1.2 Uses of *haber*

i (There is a more limited treatment of *haber* in unit 13, 1.4.v on *ser* and **estar**. See also level 2 in this unit.)

The verb **haber** has practically lost its original meaning of possession, connected as it is to the French verb *avoir* and the Italian *avere* which both retain the notion of possession. Its principal value is that of an auxiliary verb (**he hablado** = I spoke / have spoken) in forming compound tenses (see unit 5). It has one other wide acceptation, namely when it is used impersonally. Only the third person singular (**hay**), the infinitive (**haber**), the past participle (**habido**) and the gerund (**habiendo**) are used impersonally. One irregularity is that the present indicative is not **ha** but **hay**. This peculiar form is a combination of **ha** and the now obsolete **y** (there) which crops up in the French *il y a* (there is/are). **Hay** is used in the following way.

ii

Hay un coche / diez coches	There is one/a car / are ten cars
Hay un muchacho / varios muchachos	There is/are one/a/several boy(s)

It is clear from these examples that, while in English the verb agrees in number with the following noun or nouns, in Spanish it is singular throughout, like the French *il y a*. (See level 2.6. for similar use in other tenses.)

iii **Hay** followed by **que** = **hay que**, and then followed by an infinitive, denotes necessity or obligation, witness these examples:

Hay que ser prudente en carretera	I/You/We, etc., have to be careful on the road
Hay que ir mañana	I/You/We, etc., have to go tomorrow

(See level 2 for similar use in other tenses and covering personal pronouns.)

iv When a noun or equivalent word intervenes between **haber** and **que**, the idea of obligation is modified:

Hay muchos monumentos que visitar	There are lots of monuments to visit
Hay más de una dificultad que vencer	There is more than one difficulty to get over

1.3 Impersonal use of *hacer* meaning *ago* and *since*

Apart from its use with weather (see above), this verb may be followed by a measure of time, and has the value of *ago* or *since*:

Hace tres años que estoy en México	I've been in Mexico for three years
Hace más de un año que no oigo hablar de ella	I haven't heard of her for more than a year
Llegué hace cinco años	I arrived five years ago

Level 1

i **Answer the following questions:**

Example

¿Qué tiempo hace mañana? > Hace buen tiempo mañana

a ¿Qué tiempo hace hoy?
b ¿Qué tiempo hace en verano?
c ¿Qué tiempo hace en invierno?
d ¿Qué tiempo hace en primavera?
e ¿Qué tiempo hace en otoño?
f ¿Qué tiempo hace en marzo?
g ¿Qué tiempo hace en el sur de México?
h ¿Qué tiempo hace en el centro de España en julio?
i ¿Qué tiempo hace en Nueva York en febrero?
j ¿Qué tiempo hace en Arizona en agosto?

ii **Complete the following sentences with expressions related to the weather:**

Example

Juego con mis amigos en el parque cuando (_) > . . . cuando hace buen tiempo

a No salgo en el carro (**M**) / coche cuando (_)
b Mis padres y yo vamos al campo cuando (_)
c No visitamos la costa cuando (_)
d No saco buenas fotos cuando (_)
e En Londres en noviembre (_)
f En Acapulco en verano (_)
g Pasan todo el día en casa cuando (_)
h ¿Vas al colegio en camión (**M**) / autobús cuando (_) ?
i No me gustan las vacaciones cuando (_)
j Disfruto mucho cuando (_)
k Me siento muy romántico cuando (_)
l Es peligroso el mar cuando (_)

iii **Make questions from the following statements, as in the example:**
Hay una regadera (**M**) / una ducha en el baño > ¿Qué hay en el baño?

a Hay una televisión en el estudio
b Hay tres sillas en la recámara (**M**) / el dormitorio
c Hay un microondas en la cocina
d Hay unos periódicos en la mesa
e Hay una computadora (**M**) / un ordenador en el salón
f Hay varios timbres (**M**) / sellos en el paquete
g Hay un foco (**M**) / una bombilla en el techo
h Hay cuatro mesas en el comedor
i Hay un carro (**M**) / coche en el garage (**M**) / garaje
j Hay dos espejos en el baño

iv Class activity

Objective – Practice the use of impersonal verbs with reference to the weather
Method – One member of the class draws weather phenomena on the board. The class guesses what kind of weather it is.

Example

The member draws drops of water coming down
The class responds with: Llueve / Está lloviendo (*same meaning*)

1.1 above will give you plenty of help. Feel free to use your imagination to indicate heat, cold, etc. It would be easy to find ten illustrations.

Level **2**

2.1 **More on impersonal verbs** (*Más detalles sobre verbos impersonales*)
2.2 ***Ser*** **and** *estar* **used impersonally when followed by nouns and adjectives** (*Uso impersonal de **ser** y **estar** seguidos de nombres y adjetivos*)
2.3 **Modal auxiliary verbs (***Verbos auxiliares de tipo modal*)
2.4 **Uses of** *caber* **and** *soler* **(***Usos de **caber** y **soler***)
2.5 **Uses of** *bastar, faltar, quedar, sobrar* **(***Usos de **bastar**, . . .*)
2.6 **More on** *haber* **and** *hacer* **(***Más detalles sobre **haber** y **hacer***)
2.7 **Use of** *haber* + *debido* = **Ought** **and** **ought to have** (*Uso de . . .*)
2.8 **Verbs in past tenses with** *hacer* = **ago** (*Verbos en pasado con **hacer** = ago*)
2.9 ***Desde*** **= since**

2.1   More on impersonal verbs

i In addition to the weather verbs above, there is a further cluster of verbs that stand freely, and often do not have a true equivalent in English. Among the most common are:

amanecer	to dawn, to get light	*encantar*	to please, to delight
anochecer	to begin to get dark	*gustar*	to please
apetecer	to attract, to appeal (to)	*importar*	to be important
constar	to be evident	*parecer*	to seem, to appear
convenir	to suit	*ventiscar*	to be snowing (and blowing)
diluviar	to pour down		

Of course, **encantar** and **gustar** may be used in other ways:

Les encanto a mis estudiantes	My students adore me
Le gusto a mi novia	My girlfriend likes me

Ejemplos

En invierno amanece tarde	It gets light later in winter
Me gusta el verano mediterráneo porque anochece tarde	I like the Mediterranean summer because it gets dark later
¿Te apetece un helado?	Do you feel like an ice cream?
Me consta que tiene dinero	It is clear to me that he has money

Conviene firmar el contrato	It is sensible to sign the contract
Le encanta la ópera / ir a la ópera	She loves the opera / going to the opera
¿Os / les (M) gusta ir al cine?	Do you like going to the movies?
Importa mucho	It is very important
¿Les importa que fumemos?	Do you mind if we smoke?
Siempre me molesta no ayudarte	It always troubles me not to help you
Me parece que es china	It seems to me that she's Chinese
Ayer estuvo ventiscando todo el día	It was snowing hard all day yesterday

ii There are many cases where in English a verb would be used impersonally, governing an infinitive, while in Spanish the infinitive is the subject of the verb:

Me costó un ojo de la cara aprobar el examen	It cost me an arm and a leg to get through the exam
Nos tocó jugar a nosotros	It was our turn to play
A ella le correspondía ir de vacaciones en otoño	It was her turn to go on vacation in the fall/autumn
Compete a la compañía responder por el error	It is incumbent upon the company to be responsible for the error = The company takes responsibility for . . .

2.2 *Ser* and *estar* used impersonally when followed by nouns and adjectives

i The verbs *ser* and **estar** are used impersonally with special frequency when followed by nouns and adjectives:

Es una pena ver a estos niños tan enfermos	It is sad to see these children so sick
Es lástima que os tengáis que marchar	It's a pity you have to go
Es importante estudiar	It's important to study
Es esencial trabajar	It's essential to work
Es lógico terminarlo hoy	It's logical to finish it today
Es natural cuidar a tus niños	It's natural to look after your children
Estaba oscuro cuando me levanté	It was dark when I got up
Está muy nublado	It's very cloudy
Era muy tarde para ir al campo	It was very late to go into the country

ii There is an impersonal expression, of active form, but of passive value, formed by the verb **ser**, followed by *de* and the infinitive:

Es de esperar que regresen	It is to be hoped they will come back
Es de lamentar que no haya aprobado	It is to be regretted he did not pass

2.3 Modal auxiliary verbs

i English has a relatively large number of auxiliary verbs (e.g. *will, would, may, might, shall, should, must, ought*) and verbal expressions (*to be to, to have to*, e.g. *we were to arrive at nine, we have to go now*). Their main function is to express intentions or commands. There is no straightforward match between these and their Spanish counterparts. Spanish has a rather small number of auxiliary verbs (**deber**, **poder**, **querer**) and verbal expressions (**tener que hacer algo** = *to have to do something*, **haber de hacer algo** = *to have to do something*). Their main uses are:

ii Deber to have to, must (often has the value of *ought*, and less strong than **tener que** – see below; also suggests speculation = *must*)

Debo ir ahora	I must go now
Debe de ser muy pobre	She must be very poor (speculation)
Debió de hacerlo	He must have done it (speculation)

iii Poder to be able, can

Puedes ir conmigo	You can go with me
¿Puedes nadar doscientos metros?	Can you swim two hundred meters?
Podrán jugar mañana	They will be able to / can play tomorrow
Habría podido aprobar el examen	He could have got through the examination

iv Saber to know (how to)

*Sé hablar español / cocinar / nadar / usar la computadora (**M**) / el ordenador* I know how to speak Spanish/cook/ swim/use the computer

Note. **Poder** suggests physical capacity while **saber** suggests knowledge for doing something

v Conocer (to know) should also be distinguished from **saber**. If you associate it with *to be acquainted with* as in, for example, *Conozco a tu hermano / a esta autora / la ciudad de México* (I know your brother, etc) you see the difference immediately.

Bear in mind also that **saber** suggests *to know a fact*, as in: *Sé que están en la casa / que vendrán mañana* (I know that they are in the house / they will come tomorrow)

vi Querer to want, to wish

Quieren tocar los instrumentos	They want to play the instruments
Queríamos subir al monte	We wanted to go up the mountain
Yo hubiera querido acompañarlos	I would have wanted to accompany them

vii Tener que to have to / must (often stronger than **deber**)

Tengo que ir	I must go
Tenía que haberlo hecho	I ought to have done it

viii Haber + **de** has the meaning of *to be/have to*. It can also imply an assumption or a speculation = *must*. With this second meaning it fits in with **deber de**

Hemos de trabajar duro	We've got to work hard
Habrá de entregar los deberes esta tarde	We'll/He'll/She'll have to hand in the homework this afternoon
Ha de haber un baile mañana	There is to be a ball tomorrow
Había de haber un partido de fútbol al día siguiente	There was to be a football game the following day
Ha de ser muy rico	He must be very rich
La palabra ha de estar en el diccionario	The word must be in the dictionary

2.4 Uses of *caber* and *soler*

i There are two verbs which do not have an English equivalent: **caber** and **soler.** Using them is often a lot easier than translating them.

caber = to be contained in, to be enough room for, to fit

Los libros caben en la estantería	There's enough room for the books on the shelf i.e. The books fit
Este armario no cabe por la puerta	This wardrobe won't go through the door
No cabemos en el coche	There is not enough room for us in the car
¿Quepo aquí?	Is there room for me here?

ii *Caber* It also has the more impersonal meaning of *to be possible, may*:

Cabe preguntar si es suficiente	It is possible to ask if it is sufficient
Cabe suponer que cometieron un error	It is possible to suppose that they made an error

iii *Soler* to be accustomed to

Suelo venir aquí los martes	I usually come here on Tuesdays
Estos melones solían ser muy buenos	These melons used to be very good

2.5 Uses of *bastar, faltar, quedar, sobrar*

i *Bastar* to be sufficient

Basta (con) marcar el prefijo y el número	All you have to do is dial the code and number
Bastaba (con) decirle que no podemos ir	It was enough to tell her we can't come

ii *Faltar* to be lacking, to remain

Falta el postre	There remains the dessert
Aquí faltan tres tenedores	Three forks are missing here
Todavía me faltan dos horas para terminar el ejercicio	I still need a couple of hours to finish the exercise
Sólo falta(n) un par de horas para llegar	There's just a couple of hours before we arrive

iii *Quedar* to remain, to be over

Quedan tres manzanas	There remain three apples / Three apples are left over
Quedan por barrer la salita y el despacho	There just remains the living room and the office to sweep
Queda por decir que está prohibido entrar ahora	It remains to say that it is forbidden to go in now

iv *Sobrar* to be in excess, to be over

Una vez hecho el vestido me sobraron tres metros de tela	Once I had made the dress I had three meters of fabric left over
Parece que sobrarán camas	It looks as though we'll have too many beds

2.6 More on *haber* and *hacer*

i The use of *hay* extends to all tenses

Había una casa / dos casas	There was one/a house / were two houses
Hubo una explosión / varias explosiones	There was an explosion / were several explosions
Habrá una fiesta / dos fiestas	There will be a party / two parties
Habría un invitado / varios invitados	There would be a guest / several guests
*Es posible que haya un doctor (**M**) / dos doctores*	It is possible that there will be a/one physician/doctor / two physicians/ doctors
Era probable que hubiera un accidente / varios accidentes	It was probable that there would be an accident / several accidents

ii The conditional corresponds to "ought":

Habría que salir ahora	I/You/We, etc., ought to leave now

2.7 Use of *haber* + *debido* = *ought* and *ought to have*

The imperfect subjunctive of **haber** + **debido** + infinitive is frequently used with the idea of "ought to have." It has the same meaning but less weight than **tener que** above (see level 2.3)

Yo hubiera debido decirle que . . .	I ought to have told him that . . .
Hubiéramos debido ir	We ought to have gone

An alternative form of the above is:

debía + **haber** + past participle

(Yo) debía haberle dicho que . . .	I ought to have told her/him that . . .

2.8 Verbs in past tenses with *hacer* = *ago*

*Los cuates (**M**) / amigos salieron hace media hora*	The friends left half an hour ago
Visité Madrid hace un año	I visited Madrid a year ago
Hacía diez años que había ido a España	It was ten years ago when I had been to Spain

2.9 Desde = *since*

Desde hace varios siglos los árabes han colaborado con los cristianos

For centuries the Arabs have collaborated with the Christians

Desde hacía muchas horas el niño no había comido

The child had not eaten for hours

Hacer also expresses the length of time between two points:

Hace diez años que fui a España

It was ten years ago that I went to Spain

Exercises Level **2**

i **Rellena los blancos / Llena los espacios (M) con un verbo impersonal. Hay más de una posibilidad en varios casos:**

Ejemplo

El domingo (_) ir a la alberca (M) / piscina > El domingo me gustaría ir a . . .

a En verano (_) muy temprano
b En invierno (_) muy temprano
c ¿Te (_) ir al cine?
d No sé si (_) arreglar el asunto hoy
e Nos (_) ir a la ópera
f ¿Les (**M**) / os (_) aprender a coser?
g No me (_) manejar (**M**) / conducir toda la noche
h Me (_) que es de origen azteca
i Estaba (_) toda la noche cuando fui por los niños

ii **Haz frases con las siguientes expresiones:**

Ejemplo

es natural > Es natural beber cuando hace mucho calor

es una pena, es (una) lástima, es importante, es esencial, es lógico, es natural, es inevitable, es mejor, es posible, es imposible

iii **Completa las siguientes frases con uno de estos verbos. Pon los verbos en singular o plural según convenga. En algunos casos, hay más de una solución:**

caber, quedar, sobrar, faltar, bastar, tener que, haber de, poder, saber, deber, querer

a ¿(_) ir conmigo?
b (_) de equivocarse
c (_) de trabajar duro porque hay que ganar dinero
d ¿(_) más sillas aquí? Si no, nos sentamos por el suelo
e Aquí (_) cuchillos pero hay más en la cocina
f (_) nadar correctamente
g (_) que corregir tus errores
h Después del incendio sólo (_) tres muros
i (_) nadar más de un kilómetro
j (_) tocar la guitarra
k (_) tenedores. Ponlos en el cajón
l (_) media docena de huevos. Los otros los pones en el frigorífico

iv Actividad en parejas

Objetivo – Distinguir entre el uso de *saber* y *conocer*

Método – A le hace a B diez preguntas conteniendo *saber* y *conocer*, y las siguientes palabras:

1 ciudad 2 hablar portugués 3 a Teresa 4 un restaurante bueno 5 la verdad
6 tocar el piano 7 un poco de italiano 8 Chile y Colombia 9 a tu madre
10 algo de japonés

Ejemplos

París	PREGUNTA:	¿Conoces a París?
	RESPUESTA:	Conozco a París muy, muy bien
Está Juan	PREGUNTA:	¿Sabes dónde está Juan?
	RESPUESTA:	No sé donde está (Juan)

Después, se reúne todo el mundo, y el profesor le hace preguntas a toda la clase, variando las diez palabras/expresiones. Por ejemplo, en vez de usar *ciudad*, puede usar *pueblo* o *pueblito* (**M**) / *pueblecito*. En vez de *tocar el piano* puede usar *tocar la guitarra*. El profesor puede variar también los pronombres (*tú*, *Uds.*, *él/ella o ¡yo!*). Pueden descubrir así talentos ocultos de su profesor.

Unit 16 *(Unidad 16)*
Subjunctive (*El subjuntivo*)

Don't allow the term **subjunctive** to put you off. It may have all but disappeared in English though we still use it on occasions ("If I were you"), and is slowly slipping away in French, but it is still very much a mood to be reckoned with in Spanish, both in Spain and Spanish America. So it is a very necessary tool for correct expression in Spanish. Much as it is in Italian, in fact.

Before we embark on the subjunctive in Spanish, it is a good idea to see how complicated it is to express the subjunctive in English. You can be comforted by the fact that in Spanish the rules are logical whereas in English they are not. Examples in English: I want *him to go* / I wish *he would go* / It is necessary *that he go* / I am happy *that he does* it tomorrow.

Whereas the indicative (see unit 4) relates to clear knowledge and certainty, the subjunctive is linked to doubt, commands, uncertainty, desire, aspiration, risk, and danger. The indicative appears in both main and subordinate clauses but the subjunctive appears nearly always in subordinate ones. If we take the two following examples:

i *Te **he dicho** que **voy** al cine* I (have) told you I'm going to the movies

ii *Te **he dicho** que **vayas** al cine* I (have) told you to go to the movies

In the first sentence, we have a main clause (**he dicho**) and a subordinate clause (**voy**), both in the indicative. The subordinate clause is what amounts to a statement of fact. However, in the second case, we have a main clause in the indicative (**he dicho**) and then a subjunctive (**vayas**) which is determined by a command.

Two more examples will make this difference clearer.

1. (a) **Pienso** *que **viene** mi hermano* I think that my brother is coming

   (b) *No **pienso** que **venga** mi hermano* I don't think my brother is coming

2. (a) **Es seguro** *que **arregla** el problema* It's certain that he's sorting out the problem

   (b) *No **es seguro** que **arregle** el problema* It's not certain he's sorting out the problem

In 1(a) and 2(a) the probability is that the brother is coming and that the problem is being solved. However, in 1(b) and 2(b), it is far from certain that the brother is coming and that the problem is being solved, hence the use of the subjunctive in these two cases. Once you have grasped this essential difference between (a) and (b), you are well on the way to understanding the most important feature of the subjunctive. Now for the forms of the present subjunctive of the three model verbs:

	comprar – to buy	***vender*** – to sell
	*yo compr**e***	*yo vend**a***
	*tú compr**es***	*tú vend**as***
Ella quiere que . . .	*él / ella / Ud. compr**e***	*él / ella / Ud. vend**a***
She wants . . . to . . .	*nosotros / as compr**emos***	*nosotros / as vend**amos***
	*vosotros / as compr**éis***	*vosotros / as vend**áis***
	*ellos / ellas / Uds. compr**en***	*ellos / ellas / Uds. vend**an***

vivir – to live

Mi hija quiere que . . .
My daughter wants . . . to . . .

*yo viv**a** en México*
*tú viv**as** en M.*
*él / ella / Ud. viv**a** en M.*
*nosotros / as viv**amos** en M.*
*vosotros / as viv**áis** en M.*
*ellos / ellas / Uds. viv**an** en M.*

Irregular verbs offer more difficulty but they generally follow the irregularity of the indicative.

dar (to give)	*dé*	*des*	*dé*	*demos*	*deis*	*den*
decir (say)	*diga*	*digas*	*diga*	*digamos*	*digáis*	*digan*
estar (be)	*esté*	*estés*	*esté*	*estemos*	*estéis*	*estén*
haber (have)	*haya*	*hayas*	*haya*	*hayamos*	*hayáis*	*hayan*
hacer (make)	*haga*	*hagas*	*haga*	*hagamos*	*hagáis*	*hagan*
ir (go)	*vaya*	*vayas*	*vaya*	*vayamos*	*vayáis*	*vayan*
querer (want)	*quiera*	*quieras*	*quiera*	*queramos*	*queráis*	*quieran*
salir (go out)	*salga*	*salgas*	*salga*	*salgamos*	*salgáis*	*salgan*
ser (be)	*sea*	*seas*	*sea*	*seamos*	*seáis*	*sean*
tener (have)	*tenga*	*tengas*	*tenga*	*tengamos*	*tengáis*	*tengan*
venir (come)	*venga*	*vengas*	*venga*	*vengamos*	*vengáis*	*vengan*

Radical changing verbs are conjugated as follows:

volver (o–ue) (to return)	*vuelva*	*vuelvas*	*vuelva*	*volvamos*	*volváis*	*vuelvan*
cerrar (e–ie) (to shut)	*cierre*	*cierres*	*cierre*	*cerremos*	*cerréis*	*cierren*
pedir (e–i) (to ask for)	*pida*	*pidas*	*pida*	*pidamos*	*pidáis*	*pidan*

How to use the subjunctive

The use of the subjunctive falls into fifteen broad categories, six of which are treated in level 1, and nine in level 2. The first three categories in level 1 are broken down into a number of sub-categories, while the remainder are smaller, self-contained categories. These are all treated in the context of the present subjunctive, while the nine categories in level 2 are treated in the context of the present and perfect subjunctives, and the imperfect and pluperfect subjunctives.

The categories in level 1 are as follows:

Level **1**

1.1 **Influence or causation** (*Influencia o causalidad*)

1.1.1 **Command or order** (*Orden*)

1.1.2 **Request** (*Petición*)

1.1.3 **Proposal and suggestion** (*Propuesta o sugerencia*)

1.1.4 **Permission, prohibition, hindrance** (*Permiso, prohibición, oposición*)

1.2 **Emotion** (*Emoción*)

1.2.1 **After expressions of feeling** (*Tras expresiones de emoción*)

1.2.2 **After verbs of imagining and wishing** (*Tras verbos que expresan imaginación o deseo*)

1.3 **Doubt** (*Duda*)

1.3.1 **After expressions of doubt, denial and negation** (*Tras expresiones de duda, denegación y negación*)

1.3.2 **After expressions of possibility, probability, risk and danger** (*Tras expresiones de posibilidad, probabilidad, riesgo y peligro*)

1.4 **Certain impersonal verbs and expressions** (*Ciertos verbos y expresiones impersonales*)

1.5 **The verbs *ser* and *estar* used impersonally** (*Cuando se usan de modo impersonal los verbos *ser* y *estar**)

1.6 **After conjunctive expressions** (*Tras expresiones conjuntivas*)

1.1 Influence or causation

1.1.1 Command or order
(See also the imperative – unit 11.)

i The principal use of the subjunctive is after verbs expressing an action calculated to cause a person or thing to act. The force of the governing verb varies from an authoritative command to a simple request or wish. This also applies to verbs of opposite effect which involve preventing or hindering someone or something from doing something. All these verbs fall into the general category of **Influence**. We will first of all deal with **commands** or **orders**

Examples

El oficial **ordena** *que* **montemos** *guardia en el camión / que* **subamos** *al camión*
The officer orders us to be on guard in the truck/lorry / to get into the truck/lorry
Mi madre me **dice** *que* **regrese / vuelva / vaya** *temprano*
My mother tells me to return/go early
El Ayuntamiento **dispone** *que no se* **circule** *por el centro de la ciudad*
The City/Town Hall decrees that no one should drive downtown / through the center
   of the town

ii Other verbs functioning in a similar way:
decidir, decretar, establecer, exigir, insistir, mandar, necesitar, presionar (para), reclamar, recomendar, urgir, velar (por) = to see to it that . . .

iii Remarks
Some of the above verbs (**mandar**, **ordenar**, **recomendar**) may take an infinitive, instead of a subjunctive. Regrettably, there is no rule for this alternative. It is a question of usage. The possibility of an infinitive also occurs in other categories, so watch out for it.

Examples

El capitán **manda fusilar** *a los prisioneros* The captain orders the prisoners to be shot
Manda llamar *al médico / al doctor (**M**)* Send for the physician/doctor
Le **ordena salir** *inmediatamente del restaurante* He/She orders her/him to leave the
   restaurant immediately

*Te **recomiendo acostarte** temprano* I recommend you go to bed early

Note. If you were looking for a difference between the use, in these cases, of the infinitive, and the subjunctive, it could be broadly said that the infinitive is easier to manipulate (it's not all bad news) but is not necessarily more typical of the spoken language or even written language. These comments also apply to the verbs in 1.1.3.iii and 1.1.4.iii. (See 2.10 for a small table offering an analysis of some of the verbs in this unit, with reference to the infinitive or the subjunctive.)

Needless to say, there are some cases where the infinitive would **certainly not** be used. In the case of, for instance, *Le pido / digo que venga conmigo* (I ask / tell her / him to come with me), **venir** could **not** replace **venga**, as would be the case in French (*demander / dire à quelqu'un de venir*) and Italian (*chiedere / dire a qualcuno di venire*), and in English for that matter.

1.1.2 Request
i
Examples

*Te **pido** que te **acuestes** a las nueve / que lo **pagues** ahora mismo / ahorita (**M**) / que **no hagas** ruido*
I ask you to go to bed at nine / to pay for it right now / not to make a noise
*Le **suplico** que me **dé** un poco de comida*
I beg you to give me a little food
*La dirección del hotel **ruega** a los señores turistas que no **malgasten** el agua*
The hotel management requests clients not to waste water

ii Other verbs functioning in a similar way:
conseguir, lograr, necesitar, preferir

iii Remarks
a If the subject is the same for the main verb and the complement, an infinitive is used:

Examples

*El empleado pide **hablar** con el patron*	The employee asks to see the boss
*Consigo **ocultar** mis propósitos*	I succeed in hiding my intentions
*Logran **batir** el récord*	They succeed in beating the record
*Prefiero **comer** más temprano*	I prefer to eat earlier

b **Rogar** may take an infinitive when the subjects are different. The following examples are very common: *Se **ruega** no fumar / Se **ruega** a los señores clientes dejar el cuarto (**M**) / la habitación antes de las once*

1.1.3 Proposal and suggestion
i
Examples

*Juan nos **propone** que **vayamos** todos al cine* Juan suggests we all go to the movies
*Te **aconsejo** que **vuelvas / regreses** (second verb more common in **M**) antes de que oscurezca* I advise you to return before it gets dark
*¿Por qué **sugieres** que **compremos** fruta ahora?* Why do you suggest we buy fruit now?
*El comité **presiona** para que **acuda** todo el mundo a la reunión* The committee presses for everyone to attend the meeting

ii Other verbs functioning in a similar way:

agradecer, animar, bastar, convencer, invitar, más vale (que)

iii Remarks

Aconsejar, **agradecer**, **animar**, **invitar**, **proponer** and **sugerir** may take a following infinitive if the subjects are different. (See remark [**iii**] above under "Command or order.")

Examples

*Le **aconsejo** no continuar el viaje* I advise him/her not to continue the journey
*Te **agradezco** comprarme el billete / boleto (**M**)* I thank you for buying the ticket for me
*Mi mamá (**M**) / madre me **anima** a participar en el concurso* My mother encourages me to take part in the competition
*Nos **invitan** a cenar en el restaurante* They invite us to dine in the restaurant
*Les **propongo** salir con nosotros* I suggest they come out with us

1.1.4 Permission, prohibition, hindrance

i

Examples

*El profesor **permite** que **entreguemos** los deberes la semana próxima* The professor/teacher lets us hand in the homework next week
*El médico me **prohíbe** que **beba** vino* The physician/doctor forbids me to drink wine
*Este carro (**M**) / coche nos **impide** que **salgamos** del estacionamiento (**M**) / aparcamiento* This car prevents us from getting out of the parking lot / car park
*No **permito** que **regreséis** a las diez* I cannot allow you to come home at ten

ii Other verbs functioning in a similar way

consentir, dejar, oponerse a

iii Remarks

Dejar, **impedir**, **permitir** and **prohibir** may also be followed by an infinitive if the subjects are different. (See remark [**iii**] *under* "Command or order.")

Examples

*Mi padre me **deja ver** la televisión* My father lets me see television
*El médico no le **permite fumar*** The physician/doctor does not let him smoke
*¿Por qué me **prohíbes ir** a la pachanga (**M**) / fiesta?* Why do you forbid me to go to the bash?

1.2 Emotion

1.2.1 After expressions of feeling

i

Examples

*Me **alegro** de que los otros chicos **puedan** venir* I am happy that the other boys can come
*Confío en que **apruebe** sus exámenes* I trust that (s)he will get through her/his examinations
*Me **extraña** que no **lleguen*** It surprises me that they are not arriving
*(Me) temo que Pilar no **llegue** a tiempo* I fear that Pilar won't arrive in time
*Siento que **estés** obligada a irte tan pronto* I'm sorry you have to leave so soon

ii Other verbs functioning in a similar way:

celebrar, encantar, gustar, molestar, tener miedo

iii Remarks

If the subject is the same in the main clause and the complement verb then use an infinitive

Examples

Me **encanta ir** *a la ópera* I am delighted to be going to the opera

No me **gusta nadar** *después de comer tanto* I don't like swimming after eating so much

Siento *fastidiarte* I am sorry to upset you

Me **da miedo entrar** *solo en una casa tan oscura* I am frightened to go into such a dark house all alone

1.2.2 **After verbs expressing imagining and wishing**

i

Examples

Me figuro *que* **lleguen** *tarde* I imagine they will arrive late

Me imagino *que* **sepas / sepáis / sepan** (**M** = familiar form) *el camino* I imagine you know the way

Note also the very common expression *¡Ojalá!* = Oh that / I wish that. This expression comes from the Arabic **Inshallah!** (If Allah wills it)

¡Ojalá (que) **se vayan** *pronto!* I wish they'd go soon!

ii Other verbs functioning in a similar way:

desear, esperar, prever, querer

iii Remarks

Imaginarse and **figurarse** may also be followed by the indicative, depending upon the degree of certainty. It is most likely, however, that they would be followed by the subjunctive if they were in the negative

Example

Me imagino que **llega** *esta tarde* but *No me imagino que* **llegue** *esta tarde*

iv If the subject is the same for both the verb of the main clause and of the complement an infinitive is used. In the following examples, the subjunctive would **not** be used

Examples

Deseo / espero / quiero ir I want/hope/wish to go

Preveo / tengo previsto salir *esta noche* I plan to go out tonight

1.3 **Doubt**

1.3.1 **After expressions of denial and doubt or stating a negative idea**

i When the main or leading verb expresses denial, uncertainty, doubt or disbelief about the action of another person or thing, the verb expressing that action is in the subjunctive:

Examples

Niego _que mi amigo / cuate (**M**) **sea** culpable_ I deny my friend is guilty

Dudo _que **tenga** razón_ I doubt (s)he is right

Apenas puedo creer _que **diga** tal cosa_ I can hardly believe that (s)he would say such a thing

No creo _que **siga** viviendo en Nueva York_ I don't believe (s)he still lives in New York

¿Puede ser verdad _que **intente** engañarnos?_ Can it be true (s)he is trying to trick us?

No me imagino _que él **cometa** un error tan garrafal_ I can't imagine that he would make such a colossal error

¿Cree Ud. _que **quiera** rechazar mi oferta?_ Do you think that (s)he wants to refuse my offer?

No es cierto / seguro _que **regresen** hoy_ It's not certain they'll return today

ii Other verbs functioning in a similar way:

descartar, desmentir, no decir, no querer decir, no ser

iii Remarks

Certain expressions may be followed by **_si_** and the indicative

Examples

Es dudoso / Dudo si _puede venir_ It is doubtful / I doubt if (s)he can come

Ignoro si _es correcta la respuesta_ I don't know if the reply is right

No es seguro si _el camión (**M**) llegará a tiempo_ It is not certain whether the bus will arrive on time

iv One important point of usage in Mexico: when the future is implied with a degree of uncertainty, **_No sé si tengan razón_** is standard usage. In Iberian Spanish this would be: **_No sé si tienen razón_**

1.3.2 After expressions of possibility and probability, risk and danger

i

acaso	perhaps
quizá(s)	perhaps
tal vez	perhaps
posiblemente	possibly
es posible que	it is possible that
puede ser que	perhaps
(se) puede que	perhaps
probablemente	probably
es probable que	it is probable that

Examples

Quizá(s) venga _mañana_ Perhaps (s)he'll come tomorrow

Tal vez vaya _en enero_ Perhaps I'll/(s)he'll go in January

Posiblemente esté _enferma, no sé_ She's possibly sick/ill, I don't know

Probablemente _tus amigos vayan al cine_ Your pals/friends are probably going to the movies

Se puede que _tu mamá (**M**) / madre tenga prisa_ Your mother may be in a hurry

Se corre el riesgo de que pierdan el tren _si no les doy el horario_ They risk missing the train if I don't give them the schedule/timetable

*Si bajamos por aquí **correremos el peligro de que** los niños se **caigan*** If we go down
   this way there's the danger that the children will fall
*Lo peligroso es que se **extienda** la infección*
The danger is that the infection will spread

ii Note also: ***que yo sepa*** (as far as I know), ***que yo recuerde*** (as far as I remember)

iii Remark
If the expressions occur after the verb the indicative is normally used:

Examples

*Vienen esta tarde, **posiblemente / quizá(s) / tal vez / probablemente***

1.4 After certain impersonal verbs and expressions

(This often involves value judgments.)
i

Examples

Conviene *que Ud. se lo **avise*** It is wise/sensible you warn him about it
Importa *que **tomen (M) / cojan** el tren de las cinco* It is important they catch the five
   o'clock train
Basta *que yo **diga** una cosa para que ella me lleve la contraria* I only have to say one thing for
   her to say the opposite

ii Other verbs functioning in a similar way:
Hace falta, es una pena, precisar

iii Remarks
When the subject of the main verb is not properly defined, an infinitive may be used

Examples

Basta (con) meter *la comida en el horno* You only have to put the meal in the oven
*No me **conviene firmar** el contrato* It does not suit me to sign the contract
Importa inflar *las ruedas* It is important to pump up the tires

1.5 When *ser* and *estar* are used impersonally, and are followed by an adjective or an adverb

i

Examples

Es necesario/preciso *que **estemos** listos* It is important we be ready
Es inútil *que **trabajes** tanto* It is pointless working so hard
Es rarísimo *que **llegue** tan tarde* It's very rare for her/him to arrive so late
Es dudoso *que **venga / tenga** cuarenta años* It's doubtful that (s)he will come / is forty
   years old
*No **está** bien que **hagas** tus deberes tan de prisa* It's not good for you to do your homework
   so quickly
Es triste *que **sufra** tanto* It's sad (s)he is suffering so much

ii Other adjectives and expressions that function in the same way:

Es

bueno / imperativo / importante / increíble / inevitable / justo / lástima / lógico / mejor / natural / normal / previsible

But:

Está *previsto*

Examples

    Es lástima *que no **vengas*** It's a pity you can't come

    Es increíble *que **corra** los cien metros en nueve segundos coma cinco*

    It's incredible she can run the hundred meters in nine point five seconds

    Está previsto *que **salga** el tren a las tres*

    The train is due to leave at three o'clock

iii Remarks

These expressions may be followed by an infinitive if there is no properly defined subject:

Examples

    Es mejor telefonear *ahorita **(M)*** / ahora* It's better to phone now

    Es imperativo consultar *al doctor **(M)*** / médico* It is imperative to consult the physician / doctor

    No es lógico poner*te sandalias si llueve* It's not logical to put on sandals if it's raining

    No es bueno pasar *tanto tiempo al sol* It's not good to spend so much time in the sun

1.6 After conjunctive expressions

i The subjunctive follows many conjunctions and conjunctive expressions. They usually involve supposition, purpose and concession:

a fin de que	in order that	*como*	if
de manera que	so that	*como si*	as if
de modo que	so that	*con tal que*	provided that
para que / por que	in order that	*en caso de que*	in case
a condición (de) que	on condition that	*siempre que*	whenever
a no ser que	unless	*supuesto que*	supposing that
aun cuando	even if	*sin que*	without
aunque	although	*a menos que*	except
bien que	although	*excepto que*	except

Examples

    *Cierran las ventanas **a fin de que no se oigan** los ruidos de la calle*

    They close the windows so that you can't hear the noise from the street

    *Alza la voz **de manera que** todos te **oigan** bien* Speak more loudly so that everyone can hear you properly

    *Deja el libro aquí **de manera / de modo que** yo **pueda** leerlo* Leave the book here so I can read it

    *Llévame a la estación **para que** yo **compre** un periódico* Take me to the station so that I can buy a newspaper

*Cierro la puerta **por que** nadie escuche lo que **hablamos*** I close the door so that no one can hear what we are saying

*Te ayudo **a condición de que** me **reembolses*** I'll help you on condition you reimburse me

***Como no vengan** a las seis no puedo salir* If they don't come / you don't come (**M**) at six, I'll not be able to go out

***En caso de que no pueda** acudir, te aviso* In case / If I can't come, I'll let you know

ii Remarks

When the subjects of the main and subordinate clauses are the same an infinitive is used in the subordinate clause

***A fin de terminar** pronto el equipaje, lo meto todo en una maleta*

In order to finish the packing soon, I'll put it all in one suitcase

*Me quedo aquí todo el día **para concluir** el asunto*

I'll stay here all day to complete the deal

iii **Aunque.** When meaning *even if*, **aunque** is followed by the subjunctive, but when it means *although*, implying certainty, it is followed by the indicative

***aunque** pague el viaje* **even if** (s)he pays for the journey

***aunque** paga el viaje* **although** (s)he pays for the journey

iv **Como** does not always take the subjunctive. When it means *as* or *since* or *how*, it is followed by the indicative:

¿Cómo lo haces?	How do you do it?
Como llueve, es mejor no salir	As it's raining, it's best not to go out

Exercises Level 1

i Change the infinitive into the correct form of the subjunctive:

Examples

Su mamá (**M**) / madre le dice que **comer** el bocadillo > . . . que **coma** el . . .

El profesor les recomienda que **hacer** sus deberes inmediatamente > . . . que hagan sus . . .

a Mi padre me dice que **hacer** mis deberes enseguida

b Dile que **volver** a casa

c El sargento manda a las tropas que **retirarse**

d El primer ministro presiona para que su gabinete **aceptar** su juicio

e Te recomiendo que **ir** a ver la película

f Urge que (all personal pronouns) **comprar** los boletos (**M**) / billetes

g El entrenador ordena que **descansar** su equipo

h Su madre decide que **estudiar** en casa todos los hijos

i El padre vela por que los niños **acostarse** temprano

ii Translate the following sentences into Spanish. Careful, since not all these sentences need a subjunctive.

a The teacher orders the students to remain quiet

b The boss demands that we work harder

c It is urgent we take her to hospital

d I decide to do all my homework right now

viii Unravel the following jumbled sentences, and put the appropriate verb into the correct form of the subjunctive or indicative. There may be a case where the subjunctive is not necessarily required. On the other hand, if you are smart enough, you may be able to use a subjunctive in every sentence

le

casa ser cara extraña la que me > Me extraña que la casa sea cara

a él triste que tan lamentar mucho estar yo
b tú sentir no poder venir yo que
c que acompañar Uds. (**M**) / vosotros encantar nos nos
d miedo que decir la tener verdad yo él de
e hacer molestar ruido me tanto chicos los que
f ser alegrarse así que de
g la todos celebrar venir boda a que
h no no venir Navidades me para extrañar que ellos
i desear juntos ella ir nosotros que
j fin llover de esperar este semana que no
k jugar ellos (al) fútbol yo querer tarde (que) esta (*no al* in *Mexico*)
l previsto hacer semana sol está esta toda que

ix You meet a friend you have not seen for a long time. Write a small dialogue, using the subjunctive wherever you can, not forgetting that indicatives are possible too

x Here you have a puzzle. Find the verbs in the subjunctive. There are ten: five irregular verbs, one verb with a stem change, and four regular verbs. What are the infinitives of these verbs?

O	E	C	H	E	N
D	E	I	S	S	A
I	S	E	A	T	D
G	T	R	L	A	E
A	I	R	G	L	M
N	R	E	A	L	O
P	E	S	T	E	S

xi Complete the sentence by adding the correct form of the indicative leading to the subjunctive which is already in the sentence. In some cases, more than one verb, or expression, is possible

le

(_) que llegue a tiempo > No creo / Es posible / No es posible/probable que llegue a tiempo

a (_) que sepa hablar japonés
b ¿(_) que corra el riesgo de perder todo su dinero?
c (_) que quiera ir con nosotros
d (_) que su madre lo sepa
e (_) la posibilidad de que puedan ayudarnos
f (_) que sean colombianos
g (_) que me vaya a devolver los veinte dólares que le presté ayer

e I need you to help me
f The law decrees that we all do military service
g They always insist we pay for the tickets

**iii Rewrite the following jumbled sentences in the correct wc
appropriate verb in the subjunctive – if required, for it is n**

Example

tú prefiero carro (**M**) otro comprar que > Prefiero que (tú) cc

a venir le que pido
b mi Ud. petición a ruego a atender que le
c ahora tú que prefiero a yo casa regresar
d carro (**M**) manejar consigue el ella yo siempre que
e que siempre el profesor exámenes alumnos aprobar logra ;
f diez cien correr logra metros segundos en él los
g esconder mi consigo intención
h enfadarse suplico no que os

iv Translate into Spanish:
a She always encourages me to work harder (2 ways)
b We invite our friends to have an evening meal with us (2 w
c May I suggest that we all go together?
d We sometimes advise our clients to take a vacation/holida
e It is best for you to cut the grass now
f Our parents always press us into taking lots of physical exe
g It is sufficient for you to read just these three books
h I must persuade you to eat less sugar and fat, and more fr

**v Write out six sentences, using the verbs *proponer* and su;
and then followed by a subjunctive in the subordinate cla
two sentences where these two verbs may be followed b**

Examples

Su amigo nos propone que vayamos al parque / Su amigo 1
Me sugiere que cambie de trabajo / Me sugiere cambiar de

vi Put the correct form of the subjunctive in the following :

Examples

Les impide salir a la calle > Les impide que **salgan** a la ca
Mi papá (**M**) / padre me permite andar en bicicleta > . . . r

**Note. In both these cases an infinitive may be us
original sentences may stand as they are**
Les impide **salir** a la calle   Mi papá me p(
a Te prohíbo que **ver** la televisión a esta hora
b El tapón impide que **salir** el agua
c No puedo permitir que los niños **jugar** con fuegos artifi(
d El líder se opone a que se **hacer** declaraciones a los peri

**vii Write a short passage of four lines using the subjunctiv
impedir, *permitir* and *prohibir*.**

xii **You are in a restaurant, with a friend. You try to persuade your friend to agree with your choices. Write a small dialogue, using the following verbs or expressions which lead to the subjunctive.**

Querer, preferir, pedir, dudar, es raro, sugerir, es una pena, proponer

xiii **Using the words or expressions in 1.3.2 (from *acaso*), fill in the gaps in the following sentences, bearing in mind that a number of these expressions are interchangeable:**

a (_) se vayan todos

b (_) sean hermanos

xiv **Translate the following sentences into Spanish**

a It is better that you remain here

b It is predicted that all the shares will go up

c I think it is natural that children make a lot of noise

d It's incredible that they are enjoying themselves

e Why do you say that it is logical they don't want to come?

f It is always important you do your best in the examination

g She's hurt herself, so it's important we take her to hospital

h It is imperative you learn to drive safely

i It is sufficient that you work thirty-five hours a week

j It is sad they cannot come before next week

k It's not normal to drink gallons of water

l It is to be hoped that the business will/may soon be sorted out

xv **Fill in the gaps at the end of the sentences with conjunctive expressions and a subordinate clause in the subjunctive. It is possible that more than one expression will suit the meaning of the sentence**

Example

Puedo sacar los billetes ahora (_) > Puedo sacar los billetes ahora con tal que / a condición de que me des el dinero

a Preparo la cena ahora (_)

b Te doy dinero (_)

c No me muevo de aquí (_)

d Vamos a Madrid pasado mañana (_)

e Hay que sacar unos cheques de viaje (_)

f Estoy dispuesta a coger / tomar (**M**) el taxi (_)

g ¿Me puedes llevar a la estación de ferrocarril (_)

h El obrero sale de la oficina cada día (_)

i No puedo ir al cine (_)

j Le compro botas de agua al pequeño (_)

xvi **Paired activity**

Objective – To use the subjunctive following negative statements

Method – A offers ten sentences/opinions with the main verb in the affirmative. B then uses the same main verb, but in the negative. A's subordinate clause will be in the indicative but B's subordinate clause will be in the subjunctive mood.

Example

A: Pienso (main clause) que llegan (subordinate clause) esta tarde
B: No pienso que lleguen esta tarde

A can use the following verbs/expressions: pensar, creer, decir, estar seguro, es cierto, imaginarse, querer decir, figurarse, considerar, prever, afirmar, confirmar, asegurar

You can then reverse the order. B makes a negative statement with the same verbs/expressions above involving the subjunctive, and A removes the negative in the main clause and puts the main clause in the indicative mood.

Level 2

2.1 **Noun clauses** (*Oraciones con nombres*)

2.2 **Impersonal expressions of passive value made up of *ser* + *de* + infinitive + que . . .** (*Expresiones impersonales de valor pasivo*: *ser* + *de* + *infinitivo* + *que . . .*)

2.3 **After certain relative and imprecise pronouns. Similarly, after a relative when the preceding clause is negative, restrictive or interrogative** (*Tras ciertos pronombres relativos que no son precisos. Tras un pronombre relativo cuando la oración anterior es negativa, restrictiva o interrogativa*)

2.4 **After indefinite expressions formed by *quiera*, suggesting (*what)ever** (*Tras expresiones indefinidas formadas por *quiera*)

2.5 **Following the construction *por (muy) . . . que* = however** (*Tras la construcción por [muy] . . . que*)

2.6 **Perfect subjunctive** (*Subjuntivo perfecto*)

2.7 **Imperfect and pluperfect subjunctives** (*Subjuntivos imperfecto y pluscuamperfecto*)

2.8 **Imperfect and pluperfect subjunctives with conditional sentences** (*Subjuntivos imperfecto y pluscuamperfecto / antecopretérito [M] con frases en condicional*)

2.9 **Temporal clauses** (*Oraciones temporales*)

2.10 **Use of the subjunctive or infinitive after the main clause** (*Uso del subjuntivo o infinitivo después de la oración principal*)

2.1 Noun clauses

The subjunctive is used in noun clauses which correspond to uses, notably connected to verbs, described at various points in level 1.

Ejemplos

el deseo *que lo* ***haga*** the wish that (s)he do it
la necesidad de que salgamos *ahora* the need that we go out now
la esperanza de que lea *el libro* the hope that (s)he'll read the book
la duda de que lo sepa the doubt whether (s)he knows
la posibilidad de que *no* ***haya*** *agua* the possibility that there is no water
la incertidumbre de que apruebe *el examen* the uncertainty whether (s)he'll get
  through the examination

2.2 The impersonal expressions of passive value, composed of *ser* connected with a following infinitive by *de*

These constructions are of a slightly higher register value.

Ejemplos

Es de esperar *que **llegue** el tren a tiempo* It is to be hoped the train will arrive on time

Es de temer(se) *que los gastos **excedan** a los ingresos* It is to be feared that expenses will exceed income

Es de desear *que **llueva** después de una sequía tan prolongada* It is to be hoped that it will rain after such a prolonged drought

2.3 After a relative pronoun or adverb

This involves time, place or manner when this is definitely not known. Similarly, after a relative when the clause preceding it is negative, restrictive or interrogative. The real question here is uncertainty. Numerous examples are provided here for clarification of what is a more difficult area.

i

Ejemplos

Me hace falta *un guía que **hable** portugués* I need a guide who speaks Portuguese

Notice here that if you said ***Me hace falta el guía*** . . . , the rest of the sentence would be ***que habla portugués***. The indicative ***habla*** reflects the certainty of ***el guía*** as opposed to ***un guía*** (i.e. any guide).

No tardaremos *en encontrar alguien que **conozca** el camino* It'll not be long before we find someone who knows the way

El profesor ***ha prometido*** *un regalo **al primero que termine** correctamente el ejercicio* The professor/teacher has promised a present for the first one who gets the exercise right

Si quieres *un televisor que **sea** de alta calidad, elige éste* If you want a television set which is of high quality, choose this one

Me quedaré *aquí **hasta que regresen** mis papás (**M**) / padres* I'll stay here until my parents come back

Iremos *al teatro **después de que comáis / coman** (**M**)* We'll go to the theater after you have eaten

Tuerce *para la derecha **cuando llegues** al semáforo* Turn to the right when you get to the stop lights / traffic lights

¿Me puedes llamar *cuando **regreses** a casa?* Can you call me when you get home?

Haré *el trabajo **cuando quieras*** I'll do the work when you want

Yo podría organizar *la fiesta **como quieras*** I could organize the party as you like

No conozco a nadie *que **sea** capaz de* . . . I know no one capable of . . .

No hallo (**M**) / ***encuentro ningún*** *plomero* (**M**) / *fontanero que **pueda** arreglar esta llave* (**M**) / *este grifo* I can't find a single plumber who can repair this faucet/tap

Aquí ***no hay nada*** *que me **interese*** There is nothing here that interests me

Son tan parecidos en todo que ***no hay*** *quien los **distinga*** They are so similar in every way that no one can distinguish between them

Evita *que los niños no lo / lo molesten* Make sure the children don't trouble him

ii Note

The expression ***independientemente de lo que*** may be suitably dealt with here.

Ejemplos
***Independientemente de lo que hayas hecho / de lo que pienses / de lo que
crea yo . . .***
Quite apart from what you have done / of what you think / of what I believe . . .

iii Remarks

A very common alternative to the subjunctive in the subordinate clause is the use of
al + infinitive.

Ejemplos
Tuerce *para la derecha* ***al llegar*** *al semáforo* Turn right when you reach the stop lights /
traffic lights
Al terminar *mi trabajo* ***iré*** *contigo* When I finish my work I'll come with you
Al lograr *la victoria* ***disfrutaron*** *de una excelente comida* When they won they enjoyed an
excellent evening meal

iv Note also the idiomatic use of *al* when the subject is different in the main and
subordinate clause. You would logically expect the subjunctive to be used here.

Ejemplos
Al llegar yo, *(i.e.* ***Cuando llegue yo)*** ***podrás tocar el piano***
¿Puedes darme ***(M)*** */ echarme una mano* ***al volver yo*** (i.e. ***cuando vuelva / regrese [M]
yo***) ***esta tarde?***

2.4 The subjunctive follows the indefinite expressions formed by adding *quiera* to relative pronouns and adverbs

This corresponds to the idea of "-ever."

Ejemplos

quienquiera *que* ***sea***	whoever (s)he/you may be
dondequiera *que se* ***encuentre Ud.***	wherever you are
cuandoquiera *que* ***vuelvan***	whenever they return
comoquiera *que* ***trabajes***	however you work
cualquiera disculpa *que* ***ofrezca***	whatever excuse he offers

There are a number of other expressions which may suitably be mentioned here:

digas lo que digas	whatever you say
*dijera lo que dijera	whatever (s)he/you said
venga de donde venga	wherever you/(s)he come(s) from
*viniera de donde viniera	wherever she came from
sea como sea	be that as it may

*See the imperfect subjunctive later in this level

2.5 The subjunctive is also followed by the construction *por (muy) . . . que*, the interval being filled by an adjective or an adverb

Ejemplos
por (muy) listos que sean however smart/intelligent they are
por (muy) atrevida que sea however daring she is
por mucho que insistas however much you insist

2.6 Perfect subjunctive

The perfect subjunctive follows a main verb in the present or future tense. It represents an action which is completed. It is less used than the present or the imperfect subjunctive. It is made up of the present subjunctive of *haber* and the past participle of the verb in question

Ejemplos
Es un milagro que no se haya roto la pierna It's a miracle (s)he hasn't broken her/his leg
Cuando lo hayas leído, devuélveme el libro When you've read it, return the book to me

2.7 Imperfect and pluperfect subjunctives

i With the present and perfect subjunctives, we have seen the main cases where the subjunctive mood is required. All the illustrations have been confined to the present and perfect tenses. As far as the imperfect subjunctive is concerned, we only have to consider which tenses to use. For example, *para que* is followed by the present subjunctive or the imperfect subjunctive, depending on whether reference is to the present or the past. Consider the two following cases in which *para que* is used.
Me da la carta para que la eche al buzón (S)he gives me the letter so that I'll mail/post it
Me dio la carta para que la echara al buzón (S)he gave me the letter so that I would mail/post it
In the first case, *eche* is the present subjunctive because the main verb *da* is in the present tense. In the second case, *echara* is the imperfect subjunctive because the main verb *dio* is in the past or preterit tense.

ii Before we consider all the endings of the imperfect subjunctive, it should be pointed out that there are basically two forms, *-ara* and *-ase*. Take, for instance, the verb *hablar*:
Era necesario que la madre hablara con su hijo
Era necesario que la madre hablase con su hijo

For all normal purposes, the two forms are used in a similar way, but see remark 2 below.

iii Forms of the imperfect subjunctive with regular verbs

hablar	*vender*	*vivir*
hablara / *hablase*	*vendiera* / *vendiese*	*viviera* / *viviese*
hablaras / *hablases*	*vendieras* / *vendieses*	*vivieras* / *vivieses*
hablara / *hablase*	*vendiera* / *vendiese*	*viviera* / *viviese*
habláramos / *hablásemos*	*vendiéramos* / *vendiésemos*	*viviéramos* / *viviésemos*
hablarais / *hablaseis*	*vendierais* / *vendieseis*	*vivierais* / *vivieseis*
hablaran / *hablasen*	*vendieran* / *vendiesen*	*vivieran* / *viviesen*

iv Remarks

1 The two forms of the imperfect subjunctive are used after a main verb in the present or imperfect tense that refers to an action that is wholly past.

2 The *-ase* form is less used in Peninsular Spanish while in Mexico it is little used, if at all. Indeed, Mexicans do not use it in speech, only the *-ara* form.

Ejemplos

Hay / *Había gente que duda* / *dudaba que el mismo autor* **escribiera** / **escribiese** *todos estos libros*
There are / were people who doubt(ed) whether the same author wrote all these books

No creo / *creía que* **fuera** / **fuese** *culpable* I don't / didn't think he was guilty

A mí me extraña / *extrañaba que* **viviera** / **viviese** *treinta años en Los Angeles* I am / was
surprised (s)he lived in Los Angeles for thirty years

Siento / *Sentía que se* **enfadara** / **enfadase** *tanto* I am / was sorry she got so angry

Es / *Era muy triste que* **pasara** / **pasase** *toda su vida en condiciones tan difíciles* It is / was very
sad that (s)he spent her / his whole life in such difficult conditions

v There are occasions when an imperfect tense could be followed by a subjunctive in the present tense. In other words, the sequence of tenses may be broken. Take the two following cases:

Negó (past) *que* **existiera** / **exista** (universal principle) *una relación directa entre la comida y
la salud* She denied there was a direct relationship between food and health

Se le **pidió** (past) *al Presidente que* **buscara** / **busque** (he hasn't done it yet) *una solución*
The president was asked to find a solution

vi Here is a sample of the imperfect subjunctive forms of some irregular verbs. It is helpful to remember that the imperfect subjunctive *-ara* form comes from the root of the third person plural of the preterit, e.g. *dieron* > *diera*, *dijeron* > *dijera*

dar	*diera*	*dieras*	*diera*	*diéramos*	*dierais*	*dieran*
(give)	*diese*	*dieses*	*diese*	*diésemos*	*dieseis*	*diesen*
decir	*dijera*	*dijeras*	*dijera*	*dijéramos*	*dijerais*	*dijeran*
(say)	*dijese*	*dijeses*	*dijese*	*dijésemos*	*dijeseis*	*dijesen*
estar	*estuviera*	*estuvieras*	*estuviera*	*estuviéramos*	*estuvierais*	*estuvieran*
(be)	*estuviese*	*estuvieses*	*estuviese*	*estuviésemos*	*estuvieseis*	*estuviesen*
haber	*hubiera*	*hubieras*	*hubiera*	*hubiéramos*	*hubierais*	*hubieran*
(have)	*hubiese*	*hubieses*	*hubiese*	*hubiésemos*	*hubieseis*	*hubiesen*
hacer	*hiciera*	*hicieras*	*hiciera*	*hiciéramos*	*hicierais*	*hicieran*
(make)	*hiciese*	*hicieses*	*hiciese*	*hiciésemos*	*hicieseis*	*hiciesen*
ir	*fuera*	*fueras*	*fuera*	*fuéramos*	*fuerais*	*fueran*
(go)	*fuese*	*fueses*	*fuese*	*fuésemos*	*fueseis*	*fuesen*

querer	*quisiera*	*quisieras*	*quisiera*	*quisiéramos*	*quisierais*	*quisieran*
(wish)	*quisiese*	*quisieses*	*quisiese*	*quisiésemos*	*quisieseis*	*quisiesen*
ser	**SAME AS *IR***					
(be)						
tener	*tuviera*	*tuvieras*	*tuviera*	*tuviéramos*	*tuvierais*	*tuvieran*
(have)	*tuviese*	*tuvieses*	*tuviese*	*tuviésemos*	*tuvieseis*	*tuviesen*

vii Imperfect subjunctive of two radical changing verbs

dormir	**pedir**
durmiera/*durmiese*	*pidiera*/*pidiese*
durmieras/*durmieses*	*pidieras*/*pidieses*
durmiera/*durmiese*	*pidiera*/*pidiese*
durmiéramos/*durmiésemos*	*pidiéramos*/*pidiésemos*
durmierais/*durmieseis*	*pidierais*/*pidieseis*
durmieran/*durmiesen*	*pidieran*/*pidiesen*

2.8 Imperfect and pluperfect subjunctives with conditional sentences

i The imperfect subjunctive or pluperfect subjunctive (but never the present subjunctive) is used after *si* when the condition is improbable or impossible. *Por si =* *in case* is also used in this way. It should be pointed out that *por si* is followed by the indicative in the present tense: e.g., *Por si viene lo haré* In case she comes I'll do it

ii The pluperfect subjunctive is largely confined to *si* clauses, involving the imperfect subjunctive of the verb *haber* and a past participle. The pattern is:

a *Si* + imperfect subjunctive with the conditional in the second non-*si* clause
b *Si* + pluperfect subjunctive with pluperfect subjunctive **or** conditional in the past in the second non-*si* clause

Ejemplos

*Si **tuvieras**/**tuvieses*** *un millón de dólares, ¿qué **harías**?* If you had a million dollars, what would you do?

*Si **tu padre pagara**/**pagase*** *el viaje, ¿**vendrías** conmigo?* If your father paid for the journey would you come with me?

*Si yo **viniera** mañana se lo **diría*** If I came tomorrow I'd tell her/him

*Por si **hiciera** frío me llevé el abrigo* In case it was cold I took my coat

*Por si **llegara** temprano, saqué el carro del garage (**M**) / de la cochera (**M**) / coche del garaje para ir al teatro en seguida* In case (s)he arrived early I got the car out of the garage to go straight to the theater

*Si yo lo **hubiera**/**hubiese sabido** no **habría**/**hubiera**/**hubiese ido*** If I had known, I would not have gone

*Si ella **hubiera**/**hubiese tenido** bastante dinero se **habría**/**hubiera**/**hubiese** comprado una casa* If she had had enough money she would have bought a house

*Si **hubiéramos**/**hubiésemos ido** a México **habríamos**/**hubiéramos**/**hubiésemos** podido visitar a nuestros amigos/cuates (**M**)* If we had gone to Mexico we could have visited our friends

iii Remarks

Since the subjunctive is used in all temporal clauses referring to the future, an imperfect subjunctive is used in the following cases. The imperfect subjunctive is not used with a **si** clause when the future is not referred to but rather something occurring in the past. See the last two separated examples below.

iv

Ejemplos

> *Prometió llamarnos* **cuando llegara / hubiera llegado** (pluperfect of subjunctive – see level 2.8) *a casa*
> (S)he promised to call us when she (had) arrived home
> *Me comprometí a ayudarlos* **mientras estuviera** *en Chihuahua*
> I committed myself to helping them when I was in Chihuahua
> *Les dijo que les ofrecería una cena* **cuando estuvieran** *en San Cristóbal de las Casas*
> (S)he told them that (s)he would offer them an evening meal when they were in . . .
> *Me comentó que lo más fácil sería que él nos* **visitara cuando se encontrara** *en la zona*
> (S)he told me that the easiest thing to do was for him to visit us when he was in the area
>
> *Yo jugaba todo el día si mi mamá (**M**) / madre se* **quedaba** *en casa*
> I played all day long if my mother was at home
> *Si mi marido* **trabajaba** *en el jardín yo lo/le ayudaba*
> If my husband worked in the garden I would help him

2.9 Temporal clauses

i After the following conjunctive expressions of time, the subjunctive is required when uncertainty is implied. This often implies a future idea (see unit 6 for the future)

a medida que	while	*luego que*	as soon as
antes de que	before	*mientras que*	while
después de que	after	*siempre que*	whenever
en cuanto	as far as	*ya que*	as soon as
cuando	when	*hasta que*	until
una vez que	once	*(esperar / aguardar) a que*	(to wait) until
a los pocos días de que	a few days after	*a las pocas horas de que*	a few hours after
desde que	since		

Ejemplos

> *Hay que volver a casa* **antes de que llueva** We ought to go home before it rains
> *Te llamaré* **después de que** *mi mamá* **haga** *la compra* I'll call you after mom/mum has done the shopping
> **Cuando llegues** *prepara la comida* When you arrive get the meal ready
> **Luego que termine** *el trabajo iré al cine* As soon as I've finished work I'll go to the movies
> *Quédate aquí* **hasta que vuelva** *mi amigo / **regrese** mi cuate (**M**)* Stay here until my pal comes back
> *Espero en casa* **a que vuelvas** I'll wait at home until you come back

ii It must be emphasized that when the conjunctive expressions of time refer to the future and therefore imply uncertainty, the subjunctive is necessary, as seen in the examples, **but**, when **most** of these expressions refer specifically to the past, an indicative is required.

Ejemplos

Mientras que ella leía el periódico yo cocinaba While she read the newspaper I cooked

A medida que pasaba el tiempo se volvía más desagradable As time passed he became more and more unpleasant

iii However, certain conjunctions of time are followed by the subjunctive whatever the time, and however certain the events are.

Antes de que, **después de que** and **desde que** are such conjunctions.

Ejemplos

Antes de que viniera / venga hice / haré las camas Before he came / comes I made / I'll make the beds

*Desde que aprendiera a escribir compuso cuentecitos / cuentitos (**M**)* As soon as he learnt to write he made up stories

Después de que llegaran fuimos al teatro After they came we went to the movies

iv Notwithstanding the certainty implied in **desde que** and **después de que** (after all, the events have actually taken place), the subjunctive is the norm these days. Such a practice is condemned by purists. They would prefer **llegaron** in the last sentence, for example. The same goes for Mexican speakers of Spanish for whom the subjunctive is aberrant in these cases. However, nearly all Spanish newspapers, including *El País*, have adopted the subjunctive in these circumstances.

v Remarks

If the subject is the same for the main and subordinate clause the verb in the subordinate clause is in the infinitive.

Ejemplos

Escribe la carta **antes de / después de desayunar / desayunarte** *(**M**)* Write the letter before / after having your breakfast

Tendrás que crecer mucho **hasta ser** *como yo* You'll have to grow a lot until you're like me

a **Hasta que** is frequently followed, and not only in speech, by **no**, but this is condemned by purists. However, it is perfectly acceptable in Mexico

b **Hasta que** is usually followed by an indicative in the past. Compare the example with **hasta que** in (i) above, and the following one in which there is no uncertainty

Me quedé en casa **hasta que llegó** *mi amigo / cuate (**M**)*

but

Le dije que me quedaría en casa **hasta que** *regresara* I told her / him that I would remain till (s)he came back ([S]he hasn't come back yet)

2.10 Use of the subjunctive or infinitive after the main clause

In the following examples, the verbs after the main clause may be used in their subjunctive form or as an infinitive. However, Spanish speakers do have preferences, but these may vary from person to person. The examples below indicate these preferences although there is no clear-cut rule to help you. Factors such as whether the language is written, as opposed to spoken, may affect the choice, or even the tense of the main clause. To try to compare Peninsular and Mexican usage here would be going too far.

aconsejar	*Me aconseja que vaya al cine* No difference	*Me aconseja ir al cine*
animar	*Los animo a que trabajen* No difference	*Los animo a trabajar*
dejar	*Lo dejo que termine su trabajo* Infinitive preferred	*Lo dejo terminar su trabajo*
impedir	*El carro mal estacionado me impidió que saliera* No difference	*El carro mal estacionado me impidió salir*
invitar	*Nos invitaron a que cenáramos con ellos* Infinitive preferred	*Nos invitaron a cenar con ellos*
mandar	*El maestro nos mandó que saliéramos al patio* Subjunctive preferred	*El maestro nos mandó salir al patio*
ordenar	*El capitán nos ordenó que regresáramos al campamento* Subjunctive preferred	*El capitán nos ordenó regresar al campamento*
permitir	*El médico le permitió que fumara* Infinitive preferred	*El médico le permitió fumar*
prohibir	*Mi mamá me ha prohibido que beba vino* No difference	*Mi mamá me ha prohibido beber vino*
proponer	*Su amiga nos propuso que fuéramos al cine* No difference	*Su amiga nos propuso ir al cine*
recomendar	*El doctor (**M**) me recomendó que descansara* No difference	*El doctor me recomendó descansar*
sugerir	*La psicóloga le ha sugerido que cambie de trabajo* No difference	*La psicóloga le ha sugerido cambiar de trabajo*

Exercises Level **2**

i **Encuentra la forma correcta del subjuntivo en las siguientes expresiones. Elije tu verbo con un significado que convenga:**

Ejemplo

la duda de que (_) > la duda de que apruebe el examen

a el peligro de que (_)
b el riesgo de que (_)
c ¡Qué ganas tengo de que (_)!
d Tengo el temor de que (_)
e Tengo miedo de que (_)
f Existe la probabilidad de que (_)

g Me extraña el hecho de que (_)

h Es peligroso que (_)

ii Encuentra la forma subjuntiva que convenga, usando los verbos o expresiones de abajo, y completando la frase de un modo lógico:

tener que, perder, acabar, cerrar, ser, pagar, aprobar, cobrar

Ejemplo

No me parece probable que (_) > No me parece probable que apruebe el examen

a Importa que (_)

b Es dudoso que (_)

c Es inevitable que (_)

d Es lástima que (_)

e Es de esperar que (_)

f Es de temer que (_)

g Es previsible que (_)

h No está bien que (_)

iii Escribe las catorce frases de abajo, y acaba por un subjuntivo que elijas, o por una expresión alternativa:

Ejemplo

No encuentro ningún alumno que (_) > No encuentro ningún alumno que sepa resolver este problema

a Me hace falta un carro (**M**) que (_)

b ¿Conoces un electricista que (_)?

c Prometo una recompensa (_)

d No hay ningún mecánico que (_)

e Nunca he encontrado ninguna planta que (_)

f No encuentro ningún menú que (_)

g Ven a vernos cuando (_)

h Seguiré leyendo (_)

i Tendré que acostarme (_)

j Se lo agradecí con un e-mail (_)

k Te prometo ayudar a tu hermano (_)

l Iremos al parque (_)

m El precio del viaje depende del (_)

n No hay mucha gente que (_)

iv Traduce al español las siguientes expresiones:

a Whoever you are

b Wherever they are

c Whatever they do

d However you repair it

e Whatever the weather

f Whatever your opinion

g Whatever happens

h Whoever wants it

i Whatever interest you show
j Whether she goes or not
k Whatever she thinks
l Wherever you come from
m However strong she is
n However much you ask me to do it
o However much food you buy

v **Las siguientes palabras están mezcladas y no tienen sentido así. Encuentra su orden lógico:**

Ejemplo

que iremos al teatro luego acabado hayas la comida > Luego que hayas acabado la comida iremos al teatro

a arreglado hayan camión (**M**) Cuernavaca a iremos el cuando
b hayas depósito cuando vuelve casa a llenado el (*use* **tanque** *and* **regresar** *for Mexico*)
c telefoneado cuanto saldremos en Juan a hayas

vi **Traduce al español. Ten en cuenta que las formas *hubiese/hubieses*, etc., no se usan en México**

a If I had known that you were there I would have come
b If you had told me that the movie/film was so good I would have seen it
c If I had a car I would visit Spain
d If you were a millionaire, what would you buy?
e I promised her that, when I returned, we would go to the theater
f If my mom/mum made cookies/biscuits I would always invite friends home
g We agreed that, when the weather improved, we would all go to the beach
h I was frightened she would wake up when I arrived home late
i We let the children play all day so that they would be very tired and would want to go to bed early
j We advised them to use traveler's checks because the local currency was uncertain
k I denied that the bus driver had caused the accident
l In case we didn't have enough money I cashed a traveler's check

vii **Hablas / Platicas (M) con un agente inmobiliario porque quieres comprar una casa, o en la Ciudad de México, o en Madrid. Tienes una cantidad de dinero astronómica pero te interesa sobre todo una propiedad con buena relación calidad precio (*value for money*). El agente te enseña una lista de propiedades en la Ciudad de México, entre cinco estrellas (***** = excelente) y cero estrellas (poco atractivo). Hé aquí la lista, bajando de cinco a cero: Las Lomas (de Chapultepec), Santa Fe, Polanco, Jardines de la Montaña, Tlatelolcol. Escribe un diálogo que consista en cinco preguntas y cinco respuestas y que contenga (*contains*) una serie de hipótesis relacionadas con la compra de una casa. Las hipótesis deben incluir cada vez la conjunción condicional *si***

Por ejemplo

TÚ: ¿Si yo **comprara** esta casa en Las Lomas hace diez años, cuánto **valdría** ahora?

AGENTE: Bueno, vamos a ver, **habría ganado** Ud. unos quinientos mil pesos si la **hubiera comprado** en aquel entonces, y **hubiera hecho** una buena inversión (*investment*)

Podrías, si quieres, basar tu diálogo sobre las siguientes zonas de Madrid, bajando de cinco a cero estrellas:

Plaza de la Cibeles, Parque del Retiro, Puerta del Sol, Villaverde Bajo, Carabanchel

viii Traduce al español:

a I'll cook lunch before you start the housework
b We'll have a game of chess after Pedro goes to bed
c While you're in the kitchen, I'll read the newspaper
d As soon as you have had a shower we'll go to the soccer match
e Call us as soon as you get home
f Wait until they call us
g I'll wait here until they come
h We'll wash the car before we set off for the mountains
i We'll go on vacation/holiday a few days after you finish work

ix Juego de rol

Elige a un compañero / una compañera. Preparad / Preparen (**M**) para la semana próxima un diálogo que presentaréis / presentarán (**M**) a la clase. Se trata de un(a) comprador(a) que quiere adquirir una casa o en Madrid o en la Ciudad de México y que se cita con un(a) agente inmobiliario(a). Puede ser el mismo tema que el anterior (vii). Sin embargo, podríais / podrían (**M**) incluir referencias a casas en todas las zonas. Hágáis lo que hagáis / Hagan lo que hagan (**M**), se trata de una conversación presentada en clase.

Unit 17 *(Unidad 17)*

Personal pronouns (*Los pronombres personales*)

Level **1**

1.1 **Personal pronoun as subject** (*Pronombre personal como sujeto*)

1.2 **Personal pronoun as direct object** (*Pronombre personal como objeto/complemento directo*)

1.3 **Personal pronoun as indirect object** (*Pronombre personal como objeto/complemento indirecto*)

1.4 **Pronouns with prepositions / (disjunctive pronouns)** (*Pronombres con preposiciones / [pronombres disyuntivos]*)

1.1 Personal pronoun as subject

i The following personal pronouns are regularly used as the subject of a sentence:

Yo *compro una casa*	I buy a house
Tú *compras una casa*	You buy a house
Él / Ella / Ud. *compra una casa*	He/She/You buy(s) a house
Nosotros / as *compramos una casa*	We (males) / We (females) buy a house
Vosotros / as *compráis una casa*	You (males) / You (females) buy a house
Ellos / Ellas / Uds. *compran una casa*	They (males) / They (females) / You buy a house

ii A number of comments are to be made here. The first is that the **yo / tú / nosotros/as / vosotros/as** forms are not used very frequently since the verb endings make it clear who is being referred to. Secondly, if there is a mixture of males and females the masculine forms are used, i.e. **nosotros, vosotros, ellos**. The female forms **nosotras, vosotras, ellas** would only be used if females alone were referred to. The **vosotros/as** forms are not used in Spanish America and are replaced entirely by **Uds**. This is also true of Spanish spoken in the United States. This feature could be disconcerting for a Spanish speaker from Spain who would normally use the more friendly, intimate form **vosotros/as**. The present author who has experienced innumerable years of Iberian and Mexican Spanish still has some problems accommodating the **Uds.** form within an intimate or family situation. Conversely, Mexican speakers of Spanish find the **vosotros/as** forms antiquated and quaint. The younger Mexican generation would doubtless have difficulty using the corresponding verb form – **platicáis** (**habláis**) (you speak), **corréis** (you run), **pedís** (you ask for), etc. – while forms of the preterit or imperfect subjunctive would doubtless be a mystery to them: *hablasteis* (you spoke), *hablarais/hablaseis* (you should speak). Needless to say, therefore, you are in good company if you have initial problems conquering some forms of the Spanish imperfect subjunctive. Finally, the *tú* form is the familiar mode of address when you are speaking to someone you know (well), while the passage from the *Ud./Uds.* forms to this familiar *tú*, and *vosotros/as* forms is much easier in Spain and Mexico than in France, for example, where the *vous* form, instead of *tu*, still holds considerable sway. In this sense, Spain and Mexico are similar to Italy (*Lei* to **tu**). (See level 2 for further treatment of the *tú* and *Ud.* forms.)

1.2 Personal pronoun as direct object

i The following personal pronouns are all in common use as direct objects. Note that these direct objects (and indirect ones), precede the verb, apart from with the infinitive, the positive imperative, and the gerund (see level 2.1).

*Ella **me** ve*	She sees me
*Ella **te** ve*	. . . you (one person)
*Ella **lo / le** ve*	. . . him/you/it (m.)
*Ella **la** ve*	. . . her/it (f.)
*Ella **nos** ve*	. . . us
*Ella **os** ve*	. . . you (more than one person) (not in **M**)
*Ella **los / les** ve*	. . . them/you (m., or m. and f.)
*Ella **las** ve*	. . . them/you (f.)

ii The following comments are to be borne in mind. You cannot separate the direct object pronoun from the verb. In other words, you cannot put *me/te*, etc., in any other part of the sentence. Furthermore, as with the subject pronoun *tú*, *te* refers to a person whom you are addressing and you know (well). *Lo* and *le* are both used for *him* and male *you* (whom you do not know well) but the use of *lo* is much more extensive, and is used over the whole of Spanish America and therefore includes Mexico, and many parts of Spain. Castilla La Vieja and northern Spain generally, together with the traditional literature of much of Spain, still adhere to the use of *le* for *him* as direct object, and *you* as direct object for a person you are addressing but do not know well. If you read much Spanish literature of the traditional kind you will find *le* comes more readily than *lo*.

In a recent survey recorded by Manuel Seco (*Dudas y dificultades de la lengua española*), by far the higher percentage of Spanish authors use the *le* form as opposed to the *lo* form. However, this problem should not be exaggerated for both are acceptable, although you will rarely, if at all, hear *le* for *him* / male *you* as direct object in Mexico or anywhere else in Spanish America. *Lo* is used for objects, i.e. things which are masculine. *Le* is not possible here.

The remarks on *le* and *lo* also apply to the plurals *les* and *los*, although *los* is more common, even in Spain, than *les* with the meaning of *you/them* as plural direct object.

La refers to a female person = *her*, and to objects which are feminine. It is also used when addressing a female you do not know well.

Nos covers both males and females. There is no distinctive female form. The same may be said for **os**. *Os* is not used in Spanish America and is replaced by *los*, or *las*, the corresponding object pronoun forms of the subject pronouns ***ellos / ellas / Uds.***

Los and **las** are used for masculine and feminine objects, respectively.

Further examples with all the combinations:

Ellos **me** *esperan*	They are waiting for me
Ellos **te** *esperan*	They are waiting for you (one person whom you know well)
Ellos **le** *esperan*	They are waiting for you (one male person whom the speaker does not know well) / They are waiting for him (only in certain northern and central parts of Spain)
Ellos **lo** *esperan*	They are waiting for him (in all Spanish America and much of southern Spain)
Ellos **la** *esperan*	They are waiting for her
Ellos **la** *esperan*	They are waiting for you (one female person whom the speaker does not know well)
Ellos **lo** *esperan*	They are waiting for you (one male person whom the speaker does not know well, over much of southern Spain and all Spanish America)
Ellos **lo** *esperan*	They are waiting for it (masculine noun) (e.g. **un tren** = train)
Ellos **la** *esperan*	They are waiting for it (feminine noun) (e.g. **una comida** = meal)
Ellos **nos** *esperan*	They are waiting for us
Ellos **os** *esperan*	They are waiting for you (more than one person whom the speaker knows well, and in Spain, not Spanish America)
Ellos **les** *esperan*	They are waiting for them (male persons, or male(s) and female(s), in central and northern Spain)
Ellos **los** *esperan*	They are waiting for them (male persons which can include female persons and used in southern Spain and all Spanish America) (also used everywhere for masculine objects, e.g. **trenes** = trains)
Ellos **los** *esperan*	They are waiting for you (male persons, which can include female persons, whom the speaker may or may not know well, in all Spanish America)
Ellos **las** *esperan*	They are waiting for them (female persons or feminine objects)
Ellos **las** *esperan*	They are waiting for you (female persons whom the speaker does not know well in southern Spain, and knows or does not know well in all Spanish America)

1.3 Personal pronoun as indirect object

The following personal pronouns as indirect objects are all in common use:

*Ella **me** enseña el libro*	She shows the book to me
*Ella **te** enseña el libro*	She shows the book to you (singular)
*Ella **le** enseña el libro*	She shows the book to him/her/you (singular)
*Ella **nos** enseña el libro*	She shows the book to us
*Ella **os** enseña el libro*	She shows the book to you (plural)
*Ella **les** enseña el libro*	She shows the book to them/you (plural)

You will notice that **le**, as an indirect object, covers (*to / for*) *him*, *her* and the non-familiar form for *you*. **Os** is used as the familiar plural form for *you*. It is not used in Spanish America. It is replaced by **les**. The one felicitous result in these indirect forms is that they are much simpler than the direct forms. At least, no room for complaint here, compared to 1.2 immediately above.

1.4 Pronouns with prepositions (disjunctive pronouns)

i Pronouns used after prepositions are as follows:
para mí, para ti, para él, para ella, para ello, para Ud., para sí, para nosotros/as, para vosotros/as, para Uds., para ellos, para ellas (but see level 2.3).

ii These pronouns are used after a range of prepositions such as *a, ante, contra, de, dentro, hacia, por, sin, tras* (see unit 23 on prepositions for the full range)

Examples

Hablan de mí	They speak of me
Lo hago por ti	I do it for you
Voy por él	I am going (to get) him
Se dirige hacia ella	He makes his way towards her
Puedes ir sin mí	You can go without me
El detective va tras ella	The detective goes behind her

When used with **con** (with), the pronoun is modified and is attached to **con** in the following three cases:

¿Quieres ir conmigo?	Do you want to go with me?
Voy contigo	I am going with you
Mi hermana está enfadada consigo	My sister is angry with herself

Exercises Level **1**

i Replace the noun by a pronoun as in the example
Compro el periódico > Lo compro

a Hago el ejercicio
b Limpio el coche
c Barren el patio
d Cierro el libro
e Compro el boleto (**M**) / el billete
f Venden el sillón

g Oyen el ruido
h Tocamos el piano

i Rompo el vaso
j Bebo el café

ii Replace the noun by a pronoun as in the example

Canto una canción > La canto

a Toco la guitarra
b Pongo la mesa
c Doy una charla
d Abren la puerta
e Hacen la faena

f Estudiamos la lección
g Aplico la regla
h Queman la salsa
i Tomas la carne
j Coméis el pan (not in **M**)

iii Replace the noun by a pronoun as in the example

Ella barre las habitaciones > Las barre

a Nosotros abrimos las ventanas
b Uds. lavan (**M**) los platos
c Ellos friegan los cacharros
d Ellas arreglan las recámaras (**M**)
e Tú aprendes las lecciones

f ¿Comes tú chocolates?
g Yo prefiero los caballos
h Ellas traen las llaves
i Nosotras necesitamos los platos
j Uds. compran los sarapes (**M**)

iv Answer the questions as in the example

¿Por qué no compras un periódico? > Lo compro

a ¿Por qué no vendes la casa?
b ¿Por qué no pagas las facturas?
c ¿Por qué no preparas las arvejas (**M**) / los guisantes? (*peas*)
d ¿Por qué no comes la cena?
e ¿Por qué no estudias las novelas?
f ¿Por qué no visitas la ciudad?
g ¿Por qué no gastas el dinero?
h ¿Por qué no escribes el ejercicio?
i ¿Por qué no aceptan los regalos?
j ¿Por qué no aprenden los idiomas?

v Replace the indirect object (noun) by a pronoun, as in the example

(Bear in mind that, in this exercise, a Spanish speaker prefers to repeat the indirect object as a pronoun before the verb, as in the example. See Level 2.2. In this sense, you have a very artificial exercise here.)

(Le) doy el libro al chico > Le doy el libro

a Enseño el carro (**M**) al amigo
b Da el regalo a la madre
c Llevan el paquete a los estudiantes
d Muestra la página a la compañera
e Trae los platos al padre
f Compran las tazas a las madres

vi Answer the questions as in the example

¿Lo haces para mí? > Lo hago para ti

a ¿Lo compras para él?
b ¿Lo venden por mí?

c ¿Las arreglan sin ti?
d ¿La terminas conmigo?

e ¿Los acaba con ellos?
f ¿ Lo haces sin mí?
g ¿Hablan de mí?
h ¿Los compran por ellas?

i ¿Las venden por nosotras?
j ¿Va por mí?
k ¿Está enfrente de ellos?
l ¿Se sienta encima de vosotros?
   (*Wow! That's painful!*)

vii Paired activity
Objective – To use the pronouns *lo/le/la* and *los/les/las* before the verb
Method – A makes up a simple sentence with a subject, a verb and a noun, or nouns, as
object. B converts the noun into a pronoun and puts it before the verb. If you are smart,
you can change the verb ending as well

Examples

A: (Yo) Abro la puerta
B: (Tú) La abres
A: Cierras el libro
B: Lo cierro
A: Borro el pizarrón
B: Lo borras
A: Hacemos las tareas
B: Las hacen

Use verbs like: leer, hacer, cerrar, abrir, barrer (*to sweep*), coser (*to sew*), dar, preferir,
tocar, limpiar, ver, aprender, llevar, querer, comprar, vender

Level **2**

2.1 **Order of pronouns (when there are more than one)** (*Orden de los pronombres
    [cuando hay más de uno]*)
2.2 **Redundant pronouns** (*Pronombres redundantes*)
2.3 **Further remarks on disjunctive pronouns** (*Más comentarios a pronombres
    disyuntivos*)
2.4 **Further remarks on second person pronouns** (*singular and plural*) (*Más
    comentarios a los pronombres de segunda persona – singular y plural*)

2.1 Order of pronouns (when there are more than one)

i The most common order is as follows:

			le
			les
se	*te*	*me*	*lo*
	os	*nos*	*la*
			los
			las

The most important feature in this list is that ***le*** and ***les*** become ***se*** when combined with
another pronoun in this group.

Ejemplos

*Te **lo** dije ayer*	I told you yesterday
*Nos **los** mandaron el año pasado*	They sent them to us last year
*Me **lo** comunicó en seguida*	She communicated it to me immediately
*Se **lo** dije ayer*	I told her/him/them/you yesterday
*Se **la** dimos*	We gave it to her/him/them/you
*Se **las** dieron*	They gave them to you/her/him/them
*Se **me** escapa la fecha*	The date escapes me

Note that in the first example the pronoun ***lo*** is necessary, as also in, for example: ***Se lo pregunté ayer*** = I asked him/her/you/them yesterday (about it)

ii Pronouns precede all finite verbs except the affirmative imperative where the pronoun is attached to the end of the verb. Note that in the examples of pronouns attached to the verb a written accent is placed over the appropriate vowel to retain the stress:

*¿**Me** entiendes?*	Do you understand me?
***Lo** haré mañana*	I'll do it tomorrow
***La** escribiré esta tarde*	I'll write it this afternoon
*¡No **me** digas!*	You don't say!
*¡No **la** escribas!*	Don't write it!

But:

¡Escríbela!	Write it!
¡Escríbesela!	Write it to her!
¡Mándasela!	Send it to him/her!
¡Dámelos!	Give them to me!

iii Pronouns are attached to the infinitive and the present participle, but never to the past participle, as happens in Italian:

*viéndo**lo** / **la***	seeing it/him/her/you
*dándo**lo***	giving it
*al abrir**la***	on opening it
*para entender**lo** / **le***	to understand him/it

iv Pronouns may also precede an auxiliary verb, as well as being attached to the infinitive. Notice the written accent in the second example of all the five cases. Why is this?

*Te lo voy a explicar / Voy a explic**á**rtelo*	I am going to explain it to you
*Lo siguió leyendo / Siguió ley**é**ndolo*	She continued to read it
Los suelen traer / Suelen traerlos por la tarde	They usually bring them in the afternoon
*No te las puedo dar / No puedo d**á**rtelas*	I can't give them to you
*Se los quiero mandar / Quiero mand**á**rselos hoy*	I want to send them to him/her/them/ you today

2.2 Redundant pronouns

i Even when an object is expressed by a noun or a disjunctive pronoun, a pronoun is needed in Spanish in the following cases

a When a direct or indirect object is placed before the verb:

*A Juan no **le** gustó la comida*	John didn't like the meal
*A mí **me** encanta la ópera*	I love opera
*A ella **le** interesa el Siglo de Oro*	She is interested in the Golden Age

ii Very often, when an indirect object is a person or animal. As in the above cases, the repetitious nature of the pronoun may seem strange, and even unnecessary, but it is a strong feature of the Spanish language:

***Le** di el collar a la chica*	I gave the necklace to the girl
***Le** robó el coche al hombre*	He stole the car from the man
***Se lo** vendió a mi amigo*	She sold it to my friend
***Se lo** enseñó al alumno*	He showed it to the pupil
***Le** dio el hueso al perrito*	She gave the bone to the dog
***Se lo** envié al banco*	I sent it to the bank

iii When emphasis is needed, repetition also occurs:

Se lo** di a ella, no **a él	I gave it to her, not to him
***Te** llamaron **a ti** (y no a tu hermano)*	They called you (and not your brother)
*Dá**sela a ella***	Give it to her

2.3 Further remarks on disjunctive pronouns

i After a preposition, choice between *yo* (subject), *mí* (object), *tú* (subject) and *ti* (object) varies. As we have seen, the object form is used in most cases (*para mi*, *detrás de ti*) but the subject form occurs after *como* (as, like), *salvo* (save), *excepto* (except) and *según* (according to) (*como yo/tú*, *según yo/tú*).

ii There is a choice when two pronouns follow a preposition. The subject form tends to be used in these cases although the preposition may be repeated.

según tú y yo	according to you and me
para ella y yo	for her and me
delante de ti y yo	before you and me
según tú y según yo	according to you and me
detrás de ella y detrás de mí	behind her and (behind) me

2.4 Further remarks on second person pronouns (singular and plural)

The traditional labels 'familiar' and 'polite' do not adequately capture the political and social circumstances in which pronouns are used today. Since the death of Franco and the beginning of the democratization process, **tú** and **vosotros/as** have ousted **Ud.** and **Uds.** to a very large extent, except in very formal circumstances. It is unthinkable to use anything but **tú** and **vosotros** (not **vosotros** in **M**) in the following circumstances:

a addressing children and animals, God

b among relatives, friends of whatever age, workmates, soldiers of the same rank (but **not** across the ranks), colleagues in the same profession.

However, you may come across in some country areas and small towns of Mexico the use of **Ud(s).** by children when addressing their parents. This usage is fading and need not trouble you. Just recognize it, and let the author know if you ever hear it!

Tú is always used in the sense of *one*, or *you* (general).

It is normal to use **tú** and **vosotros** (**vosotros** not in **M**) in the following circumstances:

a among young people (i.e. students), whatever the circumstances

b among people of different ages in almost any informal situation, as at a party

c addressing priests

d wherever it is desirable to establish a friendly atmosphere, even in semi-formal situations as in a bank, restaurant, shop

e in public speeches, especially politicians (and particularly on the left) to their audiences

f in advertisements where someone is trying to sell you something (this is standard procedure now, and a cunning psychological device?)

g when a person addresses a stranger who is indulging in an activity the person disapproves of. If someone touches a car, for example, possibly with some evil intention, you could certainly hear the owner call out: *¡Oye! Tú de la chaqueta / chamarra* (**M**), *¿Qué haces allí?* (You with that jacket, what are you doing?) or *¡Quítate de allí!* (Clear off! / Beat it!). This is a practice you should not imitate in your early incursions into Spanish-speaking countries.

It is not going too far to say that *Ud.* and (in Spain) *Uds.* are used only:

a in very formal, public situations (a ceremony, for example)

b when writing to strangers (booking a hotel room for example)

c to old people not known to the speaker

d wherever it is desired to show respect

Compared to usage of *tu* and *vous* in France where there was a temporary flowering of the *tu* form following the social upheavals of 1968, which has now withered away, the *tú* and *vosotros/as* forms have taken on a new vigor.

Most of the foregoing comments on *Uds.* as used in Spain do not of course apply to the Spanish American countries where *vosotros/as* no longer obtains.

A word of caution

When visiting a Spanish-speaking country in your early days, you should not automatically embark on the *tú* form, when a person uses *tú* to you and is much older. Just wait and see how the conversation or relationship unfolds.

Examples with *tú* and *vosotros/as*

*El pueblo español **os** recibe satisfecho y consciente de la alta significación que este acto encierra*
(Speech of King Juan Carlos to visiting diplomats)

¿Has probado el nuevo turbo? ¡Cómprate un Chevrolet! (Have you tried the new turbo? Buy a Chevrolet!)

Cuando pases por la biblioteca ¿me recoges los libros? When you go to the library, could you collect my books?

O Dios, ayúdame a aprobar todos mis exámenes O Lord, help me to get through all my exams

Oiga, Señor, ¿sabe dónde está el Paseo de la Castellana? Excuse me, do you know where the . . . is?

A note on **vos**

In a large part of South America – Argentina, Paraguay, Uruguay and the area which goes from Chiapas in southern Mexico to Colombia – although here it is sporadic, *vos* is used instead of *tú*. It can exist side by side with *tú* in Colombia (in and around Cali for instance), Ecuador and Chile. The corresponding verb forms are: *tomás* (you take), *comés* (you eat), *vivís* (you live), *hacés* (you do). In some parts of Central America, Mexico and elsewhere, it is considered uncultured. Some Mexicans, for example, have the obscure idea that **vos** is some deformed version of *vosotros*. Such an attitude is not the case in Argentina. You will certainly come across it if you study Argentinian literature and civilization, so you should be aware of its existence.

In this context should be mentioned another colorful lingering feature of Spanish of bygone eras. *Vuestra Merced* + verb in the third person (Your grace) is still used in parts of Colombia. Interestingly enough, *Vuestra merced* derives from Old Castilian which finally leads to *Usted / Ud.*

Exercises Level 2

i Cambia el orden de las palabras, reemplazando el nombre por un pronombre como en el ejemplo

Me da un libro > Me lo da

a Te regalo un coche	f Te llevaré los guantes
b Le dio una máquina fotográfica	g Le he dado el regalo
c Me enseñaron su nuevo auto (**M**)	h Le pedí un favor
d Le devolví el dinero	i Me mandaron las tarjetas
e Te regresé (**M**) el libro ayer	j Les sugirió un paseo

ii Cambia la posición / ubicación (M) del pronombre como en el ejemplo

Me van a visitar > Van a visitarme

a Te voy a ayudar	f Se la iba a recomendar
b Les/los van a castigar	g Se lo quería proponer
c Se lo van a decir	h Me lo evitó prometer
d Me lo van a prohibir	i Se lo impidieron hacer
e Te lo voy a garantizar	j Me lo logró mandar

iii Cambia en afirmativo el orden negativo como en el ejemplo

¡No lo hagas! > Hazlo

a ¡No lo mandes!
b ¡No lo escribas!
c ¡No se las escriban!
d ¡No me lo des!
e ¡No se los devuelvas!

iv Cambia en negativo el orden afirmativo como en el ejemplo
¡Invítalos! > No los invites

a ¡Pregúntales!   f ¡Llévenselo!

b ¡Ayúdenme!   g ¡Vámonos!

c ¡Llámelos!   h ¡Salúdenlos!

d ¡Dáselos!   i ¡Arréglalo!

e ¡Espérenme!   j ¡Cántalo!

v Aquí tienes una anécdota graciosa en la cual se trata del uso constante de los pronombres personales, sobre todo **tú, Ud., vosotros,** y **Uds. (en negrilla (M) / negrita = bold)**. Explica el problema de estos pronombres en lo que se refiere a una situación que va evolucionando hacia circunstancias familiares. Es un texto más bien **mexicano**, lo que explica la confusión del Señor Pérez. ¿Por qué se confunde este señor? (Este ejercicio no ofrece un modelo por que, hasta cierto punto, la explicación se encuentra fácilmente en el texto.) Ver también ejercicio **(vi)**.

(Yo) me paseaba tranquilamente por la calle cuando, de repente, y sin darme cuenta, una señora clavó su mirada en mí como si fuera yo un bicho raro (*odd fish / strange person*), y (ella) me preguntó: "¿Disculpe señor, es **usted** el señor Pérez?"

(Yo) le dije que sí, pero me quedé "anonadado" (*stunned*). Cuando reaccioné, le pregunté: "Oiga, señora, pero ¿Cómo es que **usted** sabe quien soy yo?", a lo que me contestó: "Se parece (**usted**) mucho, por no decir que es **usted** igualito, a un señor que conozco muy bien, con quien vivo, y que tiene un hermano gemelo que desapareció cuando era niño." Luego luego, le comenté: "¡Señora mía, me ha caído **Ud.** como del cielo! Soy un gorrioncillo (*little sparrow*) que no encuentra su hogar (*home*) y, como (**Ud.**) se habrá dado cuenta (*will have realized*), estoy algo perdido. ¿Podría llevarme (**Ud.**) ante ese señor que se parece tanto a mí?"

La señora y yo llegamos a la casa del mencionado señor. Ahí, ella me presentó con él: "Oye, Juan, ¿Conoces (**tú**) al señor?"

Juan, sin vacilar, respondió: "A **usted**, yo no **lo** conozco."

Pero, yo me di cuenta que la semblanza era curiosa, así que volví a la carga: "Según la señora, **usted** y yo somos gemelos."

El señor, algo extrañado y con cara de no creer lo que sus ojos veían, me dijo: "¿Ah, sí? Sí, es cierto lo que dice, entonces **tú** eres mi hermano que desapareció hace unos veinte años . . . ¡Perdón hermanito, pero parece que me falló la memoria!"

La señora interviene: "Si es así, entonces ¿Me permite **Ud.** tutear**te**?"

Yo le contesté, aunque con cierto malestar con **Ud.** y **te** en la misma frase. "¡Claro que sí! Pero, ¿quién es **usted**?"

"¿No me reconoce**s**? Sí, salta a la vista, ¡soy **tu** madre! Y **ustedes** dos son mis hijos."

Ahora, más que anonadado, estaba yo impactado. ¡Una mamá que nos habla de **ustedes** a sus propios hijos! No es posible. Cuando mi mente (*mind*) medio digirió (*digested*) lo que estaba pasando, me dirijí a los dos: "Es imposible que **usted** sea mi mamá, y **tú** mi hermano si ella nos sigue hablando de **ustedes** a **ti** y a mí."

Él se levantó, y dijo: "¿Realmente estás tan perdido que no sabes que estamos en México y no en España?"

Pero, al final, lo que me preocupaba no era donde estábamos sino la pregunta: "¿Me permite **Ud.** tutear**te**?" Una pregunta de gran profundidad psicológica que me atormentó por mucho tiempo. ¿No sólo decirnos a los dos **Uds.**, en lugar de **vosotros**, sino también decirme a mí **Ud.** y **tú** dentro de la misma frase? Como cualquier extranjero, no acabo de entenderlo.

RB/JPL

vi Actividad para la semana que viene.

Objetivo – Aclarar en español el problema de *tú, Ud., vosotros/as* and *Uds.*

Método – Estudiar el texto de arriba. Preparar una explicación del paso de *tú/Ud.* a *vosotros/Uds.* Se les elige a tres miembros de la clase para que se dirijan a la clase y expliquen en voz alta el desarrollo y el tema de todo el texto y la confusión del Señor Pérez. ¡Es de esperar que los tres miembros no se confundan tanto como este señor!

Unit 18 *(Unidad 18)*

Possessive adjectives and pronouns, relative and interrogative pronouns *(Los adjetivos y pronombres posesivos, los pronombres relativos e interrogativos)*

Level **1**

1.1 **Possessive adjectives** *(Adjetivos posesivos)*
1.2 **Possessive pronouns** *(Pronombres posesivos)*
1.3 **Variation on possessive pronouns** *(Variación sobre pronombres posesivos)*
1.4 **Relative pronouns** *(Pronombres relativos)*
1.5 **Interrogative pronouns** *(Pronombres interrogativos)*

1.1 Possessive adjectives

i Possessive adjectives describe nouns and indicate possession, as in the following cases:

Sing: *mi* ⎫
Plur: *mis* ⎭ my   *tu* ⎫
               tus ⎭ your   *su* ⎫
                               sus ⎭ her/his/your/their/its

Sing: *nuestro/a* ⎫
Plur: *nuestros/as* ⎭ our   *vuestro/a* ⎫
                             vuestros/as ⎭ your

ii *Mi*, *tu* and *su* distinguish number only but **nuestro** and **vuestro** distinguish both number and gender. *Vuestro* and its variants are not used in Spanish America. *Su* and *sus* replace them. These possessive adjectives agree with the thing possessed, not the possessor. This can be confusing at the beginning.

Examples

mi libro	my book	*tu cuaderno*	your exercise book
mis libros	my books	*tus cuadernos*	your exercise books
mi casa	my house	*tu silla*	your chair
mis casas	my houses	*tus sillas*	your chairs
su peso	your/his/her/its/their weight		
sus pesos	your/his/her/its/their weights		
nuestro hijo	our son	*vuestro hijo*	your son
nuestros hijos	our sons/children	*vuestros hijos*	your sons/children

nuestra hija	our daughter	*vuestra hija*	your daughter
nuestras hijas	our daughters	*vuestras hijas*	your daughters

1.2 Possessive pronouns

i **Possessive pronouns** take the place of a noun. They vary like adjectives ending in **o** (see unit 21). They correspond to the English *mine, yours*, etc. Here is the complete list:

	Singular	**Plural**	
m.	*mío*	*míos* ⎫	
f.	*mía*	*mías* ⎭	mine
m.	*tuyo*	*tuyos* ⎫	
f.	*tuya*	*tuyas* ⎭	yours
m.	*suyo*	*suyos* ⎫	
f.	*suya*	*suyas* ⎭	hers / his / its / yours (for **Ud.** and **Uds.**) / theirs
m.	*nuestro*	*nuestros* ⎫	
f.	*nuestra*	*nuestras* ⎭	ours
m.	*vuestro*	*vuestros* ⎫	
f.	*vuestra*	*vuestras* ⎭	yours (for **vosotros / as**)

ii **Vuestro** and its variants are not used in Spanish America. They are all replaced by **suyo**, etc., which correspond to **Uds.**

Examples

*El carro (**M**) es mío*	The car is mine
La casa es mía	The house is mine
Los bolígrafos son míos	The (ball-point) pens are mine
*Las computadoras (**M**) son mías*	The computers are mine
El libro es tuyo	The book is yours
La silla es tuya	The chair is yours
Los cepillos son tuyos	The brushes are yours
Las pelotas son tuyas	The balls are yours

iii **Suyo**, etc. / **nuestro** and **vuestro** are used in the same way. Examples for use of **suyo** corresponding to **Uds.**, etc., in Mexico

Este changarro es suyo	This store/shop is yours (i.e. speaking to more than one person)
*Los boletos (**M**) son suyos*	The tickets are yours
*Estas chamarras (**M**) son suyas*	These jackets are yours

1.3 Variation on possessive pronouns

i There are a number of variations on this pattern. The possessive pronoun acts commonly as an adjective when it follows the noun. It has the value of *a (_) of mine / of yours*, etc.

un amigo mío	a friend of mine	*una casa mía*	a house of mine
una tarjeta suya	a card of his/hers/yours/ theirs	*un ordenador nuestro*	a computer of ours

ii The definite article is used when the verb is either other than **ser**, or if the possessive pronoun is preceded by a preposition:

Hay tres casas aquí. Me gusta más la mía	There are three houses here. I like mine most
Aquí tienes mi corbata. ¿Dónde está la tuya?	Here's my tie. Where's yours?
"¿Vamos en mi coche?" "Podemos ir en el mío"	"We'll go in my car?" "We can go in mine"
Este lápiz está estropeado. ¿Puedo escribir la carta con el tuyo?	This pencil won't work. Can I write the letter with yours?

iii Where ambiguity could arise, **suyo** is often replaced by **de** and the appropriate personal pronoun:

Los zapatos son de él y los calcetines son de ella	The shoes are his and the socks are hers
La culpa no es mía, sino de ti / Ud.	The blame is not mine, but yours
Los abanicos son de ellas, no de Uds.	The fans are theirs, not yours

If **suyo** alone were used in all these cases, shoes and socks could lose their owners, guilt would be difficult to apportion, and you could cool down (wrongly) at others' expense.

1.4 Relative pronouns

i A relative pronoun connects two parts of a sentence which have something in common. It belongs logically to the second of the two and **relates** back to a person or thing mentioned in the first, which is called the antecedent, i.e. the thing that comes before.

ii The most commonly used relative in Spanish is **que** which is a splendidly all-purpose pronoun, applicable alike as subject or object to persons or things of either gender or number. **Que** follows close after its antecedent, so that, although it is invariable in form, we are never at a loss to see what it refers to. Here are some typical examples:

La mujer que plantó aquel árbol es . . .	The woman who planted that tree is . . .
El árbol que plantaron los hombres es . . .	The tree that the men planted is . . .
Los trabajadores que hemos contratado son . . .	The workers whom we have taken on are . . .
*El pasto (**M**) que corta el hombre es largo*	The grass that the man cuts is long

In the first case, **que** relates to the subject of the clause, while in the second, it relates to the object. Do not be deceived by the position of **los hombres** in the second clause, for it is still the subject of the clause. This inversion of subject and object is very commonly associated with the use of **que** and is a characteristic of Spanish, and French and Italian for that matter. Whereas, in English, the relative pronouns *that*, *which*, *who* and *whom* are frequently omitted (The man I saw), this is not the case in Spanish.

iii **Cuyo**, and its variants, are used with the meaning of *whose* or *of whom*.

The agreement in number and gender is with the person or thing possessed:

Examples

la chica aquella cuyo padre nos invitó a cenar	that girl whose father invited us to have an evening meal
el libro cuyas páginas están rotas	the book the pages of which are torn

el culpable cuya dirección no ha sido revelada	the guilty person whose address has not been revealed

1.5 Interrogative pronouns

Spanish interrogative pronouns are as follows:

¿Quién? Who(m)?   *¿Cuál?* Which?   *¿Qué?* What?   *¿Cuánto?* How much?

(Notice the **written accent** for the interrogative form.)

They do vary in form for number and gender according to their endings.

Examples

¿Quién llama?	Who calls?
¿Con quién vas al cine?	With whom do you go to the movies? / Who are you going to the movies with?
¿A quiénes contratas?	Who(m) (more than one person) are you taking on?
¿Cuál de los / las dos prefieres?	Which of the two do you prefer?
¿Cuáles son los / las mejores?	Which are the best?
¿Qué planta(s) hay en el jardín?	Which plant(s) is/are there in the yard/garden?
¡Cuánto cambia tu hermana!	How much your sister changes!
¡Cuánto sabe!	How much she knows!

Exercises   Level 1

i Complete the following sentences with the correct possessive adjective as in the example

Leo (_) libro (yo = mi) > Leo mi libro

a Compro (_) periódico (yo)
b Uso (_) teléfono (tú)
c Escribe (_) novela (él)
d Estudian (_) lecciones (ellas)
e Tocamos (_) piano (vosotros)
f Buscan (_) llave (yo)
g Comes (_) cena (tú)
h Beben (_) coca cola (yo)
i Comen (_) helados (nosotros)
j No fumáis (_) cigarrillos (ellos)
k Reciben (_) regalo (yo)
l Manda (_) carta (nosotros)

ii Answer the questions as in the example

¿De quién es el libro? > Es mío

a ¿De quién es el periódico?
b ¿De quién son las plumas (**M**)?
c ¿De quién es la cartera?
d ¿De quién son las tarjetas?
e ¿De quién son los carros (**M**)?
f ¿De quién son las casas?

iii Complete the sentences as in the example (there may be various possibilities):
Pon tu maleta en el armario y (_) sobre la cama > . . . y la mía/suya sobre la cama

a Mi trabajo es difícil y (_) es fácil
b Tus deberes son complicados y (_) son complicados también
c Nuestras flores son bonitas y (_) están marchitas
d Nuestra casa es chica (**M**) pero (_) es grande
e Vuestros coches son caros pero (_) son baratos
f Sus sillas son pesadas pero (_) son ligeras

iv Complete as in the example
Leo mi libro ahora y (_) más tarde > Leo mi libro ahora y el tuyo más tarde

a Escribo mi carta ahora y (_) esta tarde
b Conduzco mi coche ahora y (_) esta noche
c Hago mi trabajo ahora y (_) cuanto antes

v Make a sentence from the two sentences, joining them with the relative pronoun
que. **See the example**
Leo el libro. Me das el libro. > Leo el libro **que** me das

a Hago el trabajo. Me dejas el trabajo
b Veo los programas. Ves los programas
c Preparo la cena. Comes la cena
d Comen la cena. Preparas la cena
e Pintas las casas. Compro las casas

vi The following words are all muddled. Place them in their correct order. The
important word is the relative pronoun *que*
a guapa la es que mujer canta
b listo que chico alto es el es
c es la blanca mesa que vieja es
d tienes jardín es que el grande
e que pequeña es ciudad la está cerca
f concurrida calle grande la es que está
g viejas son gafas que las uso

vii Fill in the blank spaces as in the examples

¿(_) es Ud.? > ¿Quién es Ud.?
¿(_) prefieres? > ¿Qué prefieres?

a ¿(_) haces?
b ¿(_) de los dos prefieres?
c ¿(_) viene esta tarde?
d ¿(_) cuesta?

e ¿(_) llama?
f ¿(_) son las flores que compras?
g ¿(_) escribes?

viii Class activity
Objective – to use the full range of possessive adjectives
Method – two class members address each other. This is then followed by the whole
class repeating the appropriate possessive adjective for them (*nuestro*), and then addressing

the first two. Member A says "*It's my hat.*" Member B says "*It's your hat.*" The class then says: "*It's our hat.*" The class also says: "*It's your/his/her/their hat.*"

Examples

A:	Es **mi** carro
B:	Es **tu** carro
La clase:	Es **nuestro** carro
La clase:	Es **su** carro (*his/her/their/your*)

A:	Es mi casa
B:	Es tu casa
La clase:	Es nuestra casa
La clase:	Es su casa

A:	Es mi canción
B:	Es tu canción
La clase:	Es nuestra canción
La clase:	Es su canción

You can put all the above nouns in the plural:
Son mis carros / son tus carros / son vuestros carros / son sus carros
Son mis sillas / son tus sillas / son vuestras sillas / son sus sillas
Use the following nouns: computadora (**M**), ordenador, mesa, bicicleta, periódico, guitarra, piano, flauta, plato, taza, vestido, chamarra (**M**), chaqueta, zapato, corbata

The smart ones among you can clarify what is meant by *su.* **So you could add, for example:** su casa de ellos / de Uds. / de ella / de él

Level **2**
2.1 **Further treatment of possessive pronouns** (*Más detalles sobre los pronombres posesivos*)
2.2 **Further treatment of relative pronouns** (*Más detalles sobre los pronombres relativos*)
2.3 **Use of *lo que*** (*Uso de lo que*)
2.4 **Use of *Qué* in exclamations** (*Uso de Qué con exclamaciones*)

2.1 Further treatment of possessive pronouns

i The possessive pronoun is placed after the noun for sake of emphasis, in spirited language, in contrast, or for rhetorical effect. The noun is regularly accompanied by the definite article.

Ejemplos

el derecho mío	my right	*la influencia suya*	his/her/their influence
la pasión nuestra	our passion	*según el parecer*	according to our opinion
por la patria *nuestra*	for our country	*nuestro*	

ii The possessives of the first person singular and plural are often employed in direct address.

Ejemplos

¡Hijos míos!	My sons!	*¡Amigos/oyentes míos!*	My friends/hearers!
¡Madre mía!	Heavens above!	*¡Dios mío!*	Heavens above!
¡Sí, madre mía!	Yes, mother!	*¡Adiós, amor mío!*	Goodbye, my love!

iii Similarly, the formal epistolary address:

Muy señor mío   Dear sir

iv The absolute forms of possessive pronouns are used where, in English, *of* or *from*, for example, would be required:

a pesar mío	in spite of me
Salieron en busca suya	They set out in search of him/her/them/you
No recibí carta suya	I didn't receive a letter from you/them/her/him
Fui al encuentro suyo	I went to meet him/her/them/you
en mí alrededor	around me

v When used with the neuter *lo*, *mío*, *tuyo* etc., have the value of *what is mine/yours*, etc.

Ejemplos

Lo mío es la cocina	The kitchen is my domain
Déjame en paz, que yo ando a lo mío	Leave me in peace and I'll do my own thing
Haz lo tuyo y estarás contento	Do your own thing and you'll be happy

vi When used in the plural, the possessive is frequently used to refer to the family as a group.

Ejemplo

Me esperan los míos para la cena de Navidad	My family are expecting me for a Christmas Eve meal

vii A very popular use of *mío*, etc., replacing *mí*, etc., unacceptable for purists, is the following construction where the preposition *de* disappears, **and is not to be copied in writing**:

delante tuyo instead of **delante de ti** = in front of you
enfrente mío instead of **enfrente de mí** = opposite me
a través mío instead of **a través de mí** = through me

viii This construction is not far from the perfectly acceptable

de parte mía	on my behalf
en favor nuestro	in our favor
a costa suya	to your/his/her/their cost
Miré en torno mío	I looked around me

2.2 Further treatment of relative pronouns

i As *que* governed by a preposition is not applied to persons, *quien*, *who*, is used in its place.

Ejemplos

el hombre con quien platiqué (M) / hablé ayer	the man to whom I spoke yesterday
la chica a quien te referiste	the girl to whom you referred
los políticos de quienes no me fío	the politicians I don't trust

ii A peculiarity of **quien**, either as subject or object, is that it may include its antecedent. It therefore corresponds to *he who* or *those who*:

Quien no sabe esto es francamante ignorante	Anyone who doesn't know this is frankly ignorant
La culpa no fue suya sino de quien se lo aconsejó	The blame was not hers but of the person who advised her (to do it)
Hay quien cree que esto es fácil	There are those who think this is easy
Quien no aventura no gana	Nothing ventured nothing gained
Quien paga manda	He who pays the piper calls the tune

iii The last two examples in this list illustrate how widespread this construction is. There are innumerable sayings which start with **Quien** . . .

2.3 Use of *lo que*

Lo que is used as a relative pronoun when it refers to an idea or a statement which is expressed by the previous clause. Its closest equivalent in English is *that which* although this does not always fit the Spanish. The following examples will illustrate this feature:

Dijo que no iría, lo que me enojó (M) / enfadó	He said he wouldn't come, which angered me
Pasó todo su tiempo estudiando, lo que la ayudó a aprobar sus exámenes	She spent all her time studying, which helped her to get through her examinations
Lo que no acabo de entender es su negativa a mandar la tarjeta	What I fail to understand is her refusal to send the card

2.4 Use of *Qué* in exclamations

i The use of **qué** in exclamations with the meaning of *What (a)!* occurs before an adverb, or an adjective. It corresponds to the English *How!*

Ejemplos

¡Qué bien / bueno (M)!	How splendid!
¡Qué lujo!	What luxury!
¡Qué suerte!	What luck!
¡Qué vista encantadora!	What a lovely sight!
¡Qué bien habla!	How well she speaks!
¡Qué feliz eres tú!	How happy you are!

ii Greater emphasis or vivacity is imparted by the interpolation of *más* (more) or *tan* (so) between an adjective and a noun preceded by *qué*:

¡Qué programa más malo!	What a bad program!
¡Qué partido más aburrido!	What a boring game!
¡Qué lugar tan bonito!	What a lovely spot!

Exercises Level **2**

i Cambia como en el ejemplo

el derecho (_) (yo) > el derecho mío

a Fueron en busca (_) (yo)
b Hablaron con la familia (_) (nosotros)
c Compraron los dibujos (_) (vosotros)
d Vendieron los discos (_) (tú)
e ¿Has comprado los boletos (**M**) (_) ? (ellos)
f Pintó las bicicletas (_) (ellas)
g Todavía no he encontrado los zapatos (_) (yo)
h Se le rompió la máquina (_) (nosotros)

ii Usa la forma correcta de *quien/quién* con la preposición que convenga si es necesaria

Ejemplo

¿(_) escribiste la tarjeta? > ¿A quién escribiste la tarjeta?

a ¿(_) jugaron fútbol (**M**)?
b ¿(_) escribiste al banco?
c la señora (_) te hablé
d Las mujeres (_) trabajaba
e Las personas (_) visité
f (_) le echan la culpa están equivocados
g ¿(_) firmaste el contrato?
h Los muchachos (_) diste el regalo
i ¿(_) es este bolígrafo?
j ¿Te referiste (_) esta tarde?
k ¿(_) fuiste al partido?
l No me fío (_) lo critique

iii Pon las siguientes frases en su orden correcto (una coma puede ser útil en varias frases, y en una frase, hace falta un acento escrito, entonces haz trabajo de detective)

Ejemplo

ópera que encanta la ir lo es me a > Lo que me encanta es ir a la ópera

a dijo extrañó que tu hermano lo me
b que estudié lo aprobar a ayudó el examen mucho me
c chofer (**M**) que loco manejaba (**M**) camión (**M**) como el lo miedo dio el me mucho
d permitido sé que está lo
e hice lo aconsejó que me
f quiere que le pregunta lo

iv Actividad para toda la clase

Objetivo – practicar el uso del pronombre posesivo

Método – aplicar el mismo método que el de arriba (nivel 1, ejercicio viii)

Dos miembros de la clase se dirigen la palabra el uno al otro, usando *mío* y *tuyo*. Después, toda la clase repite el nombre posesivo que le corresponde a ella (*nuestro*). Después, la clase se dirige a los dos primeros.

Miembro A dice: "Este libro es (mío)." **Miembro B dice:** "Este libro es (tuyo)." **La clase dice:** "Este libro es (nuestro)." **La clase dice también:** "Este libro es (suyo)."

Ejemplos

A:	Esta casa es mía
B:	Esta casa es tuya
La clase:	Esta casa es nuestra
La clase:	Esta casa es suya (*his/hers/theirs/yours*)

A:	Este cuaderno es mío
B:	Este cuaderno es tuyo
La clase:	Este cuaderno es nuestro
La clase:	Este cuaderno es suyo

A:	Estas bolsas son mías
B:	Estas bolsas son tuyas
La clase:	Estas bolsas son nuestras
La clase:	Estas bolsas son suyas

Use the following nouns: computadora (**M**), ordenador, mesa, bicicleta, periódico, guitarra, piano, flauta, plato, taza, vestido, chamarra (**M**), chaqueta, zapato, corbata.

Unit 19 *(Unidad 19)*

Indefinite pronouns (*Los pronombres indefinidos*)

(See also unit 26 on negation where there is an overlap.)

Level **1**

1.1 **Indefinite pronouns** (*Los pronombres indefinidos*)

1.2 **Indefinite negative pronouns** (*Pronombres indefinidos negativos*)

1.1 Indefinite pronouns

i There are a number of words of miscellaneous nature which are called indefinite pronouns. They are to some extent of a hybrid character since some of them may be used in more than one way. The following words, which never designate any particular person or thing, are regarded as indefinite pronouns, since there is nothing precise about them:

alguien	somebody, anybody	*nadie*	nobody, not anybody
alguno	some, any	*ninguno*	none, not any
algo	something, anything	*nada*	nothing, not anything

Alguien, **algo** and their opposites **nadie** and **nada** are invariable in form, have no plural and are only used absolutely, i.e. they stand alone and do not qualify nouns whereas **alguno** and **ninguno** can.

ii *Alguien* applies only to persons. It may be preceded by any preposition, and, since it denotes a person, it requires the personal *a* (see unit 22 on the personal *a*) when it is a direct object:

Alguien viene / llama a la puerta	Someone's coming / knocking at the door
¿Vas de vacaciones con alguien?	Are you going on vacation with someone?
¿Busca Ud. a alguien?	Are you looking for someone?
¿Ves a alguien?	Can you see someone/anybody?

iii *Algo* applies only to things. It may be used before an adjective just like *something* or *anything* is in English:

¿Estás buscando algo?	Are you looking for something?
Ven algo en la televisión	They see something on the television
Algo sucede en aquel lugar	Something is happening in that place
Sirve algo de vino pero muy poco	He serves a drop of wine but not much
Toca algo el piano	She plays the piano a little

iv An adjective following *algo* is often preceded by *de*:

Tiene algo de tonto	He's got something dumb about him
Tiene algo de morriña	She's a bit homesick

v *Algo* is used as an adverb before adjectives or other adverbs in the sense of *somewhat, rather*:

La casa es algo oscura	The house is somewhat dark
Este modelo es algo pequeño	This model is somewhat small

vi *Algo así* is also commonly used to mean *something like that = approximately*

Tardarán cinco horas o algo así	They'll be five hours or thereabouts

vii *Alguno* is used either alone or as an adjective, and applies to persons and things. When referring to persons, it acts similarly to *alguien*. However, *alguien* is more vague than *alguno* when the latter is used as a pronoun. *Alguno* denotes someone already referred to. It varies like an adjective in *-o*. Before a masculine noun it becomes *algún*. When it comes after a verb in the negative, it follows the noun:

Yo quiero salir, pero alguno prefiere quedarse en casa	I want to go out, but someone (of us) prefers to stay at home
Sólo quedan algunas chicos	Only a few boys remain
Compro algunas sillas	I buy a few chairs
Déjame alguna camisa	Leave me a shirt (i.e. a shirt or other)
Puede ayudarte algún vecino	Some neighbor can help you
No hay taxi alguno	There isn't a single taxi
No hay motivo alguno para que te enfades	There is no reason for you to get angry

viii *Alguno*, when referring to things, has the meaning of *some, any* or *a few*. It is omitted on occasions when in English *some*, for example, is used.

Voy a vender algunas de mis gallinas	I'm going to sell some of my chickens
*Quieren comprar algunos timbres (**M**) / sellos*	They want to buy a few stamps
Yo también quiero comprar algunos	I want to buy some as well
"¿Tienes golosinas?" "Sí, tengo"	"Have you got any candies/sweets?" "Yes, I have some / do"

1.2 Indefinite negative pronouns

i *Nadie*, *ninguno* and *nada* are, of course, negatives. When they come before the verb, they do not require *no*, but when they come after, they do require a *no* before the verb. (See also unit 26 on negation.) *Ninguno* becomes *ningún* before a masculine noun.

Examples

Nadie sabe la verdad	No one knows the truth
Nadie viene hoy	No one comes today
No viene nadie hoy	No one is coming today
No contesta nadie	No one answers
Ninguno de nuestros amigos viene	None of our friends are coming

No viene ninguno de nuestros amigos	None of our friends are coming
Nada le satisface	Nothing satisfies him
No le satisface nada	Nothing satisfies him
No veo ningún problema	I can see no problem

Note that these negative pronouns are singular. See the above examples with *ninguno*, and their English translation.

ii When **nadie** or **ninguno** are objects of a verb, or when **ninguno** is an adjective describing a person the personal **a** is used (see unit 22.2.6. on the personal **a**):

No veo a nadie	I can't see anyone
*No hallamos (**M**) / encontramos a nadie*	We can find no one
No veo a ninguno de nuestros amigos	I see none of our friends

iii **Nadie** and **nada** can stand by themselves, like *no one* and *nothing* in English:

| *"¿Quién llama?" "Nadie"* | "Who's calling?" "No one" |
| *"¿Qué cuentas?" "Nada"* | "What have you got to say?" "Nothing" |

Exercises Level **1**

i **Change the feminine noun to a masculine noun. Choose any masculine noun you like**

Example

No tengo ninguna taza > No tengo ningún plato

a No conocemos a ninguna actriz
b No necesito ninguna pluma
c No tengo ninguna hija
d No llaman a ninguna estudiante
e No hallo (**M**) / encuentro ninguna bolsa
f No tengo ninguna amiga
g No veo ninguna foto
h No te presto ninguna blusa

ii **Change the sentence into the negative**

Example

Sé algo de francés > No sé nada de francés

a Estudiamos un poco de ruso
b Hablo algo de alemán
c Tenemos algo de sed
d Sé algo de química
e Tienen algo de prisa
f Necesito algo de pan

iii **Change into the negative**

Example

Necesitamos algunos bollos > No necesitamos ningún bollo

a Veo a alguien
b Van a comprar algunos
c ¿Quieres algo?
d Viene alguien
e Quiero algunos libros
f ¿Necesitas a alguien?
g Estudio varias asignaturas
h Sabemos algo de chino

iv Change into the affirmative

Example

No vienen ningunos alumnos hoy > Vienen algunos alumnos hoy

a No esperamos a nadie

b Juan no necesita nada

c No pregunta por tu dirección nadie

d No tienen ningún libro de texto

e La muchacha no pide nada

f No viene nadie

g No quieren nada

h No tiene libro alguno

v Paired activity

Objective – To use the positive and negative forms of indefinite pronouns

Method – A asks questions of B in a positive form while B answers in a negative form

Examples

A: PREGUNTA   ¿Tienes algo?

B: RESPUESTA   (No), no tengo nada

A: PREGUNTA   ¿Llama alguien?

B: RESPUESTA   No llama nadie / Nadie llama

Use a variety of verbs like ver, contestar, saber, venir, hablar, usar, dejar, esperar, comprar, vender, alquilar, rentar (**M**), conocer, encontrar, necesitar, querer

Level **2**

2.1 **Further treatment of pronouns** (*Más detalles sobre los pronombres*)

2.2 **Use of the subjunctive when person unspecified** (*Uso del subjuntivo con una persona indeterminada*)

2.3 **Use of *cualquier*** (*Uso de **cualquier***)

2.4 **Further remarks on *nadie* and *nada*** (*Más detalles sobre **nadie** y **nada***)

2.1 Further treatment of pronouns

There are some pronouns that have a general, non-specific reference to other people, or things and have a variety of forms:

m.	*el que*	he who	*los que*	those who
f.	*la que*	she who	*las que*	those who

Ejemplos

"¿Qué pan quieres?" "El que tiene miel"

"Which bread do you want?" "The one with honey in it"

"¿Qué tren tomas?" "El que sale a las tres"

"Which train will you catch?" "The one that leaves at three"

El que llega primero recibirá el premio

The one who arrives first will get the prize

"¡Qué bonita falda!" "¿Cuál?" "La que está cerca de la ventana"

"What a lovely skirt!" "Which one?" "The one (which is) near the window"

*"¿Cuáles son tus hijas? ¿Las que están paradas?" (**M**) "No, las que están sentadas"*

"Who are your daughters? Those standing?" "No, those sitting down"

"¿Cuáles sombreros compran?" "Los que están en el mercado"

"Which hats are they buying?" "Those that are in the market"

"¡Qué maravillosas casas!" "¿Cuáles?" "Las que   "What marvelous houses!" "Which ones?"
están detrás del bosque"   "The ones behind the wood"

2.2 Use of the subjunctive when person unspecified

i If there is a degree of uncertainty in the person or object referred to, it is quite likely
that the subjunctive will be used:

Ejemplos

Los que aprueben el examen tendrán caramelos   Those who pass the exam will get some
                                                        candies/sweets

Las que terminen el trabajo antes de las cinco   Those who finish the work before five can
podrán regresar temprano   go home early

ii **Quien** is a substitute for **el que / la que**, and **quienes** for **los que / las que**, but only
with respect to persons

Quien respeta a los mayores es muy cortés   He who respects older people is very
                                                        courteous

iii When speaking of people or things where possessions are referred to, **el de / la de /
los de / las de** are used:

Ejemplos

La de la blusa roja está como un tren   The girl with the red blouse is gorgeous
Los de la camiseta blanca tienen el mejor equipo   Those with the white jerseys/shirts have the
                                                        best team
El carro de Jorge es más pequeño que el de Adriana   Jorge's car is smaller than Adriana's

2.3 Use of *cualquier*

i **Cualquiera** and its plural **cualesquiera** (little used now) have the idea of *any* when
used as a pronoun or adjective. As a pronoun, it is often followed by **de. Cualquier** is
used before a noun but **cualquiera** is used if it is not followed directly by a noun

Ejemplos

cualquier día; cualesquier estudios   any day at all; any studies at all
un día / defecto / hombre cualquiera   any day/defect/man
cualquiera de los barcos   whichever/any one of the boats
Cualquiera puede hacerlo   Anyone can do it
¿Se puede elegir cualquiera?   Can you choose any one?

ii **Cualquier/cualesquier** are often followed by the subjunctive, given the uncertainty
involved:

Ejemplos

Si ves cualquier incidente / hombre que te resulte   If you notice any incident/man which/
sospechoso . . .   who looks suspicious . . .
Cualesquiera que hayan sido sus motivos . . .   Whatever her reasons may have been . . .

Unit 20 *(Unidad 20)*

Demonstrative adjectives and pronouns (*Los adjetivos y pronombres demostrativos*)

Level **1**
1.1 **Demonstrative adjectives** (*Adjetivos demostrativos*)
1.2 **Demonstrative pronouns** (*Pronombres demostrativos*)
1.3 *Éste* and *aquél* = **the latter and the former**
1.4 **Neuter pronouns** (*Pronombres neutros*)

1.1 Demonstrative adjectives

i There are three demonstrative adjectives in Spanish. They correspond to the English *this*, *these*, *that* and *those*. They agree with the noun to which they relate, in the same manner as adjectives:

	m.	**f**.	**neuter**	
	este	*esta*	*esto*	this
sing.	*ese*	*esa*	*eso*	that (near you)
	aquel	*aquella*	*aquello*	that (further away)
	estos	*estas*	–	these
plur.	*esos*	*esas*	–	those (near you)
	aquellos	*aquellas*	–	those (further away)

ii *Este* denotes what is close by, or associated with, the speaker. *Ese* relates to the thing that is close to the person addressed and not far from the speaker or addressee. *Aquel* is far or remote from both. They precede the nouns to which they belong. However, they can follow the noun (see level 2.1).

Examples

*este timbre (**M**) / sello que tengo aquí*	this stamp I have here
*Esta recámara (**M**) / habitación está sucia*	This (bed)room is dirty
*Estos sobres no tienen timbres (**M**) / sellos*	These envelopes don't have stamps
*Estas papas (**M**) / patatas están buenas*	These potatoes are nice
*Ese coche allí es de mi papá (**M**) / padre*	That car there is my father's
Esa casa enfrente se vende	That house opposite is for sale
Esos árboles están en flor	Those trees are in blossom

Esas chicas viven muy cerca	Those girls live close by
aquel parque al otro lado del pueblo	that park on the other side of the town
aquella película que vamos a ver	that movie we are going to see
aquellos barcos que salen hoy	those boats that leave today
aquellas montañas que escaladamos	those mountains we climb

iii With reference to time, *este* refers logically to the present, *ese* to a period relatively near, while *aquel* applies to a remote period:

en este momento	at this moment
durante ese año	during that year
aquella época en que Cortés . . .	that period when Cortes . . .

1.2 Demonstrative pronouns

i *Éste*, *ésta*, *ése*, *ésa*, *aquél*, *aquélla*, etc., are often used in comparisons as in:

*Este muchacho es más abusado (**M**) / listo que ése*	This boy is cleverer than that one
Estas novelas son más interesantes que aquéllas	These novels are more interesting than those

ii As pronouns, the above forms may or may not have a written accent. There is no strict rule on this feature. It is argued that accents on pronouns avoid ambiguity. However, ambiguity is extremely rare. At the same time, the Spanish Academy considers omission of the written accent permissible, but the Spanish newspaper *El País*, for instance, does not allow this omission. Furthermore, careful writers do seem to censure its absence. So, it seems wiser to use it.

Examples

Éste (este coche) es más caro que aquél	This one (this car) is more expensive than that one
Ése es un autor de primera categoría	That is a first-class author
Aquélla es una época fabulosa	That is a fabulous period
Prefiero aquéllas en el escaparate	I prefer those in the store window

1.3 *Éste* and *aquél* = the latter and the former

A further difference between *éste* and its variants, and *aquél* and its variants is that *éste*, etc., has the value of *the latter*, while *aquél* has the value of *the former*:

Hay una lucha entre los aztecas y los españoles. Éstos tienen cañones en tanto aquéllos . . .	There is a struggle between the Aztecs and the Spaniards. The latter have cannons while the former . . .

1.4 Neuter pronouns

The neuter pronoun forms, ***esto***, ***eso*** and ***aquello*** are also used but only absolutely: that is to say, they are never found associated with nouns. They do not refer to anything specific, persons or things. They apply to statements and abstract ideas:

¿Lees esto?	Do you read this?
Eso es	That's it
Eso me parece increíble	That seems incredible to me
Aquello del vecino que pierde . . .	That business of the neighbor who loses . . .
¿Puedes solucionar aquello de tu padre?	¿Can you sort out your father's trouble/ business?

Eso may be substituted for **aquello** in the last two examples.

Ejercicios Level 1

i **Change the definite article to the correct demonstrative adjective e.g. *este*, *esta*, *estos*, *estas* (there may be more than one solution)**

Example

Mi primo quiere comprar las corbatas de ante > Mi primo quiere comprar estas corbatas de ante

a Compro los periódicos en el quiosco
b Manuel va a comprar las naranjas
c El hombre olvida los boletos (**M**) / billetes
d Los lentes (**M**) que hallo son de Jorge
e Las gafas que encuentro son de Juan
f Los jóvenes juegan fútbol (**M**) / al fútbol
g Hay que recoger a María en la estación
h Los aviones nuevos son muy cómodos
i El viaje de Barcelona a Valencia es muy cómodo
j Las fotos de Oaxaca son muy interesantes

ii **Change the demonstrative adjectives *este*, etc., to *ese*, *esa*, *esos*, *esas***

Example

Ha recibido esta carta de su hermana > Ha recibido esa carta de su hermana

a Saqué estas fotos en Málaga
b Estas naranjas son bastante caras
c ¿Pasa este tren por Córdoba?
d Esta lección es muy fácil
e Me pregunto qué hay en este paquete
f Voy a venderle los relojes a este cliente

iii **Complete the following with *aquél*, *aquélla*, etc., as in the example**
No quieren estas manzanas, sino (_) > . . . sino aquéllas

a No quieren este chocolate, sino (_)
b No quiero estos sillones, sino (_)
c No prefiero este carro (**M**) / coche, sino (_)
d No me gusta esta alfombra, sino (_)
e No compraré este disco, sino (_)
f No prefiero estas macetas, sino (_)

iv Complete the following with *éste*, *ésta*, etc

Example

Aquella computadora (**M**) es más rápida que (_) > . . . que ésta

a Ese ordenador es más caro que (_)
b Aquella lavadora es más eficiente que (_)
c Aquel camión (**M**) es más lento que (_)
d Esos mapas son más detallados que (_)
e Aquellas flores no son tan bonitas como (_)
f Esos sillones son más cómodos que (_)

v Paired activity

Objective – To use the demonstrative adjective with a noun, and then to refer to the noun with a demonstrative pronoun

Method – A asks B if (s)he can use/see, etc., "*este objeto*" = "*this object.*" B says "No" but that A can use, etc., "*ése/aquél*" = "that object," or B can see "that object" = *ése/aquél*

Examples

PREGUNTA:	¿Puedo usar este libro?
RESPUESTA:	No, pero puedes usar ése/aquél
PREGUNTA:	¿Entiendes a este autor?
RESPUESTA:	No, pero entiendo a ése/aquél
PREGUNTA:	¿Necesitas estos papeles?
RESPUESTA:	No, pero necesito ésos/aquéllos

Use the following combinations of verbs + nouns, or invent your own (by unit 20 you are doubtless able to do this):

abrir ventana, cerrar puerta, ver al chico, comprar flores, leer periódico, hacer cama, lavar pantalón, limpiar el carro, entender chiste, dibujar florero, leer libro, querer caramelo

Level **2**

2.1 **Demonstrative adjectives after the noun** (*Adjetivos demostrativos que siguen al nombre*)

2.2 **Uses of the pronoun *el*** (*Usos del pronombre **el***)

2.1 Demonstrative adjectives after the noun

The adjectival ***este***, ***ese*** and ***aquel*** and their variants may come after the noun. In these cases, they frequently, but not always, suggest a pejorative or ironic touch.

La carretera esa es muy peligrosa	That road is very dangerous
El chico aquel nunca estudia	That boy never studies
La lavadora esta funciona fatal, es un cacharro	This washing machine is hopeless, it's a piece of junk
la taimada esa	that sly so and so

2.2 Uses of the pronoun *el*

i *El*, in its several forms, when used as a pronoun, does not accompany a noun, but serves to avoid the repetition of one; it is equivalent to the English *that*, *those*, *the one*, *the ones*, referring to something already mentioned or understood:

*Compré mi computadora (**M**) y la que tiene mi hija*	I bought my computer and the one my daughter has / my daughter's
Me gusta mi ordenador y el que compraste	I like my computer and the one you bought
*Rompí la pluma (**M**) mía y la de mi cuate (**M**) / amigo*	I broke my pen and that of my friend / my friend's
Son muy bonitas las plantas en el jardín y las de al lado	The plants in the yard/garden and those at the side are very attractive

ii When a relative pronoun follows, *el*, *los*, *la*, *las* are used instead of the personal pronouns *él*, *los*, *la* and *las*:

El que habló ayer es colombiano	The one who spoke yesterday is Colombian
La que nos encontramos es muy rica	The one we met is very rich
Los que murieron eran canadienses	Those who died were Canadians
Las que te ayudaron son muy majas	Those who helped you are very nice

iii But when the relative following is governed by a preposition, *aquél* is more usual as an antecedent than *el*, when referring to persons:

Aquélla a quien he dado el regalo . . .	The person / She to whom I gave the present . . .
Aquéllos con quienes discutiste . . .	Those with whom you had an argument . . .

Exercises Level **2**

i Cambia *ese*, *esa*, etc., a *el*, *la*, etc. + noun + *ese*, *esa*, etc., como en el ejemplo

Esa carretera es muy ancha > La carretera esa es muy ancha

a Esos libros son muy pesados

b Esta cocina está muy sucia

c Ese ordenador no funciona bien

d Estas sillas están casi todas rotas

e ¿Qué vas a hacer con estas plantas?

f ¿Por qué tiraste esos botes?

g Esa computadora (**M**) soluciona todos los problemas

h No comí ese plato por que no tenía sabor

ii Completa con *el*, *la*, *los*, *las* como en el ejemplo

Mis amigos y (_) de Juan fueron al teatro > Mis amigos y los de Juan fueron al teatro

a El auto (**M**) de Ana y (_) de Guillermo están en el garage (**M**) / garaje

b Los cuadernos míos y (_) de mi prima están estropeados

c Mi radio (**M**) y (_) de mi primo son nuevos

d Mi radio y (_) de mi sobrina son caras
e Le di a mi amigo mi toalla y (_) de Jesús
f Prefiero mi departamento (**M**) a (_) de Armando
g ¿Qué vas a hacer con mi bicicleta y (_) de Carlos?
h No me convencen las ideas de Pedro y (_) de Roberto

Unit 21 (*Unidad 21*)
Adjectives (*Los adjetivos*)

Level **1**

1.1 **Agreement of adjectives** (*Concordancia de adjetivos*)
1.2 **Apocopation (shortened form)** (*Apócope*)
1.3 **Position of adjectives** (*Posición* / *Ubicación* (**M**) *de adjetivos*)

1.1 Agreement of adjectives

Adjectives in Spanish, like the definite and indefinite articles, vary in form to indicate gender and number, taking those of the nouns to which they relate. This is called *agreeing* with the noun. There are a few rare exceptions.

Adjectives form their plurals in both genders in the same way as nouns. The distinction of gender depends upon the following two principles:

i The greater number of adjectives end in *o* in the masculine, and *a* in the feminine singular, and they both take *s* in the plural:

fresco, fresca, frescos, frescas	fresh, cool
blanco, blanca, blancos, blancas	white
negro, negra, negros, negras	black

ii Those which do not end in *o* in the masculine singular have the same ending for both genders, and the plurals are the same for both genders:

cortés, corteses	courteous, polite	*dulce, dulces*	sweet
suave, suaves	soft, gentle, smooth	*útil, útiles*	useful
belga, belgas	Belgian	*azteca, aztecas*	aztec

iii Adjectives which end in a consonant, and signify nationality, add *a* in the feminine:

inglés, inglesa	English	*francés, francesa*	French
alemán, alemana	German	*escocés, escocesa*	Scottish
holandés, holandesa	Dutch	*andaluz, andaluza*	Andalusian

Notice that, quite logically, the feminine form does not take a written accent.

It also disappears in the plural of both masculine and feminine forms:

ingleses, alemanes, daneses, holandeses, franceses, escoceses, andaluces

iv Those ending in *án* or *ón* add *a* to the feminine:

holgazán, holgazana	lazy
preguntón, preguntona	inquisitive
respondón, respondona	nervy, cheeky

Notice that, quite logically, the written accent disappears in the feminine form, and that in the plural forms it also disappears: *holgazanes/holgazanas, preguntones/preguntonas, respondones/respondonas*

v Those ending in *or* and which do not have a comparative value (see unit 28 and [**vi**] below) add *a* to the feminine:

emprendedor, emprendedora	enterprising
hablador, habladora	talkative

vi The plural forms are:

emprendedores/emprendedoras, habladores/habladoras

Such words having a comparative value are the same in both genders:

exterior/exteriores	exterior	*peor/peores*	worse
inferior/inferiores	inferior/lower	*posterior/posteriores*	later, following
mayor/mayores	bigger	*superior/superiores*	superior, uppity
mejor/mejores	better	*ulterior/ulteriores*	further, ulterior
menor/menores	smaller		

vii Adjectives of nationality are used to represent the language or native of the country in question. In the latter case, they are considered as nouns. However, as both adjectives and nouns, the initial letter is in lower case:

Hablo inglés/portugués/español	I speak English/Portuguese/Spanish
Este señor es italiano/mexicano	This gentleman is Italian/Mexican
La venezolana habla francés	The Venezuelan lady speaks French

1.2 Apocopation (shortened form)

i Six adjectives assume a shortened form when standing immediately before certain nouns. This shortened form is called apocopation:

bueno	good	*grande*	big, great
malo	bad, naughty	*santo*	holy, saint
tercero	third	*primero*	first

Bueno, **malo**, **primero** and **tercero** lose the final *o* when immediately preceding any masculine singular noun:

*Tienes un buen carro (**M**)*	You have a good car
Hace buen tiempo	It's good weather
Éste es un mal vino	This is a bad wine
Hace mal tiempo	It's bad weather
estar de buen/mal humor	to be in a good/bad mood

el primer hombre	the first man
el tercer coche	the third car
San Pedro	Saint Peter
San Pablo	Saint Paul

Exceptions: **Santo** *Tomás* – Saint Thomas, **Santo** *Domingo* – Saint Dominic

ii But, of course, in the feminine form we have:

una buena comida	a good meal
una mala carretera	a bad road
la primera página	the first page
la tercera palabra	the third word

iii *Grande* drops the final *de* when it precedes a noun, masculine or feminine:

un gran amigo / general	a great friend / general
una gran casa / ciudad	a big house / city
una gran victoria	a great victory

However, **grande** becomes **grandes** before a plural noun:

los grandes almacenes	the department store
los grandes bancos	the big banks
las grandes actrices del cine	the great movie actresses

1.3   Position of adjectives

(See also "Word order," unit 29)
As far as the position of Spanish adjectives is concerned, they often follow the noun, but this is far from clear. For all general purposes, it may be safely stated that the adjective does follow the noun, at least in speech. **You are referred also to level 2 for clarification on this matter**. For our purposes here, the adjective follows the noun when it denotes a physical quality (color, size, shape, strength) or nationality, or when nationality is referred to.

Examples where the adjective clearly follows the noun:

café negro / americano	black / weak coffee
un hombre de raza blanca	a man of white race
Es una mujer alta	She's a tall woman
un hombre / vino fuerte	a strong man / wine

There are many adjectives of an intermediate character which may be used either way, the Spanish speaker being guided in their location by her/his own ideas on meaning, style, stress and so on. (**For the different values or meanings of certain adjectives when placed before or after the noun see level 2.**)

Exercises Level **1**

i Replace the first noun by those in brackets and make the agreement with the adjective

Example

el carro rojo (casa/árboles) > la casa roja / los árboles rojos

a el sarape amarillo (poncho/faldas/bolsas/bolso/cuadernos/chaqueta)
b la blusa chica (camión/guitarras/sarape/niños/alfombra)
c las cortinas largas (pluma/calles/sarapes/regla/pintura/pasillos)
d la maceta grande (coches/perlas/vestidos/sala/cómodas/árboles)
e el jardín rectangular (libro/alfombra/mesitas/radio/cuadernos)
f una toalla suave (pendiente/pelo/colores/carácter/garbanzos/temperaturas)
g un chico mexicano (chica/comida/bebidas/muchachos)
h la mejor temperatura (notas/carro/vacaciones/computadora)

ii Change the position of the adjective as in the example

Hacemos el ejercicio primero > Hacemos el primer ejercicio

a Pedro es un carpintero bueno
b Estudio el libro tercero
c El doctor es un hombre grande
d Voy a asistir al curso primero
e Pedro no es un albañil malo

f Juan es un actor bueno
g Es una casa grande
h Quiero seguir el curso tercero
i Es el martes primero del mes
j Arturo es un escritor malo

iii Put the words in their correct order

Example

café prefiero negro un > Prefiero un café negro

a atletas raza tiene negra la buenos
b blanco novia un la lleva vestido
c Mayor necesariamente mayor no calle Calle la es la
d vinos gustan me no fuertes los
e menú un apetece italiano te menú o un español?
f de verdes caen hojas las árboles los
g a puedo departamentos (**M**) / pisos no superiores subir los
h tacones le llevar gusta altos
i argentino el buen mejor mundo del es equipo un
j país tiene sistema buen financiero este un

iv Paired activity (a)
Objective – To make the adjective agree with the noun it qualifies.
Method – A says a noun and B qualifies it with an adjective. The roles can be reversed.
The noun may be masculine or feminine or plural.

Example

A: casa
B: blanca
B: flores
A: azules
A: cortinas
B: verdes

Here are some nouns and adjectives that you may use:

Nouns: sarape (**M**), bolsa, regalo, camión, canción, niño, calle, avenida, carro, coche, maceta, árbol, pelo, piel, carretera, montaña, mar, playa, zapato, calcetín, hombre
Adjectives: rojo, amarillo, blanco, negro, grande, pequeño, alto, bajo, americano, mexicano, español, inglés, rápido, cansado, fuerte, cómodo, difícil, fácil, largo, ancho

Class activity (b)

The class is divided into two groups (A and B). One member of the class asks the whole class in quick succession which adjective could qualify a noun (s)he provides. The group which calls out a correct adjective wins a point. The first group to ten wins the contest. The member giving out the nouns may also use plural nouns, and those giving the answers must offer an adjective correctly formed in the plural. Another class member keeps the score (*el tanteo*) in Spanish and records each mark on the board. This member calls out in Spanish: *(El) equipo A/B (tiene) cero puntos / un punto / dos puntos / tres puntos, etc*. Why Spanish speakers say *cero puntos*, or *cero grados** for that matter, is anyone's guess. Please tell the author if you can work it out. In the heat of battle, do not fail to observe accurate pronunciation.

*It's just as illogical in English: *zero points / degrees*

Level **2**

2.1 **Invariable adjectives** (*Adjetivos invariables*)
2.2 **Adjectives used as adverbs** (*Adjetivos usados como adverbios*)
2.3 **Invariability of two adjectives together** (*Invariabilidad de dos adjetivos juntos*)
2.4 **Variability of the meaning of adjectives according to their position**
   (*Variabilidad del sentido del adjetivo según su posición / ubicación* [**M**])
2.5 **Location of two or more adjectives** (*Posición / Ubicación* [**M**] *de dos o más adjetivos*)
2.6 **Nouns functioning like adjectives** (*Nombres que desempeñan la función de adjetivos*)
2.7 ***Lo* + adjective** (*Lo + adjetivo*)
2.8 ***El* + adjective** (*El + adjetivo*)

2.1   Invariable adjectives

A small number of adjectives are invariable. In other words, they do not change according to gender or number. The reason is largely because they are not really adjectives but nouns, or some other part of speech. The following is a short list of such adjectives:

escarlata	scarlet
hembra	female (used of animals)
hirviendo	boiling
macho	male (used of animals)
malva	mauve
modelo	model (suggesting perfection)
naranja	orange
rosa	pink
tabú	taboo
violeta	violet

Ejemplos

un color escarlata	a scarlet color
los elefantes / las ballenas hembra	the female elephants/whales
la ballena macho	the male whale
una solución modelo	a model solution (i.e. for this book)
tonos rosa	pink tones

There is some uncertainty here. For example, ***soluciones modelos*** is perfectly acceptable. (See compound nouns in unit 2, level 2, on nouns.)

2.2   Adjectives used as adverbs

i A good number of adjectives may be used as adverbs. Here is a short list:

Huele (oler) muy rico	It smells very nice
Trabaja duro	She works hard
hablar alto / bajo / claro / fuerte	to speak loudly/softly/clearly/loudly
ver claro	to see clearly
cenar fuerte	to have a big evening meal
pegar fuerte	to hit hard
jugar limpio	to play clean
El viento sopla fuerte	The wind is blowing hard

ii You will most certainly and frequently come across ***rápido*** and ***lento*** used as adverbs, notably in speech. **This is a practice not to be copied in your early stages.**

Ejemplos

Habla rápido (instead of ***rápidamente***)	He speaks quick(ly)
*El tope (**M**) obliga a la gente a manejar lento* (instead of ***lentamente***)	The speed retarder forces people to drive slow(ly)

2.3   Invariability of two adjectives together

When two adjectives are together they become invariable. This is especially true of colors:

una falda azul pálido	a pale blue skirt
ojos azul oscuro	dark blue eyes
una chaqueta marrón oscuro	a dark brown jacket

2.4   Variability of the meaning of adjectives according to their position

There are some adjectives which have a different meaning, according to whether they precede or follow the noun. Generally speaking, the following adjective is invested with a greater weight or strength than when it precedes the noun. (A fuller treatment of this question appears in unit 29.1.4, on word order.) The following list offers some of the most commonly found adjectives varying in meaning:

antiguo	costumbres antiguas	old customs
	un antiguo profesor	a former teacher
cierto	indicios ciertos	sure signs (i.e. definite)
	ciertas ideas	certain ideas (i.e. some)
diferente	cuatro hermanos diferentes	four different brothers
	diferentes ideas	different/several ideas
distinto	ideas distintas	distinct ideas
	distintas ideas	various ideas
grande	una casa grande	a big house
	un gran escritor	a great writer
medio	el hombre medio	the average man
	la clase media	the middle class
	el dedo medio	the middle finger
	medio litro	half a liter
nuevo	una canción nueva	a new song (just composed)
	Compramos una nueva casa	We buy a new (another) house
pobre	un barrio pobre	a poor district
	¡Pobre hombre!	Poor (unfortunate) man!
único	Es hija única	She's the only daughter/child
	el único problema	the only problem

2.5 Location of two or more adjectives

When two adjectives relate to one noun, each is located independently, according to its own value; one may come before, one after, both before or both after. Generally speaking, two adjectives qualifying a noun would come after, but this is by no means a hard and fast rule (see unit 29 on word order).

Un artista pobre y desgraciado	A poor, unfortunate artist
Tiene una capa negra y larga	She has a long, black cape
una nación libre e independiente	a free and independent nation
Tiene una casa pequeña y bonita	He has a small, attractive house

2.6 Nouns functioning like adjectives

It should be remembered that, contrary to English, Spanish nouns do not function like adjectives. That is the tradition. However, there is an ever-increasing number of nouns attached to nouns which produce compound nouns. The second noun in these cases does function like an adjective. (See unit 2 on compound nouns.)

To deal with the extremely common practice of two adjoining nouns in English, the usual way in Spanish, as with all Romance languages, is to place the equivalent of **of** between the two nouns, **de** in Spanish:

una bufanda de lana	a woollen scarf
una casa de madera	a wooden house
una estatua de bronce	a bronze statue
una escalera de mármol	a marble staircase

2.7 Lo + adjective

A very common feature of Spanish is the use of **lo** with an adjective, for which there is no equivalent in English. This construction has to be translated by a variety of phrases, such as *what is, the characteristic feature, the most important point*, etc. Here is a collection of adjectives used with **lo**:

Lo barato es caro	What is cheap turns out to be expensive
Lo americano es de moda	American styles are in fashion
Lo absurdo no tiene por qué ser feo	The absurd does not have to be ugly
Lo mío para mí solo, y lo de los demás, para repartir	What's mine is mine, and what remains for the rest you can share out
Lo importante es que venga hoy	The important point is he come today
Lo curioso es que los mexicanos no usan esta palabra	The funny thing is that Mexicans don't use this word

The last two examples may be extended to:

Lo bueno / malo / mejor / correcto / normal / necesario / imposible, etc., *es . . .*	The good/bad/best/correct/normal/ necessary/impossible, etc., thing is . . .

2.8 El + adjective

Adjectives may also be used with the definite article in the following way, and here again the English needs to add something, usually *one*:

Me gusta el color rojo pero no el verde	I like the red color but not the green one
Quiero el grande	I want the big one
Necesitamos el mediano	We need the medium-sized one
*Prefiero el chico (**M**) / pequeño*	I prefer the little one

Exercises Level **2**

i Completa las siguientes frases con la forma correcta de la palabra invariable que convenga. En algunos casos puede haber más de una solución

Ejemplo
La bebida tenía un color (_) poco agradable > . . . un color escarlata poco agradable

a El agua (_) es muy peligrosa para los niños
b Son rinocerontes (_)
c Es difícil saber si es una rata (_)
d Los pájaros (_) cuidan a sus pequeños en nidos
e Las soluciones (_) de este libro son útiles (We hope so)
f Su madre compró unas cobijas (**M**) / mantas (_)
g Es una palabra (_) que es muy grosera
h El sastre tenía telas (_) muy parecidas al rojo

ii Completa las frases con la misma palabra, usándola dos veces, según el ejemplo

Mi (_) profesor vivía en una casa (_) > Mi antiguo profesor vivía en una casa antigua

a Me daba (_) vergüenza aprovechar los indicios (_)
b Hay (_) soluciones pero tienes aquí dos posibilidades completamente (_)
c Es un (_) hombre que tiene una finca (_)
d El hombre (_) suele tomar (_) litro
e La (_) chica no pertenecía a una familia (_)
f Mi (_) consejo es que hables con su hija (_)

iii Contesta según el ejemplo, recurriendo a *pero* y la expresión *lo* + adjetivo que puedes elegir

Ejemplo

¿Es un buen dentista? > Sí, pero lo malo es que es impuntual

a ¿Es muy grande la universidad?
b ¿Les gusta la Ciudad de México?
c ¿Es muy trabajadora Adriana?
d ¿Son muy ricos tus primos?
e ¿Has leído mucho de este autor?
f ¿Crees que son muy abusados (**M**) / listos?
g ¿Te dio tu domingo (**M** = *pocket money*) tu padre?
h ¿Comprabas muchos libros en aquel entonces?
i ¿Me habrías ayudado si yo hubiera pedido tu ayuda?
j ¿Irás conmigo al partido de fútbol esta tarde?

Unit 22 *(Unidad 22)*

Personal or distinctive *a* (*La preposición "a" con el complemento directo*)

Level **1**

1.1 **Personal *a* when used for persons** (*La preposición a con un complemento directo*)

1.2 **Personal *a* when used with collective nouns** (*La a con nombres colectivos*)

1.3 **Personal *a* when used with animals** (*La a con animales*)

1.4 **Personal *a* when used with proper names** (*La a con nombres propios*)

1.5 **When personal *a* is <u>not</u> used** (*Cuando no se usa la a*)

1.1 Personal *a* when used for persons

In English, the distinction between a noun as subject and a noun as object is shown by its location in the sentence. In *John reads the book*, *John* is the subject and *book* is the object. *John* comes before *book*. In Latin, this was shown by what we call case endings; that is to say the endings of words changed according to their relationship with each other, and word order was not so important. In Spanish, and much more than in French or English, but similar to Italian, location has about as little effect on the meaning as in Latin. Many Spanish speakers can find themselves therefore in considerable difficulty in distinguishing between subject and object, and do not always succeed as clearly as we do in English or French.

The only device in Spanish for distinguishing a noun as direct object when referring to persons is by placing the preposition *a* before it. But, as the preposition *a* is regularly used for the indirect object (*Le doy el libro a Juan* = I give the book to Juan), most Spanish speakers end up not knowing whether the preposition *a* involves a direct or indirect object. In other words, they often fail to see the difference between *Veo a Juan* (I see Juan) and *Le doy el libro a Juan*. They think erroneously that *Juan* in *Veo a Juan* is an indirect object. The situation is further complicated because they do not have a suitable descriptive equivalent for what we call the "personal *a*." French or Italian speakers do not have an equivalent expression either. The expression "personal *a*" in English therefore helps us over a very difficult hurdle. Here are the main uses of the "personal *a*."

1.2 Personal *a* when used with persons and collective nouns

i The personal or distinctive *a* applies primarily to nouns representing determinate, known persons:

*Veo **a** Pedro*	I see Pedro
*Busco **a** la chica*	I am looking for the girl
*Quiere visitar **a** mi hija*	He wants to visit my daughter
*Lleva **a** sus hijos a la estación*	She takes her children/sons to the station

ii If the personal noun is collective, the personal *a* is often, but not always, used. However, it is safer always to use it in these circumstances:

Ana mima a su familia	Ana spoils her family
Llaman a la policía	They call the police
El político critica al gobierno	The politician criticizes the government

iii The application of the personal *a* extends to authors, painters, etc., i.e. all those in the public domain:

Leo a Cervantes con frecuencia	I read Cervantes regularly
Imita a Diego Rivera	He copies Diego Rivera
El público aplaude a la estrella	The audience applauds the star
La empresa despide a cinco obreros	The company dismisses five workers

1.3 Personal *a* when used with animals

When the direct object noun represents an animal, regarded as intelligent or rational, and especially if it belongs to a family, the personal *a* is required:

Llaman al perrito	They call the dog
Se pasa un rato acariciando al gato	She spends some time stroking the cat

1.4 Personal *a* when used with proper names

The personal *a* is also needed before proper names of persons:

Envío a Diego en su lugar	I'll send Diego in her place
Admira a Andrés	She admires Andrés/Andrew

1.5 When personal *a* is <u>not</u> used

(But see level 2.3.)
The personal *a* is **not** used when the object is an insignificant animal, or an inanimate object:

*El gato agarra (**M**) / coge (not in **M**) un ratón*	The cat catches a mouse
El niño persigue una mariposa	The child chases the butterfly
Como la carne	I eat the meat

Exercises Level **1**

i Change as in the example

Esperamos a Jorge (María / el niño) > Esperamos a María / al niño

a Vemos a los muchachos (Luisa / los señores / Manuel / la maestra / las niñas / los pajaritos)

b Llevan a las chicas (sus amigos / la niña / Carlos / las muchachas)

c Necesitas a Juan (el doctor / mis amigas / el muchacho / los alumnos)

d Oigo a los niños (la muchacha / Jorge / mis cuates [**M**] / el bebé / el gato)

e Traemos a nuestros amigos (nuestros papás [**M**] / mi abuela / tus primas / los perritos)

ii Paired activity

Objective – To practice the use of the personal *a*

Method – A gives B a verb and a noun as a direct object. B has to make a sentence with the verb and the noun, using the personal *a* when necessary. If A is smart enough, (s)he will provide some nouns where the *a* is not used. So B, be careful! (*¡cuidado!*)

Examples

A: Ver + mujer

B: Veo a la mujer

A: Admirar + pianista

B: Admiro al / a la pianista

A: Golpear + pared

B: Golpeo la pared

Here are some verbs and nouns A can use:

leer, contar, llevar, buscar, lavar, preparar, llamar, ayudar, contestar, preguntar, querer, observar, preferir, conocer, tocar, limpiar, avisar hombre, médico/doctor, enfermera, profesor, periódico, platos, gesto, ciudad, flores, guitarra, recámara (**M**) / habitación, amigo/a, familia, tío, maestro, vecinas, policía

Afterwards, you all gather together to discuss your sentences.

 Level **2**

2.1 **Use and non-use of personal *a*** (*Uso y omisión de a*)

2.2 **Use of personal *a* with personification** (*Uso de a con personificación*)

2.3 **Omission of personal *a*** (*Omisión de la a*)

2.4 **Personal *a* used with direct and indirect objects** (*Uso de a con objetos directo e indirecto*)

2.5 **Miscellaneous features** (*Varios detalles*)

2.6 **Personal *a* with *nadie, alguien, quien*** (*La a con nadie, alguien, quien*)

2.7 **More possible confusion over the personal *a*** (*Posibilidad de más confusión con la a*)

2.1 Use and non-use of personal *a*

In all cases, the employment of the personal **a** before a direct object denoting a person depends largely on how the speaker views the person. In other words, if the speaker knows the person referred to, (s)he will use the personal **a**, but if the person alluded to is not known, the **a** is not often used. Compare these two sets of cases:

Busco al doctor	I am looking for the physician/doctor
Busco un doctor	I am looking for a physician/doctor
Estoy esperando al cliente	I'm waiting for the client
Estoy esperando un cliente	I'm waiting for a client

It is of course conceivable that in all these cases **a** is used, but the further away the object is, figuratively speaking, the less likely it is that the personal **a** is used.

2.2 Use of personal *a* with personification

When the direct object is personified, the personal **a** is frequently, but not always, used. Particularly common here is the use of ***patria***, ***nación*** and ***pueblo***, especially the latter, which contains a suggestion of human beings:

Estos soldados honran a la patria	These soldiers honor the nation
Juraron defender a la nación	They swore to defend the nation
Las nuevas medidas pretenden contentar al pueblo	The new measures aim to satisfy the people
Las aves saludan a la Aurora	The birds salute the Dawn

NB   Once, towns and countries were included in this category, but this is no longer the case.

2.3 Omission of personal *a*

i The personal *a* is omitted when it would conflict with another *a* which has a true prepositional value:

El general convocó los oficiales a una conferencia	The general called the officers to a conference

Compare the two following sentences:

Abandonaron al hombre	They abandoned the man
Abandonaron el hombre a sus remordimientos	They abandoned the man to his remorse

ii When the verb has a direct and indirect object, the direct object does not take the personal *a*, thus avoiding confusion or ambiguity:

Recomendó al gobernador su hijo, Don José	He recommended his son, Don José, to the governor

Presentaré mi hermana a la señora de Vargas	I'll introduce my sister to Sra Vargas
El soldado entregó su prisionero al capitán	The soldier handed over his prisoner to the captain

2.4 Personal *a* used with direct and indirect objects

When both subject and object denote things, the object takes the personal **a**. Otherwise, confusion and ambiguity would arise. We are now in the realm of word order (see unit 29). Compare the following four sentences:

El silencio (subject) *sigue al ruido* (object)	Silence follows the noise
Al ruido (object) *sigue el silencio* (subject)	Silence follows the noise
El ruido (subject) *sigue al silencio* (object)	Noise follows the silence
Al silencio (object) *sigue el ruido* (subject)	Noise follows the silence

Compare likewise the following four sentences. (From the first four sentences above, you can work out the subject and object in each sentence below.)

El yate alcanzará al vapor	The yacht will overtake the steamer
Al vapor alcanzará el yate	The yacht will overtake the steamer
El vapor alcanzará al yate	The steamer will overtake the yacht
Al yate alcanzará el vapor	The steamer will overtake the yacht

2.5 Miscellaneous features

i When one of the terms is a person, which is usually the case, danger of ambiguity does not arise, because the person as object is accompanied by **a**.

Compare the two following sentences:

Por fin venció el joven (subject) *su pasión* (object) *por el juego*	The young man finally overcame his passion for gambling
Por fin venció al joven (object) *su pasión* (subject) *por el juego*	The passion for gambling finally overcame the young man

ii Verbs of naming, calling, considering, etc., which may take two direct objects differentiate one of these objects by the personal **a** in the following way:

¿Llaman música a este jaleo?	Do they call this ruckus music?
Consideramos pura pérdida de tiempo a la lectura de estas revistas	We consider the reading of these magazines a pure waste of time

The true object, or thing asserted, in the first case, **jaleo**, and in the second case, **lectura**, is preceded by the personal **a**.

2.6 Personal *a* with *nadie, alguien, quien*

The personal **a** is always used before **alguien**, **nadie** and **quien** when these words function as direct objects, even though they may suggest uncertainty over the person referred to:

¿Vas a invitar a alguien?	Are you going to invite someone?
No veo a nadie	I can't see anyone
¿A quién llamas?	Whom are you calling?

2.7 More possible confusion over the personal *a*

To return to the confusion generated by the personal ***a***, personal pronouns are a special case in point. Again, it is difficult for Spanish speakers who are not language conscious to know whether the following examples include pronouns (***le***, ***les***) as indirect objects or direct objects, largely because, in order to stress the pronoun, a disjunctive form of it is used before the verb:

A él le interesa el libro	The book interests him
A ella le encanta la ópera	She loves opera
A ellas les atrae la idea de . . .	They are attracted by the idea of . . .

This issue is further complicated by the following two examples based on the reflexive ***se*** (see the use of reflexives in unit 14, level 2).

Se vio el hombre en el espejo	The man saw himself in the mirror
Se le vio al hombre en el espejo	The man was seen in the mirror

Here, the reflexive ***se*** dispels any ambiguity over who is seeing whom.

Exercises Level 2

i **Sustituye un nombre por un pronombre como en el ejemplo. Puedes elegir cualquier nombre (*noun*) a condición de que sea una persona. Puede haber una gran variedad de respuestas**

Los/les oigo > Oigo a los alumnos

a Los necesito	g ¿Los acoges?
b Las ven	h Las traigo
c ¿La quieres?	i ¿Las oyes?
d Los oímos	j No lo/le entiendo
e La están esperando	k Los llevo a todos en mi carro
f Lo recibo	l Los admiramos

ii **Pon las siguientes palabras en su orden correcto. Ten en cuenta que faltan la preposición *a* y los artículos definidos en la mayoría de los casos, y que te toca insertarlos en su lugar correcto cuando sea necesario, y que puede haber más de una solución**

Ejemplos

atacó león tigre > El tigre atacó al león / El león atacó al tigre / Al león le atacó el tigre / Al tigre le atacó el león

ver familia quería hija > La hija quería ver a la familia / La familia quería ver a la hija

a verbo pronombre sigue
b doctor hallamos (**M**) sepa hijo nuestro un curar que no
c ver quería su esposa sus hijos y

 d ganso peló cocinera

 e tres mataron faisanes ciervos dos y

 f caballo comprar quisiera yo un

 g vender quería su caballo él

 h director hija María presentaron su

 i hijos colegio llevaba sus la madre

 j carro carro (**M**) rápido lento rebasó (**M**)

 k gato perro persigue

 l juez no político sobornar pudo

m quién saber llamaba quería

 n nadie yo veía no

 o le en si conocía pregunté colegio alguien

iii Actividad en parejas

Objetivo – Practicar el uso de "a" con nombres como objeto directo

Método – Se les elige a dos miembros de la clase. Escriben en el pizarrón (M) / la pizarra seis series de palabras mezcladas que contienen un verbo y un objeto directo que es una persona. Omiten adrede (*deliberately*) la *a*. Intentar no crear frases largas (seis o siete palabras como máximo). La clase tiene que reconstruir la frase, poniendo las palabras en su orden correcto y añadiendo la *a* en su lugar apropiado.

Ejemplos

Se escribe en el pizarrón:	consulta madre mi médico el
La clase reconstruye:	Mi madre consulta *a*l médico
Se escribe en el pizarrón:	amiga tu francesa conocemos
La clase reconstruye:	Conocemos *a* tu amiga francesa
Se escribe . . .	carro hombre el el maneja
La clase . . .	El hombre maneja el carro
	(**no *a* here**)

Se le corresponde al profesor intervenir si quiere.

Unit 23 *(Unidad 23)*
Prepositions (*Las preposiciones*)

Level **1**

1.1 **The basic prepositions** (*Las preposiciones básicas*)

1.2 **Uses of** *a* (*Usos de* ***a***)

1.3 **Uses of** *ante* (*Usos de* ***ante***)

1.4 **Uses of** *bajo* (*Usos de* ***bajo***)

1.5 **Uses of** *con* (*Usos de* ***con***)

1.6 **Uses of** *contra* (*Usos de* ***contra***)

1.7 **Uses of** *de* (*Usos de* ***de***)

1.8 **Uses of** *desde* (*Usos de* ***desde***)

1.9 **Uses of** *durante* (*Usos de* ***durante***)

1.10 **Uses of** *en* (*Usos de* ***en***)

1.11 **Uses of** *entre* (*Usos de* ***entre***)

1.12 **Uses of** *excepto* (*Usos de* ***excepto***)

1.13 **Uses of** *hacia* (*Usos de* ***hacia***)

1.14 **Uses of** *hasta* (*Usos de* ***hasta***)

1.15 **Uses of** *mediante* (*Usos de* ***mediante***)

1.16 **Uses of** *salvo* (*Usos de* ***salvo***)

1.17 **Uses of** *según* (*Usos de* ***según***)

1.18 **Uses of** *sin* (*Usos de* ***sin***)

1.19 **Uses of** *sobre* (*Usos de* ***sobre***)

1.20 **Uses of** *tras* (*Usos de* ***tras***)

1.1 The basic prepositions

The simplest use of prepositions is to express the relations of things to each other with respect to time and place. Such prepositions in English are *in, out, before, under, over*. They extend, however, to many other relations, and especially to the relations between adjectives or verbs and the nouns or pronouns to which they apply.

There are two sorts of prepositions in Spanish: simple and compound. The simple ones will be treated in level 1, while the compound ones will be dealt with in level 2, together with more complex expressions.

The simple prepositions are:

a	at, to, in	*hacia*	towards, about, for
ante	before	*hasta*	until, to, up to

bajo	under		*mediante*	by means of, through
con	with		*para*	for (see separate unit 24)
contra	against		*por*	for, by (see separate unit 24)
de	of, from		*salvo*	except, save
desde	from, since		*según*	according to
durante	during		*sin*	without
en	in, into, at, on		*sobre*	on, about, over
entre	between, among		*tras*	after, behind
excepto	except			

1.2 Uses of *a*

i *a* = *to, at, in*:

Vamos a Nueva York	We are going to New York
Llegamos a Los Angeles	We arrive in Los Angeles
Se sienta a la mesa/puerta	She sits at the table/door

ii *a* in time expressions:

a las tres de la tarde	at three in the afternoon
al mediodía	at midday
al día siguiente	on the following day
a la noche/mañana/tarde	tonight / tomorrow morning / this afternoon/evening
a principios de año/mes	at the beginning of the year/month
a mediados de semana/mes/año	in the middle of the week/month/year
a finales de mes/año	at the end of the month/year
a los diecinueve años	at nineteen years of age
a los cinco minutos	five minutes later
al poco rato	a little later
al mismo tiempo	at the same time
a tiempo	in time
a primera vista	at first sight

iii *a* expressing rate:

día a día	day by day
paso a paso	step by step
a docenas/millares	by the dozen/thousand
tres veces a la semana	three times a week
a razón de dos por persona	at the rate of two per person
¿A cuánto se vende el carro?	How much is the car (being sold for)?
a cuarenta pesos el kilo	at forty pesos the kilo
Lo vende al litro	She sells it by the liter
vender al por menor/mayor	to sell retail/wholesale
a cuarenta kilómetros por hora	at forty kilometers / twenty-five miles an hour

iv *a* expressing manner:

a mi manera / modo	in my way
**a la manera de Goya*	in the style of Goya
a mi costa	at my cost
***a mi juicio / entender / parecer / modo de ver*	in my opinion
a la larga	in the long run

*Notice that ***manera / modo*** does not always take ***a***, witness the following:

de una manera / de un modo elegante	in an elegant way

** but *en mi opinión*   in my opinion

v *a* expressing position:

caer al agua / suelo	to fall into the water / to the ground
al aire libre	in the open air
a mitad de camino	half-way (there)
a la derecha	on the right
a la izquierda	on the left
al otro lado	on the other side
a lo lejos	in the distance
a la mesa	at the table
al raso	in the open air
al sol	in the sun
a la sombra	in the shade
estar al teléfono	to be on the telephone

1.3 Uses of *ante*

Se arrodilla ante el altar	She kneels before the altar
ante el tribunal	before the court
Comparece ante el capitán	He appears before the captain
ante las circunstancias	in the circumstances

1.4 Uses of *bajo*

In its literal meaning, it is often replaced by ***debajo de*** (see compound prepositions, level 2) but in its figurative meaning it is very common:

dos grados bajo cero	two degrees below zero
bajo la lluvia	in the rain
bajo el puente	under the bridge
bajo el mando de	under the command of
bajo sus órdenes	at your command
bajo ningún pretexto	on no account
bajo el rey Felipe Segundo	under King Philip the Second

1.5 Uses of *con*

café con leche	coffee with milk
Paso las vacaciones con la familia	I spend the vacation with my family
Abro la lata con un desarmador (M)	I open the can with a screwdriver
Juego con el otro equipo	I play with the other team
Está contenta con el resultado	She is happy with the result
una mujer con muy mal humor	a woman in a bad mood
una tarta con fresas	a strawberry tart

1.6 Uses of *contra*

Dejo la escalera contra la pared	I leave the ladder against the wall
una campaña contra el cáncer	a campaign against cancer
Recibe un regalo contra entrega de bono	He receives a present for handing in the voucher
la lucha contra el enemigo	the struggle against the enemy

1.7 Uses of *de*

i indicating possession, origin, composition, distance

el dinero de tu madre	your mother's money
Esta casa es de mis papás (M)	This house is my parents'
una calle de Oaxaca	a street in Oaxaca
de Córdoba a Sevilla	from Cordoba to Seville
Vienen de Guanajuato	They come from Guanajuato
Es de Chihuahua	She's from Chihuahua
una estatua de bronce/mármol	a bronze/marble statute
La casa está rodeada de árboles	The house is surrounded by trees
La mesa está cubierta de un mantel	The table is covered with a tablecloth
Estamos a cien kilómetros de Puebla	We are a hundred kilometers from Puebla
Tiembla de miedo	She is trembling with fear
Llora de risa	She is crying with laughter
Su mamá muere de cáncer	Her mother is dying from cancer

ii *De* in expressions of time:

de antemano	beforehand
de día	by day
de inmediato	immediately
de joven	as a youth
de niño	as a child
de noche	by night

iii *de* in expressions of position:

estar de pie	to be standing
estar de rodillas	to be kneeling

iv *de* in expressions of price and measurement:

*un timbre (**M**) de quince pesos*	a fifteen-peso stamp
El precio del carro es de veinte mil dólares	The price of the car is twenty thousand dollars
El aumento es del diez por ciento	The increase is ten per cent
El peso es de cinco kilos	The weight is five kilos
Había más de diez chicos	There were more than ten boys

v *de* with professions:

*Hace de mesero (**M**) / camarero*	He works as a waiter

vi *de* in expressions of manner:

de todas formas / maneras / de todos modos	in any case
de cierto modo / de cierta manera	in a certain way
vestido de luto / paisano / militar / marinero	dressed in mourning / civilian clothes / military/naval uniform
La conozco de vista / nombre	I know her by sight/name
tirarse de cabeza / pie (al agua)	to dive/jump (into the water)

vii *de* expressing direction to and from:

el camino del pueblo	the way to the town
el tren * de Salamanca	the train to Salamanca
*el camión (**M**) / autocar procedente de Acapulco*	the bus from Acapulco

* The **de** in this example may be ambiguous. To make sure you don't get on the wrong train and go the wrong way, use **procedente de** for origin, as in the third example. After all, **de** can indicate *from*. **Desde** is also more clear-cut than **de** (see **desde** below, level 1.8, iii).

1.8 Uses of *desde*

i *desde* in expressions of position:

Desde la torre de la catedral se ve toda la ciudad	From the cathedral tower/spire you can see the whole city
Habla a los senadores desde la tribuna	She speaks to the senators from the platform
desde la montaña hasta el valle	from the mountain to the valley
desde mi punto de vista	from my point of view

ii *desde* in expressions of time:

Estudio desde las cinco hasta las diez	I study from five to ten

iii *desde* as expression of origin:

Vienen desde Bolivia para asistir a la boda	They come from Bolivia to attend the wedding

1.9   Uses of *durante*

*Durante la cena, platicamos (**M**)*	During the evening meal, we speak
Ha conducido este coche durante los últimos diez años	She has driven this car for the past ten years
La policía nos avisa durante la noche	The police inform us during the night

1.10   Uses of *en*

en la mesa / el tejado	on the table/roof
en la caja	in the box
*en coche / tren / autobús / camión (**M**) / moto / barco / avión / bicicleta*	in a car / on a train/bus/motorbike/boat/ airplane/bicycle
en la cárcel / en prisión	in prison
en casa	at home
en la estación	at the station
en Monterrey	in Monterrey
en todas partes	everywhere
El tren entra en el túnel	The train goes into the tunnel
el gobierno en el poder	the government in power

1.11   Uses of *entre*

*La azucarera (**M**) / el azucarero está entre la sal y el aceite*	The sugar bowl is between the salt and the oil
Se esconde entre la maleza	She hides in the undergrowth
Me deslizo entre varios coches	I slip between several cars
No hay diferencia de sueldo entre tú y yo	There's no difference in salary between you and me
Repartimos el premio entre los asistentes	We share the prize between those present

1.12   Uses of *excepto*

Como de todo, excepto pescado	I eat anything, except fish
Invitan a todo el mundo excepto a su padre	They invite everyone except his father

1.13   Uses of *hacia*

hacia Madrid	towards Madrid
hacia la izquierda	towards the left
Se lanza hacia la salida	She races towards the exit
Miro hacia el otro lado	I look towards the other side

Llegamos hacia las diez de la mañana	We'll arrive at about ten in the morning
su amor hacia su hija	his love for his daughter

1.14 Uses of *hasta*

Inés pasea hasta la playa	Ines goes for a walk as far as the beach
Llego hasta donde estás	I'll go to where you are
Esperamos hasta las diez	We'll wait until ten
Sólo puedo gastarme hasta cien euros	I can only spend up to a hundred euros

1.15 Uses of *mediante*

Consigo la beca mediante la ayuda de su papá (***M***) / *padre*	I receive the grant with his father's help
los resultados obtenidos mediante este proceso	the results obtained through this process

1.16 Uses of *salvo*

Salvo tú, todos los demás están comiendo	Excepting you, everyone is eating
Ésta es la cantidad, salvo error	That's the quantity, save error (if I'm not mistaken)

1.17 Uses of *según*

según las normas de la empresa	according to the company's rules
según la Secretaría de Economía (***M***)	according to the Treasury

1.18 Uses of *sin*

Estoy sin trabajo	I am without work
Abren la puerta sin la llave	They open the door without the key
Voy de vacaciones sin la familia	I go on vacation without the family

1.19 Uses of *sobre*

Hay un libro sobre la mesa	There's a book on the table
las manos sobre las rodillas	with hands on knees
posarse sobre la luna	to land on the moon
El avión vuela sobre la ciudad	The airplane flies over the city
el puente sobre el río	the bridge over the river
un libro sobre Carlos Fuentes	a book on C. F.
sobre las cinco de la tarde	about five in the afternoon
Saco ocho sobre diez	I get eight out of ten (in marks)

1.20 Uses of *tras*

Veo una película tras otra   I see one movie after another
Se esconden tras la puerta   They hide behind the door
Se protegen de los disparos tras los camiones   They seek protection from the shots behind
                                              the trucks

Exercises Level **1**

i Complete the sentences with the appropriate preposition, as in the example

Vamos (_) Palenque > Vamos a Palenque

a Llegamos (_) las dos (_) la tarde
b Este libro no es mío, es (_) Armando
c Es una cabaña (_) barro
d Acabo de ver a la Sra (_) Jiménez
e No pensaba más que (_) sí
f ¿Qué piensas (_) la película?
g El chico es menor (_) edad
h Pasó todo el día (_) sol
i Tiene cariño (_) su gato
j Es un tesoro y lo guardo (_) llave
k Salieron y (_) poco rato regresaron
l Lee y (_) mismo tiempo canta
m El camino tuerce (_) la derecha
n (_) la luz de la lámpara lee el periódico
o El culpable comparece (_) el director del colegio
p Vamos al cine (_) mi hermano
q Esta bicicleta es (_) su hermana
r ¿Tienes un remedio (_) la tos?
s La caja está cubierta (_) una lona
t Son doce kilómetros (_) aquí (_) la costa
u Me dirigía (_) el pueblo cuando se me descompuso el carro
   (*I was going . . .*)   (*my car broke down*)

ii Paired activity

Objective – Practice the use of basic prepositions

Method – A asks B, and vice versa, where (s)he comes from, what her/his clothes are made of, where (s)he goes in the evening, where (s)he eats, where (s)he puts her/his books, how long (s)he works for, whom s(he) goes to the theater with. Use the prepositions *de / a / con / durante / sobre / a / en*.

Examples

A asks: ¿De dónde vienes ahora?
B replies: Vengo de la alberca (**M**) / piscina
A . . .   ¿Adónde vas a las doce?
B . . .   Voy a la biblioteca

One member of the class then asks the rest, in Spanish, what their answers are. These answers are put on the board.

Level **2**

2.1 **Some compound prepositions** (*Algunas preposiciones compuestas*)

2.2 **Uses of** *acerca de* (*Usos of acerca de*)

2.3 **Uses of** *antes de/que* (*Usos of antes de/que*)

2.4 **Uses of** *debajo de* (*Usos de debajo de*)

2.5 **Uses of** *delante de* (*Usos de delante de*)

2.6 **Uses of** *detrás de* (*Usos de detrás de*)

2.7 **Uses of** *encima de* (*Usos de encima de*)

2.8 **Uses of** *enfrente de / frente a* (*Usos de enfrente de / frente a*)

2.9 **Uses of** *junto a* (*Usos de junto a*)

2.10 **Uses of** *lejos de* (*Usos de lejos de*)

2.11 **Uses of** *dentro de* (*Usos de dentro de*)

2.12 **Uses of** *fuera de* (*Usos de fuera de*)

2.13 **Uses of** *después de* (*Usos de después de*)

2.14 **Uses of** *a través de* (*Usos de a través de*)

2.15 **Other compound prepositions** (*Otras preposiciones compuestas*)

2.16 **Adverbial idioms with** *a* (*Locuciones adverbiales con a*)

2.17 **Adverbial idioms with** *con* (*Locuciones adverbiales con con*)

2.18 **Adverbial idioms with** *de* (*Locuciones adverbiales con de*)

2.19 **Adverbial idioms with** *en* (*Locuciones adverbiales con en*)

2.20 ***A* + following infinitive** (*A con infinitivo*)

2.21 ***De* + following infinitive** (*De con infinitivo*)

2.1 Some compound prepositions

acerca de	about, concerning	*dentro de*	within
antes de / que	before (in time)	*encima de*	on top of, above
debajo de	under, beneath	*enfrente de*	opposite
delante de	in front of	*frente a*	opposite, off
detrás de	behind	*fuera de*	outside of
lejos de	far from	*después de*	after
junto a	close to	*a través de*	across, through

2.2 Uses of *acerca de*

Escribe libros acerca de los insectos	She writes books on insects
Habló media hora acerca de este asunto	He spoke half an hour on this topic

2.3 Uses of *antes de/que*

antes de las cuatro	before four o'clock
Lo hizo antes que yo	She did it before me

2.4 Uses of *debajo de*

debajo de la mesa	under the table
¿Qué escondes debajo del abrigo?	What are you hiding under your coat?

2.5 Uses of *delante de*

Estoy delante de Uds. en la cola	I'm in front of you in the line/queue
Delante de la casa hay un jardín	In front of the house there is a yard/garden
Tienes el libro delante de ti	You've got the book in front of you

2.6 Uses of *detrás de*

Detrás del chalé tienen un huerto pequeño	They have a small vegetable garden behind the chalet
Lleva el precio detrás de la etiqueta	It's got the price behind the tab

2.7 Uses of *encima de*

Coloca estos libros encima de la mesa	Put these books on the table
Llevaba una americana encima de la camisa	He wore a jacket over his shirt

2.8 Uses of *enfrente de / frente a*

El cine está enfrente del supermercado	The movie theater is opposite the superstore
El carro paró frente a la casa	The car stopped opposite the house
Hubo un accidente frente a Veracruz	There was an accident off Veracruz (out at sea)

2.9 Uses of *junto a*

Se sentó junto a la ventana	She sat down near the window
Pasó las vacaciones junto a la familia	She spent her vacation with her family

Note. Try not to confuse ***junto a*** meaning *next to* and ***junto*** meaning *together*. ***Junto a*** is an adverb and therefore does not agree with the noun while ***junto*** meaning *together* is an adjective and does agree, e.g. *Fuimos juntos* = We went together.

2.10 Uses of *lejos de*

La casa estaba lejos del pueblo	The house was far from the town
Colóquense lejos del edificio incendiado	Move away from the burning building

2.11 Uses of *dentro de*

El dinero está dentro de la caja	The money is in(side) the box
Guarda mucho rencor dentro de sí	He keeps a real grudge within him

2.12 Uses of *fuera de*

Los leones están fuera de las jaulas	The lions are outside the cages
El preso estuvo fuera de control	The prisoner was out of control
Un coche nuevo está fuera de mis posibilidades	A new car is beyond my possibilities

2.13 Uses of *después de*

Entrarás después de mí	You'll go in after me
Los corredores africanos llegaron dos segundos después de los chinos	The African runners arrived two seconds after the Chinese

2.14 Uses of *a través de*

La luz entraba a través de una claraboya	The light entered through a skylight
Me enteré a través de un amigo	I learnt about it through a friend

2.15 Other compound prepositions

además de = besides, in addition to	*respecto a* = with respect to
alrededor de = around	*a causa de* = on account of
conforme a = according to	*en vez de* = instead of
contrario a = contrary to	*en cuanto a* = as for
a pesar de = in spite of	

2.16 Adverbial idioms with *a*

There are many adverbial idioms of manner in Spanish formed on the pattern ***a*** + singular or plural noun, and ***a*** + feminine plural adjective or noun. Some of the most common are:

estar a sus anchas	to be at ease	*tomar a pecho*	to take to heart
Lo/Le mataron a balazos	They shot him dead	*a duras penas*	with great difficulty
		saber a punto fijo	to know for certain
a caballo	on horseback	*a regañadientes*	reluctantly
Llueve a cántaros	It's pouring with rain	*a solas*	alone
		Avanzó a tientas	He groped his way
avanzar a ciegas	to go forward blindly	*a todo meter*	forward with great intensity

215

a ciencia cierta	for sure	*a trechos*	occasionally
a la corta o a la larga	sooner or later	*a trompicones*	in fits and starts
* Se abrió paso a empujones	He pushed his way through	*al otro lado de*	on the other side of
a escondidas	covertly, stealthily	*a raíz de*	immediately after
* Entró a hurtadillas	He crept in		
a oscuras	in the dark		
estar a la altura de las circunstancias	to rise to the occasion		
a favor de	in favor of		
al lado de	at the side of		
a partir de	starting from		

*Notice here that the English and the Spanish are quite different. We see an inversion of the verb and the adverbial expression. The Spanish verb corresponds to the English adverbial expression, while the Spanish adverbial expression corresponds to the English verb. This difference marks a real difference in the two languages, so watch out for it.

2.17 Adverbial idioms with *con*

con arreglo a la ley	in accordance with the law
con miras al futuro	with a view to the future
con motivo de escaparse	with the intention of escaping
con vistas a	with a view to
El barco salió (con) rumbo a Londres	The boat set out for London

2.18 Adverbial idioms with *de*

de costumbre	usually
de buena / mala gana	willingly/unwillingly
de buen grado	willingly
de improviso	unexpectedly
Es de lejos el mejor	It's by far the best
estar de moda	to be in fashion
de nuevo	again
de pronto	suddenly
estar de viaje	to be traveling
estar de visita	to be visiting

2.19 Adverbial idioms with *en*

en ausencia de	in the absence of
en presencia de	in the presence of
en busca de	in search of
en cambio	on the other hand
en carretera	on the (main) road

en todo caso	in any case
en consecuencia	consequently
en cuclillas	squatting
estar en condiciones de	to be in a position to
emisión en diferido	recorded broadcast
emisión en directo	live broadcast
*en el radio (**M**) / la radio*	on the radio
en virtud de	by virtue of
en lo que va de año	as far as this year is concerned
en resumen	in short
tomar en serio	to take seriously

2.20 *A* + following infinitive

alcanzar a	to succeed in
No alcanzo a comprender por qué no se ha casado antes	I can't understand why she didn't marry before
aprender a	to learn to
*Aprendí a manejar el carro (**M**)*	I learnt to drive the car
apresurarse a	to hurry to
Se apresuró a entrar	She hurried in
arriesgarse a	to risk
Me arriesgué a nadar hasta el puente	I risked swimming as far as the bridge
atreverse a	to dare
Se atrevió a atravesar el foso	He dared to cross the ditch
comenzar a	to commence
Comenzó a estudiar en Granada	He began to study in Granada
decidirse a	to decide to
Por fin se ha decidido a terminar la tesis	She's finally decided to finish the thesis
empezar a	to begin to
Empezó a hablar con los asistentes	She began to talk with those present
llegar a	to end up
Llegó a insultarnos	He ended up insulting us
ponerse a	to start to
Irene se puso a servir/estudiar	Irene began to serve/study
romper a	to burst out (doing something)
El niño rompió a llorar	The child burst out crying
Ir a	to go to
Fui a verla	I went to see her
Salir a	to come/go out to
Salieron a acogernos	They came out to greet us

2.21 *De* + following infinitive

***acabar de**	to have just
Acaba de llegar	He has just arrived

Acababa de llegar	He had just arrived
***dejar de**	to stop
Ha dejado de estudiar	She's stopped studying
terminar de	to finish
Hemos terminado de hacer el trabajo	We have finished doing the work

*Note the difference in the negative:

No acabo de entender su intención	I fail to understand her intention

**Note the difference in the negative:

No dejes de venir	Don't fail to come

Exercises Level **2**

i Completa la frase con una preposición compuesta como en el ejemplo:

Habló media hora (_) este asunto > Habló media hora acerca de este asunto

    a Las pruebas fueron largas (_) difíciles
    b El gato está dormido (_) la silla
    c La insultó (_) mí
    d El chico se escondió (_) los árboles
    e Alaska está muy (_) Tierra del Fuego
    f Pon la mesa (_) la puerta
    g Busqué la carta (_) el cajón
    h La nariz está (_) la boca
    i Había un terreno de fútbol (_) la casa nuestra
    j ¿Quién dejó el helado (_) el congelador?
    k Vendrá (_) la clase
    l Reembolsó el empréstito (_) el banco
  m Lo miraba (_) una celosía
    n (_) lo que María había argumentado, se aprobó la propuesta

ii Pon las palabras en su orden correcto. Al mismo tiempo inserta la preposición que conviene después del verbo. Sigue el ejemplo:

nadar alberca aprendió en mi > Aprendió a nadar en mi alberca

    a deberes acabar apresuró se sus
    b cumbre sin atrevería no la subir se ayuda hasta
    c se se casa en aburría decidió que dado salir
    d tobillo se el en niña la hizo llorar rompió daño y
    e paisaje pintar puso un se
    f autobús echó del correr detrás
    g trabajo acababa su regresé cuando su terminar
    h entramos dejado había comer cuando
    i convencerme razonamiento termina no su
    j vecino paró hablar el con se

iii Actividad en común

Objetivo – Practicar el uso de preposiciones compuestas

Método – Un miembro de la clase (mejor que sea extrovertido/a) se mueve en el salón, y después de cada desplazamiento, pregunta: *¿Dónde estoy?* La clase contesta con preposiciones compuestas. El estudiante que puede hacer de payaso se desplaza diez veces. Se encuentran numerosos ejemplos de preposiciones compuestas al principio de este nivel.

Ejemplos

**Después de subirse a una silla o a
  una mesa hace la siguiente
    pregunta:**   ¿Dónde estoy?

Respuesta: Estás encima de una/la silla/mesa

Se acerca a la ventana y pregunta: ¿Dónde estoy?

Respuesta: Estás cerca de la ventana

It goes without saying that you must be very careful in the actions you perform. For example, it would be unwise to climb on to a chair if the chair were in a poor condition.

Unit 24 (Unidad 24)

Prepositions *por* and *para* (*Las preposiciones **por** y **para***)

Level **1**

1.1 **Basic differences between *para* and *por*** (*Diferencias básicas entre **para** y **por***)

1.2 **Basic uses of *para*** (*Usos básicos de **para***)

1.3 **Basic uses of *por*** (*Usos básicos de **por***)

1.1 Basic differences between *para* and *por*

The two Spanish prepositions **para** and **por** cause a great deal of confusion, partly because they can sometimes be translated by the same English preposition *for*. They are treated apart from the other prepositions since, by comparing and contrasting them, it is hoped that you will be able to distinguish between them more clearly. The first most important feature that separates them is that ***para*** indicates direction or purpose while ***por*** indicates cause or an act performed on behalf of or through someone. Three contrastive examples will illustrate this point.

i

Mi hermana tiene un e-mail para mí	My sister has an e-mail for me (and is waiting to give it to me, for example)
Mi hermana escribe un e-mail por mí	My sister writes an e-mail for me (i.e. on my behalf or because I do not do it myself)
Vamos para las montañas	Let's head towards the mountains
Vamos por las montañas	Let's go through the mountains
Dale el dinero para el carro	Give him the money for the car (i.e. so that he can buy it)
Dale el dinero por el carro	Give him the money for the car (i.e. in exchange for)

ii A further example containing both prepositions in the same sentence will make the difference even clearer:

Mi hermano hizo la tarea por mí para la maestra	My brother did my homework for me for the teacher

In this sentence, ***por*** suggests *on behalf of* while ***para*** suggests destination. We shall firstly consider the uses of ***para*** and then those of ***por***.

1.2   Basic uses of *para*

i Purpose

Mi prima estudia para (ser) ingeniero My cousin is studying to be an engineer
Llamo para felicitarte I call to congratulate you

ii Destination

Tengo un mensaje para ti I've got a message for you
Saca un billete para Santander He's buying a ticket for Santander

iii Going towards a place

La veo cuando voy para la facultad I see her on my way to the university

iv Changing direction

Tuerces para la derecha cuando . . . Go to the right when . . .

v Indicating a point in time (usually in the future)

*Te dejo mi departamento (**M**) para las vacaciones* I'll leave my apartment for you for the vacation

vi Indicating limit of date, month, etc.

Acaban las obras para Semana Santa The (road)works will be finished by Holy Week

vii Expressing opinions

Para mí, todo el mundo se equivoca As far as I'm concerned, everyone's wrong

1.3   Basic uses of *por*

i In passive statements when a person is the agent

El teatro fue construido por un buen arquitecto The theater was built by a good architect

ii Indicating passing through or across

Vamos a Madrid por Ávila We go to Madrid via Avila
Miro por la ventana I look out of the window
Me paseo por la calle I walk down the street

iii Indicating a vague idea with respect to place

Los soldados se esconden por algún pueblo de Zamora The soldiers hide in some village in (the province of) Zamora
¿Pasamos por aquí, verdad? We go this way, don't we?
¿Hay un banco por aquí? Is there a bank (around) here?

iv Indicating approximate time

*Regreso (**M**) / Vuelvo por Semana Santa* I'll be back for Holy Week

v Indicating a specific point of time in the day

Los jefes se reúnen por la mañana / tarde / noche   The leaders meet in the morning/ afternoon / at night

vi Indicating frequency or speed with respect to time

Corre a ciento cincuenta kilómetros por hora   She's traveling/racing at a hundred miles an hour

Hace dieta dos veces por semana   She diets twice a week

vii Indicating cause

¿Por qué lo haces?   Why do you do it?

viii Indicating "on behalf of," "for the sake of"

Voy al supermercado por ti   I go to the superstore for you
Celebran una misa por su alma   They say mass for his soul
Firma por su esposa   He signs for his wife

ix Suggesting "by means of"

Me entero por la prensa   I learn of it through the newspapers
Me llama por teléfono   She phones me
Lo pago por el banco   I pay it through the bank

Exercises Level **1**

i Insert *para* or *por* in the space. In some cases, both *para* and *por* are possible but the meaning can be different. Indicate where the possibilities exist.

a Alquilé una bicicleta (_) ir de paseo
b Lo saludé (_) tu parte
c Mamá prepara la fiambrera (_) la comida
d Creo que los chicos perdidos están (_) allí
e El pequeño duerme un par de horas (_) la tarde
f Es un bar (_) estudiantes
g Hay que pagar cinco euros (_) persona
h ¿Tiene dos boletos (_) Tijuana?
i Es casi seguro que terminaré mi tarea (_) enero
j Les dimos la casa (_) dos meses
k Perdieron (_) cinco goles a uno
l Pasamos por Oaxaca (_) ir a Palenque
m Se compró un apartamento (_) ciento cincuenta mil euros
n Ve (_) la izquierda al llegar a la esquina
o Todo el mundo es loco (_) él
p Este edificio fue derribado (_) la empresa
q Con tanto bulto no pasas (_) la puerta
r Lo supe (_) tu padre

ii Paired activity

Objective – To understand the differences between *por* and *para*

Method – Engage in a discussion to work out why *por* and *para* are used in the following five pairs of sentences. Try to distinguish their use and meaning.

a (1) Quieren ir por el museo   (2) Quieren ir para el museo
b (1) Estoy limpiando la casa por la fiesta   (2) Estoy limpiando la casa para la fiesta
c (1) Dale el dinero por el regalo   (2) Dale el dinero para el regalo
d (1) El hombre está por confesar la verdad   (2) El hombre está para confesar la verdad
e (1) Hace la tarea por mí   (2) Hace la tarea para mí

Now, each pair finds two more pairs of sentences like these above to present to the class.

Level 2

2.1 More information on *para* (*Más datos sobre **para***)
2.2 More information on *por* (*Más datos sobre **por***)

2.1 More information on *para*

i Indicating "as" or "with the status of"

Nuestra candidata no salió para alcaldesa   Our candidate did not get the mayor's post

ii Suggesting some undisclosed thought

Aquel lugar es ideal, pensó el conde para sí   That's an ideal spot, the count thought to himself

"No me atrevo," dije para mí   "I dare not," I said to myself

iii Suggesting comparison or contrast

No hace demasiado calor para ser agosto   It's not hot enough to be August

iv Corresponding to "in order to"

Trabaja mucho para ascender a jefa   She works a lot to become the boss
Estudio bastante para ir a la universidad   I work quite a lot to go to university

v Suggesting sufficiency or necessity

El agua es necesaria para la vida   Water is necessary for life

vi Used with verbs like *quedar*, *faltar*, and *restar* indicating time left to do something or distance to be covered

Faltan dos horas / diez kilómetros para llegar al pueblo   There are two hours / six miles left to reach the town
*Quedan/restan dos semanas para las vacaciones   There are two weeks before the vacation

*****Quedar*** is used much more than ***restar*** in this context

vii Indicating mood or opportunity to do something (usually this has a negative idea)

No estoy para bromas	I'm not in the mood for joking
La oficina está para pocos gastos	The office is not keen on spending money

viii Used in conjunction with *demasiado* and *suficiente*

Esta casa es demasiado grande para mí	This house is too big for me
No tengo suficiente dinero (como) para comprártelo	I haven't enough money to buy it for you

ix Other uses

Es para volverse loco	It's enough to send you mad
No es para creerlo	You really can't believe it

x *Para* is also used in conjunction with *con* = *towards*

Es muy simpático para con todo el mundo	He's very nice with everyone

2.2 More information on *por*

i Indicating cause

Detuvieron al alcalde por el asesinato de su mujer	They arrested the mayor for the murder of his wife

ii Used frequently before an abstract noun

Lo hice por placer	I did it for pleasure
Le dio todo su dinero por amor	He gave her all his money out of love
Les pagué las vacaciones por cariño	I paid for their vacation out of affection
Lo hizo por inadvertencia	She did it by mistake
No escribí la carta por descuido	I didn't write the letter by an oversight
No contestó por dignidad	She didn't answer out of dignity
Visitaba al enfermo por compasión	I would visit the sick person out of compassion
Lo acompañé por amistad	I accompanied him out of friendship
No felicitó al ganador por despecho	He didn't congratulate the winner out of spite

iii Indicating intensification and followed by an infinitive

Gritaba por gritar	He shouted for shouting's sake

iv Indicating rate

Se vende por docenas	It's sold by the dozen
La tasa es del ocho por ciento	The rate is eight percent

v Indicating manner and means

Es mexicano por adopción	He's Mexican by adoption
por aire/carretera/ferrocarril/mar/tierra	by air/road/railroad/sea/land
La informaron por carta	They informed her by letter

Les mandé el dinero por correo	I sent them the money by mail		
Lo oímos por la radio / televisión	We heard it on the radio/television		
La conocí por su sombrero	I recognized her by her hat		
Lo informó por escrito	She informed him in writing		

vi Used in adverbial idioms of manner

por cierto	certainly	*por un lado / una parte*	on the one hand
por consiguiente	in consequence	*por otro lado / otra parte*	on the other hand
por el contrario	on the contrary	*por lo tanto*	therefore
por desgracia	unfortunately	*por último*	at last
por fortuna	fortunately	*por fin*	at last
por lo general / regla general	generally	*por lo visto*	apparently
por supuesto	of course	*por separado*	separately

Ejemplos

Por desgracia murió antes de acabar la novela	Unfortunately she died before finishing the novel
El jefe nos fue entrevistando a todos por separado	The boss went on interviewing us all separately
¡Por fin / último ha llegado!	She has finally arrived!
Por un lado no tengo el dinero y ¡por otro no quiero dártelo!	On the one hand I haven't the money and on the other I don't want to give it to you!

vii *Por* with other prepositions, usually suggesting movement

Corrieron por entre los árboles	They ran among trees
Pasó por detrás de la silla	He went round the back of the chair
El avión voló por debajo del puente	The airplane flew under the bridge
Saltó por encima del muro	She jumped over the wall
Me preguntó por mediación de su amigo	She asked me via a friend
Salí a por el periódico	I went out to get the newspaper

The last example in this list is colloquial, but the construction is very common. The alternative, perhaps more acceptable, is ***Salí por el periódico*** which is what a Mexican would say.

viii Used with a variety of verbs

Tengo una novela por terminar	I have a novel to finish
Me quedan varias cosas por comprar	I've got a few things to buy
Empezaré por exponer el nuevo plan	I'll begin by developing the new plan
Acabarán por despedirte	They'll end up dismissing you
Votaron por los demócratas	They voted for the democrats
Me he decidido por el coche blanco	I've decided on the white car

Exercise Level 2

i **Inserta *para* o *por* en el blanco. En algunos casos, cabe tanto *para* como *por*. Indica donde existen las dos posibilidades**

   a Me pongo nerviosa al leer en voz alta, prefiero leer (_) mí

   b Pasaron (_) entre las columnas

c Lo dije (_) gestos

d Gloria tiene muy buen aspecto (_) lo enferma que está

e El autocar chocó (_) ir demasiado rápidamente

f El científico recibió dinero (_) sus investigaciones

g Pasé todo el día en casa (_) preparar la cena

h ¡(_) Dios!

i Sus papás lo castigaron (_) llegar demasiado tarde

j La comida era suficiente (_) diez personas

k Tan sólo quedan dos meses (_) las vacaciones

l (_) la cara que traes yo diría que estás enfadada

m No (_) mucho hablar te vas a ganar su confianza

n Restaban dos semanas (_) el fin de las clases

o Se puso un mandil (_) no mancharse

p (_) Antón esta ciudad es todo lo que puede soñar cualquier persona

q Los beneficios se multiplican (_) diez

r ¿(_) quién es la misa?

s (_) Navidades ya estarás completamente curado

t (_) ser profesionales juegan bastante mal

u La chica salió de casa (_) propia iniciativa

v No me encuentro bastante bien (_) ir al trabajo

w ¿Quién eres tú (_) darme órdenes?

x Los socios preguntan (_) el supuesto

y (_) una vez que me invitas podía haber sido en un restaurante mejor

z Me agarró (_) los hombros

aa Sujetó la olla (_) el asa

bb Te doy mi carro (_) tu moto

cc Éste no es motivo (_) despedirla

dd Pregunté (_) Juana

ee Pongo a Dios (_) testigo

ff El futuro está (_) llegar

Unit 25 *(Unidad 25)*

Adverbs (*Los adverbios*)

Level **1**
1.1 **Formation of adverbs** (*Formación de adverbios*)
1.2 **Adverbial expressions** (*Expresiones adverbiales*)
1.3 **Other adverbs** (*Otros adverbios*)

1.1 Formation of adverbs

i Adverbs in Spanish, as in English, are formed in different ways. However, the most common way for creating an adverb in Spanish is by adding *-mente* to the feminine form of the adjective:

rápidamente	quickly		*perfectamente*	perfectly
lentamente	slowly		*públicamente*	publicly
solamente	only			

Examples

Corre rápidamente / lentamente	She runs quickly / slowly
Habla perfectamente el alemán	He speaks German perfectly
Come solamente verduras	She only eats vegetables
Anuncia públicamente que . . .	He announces publicly that . . .

It is obvious from these examples that, in Spanish, there are almost as many adverbs as there are adjectives. It should be added that Spanish adverbs are invariable, that they modify verbs, and are frequently placed next to them.

ii Adjectives which have no distinctive feminine form add *-mente* in the usual way:

felizmente	happily		*constantemente*	constantly
útilmente	usefully		*amablemente*	pleasantly

Examples

Regresa felizmente a casa	She returns home happily
Hay que trabajar constantemente	You have to work constantly

iii Adverbs formed with *-mente* are pronounced as two words, each part retaining its accent, both written and spoken:

sólidamente	solidly		*cortésmente*	courteously
poéticamente	poetically		*originalmente*	originally

227

iv When two or more of these adverbs occur in immediate succession, only the last receives the ending *-mente*, the others assuming the form they would have if *-mente* were to be added. This takes place when more than one adverb of the *-mente* type modify the same verb:

Escribe clara, concisa y elegantemente	She writes clearly, concisely and elegantly
gradual pero insensiblemente	gradually but imperceptibly

v The adverb **recientemente** is shortened to **recién** before past participles used adjectivally:

Llegó recientemente	She arrived recently **but**
los recién casados	the newly weds
un recién nacido	a newborn child
pan recién cocido	freshly baked bread
con la cara lavada y recién peinada	with a face freshly washed and recently combed hair

vi Often Spanish adverbs can be clumsy with the ending *-mente*, unlike the lighter English *-ly*, and there is always the possibility of avoiding this clumsiness. For instance, a noun preceded by **con** is often a suitable alternative:

industriosamente>	*con industria*	industriously
orgullosamente>	*con orgullo*	proudly
prudentemente>	*con prudencia*	prudently
El chico anuncia con orgullo que ha ganado el premio		The boy proudly announces that he has won the prize
Es importante manejar con prudencia		It's important to drive carefully

1.2 Adverbial expressions

i A further variety may be obtained by a phrase composed of *de (una) manera*, *de (una) forma* or *de (un) modo*:

de (una) manera uniforme	in a uniform manner
de (una) manera amistosa	in a friendly manner
de (un) modo elegante	in an elegant way
de (una) forma brusca	in a rough way

The inclusion of the indefinite article before these nouns makes the expression more formal.

ii Some adjectives which do not end in **o** or have a distinct feminine form cannot take the suffix *-mente*:

de (una) manera preguntona	inquisitively
de (una) forma holgazana	in an idle way

1.3 Other adverbs

There is of course a whole range of Spanish adverbs which do not derive from adjectives and which are adverbs in their own right. These include:

bien	well	*mucho*	much	*muy*	very
mal	badly	*poco*	little	*pronto*	soon
mejor	better	*más*	more	*a tiempo*	in time
peor	worse	*menos*	less	*tarde*	late
temprano	early	*siempre*	always	*nunca*	never
sólo	only	*casi*	almost	*luego*	then

Pocos hablan bien dos idiomas	Few people speak two languages well
El niño come mal	The child eats badly
*Con estos lentes (**M**) veo mejor*	With these glasses I can see better
Veo peor que antes	I see worse than before
Me levanto temprano	I get up early
Me quedan sólo tres	I've only got three left (Only three remain to me)
Como sólo legumbres	I only eat vegetables
Toca mucho el piano	She plays the piano a lot
Siempre salgo de casa a las ocho	I always leave home at eight
Es importante llegar a tiempo	It's important to arrive on time

Exercises Level **1**

i **Complete the sentences with adverbs based on the following adjectives. There can be an alternative:**

directo, inmediato, paciente, posible, rápido, fácil, puntual, tranquilo, total, constante, único, cariñoso, afectuoso, amable, respetuoso, cruel, sumo, alto, dulce, largo, ciego, independiente, nuevo, feliz, cortés

Example

lento

¿Puedes hablar un poco más (_) ? > ¿Puedes hablar un poco más lentamente?

a Viven (_) con sus tres niños
b Su padre (_) lee periódicos
c Los novios se despidieron (_)
d Nos acogieron (_)
e Deberás sonreírle (_)
f Su padre le pegó (_)
g Hay que saludarlos (_)
h El problema es (_) difícil
i Subir por allí es (_) peligroso
j La madre le dijo (_) que le tenía mucho cariño
k La cuestión ha sido (_) debatida
l Confía (_) en su padre
m Le contesté (_) que era muy amable
n La familia está esperando (_) en la cola

o Hay examen mañana y tengo que empezar a estudiar (_)

p Se vive (_) en aquel pueblo en la sierra

q ¿Las enchiladas? Se preparan (_)

r "¿El hombre va a vivir en la luna algún día?" "(_)"

s ¿Qué pasa? Estoy (_) confundido

t Un vuelo que hace escalas no va (_) a su destino

u Cuando ve la televisión, mi hermano cambia de canal (_)

v Es necesario que las clases empiecen (_)

w ¡Híjole! (**M**) (_) se producen disturbios en la ciudad

x Salen (_) para tomar (**M**) / coger el autobús

y (_) de lo que digas, lo haré

ii Put the correct form of the adverb in the following sentences:

Examples

Es una casa (_) pintada > Es una casa recién pintada

Se puede hacer **individual** o **colectivo** > Se puede hacer individual o colectivamente

a Los (_) venidos son muy amables

b Voy a ver la obra de teatro (_) estrenada

c Me contesta **correcto** y **cortés**

d Duerme como un (_) nacido

e (_) iniciada la charla, sonaron los aplausos

f Estudiaba **constante** y **lento**

g (_) llegado del servicio militar, se casó

h Se expresaba **firme** e **insistente**

i (_) salidos del aeropuerto, empezó a relampaguear

j El (_) galardonado donó su premio a una obra de caridad

k (_) construida la torre, hubo que reforzarla

iii Complete the sentence with a suitable adverb. There can be more than one adverb.

Example

Habla (_) el chino > Habla bien el chino

a Habla (_) el japonés

b Pedro maneja muy (_) y tendrá un accidente

c ¿Por qué te levantas tan (_)? Son (_) las cinco

d ¿Por qué te levantas tan (_)? ¡Es la hora del almuerzo!

e Si no llegas (_) no podrás ver la película

f Te echo de menos (_)

iv Paired activity

Objective – To find adverbs corresponding to adjectives

Method – A says ten adjectives and B provides ten corresponding adverbs. It's as simple as that.

Examples

A:	buen	B:	bien
A:	alegre	B:	alegremente
A:	claro	B:	claramente

The class then comes together, and uses the adverbs in sentences. A member of the class writes the sentences on the board. Remember that the adverb, particularly if it is short, frequently follows the verb as in the sentence below:

Canta bien esa canción

Level 2

2.1 **Adverbs of time, place and degree** (*Adverbios de tiempo, de lugar y adverbios restrictivos*)

2.2 **Preposition + definite article + word** (*Preposición + artículo definido + palabra*)

2.3 **Without the article and in the singular** (*Sin artículo y en singular*)

2.4 **Without the article and in the plural** (*Sin artículo y en plural*)

2.5 **Some adverbial phrases** (*Algunas expresiones adverbiales*)

2.6 **More adverbs of time** (*Otros adverbios de tiempo*)

2.7 **Adverbs of place** (*Adverbios de lugar*)

2.8 **Adverbs of manner** (*Adverbios de modo*)

2.9 **Adverbs of degree** (*Adverbios restrictivos*)

2.10 **Adverbs involving doubt** (*Adverbios expresando duda*)

2.11 **Adverbs involving affirmation and negation** (*Adverbios expresando afirmación y negación*)

2.12 **Further adverbs expressing time and movement** (*Otros adverbios expresando el tiempo y movimiento*)

There is a further range of adverbs which express time, place, degree, doubt, affirmation and negation. These may be subdivided into the following categories.

2.1 Adverbs of time, place and degree

Those that may be regarded as simple and original:

así	thus	*hoy*	today
aún	yet, still	*mañana*	tomorrow

Other words used adverbially without change. This includes several adjectives used with verbs, examples of which may be found in the unit on adjectives (see unit 21, level 2.2). It also includes the following:

algo	somewhat	*nada*	not at all

Preposition *a* joined to a following word:

abajo	down	*apenas*	scarcely
acaso	perhaps	*arriba*	up
adelante	forwards	*atrás*	backwards
ahora	now	*anoche*	last night

Ejemplos

Espérame abajo	Wait for me downstairs
Acaso hayan muerto ya	Perhaps they have already died
El batallón siguió adelante	The batallion went forward
Apenas se le oye	You can hardly hear him/her
*Tus papás (**M**) están arriba*	Your parents are upstairs
*Anoche la (**M**) / lo pasamos muy bien*	We had a good time last night

2.2 Preposition + definite article + word

a la ligera	lightly		*en el acto*	instantly
al contado	in cash		*por lo pronto*	for the time being
al momento	instantly		*por lo regular*	usually
al raso	in the open air		*por lo tanto*	consequently

Ejemplos

Te tomas las cosas demasiado a la ligera	You take things too lightly
¿Quieres pagar al contado?	Do you want to pay cash?
*Llamamos al mesero (**M**) / camarero y vino al momento*	We called the waiter and he came straightaway
Tuvimos que pasar la noche al raso	We had to spend the night in the open air
El conductor del vehículo falleció en el acto	The vehicle's driver died at the wheel

2.3 Without the article and in the singular

de balde	gratis, free		*de inmediato*	immediately
de mala gana	unwillingly		*en resumen*	in short
de buena gana	willingly		*en seguida*	at once
de buen grado	willingly		*por consiguiente*	consequently
de nuevo	again		*por supuesto*	of course
por fin	finally		*por último*	at last

Ejemplos

Yo no hago ese trabajo de balde	I won't do that work for nothing
De mala gana iría allí	I won't go there willingly
De buena gana me iría de vacaciones	I'd willingly go on vacation
Cuando lo veas de nuevo, dile que llame	When you see him again tell him to give me a call
"¿Puedo sentarme?" "Por supuesto"	"May I sit down?" "Of course"
Y ya, por último les hablaré de . . .	And then, finally, I'll speak to them about . . .

2.4   Without the article and in the plural

a ciegas	blindly		*de oídas*	by hearsay
a escondidas	secretly		*de rodillas*	on your knees
a gatas	on all fours		*de pie*	standing
a medias	by halves		*en ayunas*	fasting
a solas	alone, privately		*en cueros*	naked

Ejemplos

*No había luz y fui a ciegas a mi recámara (**M**) / habitación*	There was no light so I couldn't see when I went to my room
Me dijo a escondidas que . . .	She told me in secret that . . .
Los niños aprenden a andar a gatas muy pronto	Children learn to crawl on all fours very quickly
Todo lo arregla a medias	He only does things by halves
Marta pasó toda la noche a solas	Martha spent all night alone

2.5   Some adverbial phrases

i

a más no poder	with all your might		*de par en par*	wide open (door)
a más tardar	at the latest		*de vez en cuando*	occasionally
a sus anchas	at your ease		*gota a gota*	drop by drop
cuanto antes	as soon as possible		*poco a poco*	little by little

Ejemplos

Disfrutamos a más no poder	We enjoyed ourselves enormously
Regresaremos el lunes a más tardar	We'll be back by Monday at the latest
En tu casa me siento a mis anchas	I feel really at home in your house
Mándamelo cuanto antes	Send it to me as soon as possible
La puerta estaba abierta de par en par	The door was wide open
Voy al teatro de vez en cuando	I go to the theater on occasions

ii Many of these adverbial phrases are restricted to certain verbs:

Lo miró de hito en hito	She stared at him
Le hizo la pregunta a quemarropa	He suddenly shot the question at her

iii Many of these adverbial expressions may be further extended by the addition of other adverbs:

Entró muy de golpe	He suddenly came in
Lo toma demasiado a la ligera	She takes it too lightly

2.6 More adverbs of time

*ahora / ahorita (**M**)*	now	*jamás*	never
a menudo	often	*nunca*	never
de día	by day	*luego*	soon
de noche	by/at night	*pronto*	soon
después	afterwards	*raras veces*	seldom
entonces	then	*siempre*	always
últimamente	lately	*luego luego (**M**)*	straightaway
justo cuando	just when		

Ejemplos

No está lloviendo ahorita	It's not raining now
Nos visitan a menudo	They often visit us
Llegué pronto a la cita	I arrived early at the rendez-vous
Luego luego me contestó que . . .	He immediately answered that . . .

2.7 Adverbs of place

acá	here (vague)	*a la derecha*	to the right
aquí	here (precise)	*a la izquierda*	to the left
allá	there (vague)	*en otra parte*	elsewhere
allí	there (precise)	*lejos*	faraway
más acá	more this way	*cerca*	near
más allá	more that way	*por aquí*	near here
por todas partes	everywhere		

Ejemplos

Ven acá / aquí	Come here
Fue hacia allá hace un rato	He went over there some time ago
Está más acá / allá	It's more this way / that way
Hay polvo por todas partes	There's dust everywhere

2.8 Adverbs of manner

The adverbs of manner are much more numerous than all the others. The greater part of them are adverbial phrases, or adverbs formed from adjectives by the addition of **-mente**:

al por mayor	wholesale	*bien*	well
al por menor	retail	*de antemano*	beforehand
a sabiendas	wittingly	*de improviso*	unexpectedly
así	thus	*de propósito*	on purpose
a tientas	groping, tentatively	*adrede*	on purpose

Ejemplos

vender al por mayor/menor	to sell wholesale/retail
Yo sabía de antemano que . . .	I knew beforehand that . . .

2.9 Adverbs of degree

algo	somewhat	*harto*	enough
apenas	hardly	*más bien*	rather
bastante	enough	*menos*	less
casi	almost	*muy*	very
demasiado	too, too much	*sobradamente*	excessively

Ejemplos

Es algo difícil	It's somewhat difficult
Apenas duerme	She hardly sleeps
Está casi terminado	It's almost finished
Lo conozco sobradamente	I know him only too well

2.10 Adverbs involving doubt

acaso / quizá(s) / tal vez	perhaps	*difícilmente*	hardly, improbably
apenas	scarcely		

Ejemplos

Acaso / quizá(s) / tal vez venga hoy	Perhaps she'll come today
Los distingo difícilmente	I can hardly make them out

2.11 Adverbs involving affirmation and negation

¡Así es!	That's it!	*ni . . . ni*	neither . . . nor
¡Claro!	That's right!	*por cierto*	certainly
¡Eso no!	Not that!	*por supuesto*	of course
¡Eso sí!	That's it!	*sin duda*	undoubtedly
jamás/nunca	never	*tampoco*	neither
nada	not at all		

Ejemplos

"¿Puedes venir?" "Por supuesto"	"Can you come?" "Of course"
No conozco a su madre. A su padre tampoco	I don't know her mother, or her father

2.12 Further adverbs expressing time and movement

Adverbs expressing time or direction of a movement may be placed after nouns, thus forming adverbial expressions of time and place:

años antes	years before	*meses después*	months afterwards
calle adelante	up the street	*río abajo*	downriver
calle abajo	down the street	*siglos atrás*	centuries ago
calle arriba	up the street	*tierra adentro*	inland
cuesta arriba	up the hill	*campo a través*	across country
a lo largo de	along		

Ejemplos

Anduvieron calle abajo	They walked down the street
Fueron cuesta arriba	They went up the hill
Caminaron campo a través	They walked across country
Mucha gente esperó a lo largo de la avenida	Many people waited along the avenue

English and Spanish differ greatly in the ways in which they convey manner and direction of movement. English tends to use a verb to express manner, and a preposition to express direction; in Spanish, the verb normally expresses direction while a gerund or other adverbial phrase expresses manner:

Ejemplos

Avanzó a gatas hacia la pared	She crawled towards the wall
Cruzó el río a nado	She swam across the river
Bajé de puntillas la escalera	I tip-toed down the stairs
Pasaron por encima del muro	They climbed over the wall
Avanzó a ciegas	He went blindly forward

Exercises Level 2

i **Forma frases completas con las siguientes palabras y usa un adverbio o una expresión adverbial que no aparece en el conjunto de palabras. Hace falta también cambiar el infinitivo al indicativo o al subjuntivo**

Ejemplo
Irse calle > Se fue calle abajo

a estar nevando
b sentir miedo
c si nos dejar dormir
d mira hacia
e échate para, hay una culebra allí
f pagarme o con cheque, es igual
g nos sorprender noche en montaña y tener que pasarla
h pasearse por el río
i Siempre hacer deberes, no le gusta estudiar
j Saltar la tapia

ii Completa las siguientes frases con un verbo adecuado

Ejemplo

Tuvo que (_) a gatas para no ser visto > Tuvo que andar a gatas para no ser visto

a (_) a nado el estrecho de Gibraltar
b No se le oyó porque (_) de puntillas
c Vivir solo (_) por encima de sus posibilidades
d (_) de oídas el documento pero no lo he podido leer
e Tengo que (_) un análisis de sangre en ayunas
f Le gusta (_) en la playa en cueros
g (_) a las cinco, o a más tardar, a las seis
h ¡Oye! ¡(_) las ventanas de par en par!
i Le (_) a quemarropa y (_) en el acto
j La cartera no la (_) por allá, está más acá

iii (a) Actividad en parejas

Objetivo – Practicar adverbios de tiempo (*time*). Ver 25.2.6.

Método – A le hace a B diez preguntas relacionadas con el tiempo (*time*). La respuesta contiene un adverbio de tiempo

Ejemplos

A: ¿Cuándo vas al cine?
B: Voy al cine a menudo
A: ¿Cuándo vas a hacer tu tarea?
B: La haré después

(b) Hacer igual con adverbios de lugar. Ver 25.2.7.

Ejemplos

A: ¿Dónde vives?
B: Vivo cerca
A: ¿Dónde está la pelota?
B: Está aquí

Unit 26 (*Unidad 26*)

Interrogative and negative sentences (*Las frases interrogativas y negativas*)

Level **1**

1.1 **Interrogative sentences** (*Frases interrogativas*)

1.2 **Use of ¿*Verdad?* (*Uso de* ¿*Verdad?*)

1.3 **Negation** (*Negación*)

1.1 Interrogative sentences

i A question is regularly formed in Spanish by placing the verb before its subject:

singular		plural	
¿Hablo yo?	Do I speak?	*¿Hablamos nosotros/as?*	Do we speak?
¿Hablas tú?	Do you speak?	*¿Habláis vosotros/as?*	Do you speak?
¿Habla él/ella/Ud.	Does (s)he / do you speak?	*¿Hablan ellos/ellas/Uds.?*	Do they/you speak?

Examples

¿Habla Ud. español?	Do you speak Spanish?
¿Vas al cine?	Do you go to the movies?

ii Notice that Spanish speakers have the clever idea of warning you of a question in the making by requiring an upside-down question mark at the beginning of the sentence, as well as at the end. This also holds for exclamation points/marks: ¡*Híjole!* (**M**) / ¡*Jolín!* / ¡*Jolines!* (only in Spain) = Jees! / Heavens above!, ¡*Dios mío!* = Jees / Heavens above! (*My God!* is stronger in English than ¡*Dios mío!* The same goes for the English *Jesus!* which is much stronger than ¡*Jesús!*, commonly used when someone sneezes = Bless you!)

iii As a point of interest, this practice of having a question mark at the beginning of a question corresponds to the English of a few centuries ago, while the introduction of *do* as part of a question, a veritable headache for foreign learners of English, is comparatively modern. No construction like *do* exists in Spanish. The same goes for the other Romance languages.

When an interrogative word is used, it begins the sentence, just as in English:

¿Quién quiere cenar ahora?	Who wants to eat now?
¿Qué dices?	What do you say?
¿Por qué canta ahora?	Why's she singing now?

iv In the absence of an interrogative word, the verb may come first, although in speech the subject could very easily precede the verb. When the subject comes before the verb, there is a rise in the intonation at the end of the sentence:

¿Viene la chica ahora?	Is the girl coming now?
¿La chica viene ahora?	Is the girl coming now?
¿Arregla el carro el mecánico?	Does the mechanic repair the car?
¿El mecánico arregla el carro?	Does the mechanic repair the car?
¿Corrige los deberes la profesora?	Does the teacher correct the homework?
¿La profesora corrige los deberes?	Does the teacher correct the homework?

Notice the word order in the second and third examples. In *¿Arregla el carro el mecánico?*, it is very unlikely that *mecánico* would precede *carro*, any more than *profesora* would precede *deberes*. However, if *carro* or *deberes* is qualified in any way, and that part of the sentence lengthened, these two words could come after the subject (see unit 29 on word order).

1.2 Use of *¿Verdad?*

Fortunately for English speakers, and unfortunately for Spanish speakers learning English, the all-purpose *¿verdad?* covers approximately 200 English possibilities. So have sympathy with Spanish speakers of English. Or any foreigner tackling English for that matter.

Examples

Vas al teatro ¿verdad?	You're going to the theater, aren't you?
Es tarde ¿verdad?	It's late, isn't it?
Son colombianos ¿verdad?	They're Colombians, aren't they?

1.3 Negation

i The Spanish verb is negated by placing *no* in front of it:

No veo la luna	I can't see the moon
No va al partido	He's not going to the game
No entienden el italiano	They don't understand Italian

ii Other words which form a negative sentence are *nadie* (no one), *nada* (nothing), *ninguno* (none), *nunca* (never) and *jamás* (never).
When these words follow the verb *no* precedes the verb:

No ve a nadie	She doesn't see anyone
No encontramos a nadie	We don't meet anyone
No esperan nada de ti	They don't expect anything from you
No veo nada aquí	I can't see anything here
No pasa nada	It's O.K., Don't worry
No muestra ningún interés	She shows no interest
No voy nunca a Argentina	I never go to Argentina
No nos visita jamás	She never visits us

iii However, if *nadie*, *nada*, *ninguno*, *nunca* and *jamás* precede the verb, *no* is not used:

Nadie lo sabe	Nobody knows it
Nadie sale a encontrarnos	No one comes out to meet us
Nada le satisface	Nothing satisfies him
Nada me falta	I need nothing (i.e. nothing is lacking to me)
Ninguna persona quiere ayudarnos	No one wants to help us
Nunca viene	He never comes
Nunca me llama	He never calls me
Jamás trabajo de noche	I never work at night

Exercises Level **1**

i Find a question that fits the following replies

Example

Tengo veinte años > ¿Cuántos años tienes / tiene Ud.?

a Voy a México este verano
b Vamos al cine a las siete
c Comen más tarde
d Van a jugar (al) fútbol esta mañana (**al** *in Spain, not in* **M**)
e Escribo con la computadora
f Prefieren estas flores
g Este libro cuesta cien pesos
h Porque estoy cansado
i Este chico es el alumno más listo
j Estoy leyendo

ii Change the following sentences into the negative. There may be more than one possibility.

Example

Anda por la calle > No/nunca anda por la calle

a Veo a alguien
b Trabajan toda la semana
c Estoy leyendo un libro
d Entienden todo lo que digo
e Vamos siempre a la alberca (**M**) / piscina el viernes
f Todo el mundo cena aquí esta noche

iii Change the position of the second negative word so that all the negative expressions precede the verb.

Example

No he querido nunca visitar aquel museo > Nunca he querido visitar aquel museo

a No ha venido nadie
b No he visto nunca Las Barrancas del Cobre

c No hemos estudiado nunca el japonés
d No me interesa nada
e No me ha escrito ningún banco

iv Create questions with *¿verdad?* to precede the following sentences.

Example

Sí, es tarde > Es tarde, ¿verdad?

a Sí, vamos al teatro esta noche
b Sí, sale con toda la familia
c No, no compramos verduras hoy
d Sí, me duele la espalda
e Sí, fuimos a Albuquerque / Nuevo México el año pasado
f No, mi mamá vive en San Francisco

v Paired activity (a and b)

(a) Objective – To practice use of the negative in sentences
Method – A makes a statement and B puts it in the negative

Examples

A: Voy al parque
B: No voy al parque
A: Veo a alguien
B: No veo a nadie
A: Tengo un libro
B: No tengo ningún libro

(b) Objective – To practice the use of the interrogative. (In fact, we have been practicing this all along with these paired activities, so it will be easy.)
Method – A makes ten statements and B converts them into questions

Example

A: Preparo la comida
B: ¿Preparas la comida?
A: Voy al estadio
B: ¿Adónde vas?

Level **2**

2.1 **Uses of *no . . . ni . . . (ni)*** (*Usos de no . . . ni . . . [ni]*)

2.2 **Uses of *sino, no sólo . . . ,* and *tampoco*** (*Usos de . . .*)

2.3 **Uses of *ni siquiera*** (*Usos de . . .*)

2.4 **Order with *no*** (*Orden con no*)

2.5 ***No* with negation and repetition** (***No* con negación y repetición**)

2.6 **Miscellaneous features** (*Varios detalles*)

2.7 **Negative prefixes** (*Prefijos negativos*)

2.8 **Order with *no* and compound verbal forms** (*Posición / Ubicación* **[M]** *de no con formas verbales compuestas*)

2.1   Uses of *no . . . ni . . . (ni)*

i Ni . . . ni . . . is the equivalent of *neither . . . nor . . .* (or *not . . . either . . . or*):

No tengo ni pasteles ni caramelos	I haven't got cakes or candies
*No lo encontré ni en el departamento (**M**) / piso ni en el jardín*	I couldn't find it either in the apartment or in the yard/garden
No bebo ni fumo	I neither drink nor smoke
Nunca riñes ni protestas	You never quarrel or protest
No lo saben ni Celia ni Pablo	Neither Celia nor Pablo know it

ii *No* is also followed by ***ni*** in the following way when used with ***tener****:

No tengo ni idea	I have no idea / I haven't a clue

It also occurs in the idiomatic *¡**ni hablar!*** used to reject a suggestion:

"¿Vienes al cine?" "Ni hablar"	"Are you coming to the movies?" "Nothing doing"

iii *Ni* takes the place of ***o*** = *or*, after all negatives or clauses embodying a negative or restrictive idea:

Apenas podía respirar ni moverse	He could hardly breathe or move
Salió sin decirme nada ni cerrar la puerta	She went out without saying anything to me or closing the door

2.2   Uses of *sino, no sólo . . .* and *tampoco*

i Notice how *sino* combines with ***no*** = *not . . . but*, and ***no sólo*** = *not only . . . but also*:

Hoy no es mi cumpleaños sino mi santo	Today is not my birthday but my saint's day
No sólo era buen cocinero sino también un fantástico anfitrión	He wasn't only a good cook but also a fantastic host

ii Use of *tampoco* which is often the equivalent of *either*. ***Tampoco*** negates something in addition to a previous negation:

Pepa no ha comido, Juan tampoco	Pepa hasn't eaten, Juan hasn't either
"No he visto ninguna película." "Y la última de Cantinflas?" "Tampoco"	"I haven't seen a single movie." "And the last one of Cantinflas?" "Not that one either"

2.3   Uses of *ni siquiera*

Uses of ***ni siquiera*** = not even. It strengthens the negation of ***ni***:

No lo/le conozco (ni) siquiera de vista	I don't know him, not even by sight
Se lo entregué y (ni) siquiera me dio las gracias	I gave it to him and he didn't even thank me
La niña no sabe (ni) siquiera sumar	The child doesn't even know how to add up

2.4 Order with *no*

With the exception of object personal pronouns, no word intervenes between the verb and the negative:

Su proyecto no me parece rentable	Her plan doesn't seem viable to me
No se lo he conseguido todavía	I haven't obtained it for him/her yet
Parecen distintos pero no lo son	They look different but they aren't

2.5 *No* with negation and repetition

i *No* neutralizes any adjectives, adverbs or proposition of negative value, and is itself neutralized by repetition:

detalles no importantes (see lower down)	unimportant details
No le fue permitido no asistir	He was not allowed not to go
No podemos no admitir su razonamiento	We cannot but admit his reasoning

ii There can be more than one set of negatives in a Spanish sentence. In the second example below there are four, and three in the first:

Ella no me ha dicho nunca nada	She has never told me anything
No toleraba nunca ninguna	He never tolerated any intervention from
intervención de nadie	anyone

The positive forms *anything* (**algo**) and *anyone* (**alguien**) in English are not possible in these Spanish sentences.

iii Note also the use of *alguno* which, when it occurs after the noun, has a negative connotation:

No he visto a persona alguna en la calle	I haven't seen anyone in the street
No tengo idea alguna sobre el asunto	I have no idea on the affair
No le interesa sugerencia alguna	He's not interested in any suggestion

2.6 Miscellaneous features

In verbal expressions at least, **no** does not give an exactly opposite meaning:

Acabo de entender por qué lo hizo	I have just understood why he did it
No acabo de entender por qué lo hizo	I fail to understand why he did it
Dejé de fumar	I stopped smoking
No dejé de seguir estudiando	I didn't fail to go on studying

2.7 Negative prefixes

i Often an adjective or noun can be negated by using a negative prefix *in-* or *des-:*

cómodo–incómodo suitable–unsuitable	*conocido–desconocido* known–unknown

If such a ready-made word does not exist, a variety of negatives, **no**, **nada** and **poco** can be used. Sometimes, in the case of **no**, this can have a euphemistic effect:

los no creyentes (los infieles)	the unbelievers (non-believers)
los no violentos (partidarios de la paz)	those who are non-violent (peace supporters)
fuerzas no identificadas	unidentified forces
ciudadanos no votantes	non-voting citizens
una costumbre nada frecuente	a rare custom
un empleo nada lucrativo	a poorly paid job
una idea nada convincente	an unconvincing idea
un profesor poco divertido	a dull teacher
un coche poco rápido	a slow car

ii Note also the use of **sin** + infinitive:

una cuestión sin resolver	an unresolved question
misterios sin aclarar	unclarified mysteries
La cena está sin hacer	The evening meal remains to be prepared

iii Spanish has a number of other expressions which have the value of a negative and sometimes, but not always, require **no** before the verb:

No dijo palabra	She didn't say a word
sin decir nada a nadie	without saying anything to anyone
antes de hacer ningún gesto	before making a single gesture
Es imposible contestar nada	It's impossible to answer anything
En mi vida he visto tantas arañas	I haven't seen so many spiders in my life
En toda la noche he podido dormir	I haven't slept all night
En todo el año ha hecho tanto frío como hoy	In the whole year it has not been so cold as today
No veo ni gota	I can't see a thing
No entiende ni gota de inglés	He doesn't understand any English at all

2.8 Order with *no* and compound verbal forms

In the case of compound verbal forms with **ser**, **estar** and **haber**, **no** precedes the auxiliary:

No he querido ir	I haven't wanted to go
No están dispuestos a aceptar la oferta	They aren't ready to accept the offer
El regalo no fue aceptado	The present was not accepted

Finally, for any philosophers among you, the indefinite negative pronoun **nada** may also be construed as a noun = *nothing(ness)*. Carmen Laforet's novel *Nada* and Sartre's monumental treatise (if you can face it) called in Spanish *El ser y la nada* (*L'Être et le néant / Being and Nothingness*) illustrate this point.

Exercises Level **2**

i Pon las palabras de las siguientes frases en un orden adecuado. Dichas frases siguen una secuencia lógica y conducen naturalmente al segundo ejercicio

Ejemplo

siquiera de lavarse sin salió casa > Salió de casa sin siquiera lavarse

a toalla playa a *playeras/playera sin ni llegó la
b aletas gafas / visor (**M**) a ni sin nadar empezó
c tabla la guantes sin ni subió windsurf a de se arnés
d del sin baño zapatillas de traje agua ni salió
e padre / papá (**M**) madre / mamá (**M**) ni no su su protestó ni
f ponerse quiso baño de no traje pantalón ni corto ni
g convencer dificil mal sino sólo educado también era no de

*Playeras = *sneakers/trainers* in Spain. Playera = *T-shirt* in **M**.

ii Dadas las circunstancias referidas en las frases de arriba, y a la luz de ellas, llena los espacios (M) / rellena los blancos con una expresión negativa.

Ejemplo

(_) he visto tal espectáculo > En mi vida / Nunca he visto tal espectáculo

a (_) entiendo (_) el comportamiento del niño (_) su modo de hablar
b Este chaval / jovencito (**M**) (_) tiene (_) para cubrirse
c (_) he visto (_) igual en la vida
d (_) yo tampoco
e ¿(_) le puedes prestar (_) de ropa?
f Pero (_) acepta (_) ayuda (_) sugerencia
g (_) acabo de entender por que se comporta así
h (_) dejes de decirle que es un mal educado por (_) cubrirse
i (_) he podido (_) hacerle entrar en razón bajo (_) motivo
j ¿(_) sería posible llamar a un policía?
k Sí, pero el policía diría que "(_) es nada, y el chaval / jovencito (**M**) (_) sabe (_) de (_)"
l Entonces en una democracia, ¿Las autoridades admiten tal conducta como si (_)?
m Pero, hay que decirle al niño "¡(_) de tonterías!"
n Yo que tú, diría que (_) (_) permitiría eso

iii Actividad en parejas

Objetivo – Usar la estructura *ni . . . ni*

Método – A le ofrece a B un verbo y dos nombres (diez frases en total). B usa un verbo al que siguen dos nombres separados por *ni . . . ni*

Ejemplos

A: Comer carne queso
B: No como ni carne ni queso
A: Ver árboles flores
B: No veo ni árboles ni flores

Después se reúne toda la clase, y el profesor recaba todos los ejemplos

Unit 27 *(Unidad 27)*

Numbers and measurements. Time and dimensions *(Los números y las medidas. El tiempo [duración = la hora] y las dimensiones)*

Level **1**

1.1 **Cardinal numbers** *(Números cardinales)*

1.2 **Telephone numbers** *(Números de teléfono)*

1.3 **Ordinal numbers** *(Números ordinales)*

1.4 **Days, weeks, months and seasons** *(Días, semanas, meses y estaciones del año)*

1.5 **Time and the clock** *(La hora y el reloj)*

1.1 Cardinal numbers

(Note the figures/letters in bold.)

i

Un(o), una	1	*veinte*	20
dos	2	*veintiún/uno/una*	21
tres	3	*veintid**ó**s*	22
cuatro	4	*veintitr**é**s*	23
cinco	5	*veinticuatro*	24
seis	6	*veinticinco*	25
siete	7	*veintis**é**is*	26
ocho	8	*veintisiete*	27
nueve	9	*veintiocho*	28
diez	10	*veintinueve*	29
once	11	*treinta*	30
doce	12	*treinta y un/uno/una*	31
trece	13	*cuarenta*	40
catorce	14	*cuarenta y un/uno/una*	41
quince	15	*cincuenta*	50
*diecis**é**is*	16	*sesenta*	60
diecisiete	17	*setenta*	70
dieciocho	18	*ochenta*	80
diecinueve	19	*n**o**venta*	90

cien / ciento	100	*dos mil*	2.000
ciento un / uno / una	101	*ochenta mil*	80.000
ciento dos	102	*ciento sesenta mil*	160.000
doscientos / as	200	*un millón*	1.000.000
trescientos / as	300	**un billón (americano)*	1.000.000.000
cuatrocientos / as	400	*un billón*	1.000.000.000.000
quinientos / as	500		
seiscientos / as	600		
*se**t**ecientos / as*	700		
ochocientos / as	800		
*n**o**vecientos / as*	900		
mil	1000		
mil cincuenta	1050		
mil quinientos veinte	1520		

*This figure may be recorded as *mil millones*
Notes. Thousands are separated by periods / full stops. Decimals are separated by a comma: *Corre los cien metros en nueve coma nueve* = 9,9 (He runs . . .). Millions are written in letters: *50 millones / 500 millones / 500.000 millones*, to avoid a confusing series of zeros

ii Mexico uses the Anglo-American system of commas for thousands: 10,000 = *diez mil*. Furthermore, and still consistent with the Anglo-American practice, a Mexican would use periods / full stops for decimals: *Corre los doscientos metros en veintitrés punto tres* = She runs the two hundred meters in . . .

Once, from **dieciséis** to **veintinueve**, the numbers were frequently written thus: **diez y seis** > **veinte y nueve** but this practice has recently faded.

Uno becomes **un** before a masculine noun   *Tengo un coche* = I have a car
Uno becomes **una** before a feminine noun   *Tengo una casa* = I have a house

iii The cardinal numbers are all invariable except for **uno** (see above) and **ciento**. **Ciento** drops the final **to** when it comes before a masculine or feminine noun:

Examples

Veo treinta y tres árboles	I can see thirty-three trees
Acuden cien mujeres / hombres	One hundred women / men come
Tengo quinientos euros	I have five hundred euros
Llegan seiscientos espectadores	Six hundred spectators arrive
Hay mil soldados	There are a thousand soldiers
Veo a dos mil soldados	I see two thousand soldiers
Hay cien mil en el estadio	There's one hundred thousand in the stadium

iv Note also the way of rendering percentages:
*Sube la inflación **en** un diez por ciento* Inflation goes up by ten percent

v When **uno** follows a noun it retains its full form:

"¿Cuántos libros tienes?" "Sólo uno"	"How many books have you got?" "Only one"
En cuanto a chicas, hay cuarenta y una	As far as girls are concerned, there are forty-one

vi *Millón* and *billón* are considered as nouns:

Hay un millón de kilómetros desde aquí hasta . . .	There are a million kilometers from here to . . .
Hay millones de mosquitos	There are millions of mosquitos
*Nuestro déficit es **de** dos billones de dólares* (Note the **de** here)	Our deficit is two million dollars

1.2 Telephone numbers

With respect to telephone numbers and in writing, if there is an uneven number of digits, the first set (see below in bold) for the local number consists of three digits and the remainder of a series of two digits. For example, in Spain, a Madrid number could read from abroad: (00 34) 91 **754** 92 81. There are various ways of reading these figures out aloud, but by far the simplest, and certainly one of the most common ways, is merely to treat each digit individually. The figure above would therefore read: ***cero cero tres cuatro nueve uno siete cinco cuatro nueve dos ocho uno***. An alternative could be to read off the first three local numbers **754** as ***setecientos cincuenta y cuatro*** and the rest as ***noventa y dos ochenta y uno***. A number for Mexico City from outside the country would read: (00 52) 55 57 68 53, and the likelihood in Mexico would be to read the figures off in twos, apart from the initial ***cero cero***.

1.3 Ordinal numbers

Considerable uncertainty exists over ordinal numbers, since once you go over ten, and reach, say, twelve, these become unmanageable and end up in quiz shows. For all normal purposes, cardinal numbers are used instead of the ordinal numbers when you reach twelve. Ordinal numbers are:

primero/a	first	*duodécimo*	twelfth
segundo/a	second	*decimotercero*	thirteenth
tercero/a	third	*decimocuarto*	fourteenth
cuarto (etc.)	fourth	*decimoquinto*	fifteenth
quinto	fifth	*decimosexto*	sixteenth
sexto	sixth	*decimosé(p)timo*	seventeenth
sé(p)timo	seventh	*decimoctavo*	eighteenth
octavo	eighth	*decimonoveno*	nineteenth
noveno	ninth	*vigésimo*	twentieth
décimo	tenth	*centésimo*	hundredth
undécimo	eleventh	*milésimo*	thousandth
último	last		

Note that all the above are really adjectives and all the ordinal numbers agree in number and gender. They therefore all have four forms, in principle, although it would be exceedingly rare for ***segundo***, ***tercero***, ***cuarto***, etc., to be put in the plural. ***Primero*** and ***último*** are logically the only ordinal numbers to be used regularly in the four forms. ***Primero*** and ***tercero*** lose the ***o*** before a masculine noun.

Note that **séptimo** and **decimoséptimo** may be written and pronounced without the **p**, but this is not the case in Mexico. In the "**decimos**," the teens, there are two spoken tonic accents, one on the **e** in **decimo** and one on the penultimate syllable, except for **decimoséptimo** which has a written accent on the antepenultimate syllable.

Examples

el primer libro	the first book
la primera página	the first page
los primeros coches	the first cars
las primeras casas	the first houses
Soy el primero / la primera	I am the first
por primera vez	for the first time
el primer niño	the first child
el tercer chico	the third boy
la tercera palabra	the third word
la niña trece	the thirteenth girl
la niña catorce	the fourteenth girl
la niña veinte/vigésima	the twentieth girl
la niña treinta y una	the thirty-first girl
la niña cuarenta	the fortieth girl
la centésima niña	the hundredth girl
el centésimo niño	the hundredth boy
la milésima mujer	the thousandth woman
el milésimo espectador	the thousandth spectator
la última plaza	the last place
el último cuchillo	the last knife
*las últimas chamacas (**M**)*	the last girls
*los últimos chamacos (**M**)*	the last boys/kids
por última vez	for the last time

Note also: *por la enésima vez*   for the nth time

It is not uncommon to see certain ordinal numbers come after the noun. This is especially so in literary writings.

capítulo primero	first chapter
capítulo tercero	third chapter

1.4   Days, weeks, months and seasons

i Days of the week

In civil life, the week starts on Monday, but from the religious and traditional point of view, it starts on Sunday. All days of the week are masculine and are written in lower case:

lunes	Monday
martes	Tuesday
miércoles	Wednesday
jueves	Thursday

viernes	Friday
sábado	Saturday/Sabbath
domingo	Sunday

When you are referring to a specific day near to you – say, "this Thursday" – the singular definite article is used with no preposition:

el jueves (próximo)	(next) Thursday

When you are referring to Thursdays in general, the plural definite article is used:

Los viernes voy al teatro	On Fridays I go to the theater

ii Months of the year

These are all masculine and are written in lower case:

enero	January	*julio*	July
febrero	February	*agosto*	August
marzo	March	*se(p)tiembre*	September
abril	April	*octubre*	October
mayo	May	*noviembre*	November
junio	June	*diciembre*	December

Note. You have noticed that ***se(p)tiembre*** has two spellings. Certainly, many speakers from Spain do not pronounce the "p." This is not the case in Mexico, however, where the omission of "p" is odd.

iii Seasons of the year

Seasons are all masculine, save the first, and are written in lower case:

primavera f.	Spring
verano m.	Summer
otoño m.	Fall/Autumn
invierno m.	Winter

En is used for *in* with reference to months and seasons:

En enero cae mucha lluvia	It rains a lot in January
Las cigüeñas vuelven a España en primavera	The storks come back to Spain in Spring

1.5 Time and the clock

a las diez de la noche	at ten o'clock at night
Acaban de dar las siete	It has just struck seven o'clock
al cuarto para las cinco (**M**)	at a quarter to five
al veinte para las diez (**M**)	at twenty to ten
El tiempo pasa despacio	Time passes slowly
El tiempo pasa lentamente	Time passes slowly
El tiempo pasa rápidamente	Time goes quickly
Son las cinco de la tarde	It is five o'clock in the afternoon
Es la una de la tarde	It's one o'clock in the afternoon

Es mediodía	It's midday
Es la una y tres minutos	It's three minutes past one
Es la una y media	It's half past one
Es medianoche	It's midnight
Es la una y cuarto	It's a quarter past one
Están dando las cinco	It's striking five o'clock
hora f. exacta	exact time
hora f. punta	commute/rush hour
hora f. pico (**M**)	commute/rush hour
horario m.	schedule, timetable
huso m. horario	time zone
llegar a deshora	to come unexpectedly
Mi reloj no anda	My watch isn't working
¿Qué hora es?	What's the time?
reloj m.	clock
Son/Es cuarto para las tres (**M**)	It's a quarter to three
Son las cinco en punto	It's exactly five o'clock
Son las seis de la tarde	It's six o'clock in the afternoon/evening
Son las ocho y cuarto	It's a quarter past eight
Son las dos de la madrugada	It's two o'clock in the morning
Son las seis de la mañana	It's six o'clock in the morning
Son las cinco menos cuatro minutos	It's four minutes to five
Son veinte para las nueve (**M**)	It's twenty to nine
una hora f. fija	a fixed time

NB   Note the difference between **M** and Spain with respect to times to the hour. Spanish speakers do not have *am* and *pm* for official times. They use the twenty-four-hour timetable for traveling purposes, for instance.

El tren sale a las quince horas	The train leaves at three o'clock/pm

Spanish speakers differentiate between early morning (**madrugada**) and later morning (**mañana**):

Volvemos a las dos de la madrugada	We return at two in the morning

Mañana could be used here but in the following two examples **madrugada** could not replace **mañana**:

Salgo a las once de la mañana	I leave at eleven in the morning
Trabajo por la mañana	I work in the morning

Conversely, Spanish speakers cannot differentiate, as English speakers can, between *afternoon* and *evening*. **Tarde** covers them both. It stretches from about afternoon meal time (two/three/four o'clock) to dusk. But, of course, dusk can vary considerably in Spain between winter and summer, and Spaniards have the reputation of not keeping time when it comes to the midday meal, a misnomer in Spain. The actual time stated eliminates all confusion if *por la tarde* is not good enough, as in:

¿Nos vemos a las seis de la tarde?	We'll see each other at six this evening?

The usual time greetings are:

¡Buenos días!	Good morning/day!
¡Buenas tardes!	Good afternoon/evening!
¡Buenas noches!	Good evening/night!

¡Buenos días! is restricted to the morning, while ***¡Buenas noches!*** applies to both meeting someone and taking leave of him/her.

Exercises Level **1**

i Practice your numbers.

Example

5 niños > cinco niños

a	3 hombres	i	30 bebidas
b	1 clase	j	45 árboles
c	8 casas	k	100 vehículos
d	11 alumnos	l	1.000 (1,000 **M**) espectadores
e	15 carros (**M**)	m	500 tazas
f	21 ideas	n	10.000 (10,000 **M**) pesos
g	11 mesas	o	150.000 (150,000 **M**) libras
h	28 estudiantes	p	1.000.000 (1,000,000 **M**) dólares

ii How's your math(s)? Write out the figures in letters and do the calculations.

Examples

$2 + 3 = ?$ >		dos y tres son cinco
$7 - 3 = ?$ >		siete menos tres son cuatro

a	$4 + 5 = ?$	f	$17 - 3 = ?$
b	$5 - 3 = ?$	g	$25 + 3 = ?$
c	$2 + 6 = ?$	h	$23 - 3 = ?$
d	$11 - 7 = ?$	i	$30 - 11 = ?$
e	$16 + 4 = ?$	j	$29 - 15 = ?$

iii Read out loud the following fictitious telephone numbers:

00 34 943 20 45 32 (España)
00 52 80 21 71 93 (México)

iv What are the following days called? Use Sunday as the first day.

Example

el cuarto día de la semana > miércoles

a el tercer día de la semana
b el segundo día de la semana
c el sexto día de la semana
d el séptimo día de la semana

v What day is it? Use Sunday as the first day.

Example

jueves > el quinto día de la semana

a viernes   b miércoles   c sábado   d lunes

vi What month is it?

Example

marzo > el tercer mes del año

a noviembre   b diciembre   c julio   d abril   e febrero   f septiembre   g enero
h mayo

vii What time is it? (*¿Qué hora es?*) You may use the Mexican system as well.

Examples

3.20 > Son las tres y veinte / 4.45 > Es cuarto para las cinco (**M**) / Son las cinco menos
cuarto

a 2.15   f 3.45
b 12.10   g 10. 50
c 4.40   h 1.05
d 1.20   i 9. 55
e 11.54   j 6.15

viii Class activity
Objective – To recognize numbers as words
Method – Two teams (A and B) are constituted. One member of the class writes a
number on the board. The first person who calls out the correct number in Spanish
gains a point. The team reaching ten points is the winner

Examples

Class member:	37
Answer:	treinta y siete
Class member:	253
Answer:	doscientos cincuenta y tres
Class member:	581
Answer:	quinientos ochenta y uno

**ix Class activity. Exactly the same procedure as above with time and the clock. Use *de
la madrugada, de la mañana, de la tarde, de la noche*. Use also the verb *ser*. You
may use the Mexican or Spanish way of referring to time "to the hour."**

Examples

Class member:	5.30 am
Answer:	Son las cinco y media de la mañana
Class member:	2.40 pm
Answer:	Son las tres menos veinte de la tarde
	Son cuarenta para las tres (**M**) de la tarde

Level **2**

2.1 *Dar* and the clock (*Dar y el reloj*)
2.2 **Division of time** (*División del tiempo*)
2.3 **Expressing dimensions** (*Expresando dimensiones*)
2.4 **Age** (*Edad*)
2.5 **Collective numbers** (*Números colectivos*)
2.6 **Fractions** (*Fracciones*)
2.7 **Mathematical expressions and signs** (*Expresiones matemáticas y signos*)

2.1 *Dar* and the clock

The verb ***dar*** is used when speaking of the striking of the hour:

Dieron las tres	It struck three o'clock
Han dado las cinco	It has struck five o'clock

2.2 Division of time

i The division of time in the immediate future is expressed by ***próximo*** and ***que viene***. The present time is represented by ***actual*** (which does not mean *actual*), ***presente*** or ***corriente***, while the past is referred to as ***pasado***. Thus:

el siglo pasado	the last century	*el mes que viene*	next month
el año pasado	last year	*el viernes que viene*	next Friday
el mes pasado	last month	*el jueves próximo*	next Thursday
el año próximo	next year	*el lunes de la semana que*	Monday of next
la semana próxima	next week	*viene*	week
la próxima vez	next time		

Ejemplos

La reunión se celebrará a finales del mes corriente	The meeting will take place at the end of the current month
El cinco de diciembre del corriente se producirá el próximo eclipse	On the fifth of December of the current year the next eclipse will appear

ii Próximo can come before the noun with no difference in meaning –
la próxima semana, el próximo mes.

iii Quince días / quincena are used for a *fortnight*. There seems little logic in this for, as in French and Italian, one day is counted twice. Spanish speakers do, however, insist that the system is logical. Choose yourself. A similar mathematical but confusing operation takes place for a week which, of course, is ***una semana***, but also ***ocho días***, again as in French and Italian:

de hoy en quince días	a fortnight from today / in a fortnight's time
de hoy en ocho días	a week from today / in a week's time

de mañana en ocho días	a week from tomorrow
Llegará dentro de ocho días	She'll arrive in a week's time

iv Expressions for the beginning, middle and end of any indefinite period of time are the following:

a primeros / mediados / finales / últimos de mes / año	at the beginning/middle/end of the month/year

v Nouns expressing time in its various aspects

Tiempo is *time* in its widest and most general sense, but not with specific reference to the clock. It is used in philosophy and science:

Este trabajo me llevará poco tiempo	This work won't take me long
Todavía tengo tiempo de arreglarme	I've still got time to get ready
No llegará a tiempo	She'll not arrive in time
Ha llegado ya el tiempo de la cosecha	The time for harvest has now arrived
Según los científicos el tiempo es infinito	According to scientists time is infinite

NB   Be careful not to mix up **tiempo** for time and **tiempo** for weather. If you ever need to separate the two phenomena, you could say **tiempo duración** (time) and **el tiempo que hace** (weather).

Plazo is a period of time generally agreed upon or appointed:

Hay que dármelo dentro de un plazo de tres días	You have to give it to me within three days
el plazo de entrega	the delivery time
acortar / alargar el plazo	to shorten/lengthen the period
a corto / largo plazo	in the short/long term
comprar a plazos	to buy in installments

Rato is an undetermined, generally short space of time, equivalent to the English *while*:

al cabo de un rato	after a while
después de un buen rato	after a good while
Pasé un rato ideal allí	I had a splendid time there
Lo esperamos un rato	We waited for him for a while
Cuando tenga un rato te llamo	When I'm free I'll call you

Note that **época** is used much more than than *epoch*:

en la época de los Reyes Católicos	during the period of the Catholic Monarchs
Fue una época de grandes convulsiones	It was a period of great upheaval

Vez is a point of time considered as one of a series:

Esta vez te perdono	This time I'll forgive you
Es muy simpática pero, a veces, dice unas bobadas increíbles	She's very nice but, sometimes, she says the dumbest of things
Es la primera vez que te veo aquí	It's the first time I've seen you here

Note the present tense in the last example. Similarly, the imperfect with **fue**:

Fue la primera vez que la veía allí	It was the first time I'd seen her there

2.3 Expressing dimensions

i Manner of expressing dimensions

The principal nouns and adjectives used are as follows:

Nouns	**Adjectives**
la altura – height	*alto* – high/tall
la longitud/largura – length	*largo* – long
la anchura – width/breadth	*ancho* – wide/broad
la profundidad – depth	*profundo* – deep
el espesor – thickness	*grueso* – thick

The adjective ***espeso*** exists but it is less used than ***grueso*** when referring to thickness of materials, walls, wood, etc. It is largely used for liquids, shrubs or a wooded area.

The nouns and adjectives are used in the following way:

Esta fachada mide treinta metros de altura	This facade is thirty meters / one hundred feet high
Esta fachada mide treinta metros de alto	This facade is thirty meters / one hundred feet high
El muro mide veinte metros de longitud	The wall is twenty meters / sixty feet long
El muro mide veinte metros de largo	The wall is twenty meters / sixty feet long
La calle tiene diez metros de anchura	The street is ten meters / thirty feet wide
La calle tiene diez metros de ancho	The street is ten meters / thirty feet wide
El pozo tiene veinticinco metros de profundidad	The well is twenty-five meters / eighty feet deep

A meter is just over three feet. Thus, the last example could be translated as "approximately eighty feet deep."

ii Another way of expressing measurements is as follows:

una torre de cincuenta metros de altura *una torre de cincuenta metros de alto* *una torre alta de cincuenta metros*	a tower fifty meters / one hundred and fifty feet high
un muro de trescientos metros de longitud *un muro de trescientos metros de largo* *un muro largo de trescientos metros*	a wall three hundred meters / nine hundred feet long
un foso de tres metros de anchura	a ditch three meters / nine feet wide
un foso de tres metros de ancho	a ditch three meters / nine feet wide
un pozo de veinticinco metros de profundidad	a well twenty-five meters / eighty feet deep
un pozo profundo de veinticinco metros	a well twenty-five meters / eighty feet deep
un muro de un metro de espesor	a wall a meter / three feet thick
un muro grueso de un metro	a wall a meter / three feet thick

iii After the verb *ser*, numerals denoting dimensions, weights and prices are preceded by the preposition *de*:

El tamaño de este hombre es de dos metros	The size of this man is two meters / six feet six

La distancia es de treinta kilómetros	The distance is thirty kilometers / twenty miles
El precio de este coche es de cuarenta mil dólares	The price of this car is forty thousand dollars

iv Other common statements of measurement:

¿Cuánto mides?	How tall are you?
¿Qué número calzas?	What size shoe do you take?
Mi talla es la treinta y cinco	My size is thirty-five

2.4 Age

i Age is expressed with the verb **tener** + cardinal number + **años**:

¿Cuántos años tienes?	How old are you?
Tengo quince años	I am fifteen years old

Note also the very common use of ***cumplir***:

Ha cumplido diez años	He is / has reached ten (years of age)

ii Tiempo is also used of very small children, but not in Mexico, when their age is measured in months, weeks or days:

¿Cuánto tiempo tiene el niño / el bebé?	How old is the child/baby?

iii Not only is a birthday celebrated in Spanish-speaking countries but also the day of the saint after whom the person is named, although this practice has faded recently, and is only applied to the names of very important saints, as with San José or San Ignacio in the Basque country. This could lead, of course, to two sets of presents *¡Qué alegría!* (O joy!), as with the celebration of Christmas Day and the sixth of January, the **Reyes Magos** = Epiphany (i.e. the *Three Kings*):

¡Feliz cumpleaños!	Happy birthday!
Hoy es mi cumpleaños	Today is my birthday
El tres de marzo es el santo de José	José's Saint's day is the third of March

2.5 Collective numbers

i There are a number of nouns in Spanish which correspond to the English *about*:

una decena	about ten		*una treintena*	about thirty
una quincena	about fifteen		*una cuarentena*	about forty days
una veintena	about twenty		*una centena*	about a hundred
un millar	about a thousand		*un centenar*	about a hundred

ii These collective nouns are not greatly used between thirty and a hundred, although **cincuentena** exists, for example. **Docena** = *dozen* is less used than **decena** but survives in **la docena del fraile** = *baker's dozen*, i.e. thirteen.

257

Considerable uncertainty exists over the use of a singular or plural verb with these collective nouns. There are many examples for both forms of the verb but usage seems to outweigh grammatical logic. In other words, ***veintena***, while yet a singular noun, is more easily followed by the plural:

Apenas si quedaban una veintena de personas	Hardly twenty people remained
Es la primera vez que se reúne(n) un número de	It's the first time that a number of specialists
especialistas	have gathered

(See unit 3, level 2.4, for more information on this point.)

2.6   Fractions

i Increasingly abandoned in the interests of percentages, fractions appear as follows: *la mitad* (half), *el tercio / la tercera parte* (third), *el cuarto / la cuarta parte* (quarter), *la quinta parte* (fifth), *la sexta parte* (sixth), *la décima parte* (tenth), *la centésima parte* (hundredth), *los dos tercios / las dos terceras partes* (two thirds), *los tres cuartos / las tres cuartas partes* (three quarters), *las dos quintas partes* (two fifths), *las tres séptimas partes* (three sevenths), *las dos centésimas partes* (two hundredths), *las nueve milésimas partes* (nine thousandths)

ii The same uncertainty as above (level 2.5.ii) exists with *la mitad*, etc., with respect to plural and singular verbs.

Ejemplos

Un tercio de los hombres dijeron / dijo que no	A third of the men said no
La mitad de los habitantes se opusieron/opuso al proyecto	Half the inhabitants opposed the plan

2.7   Mathematical expressions and signs

Here are the basic mathematical expressions and signs:

$+$	*más*	$:$	*dividido por / entre*
$-$	*menos*	$\times$	*(multiplicado) por*
^{2}	*al cuadrado*	$\%$	*por ciento*

Note the division sign is different from the Anglo-American $\div$.
   Note also the following terms:

la adición	the addition	*Sobran cinco*	There's five left over
Quedan diez	The remainder is ten	*Suma y sigue*	Add and carry
la resta	the subtraction	*sumar*	to add
restar	to subtract		

Examples

Tres más dos son cinco	$3 + 2 = 5$
Nueve dividido por tres son tres	$9 : 3 = 3$
Cuatro multiplicado por seis son veinticuatro	$4 \times 6 = 24$

Dieciséis son cuatro al cuadrado $16 = 4^2$

La tasa es del cinco por ciento   The rate is 5%

Exercises Level **2**

i Más problemas de matemáticas. Calcula los siguientes problemas y escribe tus respuestas con todas sus letras.

Ejemplo

$80 - 30 >$ ochenta menos treinta son cincuenta

a $30 + 50 =$	j $20 \times 30 =$
b $45 + 45 =$	k $27 \times 40 =$
c $32 + 58 =$	l $50 \times 60 =$
d $77 + 23 =$	m $73 \times 41 =$
e $100 - 40 =$	n $45 : 15 =$
f $99 - 59 =$	o $60 : 20 =$
g $84 - 34 =$	p $200 : 5 =$
h $78 - 36 =$	q $1.000 : 25 =$
i $88 - 28 =$	r $10.000 : 1.000 =$

ii Llena (*M*) / rellena los blancos con expresiones de tiempo y de dimensión.

Fui a Cuernavaca la semana (_), y la (_) voy a Guanajuato. A (_) año pasaré quince días en las Barrancas del Cobre, y el año que (_) me gustaría ir al Gran Cañón. Quisiera pasar ahí (_) ya que ocho días no son suficientes. La mejor (_) del año para visitar estos dos cañones es junio.

    Me gustaría mucho visitar el Gran Cañón porque tiene casi dos mil metros de (_) y muchos kilómetros de (_). Desde abajo, tiene dos mil metros (_). Lo más impresionante es que es tan (_) que cubre centenares de kilómetros.

    Yo quisiera visitar nuevamente las Barrancas del Cobre (_) unos meses. Este cañón es tan (_), tan (_) y tan (_) como el Gran Cañón. El año (_), bajé hasta el fondo de las Barrancas del Cobre con una (_) de cuates (**M**) / amigos. La mitad de ellos, o sea diez, se quedaron / quedó en el fondo, y los otros, o sea una (_), volvieron a subir. Hay trayectos del río que está en el fondo hasta con diez metros (_), cincuenta (_), y varios kilómetros (_).

    Planeamos pasar (_) días en el fondo de las Barrancas. Estando abajo, el tiempo apremiaba, y pensamos que nos (_) poco tiempo. Salimos rápidamente del cañón, y arriba, nos dimos cuenta de que habíamos calculado muy mal y que nos (_) cuatro días. ¿Qué haríamos con estos cuatro días?

iii Actividad en común

Objetivo – Practicar el cálculo de números en todas sus letras

Método – Un miembro de la clase escribe diez problemas matemáticos en el pizarrón (***M***). Escribe en cifras. La clase, ya dividida en dos equipos, calcula la solución. El primer equipo en facilitar la solución en palabras gana el punto. El primero en alcanzar diez puntos gana el partido.

Ejemplos

Miembro de la clase:	$25 + 73 = ?$
Clase:	noventa y ocho
Miembro de la clase:	$199 + 241 = ?$

Clase: cuatrocientos cuarenta
Miembro de la clase: $15 \times 20 = ?$
Clase: trescientos

No olvidar usar las seis operaciones que aparecen en 2.7. Si es listo, el miembro que puede escribir en el pizarrón hace preguntas relacionadas con el porcentaje.

Unit 28 *(Unidad 28)*

Comparatives and superlatives *(Los comparativos y superlativos)*

Level **1**

1.1 **Comparison of adjectives indicating inequality and equality** (*Comparación de adjetivos indicando desigualdad e igualdad*)

1.2 **Comparison of adverbs indicating equality and inequality** (*Comparación de adverbios indicando igualdad y desigualdad*)

1.3 **Superlatives + adjectives** (*Superlativos + adjetivos*)

1.4 **Other features** (*Otros detalles*)

1.1 Comparison of adjectives indicating inequality and equality

i The comparison of adjectives is formed by using **más** (more) and **menos** (less) before the adjective. **Que** (than) is used after the adjective.

Examples

Carlos es más rápido que tú	Carlos is faster than you
Este chico es más listo que su hermano	This boy is smarter than his brother
Son menos ruidosos que las muchachas	They are less noisy than the girls
Es un hotel menos tranquilo que el otro	It's a less quiet hotel than the other one
negro / más negro / menos negro	black / blacker / less black
capaz / más capaz / menos capaz	capable / more capable / less capable

ii Four adjectives, in addition to their regular comparatives, have other, and, in two cases, preferred, forms:

Positive	**Comparative**
bueno (good)	*mejor* (better)
malo (bad)	*peor* (worse)
grande (big, large)	*mayor* (bigger, larger)
pequeño (small)	*menor* (littler, smaller)

Examples

Esta novela es mejor que la otra	This novel is better than the other one
Isabel es peor estudiante que María	Isabel is a worse student than María

Tu niña es mayor que la mía	Your girl (daughter) is bigger than mine
Mi prima es menor que yo	My cousin is smaller than me

iii Comparison of adjectives (indicating equality)
Tan (as/so) is used here, followed by ***como*** (as):

*Es tan abusado (**M**) / listo como su papá (**M**) / padre*	He's as smart as his father
Es tan caro como el caviar	It's as dear as caviar

1.2 Comparison of adverbs indicating equality and inequality

i Equality. As with adjectives, ***tan*** + ***como*** is used:

Habla español tan bien como su profesora	She speaks Spanish as well as her teacher
La niña escribe tan perfectamente como su hermano mayor	The little girl writes as perfectly as her older brother

ii Inequality. *Más* (more) and ***menos*** (less) are used here, followed by ***que*** (than), as with comparisons of adjective:

Corre más rápidamente que yo	She runs faster than me
Lee más lentamente que su primo	She reads more slowly than her cousin
Lo arregla menos fácilmente que yo	He sorts it out less easily then me
Trabaja menos seriamente que su hijo	She works less seriously than her son

1.3 Superlatives + adjectives

i The superlative is usually expressed by placing the definite article with the comparative:

Son los más inteligentes	They are the most intelligent
Este hotel es el más caro de la ciudad	This hotel is the dearest in town
Este es el peor jugador del equipo	This is the worst player in the team
El tiempo que hace es el mejor del año	The weather is the best this year

ii *De* follows a superlative in cases where in English we would have *in*:

Texas es el estado más extenso de los Estados Unidos	Texas is the biggest state in the United States
El Nilo es el río más largo del mundo	The Nile is the longest river in the world

1.4 Other features

i Frequently, ***menos*** is replaced by ***no*** + ***tan*** + adjective or adverb + ***como***:

No es tan alto como su hermana	He's not so tall as his sister
No trabaja tan seriamente como yo	He doesn't work as seriously as me

ii *Más de* and *menos de* are used before quantities and numbers:

Hay más de un millón de libros en aquella biblioteca	There are more than a million books in that library
¿Por qué compras menos de dos kilos?	Why do you buy less than two kilos?

iii *Tanto ... como*, with its three other forms (*tanta / tantos / tantas ... como*), as much / many ... as, is used with equality of nouns:

No tengo tanto pan como Jorge	I haven't got as much bread as Jorge
No traes tantos discos como Elena	You don't bring as many discs as Elena
Hay tanta mantequilla como en casa	There's as much butter as at home
Tienes tantas cucharas como yo	You have as many spoons as me

Exercises Level 1

i Make three separate sentences from the two available. Follow the example

Juan disfruta mucho. Armando disfruta poco > **1.** Armando disfruta *menos que* Juan + **2.** Juan disfruta *más que* Armando + **3.** Armando *no* disfruta *tanto como* Juan

a Alicia se divierte mucho. Rosa se divierte poco
b Los muchachos descansan mucho. Yo descanso poco
c El doctor se cansa mucho. Su hijo se cansa poco
d Los niños gritan mucho. Juanito grita poco
e Me preocupo mucho. Tú te preocupas poco
f La señora trabaja mucho. Marta trabaja poco
g Tus amigas platican (**M**) / hablan mucho. Tú platicas/hablas poco
h Teresa gasta mucho. Sus hijos gastan poco
i Ellos comen mucho. Yo como poco
j La niña se queja mucho. Su hermano se queja poco

ii Put the following sentences in the negative. Use *tanto/a/os/as.*

Example

Escribí dos cartas. Juan escribió cuatro cartas > No escribí tantas cartas como Juan

a En mi país hay muchas montañas. En el tuyo hay menos
b Alicia salta tres metros. Lupe salta dos
c En las ciudades hay mucha niebla. En los pueblos hay poca niebla
d Luis toma mucha leche. Alicia toma poca
e Practicamos varios deportes. Lucía practica pocos
f Eché a perder mucho papel. Rosa echó a perder poco
g Jorge tiene mucho dinero. Nosotros tenemos poco
h En mi coche hay mucho lugar. En el tuyo hay poco
i Elena recibió muchos regalos. Tere recibió pocos
j Mis sobrinos comieron muchas aceitunas. Los tuyos comieron pocas

iii Paired activity
Objective – To practice statements of comparison
Method – A and B ask each other questions using ten expressions such as *tan ... como,* *más ... que, menos ... que, tantos ...*

Examples

A: ¿Eres más listo que yo?

B: No soy tan listo como tú

A: ¿Mi hermana es menos inteligente que yo?

B: Tu hermana no es tan inteligente como tú

 Level **2**

2.1 **Como** = *like* **or** *as* in English (**Como** = . . .)

2.2 **Que** replaced by **de lo que** (**Que** *reemplazado por* . . .)

2.3 **Cuanto . . . tanto**

2.4 **Superlatives of adverbs** (*Superlativos de adverbios*)

2.5 **Absolute superlative of adjectives** (*Superlativo absoluto de adjetivos*)

2.6 **Absolute superlative of adverbs** (*Superlativo absoluto de adverbios*)

2.1   *Como* = *like* **or** *as* in English

Corre como un conejo	She runs like a rabbit
Lucha como un tigre	He fights like a tiger
Hazlo como lo quieras	Do it as you wish

2.2   *Que* replaced by *de lo que*

i When each part of the comparison contains a different verb, **que** is replaced by **de lo que**:

Es menos fácil de lo que dice	It's less easy than he says
El examen fue más difícil de lo que habíamos temido	The examination was more difficult than we had feared
Es más tonto de lo que parece	He's dumber than he looks

ii This is also true with nouns:

Tiene menos dinero de lo que dice	She has less money than she says
Ha cometido más delitos de lo que piensas	He's committed more crimes than you think

2.3   *Cuanto . . . tanto*

i *Cuanto . . . tanto* followed by any comparative are used in correlatives to express ratio, corresponding to the English *the . . . the*:

Cuanto más viejo es el vino, tanto mejor	The older the wine, the better it is
Cuanto más largo es el día tanto más corta la noche	The longer the day, the shorter the night

ii *Tanto más/menos . . . cuanto que* corresponds to *all the more/less . . . because . . .*:

El delito es tanto más grave cuanto que acaba de salir de la cárcel	The crime is all the more serious because he's just come out of jail

Estoy tanto menos satisfecho de su conducta cuanto que le di dinero — I am all the less satisfied with her conduct because I gave her money

2.4 Superlatives of adverbs

The superlative of adverbs is formed in the same manner as those of adjectives:

Los mejores alumnos son los que hablan menos — The best pupils are those who speak least

Esa era la respuesta que menos esperaba oír — That was the reply I was least expecting to hear

Amo el mar cuando más alto suben las olas — I love the sea when the waves rise up even more

2.5 Absolute superlative of adjectives

i The absolute superlative of adjectives, when formed regularly, is made by adding *-ísimo*. It is then varied like any adjective ending in **o**. This ending has an intensive value, equivalent to the English *very* or *most*. As with the common Italian *-issimo*, and the occasional *-issime* in French, this form derives from the Latin.

Ejemplos

El acero es durísimo — Steel is very hard/tough

El oro es purísimo — Gold is very/most pure

La casa es altísima — The house is very tall

Las flores son hermosísimas — The flowers are really lovely

Es una construcción feísima — It's a really ugly building

ii The following distinctions are to be observed in the formation of the absolute superlative of adjectives:

a If the positive adjective ends in a consonant, it receives **-ísimo** without changing, unless the final consonant is **z**, which changes to **c** before **i**:

hábil / habilísimo — skillful / most skillful

feliz / felicísimo — happy / very happy

feroz / ferocísimo — fierce / most fierce

b A final vowel or diphthong is omitted before **-ísimo**. When the adjective ends in two vowels, as in **io**, both are omitted, although it could be maintained that the **i** remains but receives a written accent, and therefore a spoken stress.

importante / importantísimo — important / most important

limpio / limpísimo — clean / very clean

sucio / sucísimo — dirty / very dirty

amplio / amplísimo — wide / widest, full/fullest

pobre / pobrísimo — poor / very poor

Ejemplos

*una recámara (**M**) amplísima* — a very spacious bedroom

una mujer pobrísima — a very poor woman

Tiene manos limpísimas — She's got very clean hands

iii If, after dropping the final *a* or *o*, the last remaining letter is *c*, it is changed to *qu*, and similarly *g* to *gu* to preserve the hard sound:

blanco / blanquísimo	white / very white
rico / riquísimo	rich / very rich
fresco / fresquísimo	fresh / very fresh
largo / larguísimo	long / very long

Ejemplos

una piel blanquísima	a very white skin
un río larguísimo	a very long river
unas fresas fresquísimas	some very fresh strawberries

iv An unresolved issue. In principle, the diphthongs *ie* and *ue* revert to their original vowels *e* and *o* since the stress is transferred to the ending:

cierto / certísimo	certain / most certain
tierno / ternísimo	tender / most tender
ferviente / ferventísimo	fervent / most fervent
bueno / bonísimo	good / very good
nuevo / novísimo	new / very new
fuerte / fortísimo	strong / very strong

However, there has been a major shift in contemporary practice here. In the author's experience, ***ciertísimo***, ***tiernísimo***, ***buenísimo***, ***nuevísimo*** and ***fuertísimo*** have replaced the above, with the result that many Spanish speakers no longer know which is the correct one, suffering some residual sense that the original form is the *correct* one and the new one the *wrong* one. In any case, the so-called *wrong* form holds sway. This topic is another question for the quiz program, in both Spain and Mexico, for there are many other examples of these doublets (***dobletes***). It should be added that the author has never met with any form of the absolute superlative of ***viejo*** but ***viejísimo***.

This innovation was strenuously resisted by the members of the Real Academia and more conservative writers but they have lost the battle.

v The following is just a small sample of adjectives (there are many more) reverting to the original Latin for their entire form:

acre / acérrimo	bitter / very bitter
áspero / aspérrimo	harsh / very harsh
célebre / celebérrimo	most celebrated

Needless to say, these last three are only in literary use.

2.6 Absolute superlative of adverbs

i These are created by adding *-mente* to the superlative form of the adjective. They are not very common. It is felt that you should at least be aware of their function. Here are two examples:

noblemente / nobilísimente	nobly / most nobly
ricamente / riquísimamente	richly / very richly

ii Since these forms are very cumbersome, they are generally replaced by, for example, *muy, altamente, sumamente, extremamente, en extremo, en gran manera*:

Las pruebas resultaron altamente peligrosas	The tests turned out to be highly dangerous
El problema es sumamente difícil	The problem is most difficult
*Se enoja (**M**) / enfada en extremo por cualquier cosa*	She gets angry over the slightest thing

iii Many adjectives do not admit of comparisons. The principal ones are those that involve the idea of infinity and therefore express in themselves the idea of a superlative degree, or denote origin, material, shape or class. Such adjectives are:

supremo	*metálico*	*principal*	*inmortal*
italiano	*circular*	*triangular*	*celestial*

Of course, ***italiano*** is only one example among hundreds related to adjectives of countries: *mexicano, español, norteamericano, inglés, francés*, and so on

Exercises

Level **2**

i **Completa los blancos con una de las siguientes expresiones. Puede haber más de una respuesta**

como, tanto . . . como, más . . . que, menos . . . que, de lo que

Ejemplos

Tiene seis años pero escribe (_) una persona mayor > Tiene seis años pero escribe como una persona mayor

Hay . . . caballos . . . vacas > Hay tantos caballos como vacas

a Trabaja (_) un loco
b Me baño (= nado in **M**) en el mar (_) veces (_) tú
c Recibió (_) regalos (_) parientes tenía
d Envía (_) postales (_) envía su amigo
e Coge / Toma (**M**) (_) (_) (dos palabras) puedas
f Coge / Toma (**M**) (_) flores (_) puedas
g Estoy (_) (_) (dos palabras) ronco que no dejé de hablar / platicar (**M**) en toda la noche
h Llegó con mucho (_) retraso (_) (_) (_) (cuatro palabras) solía llevar
i Es (_) culto (_) (_) (_) (cuatro palabras) yo pensaba
j Tiene (_) dólares (_) yo, de suerte que me invita a cenar
k Le ofrecí un helado por que tenía (_) dinero que yo
l Había (_) (_) (dos palabras) mil espectadores y no cabían todos
m Había (_) (_) (dos palabras) veinte nadadores en la alberca (**M**) / piscina y había mucho espacio
n Compré (_) peras por que tenía (_) dinero (_) (_) (_) (cinco palabras) pensaba
o Aprobó todos sus exámenes, es (_) listo (_) (_) (_) (cuatro palabras) pensaba

ii **Actividad en clase**

Objetivo – Usar el superlativo de adjetivos

Método – Se le elige a un miembro de la clase. Se divide la clase en dos equipos. El miembro de la clase escribe un adjetivo en el pizarrón (**M**) / la pizarra. La clase tiene que encontrar el superlativo correspondiente. Huelga decir (*Needless to say*) que el primer equipo que alcance diez puntos gana el concurso

Ejemplos

Miembro de la clase:	¿Cuál es el superlativo de "bueno"?
Respuesta:	Mejor
Miembro de la clase:	¿Cuál es el superlativo de "malo"?
Respuesta:	Peor

Después, el profesor le pide a cada equipo que forme una frase con los superlativos encontrados. El miembro de la clase se queda cerca del pizarrón para indicar los puntos ganados en este concurso. Diez puntos es la meta.

Unit 29 *(Unidad 29)*

Word order (*El orden de las palabras*)

(It is recommended that, to take full advantage of this unit on word order, it be studied after most of the other units, since it suggests a degree of sophistication which can only be acquired from some previous penetration into the language.)

Level **1**

1.1 **Subject + verb + object** (*Sujeto + verbo + objeto/complemento*)
1.2 **Verb + subject** (*Verbo + sujeto*)
1.3 *Bien* **and** *mal* **with verbs** (*Bien y mal con verbos*)
1.4 **Adjectives with nouns** (*Adjetivos con nombres*)
1.5 **Pronouns + verbs** (*Pronombres y verbos*)
1.6 **Numbers +** *Otros/as* (*Números + otros/as*)
1.7 **Some flexibility with numbers** (*Alguna flexibilidad con números*)
1.8 **Dates** (*Fechas*)

1.1 Subject + verb + object

Essentially, Spanish word order is like English word order in that the subject precedes the verb that precedes the object: Juan lee el libro – *John reads the book*. However, the flexibility of the Spanish language frequently means that this order is not respected. It can be affected by a whole range of considerations such as the written word as opposed to the spoken word, the intention of an author in stressing an idea, length of sentences, questions of balance, the need to avoid clumsiness, short words as opposed to long words, use of punctuation, repetition – the list is endless.

The first feature to notice in Spanish word order is that the verb does not necessarily follow the subject. Compare the following two sentences:

El amigo se va	The friend goes away
Se va el amigo	The friend goes away

In these two sentences, the emphasis switches from ***El amigo*** in the first to ***Se va*** in the second since both of these sets of words appear at the beginning of their respective sentences. Much of the complexity and variability of the Spanish sentence flows from this simple but important inversion.

1.2   Verb + subject

Conditions when the subject comes after the verb:

i Where the subject is much longer than the verb or verb phrase, and often when the verb is reflexive. This is designed to create a sense of balance:

Durante mucho tiempo se oye un ruido ensordecedor	You can hear a deafening noise over a long period of time
Del latín vienen el español, el francés, el italiano y el portugués	Spanish, French, Italian and Portuguese come from Latin

ii Where the verb does not take a direct object. These verbs include:

doler (to hurt), *faltar* (to be lacking), *gustar* (to please = to like), *quedar* (to remain), *sobrar* (to be over / in excess)

Me duele la cabeza	My head hurts (i.e. I have a headache)
Me duelen los dientes	I've got toothache (i.e. more than one)
Faltan dos tenedores aquí	We need two more forks here
Me gusta este pan	I like this bread
Quedan doscientos metros hasta la cumbre	There are another two hundred meters to the top
Por lo visto sobran camas	Apparently there are beds left over

iii When a plural subject is used without an article: this often occurs when the verb is reflexive or intransitive:

En el mercado se venden peras	Pears are sold in the market
*Se ponen las cáscaras en el bote (**M**) / cubo*	The peelings are put in the can
Corren conejos por todas partes	Rabbits are running everywhere
Llegan niños de muy lejos	Children come from a long way away

1.3   *Bien* and *mal* with verbs

Whereas, in English, the adverb can be separated very easily from the verb, such is not the case in Spanish, unless the adverb or adverbial phrase is a long one. Again, it is a question of balance.

Compare the two sentences in each of the following pairs of sentences:

Habla bien el chino	She speaks Chinese well
Habla el chino estupendamente bien	She speaks Chinese marvelously well
Escribe mal el inglés	He writes English badly
Escribe el inglés increíblemente mal	He writes English incredibly badly

In the first sentence, **bien** immediately follows the verb, but in the second it follows the object since, accompanied by another adverb, it would be cumbersome and sound odd if it preceded the object. The same comments apply to the second set of sentences with **mal**.

1.4   Adjectives with nouns

(See also unit 21 on adjectives, levels 1 and 2)

i An adjective following a noun usually has a "distinctive" overtone, a nuance which is often conveyed by contrastive stress:

"¿Cómo es tu casa?"	"What's your house like?"
"Es una casa pequeña"	"It's a small house"

Pequeña is emphasized with rising intonation at the end of the sentence.
   However, in the sentence

Vivía en una pequeña casa cerca de la catedral	He lived in a small house near the cathedral

pequeña may be used before or after the noun with little difference of meaning or stress.

ii Note the difference between the two following sentences:

Las hojas secas caen	The dry leaves fall
Las secas hojas caen	The dry leaves fall

Here, it is a case of some of the dry leaves, as in the first case, or of all the dry leaves, as in the second case. The distinctive feature of the leaves in the first sentence is that some of them are dry. **Secas** is invested with greater importance in the first sentence and therefore comes after **hojas**.

iii But, the difference in adjectives before or after the noun is by no means clear cut.

Largo, for instance, precedes the noun in the sentence below:

Damos un largo paseo por el campo We go for a long walk in the country

Here, **largo** would sound odd after the noun. However, if **muy** were introduced to qualify **largo**, **largo** before or after the noun would be acceptable:

Damos un muy largo paseo / un paseo muy largo por el campo

iv There are some adjectives in Spanish which differ in meaning according to whether they precede or follow the noun. As a rule, the adjective after the noun receives more emphasis than were it before the noun. Here is a short list:

antiguo	*costumbres antiguas*	old customs
	un antiguo presidente	a former president
cierto	*indicios ciertos*	sure / definite signs
	ciertas personas	certain people
diferente	*libros diferentes*	different books
	diferentes libros	several books
distinto	*ideas distintas*	distinct ideas
	distintas ideas	various ideas
grande	*una casa grande*	a big house
	un gran escritor	a great writer
ligero	*una mesa ligera*	a light table
	de ligera importancia	of slight importance
nuevo	*una canción nueva*	a brand new song

	hemos comprado una nueva casa	We've bought a new / another house
pobre	un barrio pobre	a poor district
	¡Pobre mujer!	Poor woman!
único	su hija única	their only daughter
	la única solución	the only solution

v Some adjectives are always distinctive and rarely, if ever, precede the noun. Such adjectives typically denote nationality, membership of a political or religious ideology, color, etc.

Es de nacionalidad mexicana	He's of Mexican nationality
un carro (**M**) / coche francés	a French car
el partido socialista	the socialist party
la religión musulmana	the Muslim religion
Me gusta el vino tinto / blanco	I like red/white wine
una casa amarilla	a yellow house
un estudio literario	a literary study
una servilleta inútil	a useless napkin/serviette
ácido sulfúrico	sulphuric acid

1.5 Pronouns + verbs

Spanish pronouns precede the verb, except in the case of the imperative. For a full treatment of the topic see the units on pronouns (unit 17) and the imperative (unit 11).

Examples

Te doy el libro	I give you the book
Te lo doy	I give it to you
Se lo doy	I give it to her/him/you
Dámelo	Give it to me

1.6 Numbers + otros/as

Otros / as precedes the number, witness the examples:

otros cuatro hombres	another four men
otras cinco mujeres	another five women
otros tantos árboles	just as many other trees
otras pocas chicas	a few other girls

1.7 Some flexibility with numbers

There is some flexibility with numerals when used with **primero** and **último**.

| los dos primeros/últimos años | the first/last two years |
| los primeros / últimos dos años | the first/last two years |

1.8 Dates

The order of the definite article in dates:

*Hoy es **el** sábado 5 (cinco) de enero*   Today is Saturday the fifth of January
*Llegan **el** martes 4 (cuatro) de abril*   They arrive on Tuesday the fourth of April

Exercises Level **1**

i **Put the following words in their correct order. There may be more than one order in many cases.**

Example

cansado se chico temprano el acuesta > El chico cansado se acuesta temprano / Se acuesta temprano el chico cansado

   a tranquilidad médico recomienda le el
   b bicicleta en me andar gusta
   c dos quedan vacaciones las para semanas me
   d tela metros tres sobran de
   e idiomas pocos dos bien hablan
   f canción chica la la mal canta
   g de tiempo corre el prisa
   h río carretera el la corre a junto
   i cambios partido los el opone a se conservador
   j México brasileña queda familia se en la
   k salita despacho el la barrer por queda y
   l árboles casas tapan nos vista las los y la verdes negras
   m montañas las altas las alcanzar podemos cumbres de
   n doscientos da otros euros me
   o premios diez ganaron primeras chicas las
   p octubre llegamos dos el de sábado

ii **Actividad en común (the information for these last exercises is in Spanish)**
Objetivo – Estudiar el orden de las palabras
Método – Un miembro de la clase, con ayuda del profesor, escribe en el pizarrón (**M**) / la pizarra, diez frases pero con las palabras mezcladas. *Las frases no son largas*, con un máximo de seis palabras. Dos equipos, ya formados, adivinan (*guess*) el orden correcto de las frases. El equipo que alcance primero seis frases correctas gana el concurso.

Ejemplos

la duele mano me   > Me duele la mano
me dólares cien quedan   >Me quedan cien dólares
portugués mal muy escribe el   > Escribe muy mal el portugués

Level **2**
2.1 **Adjective + (i.e. that precedes) noun** (*Adjetivo* + [*que se antepone al*] *nombre*)
2.2 **Two adjectives + noun** (*Dos adjetivos + nombre*)

2.3 **Verb + subject** (*Verbo + sujeto*)

2.4 **Meaning of adjective according to position** (*Sentido del adjetivo según su posición / ubicación* [**M**])

2.5 **Changing position of words with little difference in meaning** (*Posición / Ubicación* [**M**] *cambiante de palabras sin diferencia de sentido*)

2.6 **Word order with the reflexive *se*** (*Orden de palabras con **se***)

2.1 Adjective + (i.e. that precedes) noun

i Other factors favoring the adjective preceding the noun
When adjective and noun make a familiar or set phrase:

los altos Alpes	the high Alps
un ligero aumento en el coste de la vida	a slight rise in the cost of living
el presunto culpable	the alleged guilty person
las pequeñas y medianas empresas	small and medium-sized companies

ii When the adjective is an expected attribute:

un lamentable accidente	a lamentable accident
con enormes dificultades	with enormous difficulty

2.2 Two adjectives + noun

When there is more than one adjective, the most distinctive one is placed furthest away from the noun. This, again, conforms to the notion of emphasis placed at the end of the sentence:

la política contemporánea mexicana	contemporary Mexican politics
la situación militar africana	the African military situation
la literatura argentina actual	present Argentinian literature
la opinión política popular	popular political opinion

2.3 Verb + subject

The subject frequently follows the verb in the following circumstances
i When a preposition such as *a* or *de* begins the sentence:

Al hombre le vino la idea de salir enseguida	The man had the idea of going out immediately
A todos los chicos se les ocurrió jugar (al) fútbol	All the boys had the thought of playing football
A mí no me gusta la música popular	I don't like popular music
De su silencio se deduce que no vendrá	We can deduce from his silence that he's not coming

ii When the sentence begins with the "impersonal" *se*:

Se nos está acabando el lavavajillas	Our dishwasher is wearing out
Se alquilan bicicletas	Bicycles for rent
Se venden departamentos (**M**) / *pisos*	Apartments for sale
Se ha confirmado el terremoto	The earthquake has been confirmed

2.4   Meaning of adjective according to position

Further adjectives the meaning of which can vary (but not always) according to their position before or after the noun:

medio	*el hombre medio*	the average man
	la clase media	the middle class
	el dedo medio	the middle finger
	medio litro	half a liter
mismo	*Roma misma* / ***la** misma Roma*	Rome herself
	su mismo pueblo / *su pueblo mismo*	his very village
	el mismo sentido	the same meaning
propio	*en defensa propia*	in self defense
	Tiene casa propia / *su propia casa*	She has her own house
	sus propias palabras	his very words
	obra del propio Unamuno	a work of Unamuno himself
puro	*la verdad pura*	the unadulterated truth
	de pura envidia	through sheer envy
simple	*un corazón simple*	a simple heart
	un procedimiento simple	an easy procedure
	una simple razón	a simple reason

2.5   Changing position of words with little difference in meaning

Further examples of changing word order with little change in meaning, except for, possibly, slight shift in emphasis. Note the great variety in the first example:

Las maniobras militares terminaron sin incidencias / *Terminaron las maniobras militares sin incidencias* / *Terminaron sin incidencias las maniobras militares* / *Sin incidencias terminaron las maniobras militares*	The military maneuvers ended without incident
Intervinieron muchos factores en mi decisión / *Muchos factores intervinieron en mi decisión* / *En mi decisión intervinieron muchos factores*	Many factors affected my decision
Se ha inundado la bodega / *La bodega se ha inundado*	The cellar / warehouse (**M**) has been flooded
Han inundado el sótano las aguas / *Las aguas han inundado el sótano*	The water has flooded the basement

Me irrita la garganta el humo de la fábrica / El   The factory smoke irritates my throat
humo de la fábrica me irrita la garganta

Le dijo el médico que debe guardar cama / El   The physician/doctor told him that he
médico le dijo que . . .   must stay in bed

2.6   Word order with the reflexive *se*

Further examples of variety in word order involving the reflexive, and untranslatable, **se**. This is probably the most complicated series of expressions in the present work, and this usage looks forward to a more advanced tackling of Spanish grammar. It is difficult to explain the constructions below and it seems wiser to let them speak for themselves. The following three sentences that one would find in the written language have exactly the same meaning:

A todos los chicos se les permite salir
Se les permite salir a todos los chicos } All the boys are allowed to go out
Se les permite a todos los chicos salir

If the noun **chicos** governs a subordinate clause the result is the following. Again, this is more the written language:

A todos los chicos que tengan más de doce años se les
permite salir } All the boys who are more than twelve
Se les permite salir a todos los chicos que tengan más years old are allowed to go out
de doce años

If you can grasp this structure you are well on the way to conquering Spanish grammar.

Exercises Level 2

i **Escribe las siguientes frases cambiando el orden de las palabras, una o dos veces. Ten en cuenta que se trata sobre todo del equilibrio de la frase.**

Ejemplo

A todos los jóvenes se les permite nadar en la alberca (**M**) / piscina > Se les permite a todos los jóvenes nadar en la alberca / Se les permite nadar en la alberca a todos los jóvenes

a A los soldados se les prohíbe salir del campamento militar
b A algunos de los policías no se les deja regresar temprano
c A la mayoría de los profesores no se les recomienda trabajar más de cuarenta horas
d A los clientes no se les prestan más de diez mil euros
e A casi todos los conductores se les impidió usar la autopista
f A todos los clientes se les avisará sobre el valor de sus acciones
g A toda la familia se le ayudó a pagar los gastos médicos
h Al estudiante colombiano se le animó a estudiar más horas

ii Actividad en común

Objetivo – Estudiar el orden de las palabras

Método – Se trata del mismo método que en el ejercicio de arriba (29, ejercicio ii). Cambia una condición. La frase puede consistir en ocho palabras, en lugar de seis.

Ejemplo

tarea profesor hagamos que la pide nos el >
El profesor nos pide que hagamos la tarea

Unit 30 *(Unidad 30)*

Augmentatives and diminutives (*Los aumentativos y diminutivos*)

(Although this is the last unit, don't think that its contents are less important than those of the other units. Augmentatives, and especially diminutives, are very common in the Spanish language.)

Level **1**
1.1 **Diminutives** (*Diminutivos*)

1.1 Diminutives

i One of the characteristic features of Spanish, especially in the spoken language, is its use of suffixes which can express a wide range of affective notions (size, affection, disapproval, irony, etc.). Some suffixes are so firmly associated that they form words in their own right. Here is a small list:

bocadillo	sandwich in form of a roll	*panecillo*	bread roll
caballete	easel	*platillo*	saucer
camarín	dressing room (in theater)	*ramita*	twig
cucharita	teaspoon	*ventanilla*	window (of car/train), ticket
golpecito	tap (small blow)		office
hoyuelo	dimple		
mesita	small/bedside table		

ii The two main diminutive suffixes are as follows:

-ito/a – -ecito/a

These are among the most common suffixes, especially in Spanish America, and therefore Mexico. Their predominant meaning is diminutive. However, this does not necessarily mean that the object is smaller. It can sometimes merely be an affectionate way of expressing yourself:

Examples

*Tengo rentado (**M**) un carrito / alquilado un cochecito*	I've rented a (small) car
*Hernani es un pueblito (**M**) / pueblecito en el País Vasco*	Hernani is a small village in the Basque Country
*Acabo de leer un cuentito (**M**) / cuentecito*	I've just read a short story/tale

iii As for a choice between *-ito / a* and *-ecito / a*, Mexican speakers seem to choose the *-ito / a* form – witness the second and third examples above.

Note also the pervasive use in Mexico and all Central America of **ahorita** with the meaning of *now*, **ahora** in Spain. It should be added that the present author has never heard the Peninsular **ahora** in Mexico. Similarly, Mexicans seem to use **prontito** (soon) much more than **pronto**. This ubiquitous use of the *-ito / a* form is viewed by some Spaniards as too sentimental, while conversely, Mexicans may consider the Spaniards' use of language as aggressive or harsh-sounding. What is clear is that the Spanish of Mexico, especially in the north, is much more melodious than the Spanish of Castile.

It should be added that diminutives and augmentatives form such an integral part of the Spanish language that few of them appear in dictionaries since dictionary sizes would probably double.

iv *-Ito* and *-ecito* also indicate genuine affection, and are particularly associated with language used to, and by, children.

Examples

Dale un besito a Papá	Give Daddy a kiss
¡Oye, niño, déjalo al caballito!	Hey, leave the horse alone!
Le duele el dientecito al pequeño	The child's tooth is hurting

You must have read when you were small: *Los Tres Cerditos* (*The Three Little Pigs*), *Pulgarcito* (*Tom Thumb*), *La Caperucita Roja* (*Little Red Riding Hood*), *El Patito Feo* (*The Ugly Duckling*) and *Blancanieve y los Siete Enanitos* (*Snow White and the Seven Dwarves*).

-Ito / a can also have an intensifying effect:

Examples

Hace un poco fresquito, ¿verdad?	It's a bit chilly, isn't it?
Allí tienes un café calentito	There's some nice hot coffee for you
¡Ay, el pobrecito!	Poor old thing!

v An alternative form for certain nouns ending in *-ito/a* is *-illo/a*. For example, there is a choice between **cucharita** and **cucharilla**, and between **mesita** and **mesilla**, to the point that there is often a discussion as to which one is the correct one. Of course, both are, although it depends on the region of Spain or elsewhere.

vi Affective suffixes are used most often with nouns and adjectives, although the use of *-ito / a* extends to past participles used adjectivally and even to adverbs.

Examples

El niño está dormidito	The child is sound asleep
*Hay que platicar (**M**) / hablar bajito*	You must speak really quietly
Lo haré en seguidita	I'll do it right away

Exercises Level **1**

i **Find diminutives for the following words. In some cases, there can be more than one diminutive.**

Example

casa > casita

almohoda	flor	papá	salón
bajo	guerra	piedra	señor
campana	jardín	pobre	silla
chico	joven	poco	taza
cigarro	lugar	pedazo	trozo
copa	mamá	pastel	vaso
farol	nube	reloj	

ii Actividad en clase

Objetivo – Familiarizarse con la construcción de diminutivos

Método – *A* escoge un nombre (*noun*), y le pide a *B* que encuentre un diminutivo que corresponda a este nombre (y vice versa). Sería fácil encontrar quince nombres con sus diminutivos.

Ejemplos

A: casa
B: casita
A: hombre
B: hombrecito
A: chico
B: chiquito

Después, el profesor los (*you*) **reúne y pide a un voluntario que recabe** (*collect*) **todos los diminutivos para escribirlos en el pizarrón (M).**

Level **2**

2.1 **More on diminutives** (*Más detalles sobre diminutivos*)

2.2 **Augmentatives** (*Aumentativos*)

2.1   More on diminutives

i *-illo/a – ecillo/a*

These are diminutive suffixes which may have a pejorative overtone. In Spanish America they are almost exclusively pejorative.

Ejemplos

No me gusta este tonillo de superioridad / ironía	I don't like this touch of superiority/irony
Había en la tienda un hombrecillo que se quedaba callado	In the shop was a(n insignificant) little man who said nothing
Me parece un poco complicadillo	It seems a bit complicated/awkward to me
Es una novela fuertecilla	That novel's heavy-going

ii The pejorative overtone is not always the case. See *panecillo*, etc., in the first paragraph of level 1.

More examples of a non-pejorative use of **-*illo*:**

Seguí un cursillo de español en Salamanca	I followed a Spanish course in Salamanca
Soplaba un airecillo / vientecillo muy agradable	A pleasant, light breeze was blowing

iii -uelo/a, –(e)juelo / a, -chuelo / a, -ete, -ecete, oleto

These are diminutive and may be pejorative, but it depends on the context and tone of voice or style of writing. For example, in all the following examples, the suffixes do not suggest any pejorative meaning.

Examples

Por el pueblecito bajaba un riachuelo que a veces estaba seco	A brook that was often dry came running down through the village
Un arroyuelo corre junto a los árboles	A stream runs past the trees
Mis hijos suelen montar en los columpios de una plazoleta / plazuela cercana	My children often get on the swings in a small square nearby
Las modernas oficinas bancarias han sustituido a los antiguos palacetes del Paseo de la Castellana en Madrid	The modern banking offices have replaced the old luxury villas of the Paseo de la Castellana in Madrid
Tiene los dedos regordetes	He's got chubby fingers

2.2 Augmentatives

i -ón / a

This suffix has a number of values. It may simply be an augmentative as in **sillón** (arm chair) or **hombretón** (well-built man). As an augmentative, it takes on most frequently a pejorative overtone, since largeness or excess is often thought to be bad:

solterón / ona	confirmed bachelor / unmarried woman
cabrón / ona	son of a bitch, bastard, bitch (care needed here)
dulzón	oversweet, sickly sweet, maudlin

Ejemplos

Es un solterón empedernido	He's a confirmed bachelor
Esa tía es una cabrona que me las pagará	That broad is a bitch who will pay for what she has done to me
Es una bebida dulzona que no me gusta	It's a sickly drink I don't like
No me gustó el final de la película, fue muy dulzón	I didn't like the end of the movie, it was very slushy / schmaltzy

ii -ón can also form pejorative adjectives from nouns

cabezón	stubborn

and pejorative nouns and adjectives from verbs:

llorón	cry-baby
empollón	grind, swot, swotty (not in **M**)

Ejemplos

Antonio es un cabezón y no va a cambiar de idea	Antonio is stubborn and won't change his ideas
Estas últimas noches el niño ha estado muy llorón	These last few nights, the child has been crying

Sólo han aprobado el examen los cuatro empollones   Only the four grinds/swots passed the examination

iii *-azo*
This suffix is similar to **-ón**, but is less common:

bigotazo	big moustache		*cochazo*	big car
acentazo	bad accent		*carrazo (**M**)*	big car
exitazo	great success			

Ejemplos

El bigotazo le cubría la cara hasta las orejas   His mustache covered his face right up to his ears

Su último DVD fue un exitazo tremendo   His last DVD was a tremendous hit

-azo can also have the meaning of *a (big) blow*:

codazo	blow with the elbow		*golpazo (**M**)*	big blow, thump
mazazo	blow with a cudgel		*puñetazo*	punch
golpetazo	a big blow			

Ejemplos

Dio un golpetazo en la pared con el puño   He banged his fist on the wall

Al carpintero se le escapó el mazo y se dio un mazazo en la mano   The hammer slipped from the carpenter's grasp and he banged his hand

iv *-ote/a*
This is augmentative and pejorative:

librote	dull book
palabrota	swear/dirty word
cabezota	stubborn
brutote	rough, clumsy, dumb
francote	very easy-going

Ejemplos

Ese hombre tiene costumbre de decir palabrotas   That man often says swearwords

María es una cabezota y no cambiará de idea   Maria is stubborn and won't change her ideas

However, **amigote** has the meaning of *buddy/mate* and is familiar rather than pejorative.

Ejemplo

Se fue por allí con los amigotes   He went that way with his buddies

v *-ucho / a, -acho / a, -uco / a, -aco*
These are clearly pejorative

casucha	hovel, dump
cuartucho	squalid room
populacho	populace, common herd
ricacho	stinkingly rich
frailuco	stupid little monk

mujeruca	old woman
pajarraco	big, ugly bird
But *picachos*	fierce-looking peaks

Ejemplos

Vivía en un barrio de casuchas	She lived in a slum shack
¿Cómo pueden vivir en el cuartucho ese?	How can they live in that dump of a room?
Le han regalado un pajarraco que no para de chillar	They have given him a wretched bird that squeals and squeals

vi The above are just some of the ways in which Spanish speakers manipulate verbs, nouns and adjectives to suit their emotional reactions to things and events. Some simple illustrations, among countless others, of the flexibility (describing small and big things) of these suffixes, are, going from small to large:

small	**average**	**(very) big**
botellín/botellita (**M**)	*botella*	*botellón*
casita (small house)	*casa*	*casona* (large country dwelling)
casilla (pigeon hole)	*caseta* (hut)	**casucha* (hovel)
cochecito	*coche*	*cochazo* (enormous car)
carrito (**M**)	*carro*	*carrazo* (enormous car)
disgustillo (minor trouble)	*disgusto* (annoyance, grief)	*disgustón* (most serious disturbance/ upset)

*here suffix has meaning of "unpleasant," "dirty," "ugly," rather than "big"

Neither the English language nor the French or Italian languages can match this flexibility, although Italian has a large and varied number of diminutives like ***piazzetta*** (little square) or ***Pinocchio*** (and you must have heard of him = Little Pine). However, do not allow this particular deficiency in French and Italian to prevent you from studying them. The present author has benefited enormously from them.

Finally, a few comments on diminutives as used in Mexico. As stated at the beginning of level 1, the Mexicans use the suffix ***-ito*** with great frequency, to the extent that the Peninsular speakers of Spanish may sometimes find it just too affectionate or warmhearted. Conversely, Mexicans can find the Spanish of Spain, and notably Castile, rough and abrupt, too harsh for the mellifluous tones of Mexican Spanish, and especially that of northern Mexico. It is all a question of personal choice and taste. ***Un carrito*** may be a *toy car* in Mexico, when being bought for a child, but it can equally well reflect the Mexican's love for his/her car, however big the engine size (***la cilindrada***). ***Agua*** is indeed the standard term for *water* in the whole of the Spanish-speaking world but the Mexicans seem to prefer ***agüita***, unusual in Spain. Similarly, ***frijoles*** (*beans*, but ***judías*** in Spain) is often replaced by ***frijolitos***, although this has nothing to do with size but, rather, with their culinary importance. This variety of choice in suffixes contributes to an unparalleled richness in Spanish which, in turn, provides the student with a treasure that is the cultural experience of the Spanish-speaking peoples.

Language is your point of entry into a wealth of personal experiences which you are now able to develop and promote. You have done well to progress to this point. But, don't stop here. ***¡Suerte en tu aventura lingüística!*** (Happy hunting!)

Exercises Level **2**

i Reemplaza las palabras donde puedas por diminutivos que convengan. Se trata aquí de un texto mexicano que puedes adaptar un poco

El domingo pasado, decidimos dar un paseo en el carro y visitar nuestra casa en el campo que está muy cerca de un pequeño y hermoso pueblo llamado Tepoztlán. Llamé a los abuelos a quienes siempre les gusta acompañarnos, sobre todo para ver a los nietos. Saqué el carro del garage. Dejamos en casa a los perros y los gatos por que no cabían en la cajuela del coche que tenemos. En el trayecto, por una carretera muy angosta, nuestra hija María preguntó a su Mamá: "¿Mamá, preparaste bocadillos, pasteles, y tenemos agua de naranja también?" Mamá contestó: "Sí, mi amor, preparé panecillos con queso y jamón."

Salimos en el carro para la casa de campo que está cerca de un bosque lleno de flores y donde zumbaban todo tipo de bichos y piaban muchos pájaros. Nuestros niños, María, Carlos y Juan fueron a jugar cerca de un lago donde había patos con sus patitos. Un arroyo desembocaba en el lago. Al lado, en el prado, había caballos y burros y todo tipo de animales.

Después de comer, los niños se acostaron y, al poco rato, estuvieron dormidos. Después de una hora, se despertaron, y Carlos se quejó, diciendo que le dolía la panza. Le dimos una pastilla y se le quitó el dolor. Por la tarde, caminamos por el pueblo, viendo las artesanías hasta que se nos hizo de noche. Regresamos a casa bajo unas estrellas centelleantes, admirando las luces emitidas por las luciérnagas. Cuando llegamos a casa, se despidieron los abuelos. Los tres chamacos nos dijeron: "Mamá, Papá, estamos cansados. Queremos acostarnos." Les dijimos a los niños: "Antes de que se vayan los abuelos, denles un beso." Y se fueron a la cama para dormir y soñar con los ángeles.

RB/JPL

ii Actividad en común (preparen esta actividad con quince días de anticipación).
Objetivo – Practicar el uso de diminutivos
Método – Se divide la clase en grupos de siete. Cada miembro del grupo representa a un personaje que aparece en el trozo de arriba (Level 2, i), o sea papá, mamá, los tres niños, abuelo y abuela. Se crea una conversación entre estos siete personajes. La conversación pone de relieve todos los diminutivos que salgan del trozo referido. La conversación puede tener un contexto mexicano o español.

Posible principio de la conversación:

Papá: Oigan, niños, vamos a pasar algunos días en la casita de campo
María: ¡Qué bueno! ¿Vendrán nuestros abuelitos?
Mamá: Sí, y también los perritos

Cuando cada grupo haya creado y practicado la conversación, la presentará a la clase entera. La dramatizará.
El profesor ofrecerá su opinión sobre la mejor actuación y el uso de los diminutivos.

Los más ambiciosos podrían crear una pequeña obra de teatro. Se trata de la última actividad del libro. Entonces ¡ánimo!

Model Answers / Soluciones y modelos

Unit 1 Level 1

ii Viajando a través de la ciudad de México

La ciudad de México es una de las más grandes del mundo, y como en toda gran ciudad, el transporte es muy diverso, y ofrece muchas opciones para viajar de un lugar a otro. Se puede viajar en automóvil, taxi, colectivo, camión, bicicleta, y trolebús. La mayoría de la población hace uso del transporte público. Los vehículos más utilizados de manera privada son los automóviles y los taxis.

  i Yes: *opción*

  ii No

  iii No: *lugares* (*lugar* is correctly spelt); *camión* needs an accent in the singular, plural = *camiones;* *trolebús* needs an accent in the singular, plural = *trolebuses; población* needs an accent in the singular, plural = *poblaciones*

Unit 1 Level 2

i

A través de su‿ historia, los Estados Unidos se‿ han caracterizado como‿ un gran crisol étnico. Esto quiere decir que‿ aunque la población está constituida de muchos grupos de personas de distinto‿ origen, existe no‿ obstante un pueblo norte‿americano. Tradicionalmente, los inmigrantes se‿ han asimilado‿ a la cultura norte‿americana después de‿ una‿ o dos generaciones. Debido‿ a la‿ insistencia de los padres, los hijos han hablado‿en inglés y, gradualmente, han adoptado las nuevas costumbres de la patria‿ adoptiva.

iv

Cada vez que me visita mi cuate (*pal*), siempre me pregunta por qué no tengo una buena chamba (*job*). Le pregunto: "¿Por qué me preguntas siempre lo mismo?" Me contesta: "Como tu cuate, puedo preguntarte cualquier cosa." Pero contesto a mi vez "¿Quién te crees tú para preguntarme qué chamba tengo?" "Bueno, si no quieres responderme, ¿Dónde trabajas y cuál es tu trabajo?" "Me enoja (*annoys*) que insistas tanto. Yo sé donde trabajo y como es, y ¡párale! (*that's enough*). ¿Cuándo te vas?"

Unit 2 Level 1

i (gender only)

la/una casa/silla/mesa/bombilla/botella/habitación/costa/fuente/reina/víctima; el/un / área/arma (these two are feminine); el/un plato/foco/libro/cuaderno/mapa/burro/caballo/jardín/amigo/rey

ii (gender only)

de la/a la casa/mesa/habitación/víctima/calle/pared/taza/escuela/anchoa;
del/al caballo/mapa/árbol/pájaro/departamento/apartamento/ángel; del/al área/
arma/águila/alga

iii La chica trabaja todo el día / En el suelo hay un gato / El padre está sentado en el
sillón / ¿Ves el reloj en la mesa? / La flor está en el jardín / Una mujer está en la calle /
Veo un árbol en el parque / Un(a) estudiante habla con la profesora / el profesor / Un
pájaro canta en el cielo / La casa está detrás del jardín

Unit 2 Level 2

i México es una gran nación / La muchedumbre está en la plaza / El/La estudiante
prepara la tesis / La ambición del hombre no tiene límites / El alma es eterna / El avión
imita al gorrión / La cocinera prepara la comida / Es médico y muy listo / Los padres
tienen cuatro hijos, dos hijas y dos hijos / El físico estudia la física / El ministro llega
con la ministra / La abogada habla con el alcalde / Voy a El Cairo / a El Cabo / La / El
policía forma parte de la policía / Lo bueno es que habla muy bien el español / Me
impresionó mucho lo ocurrido

ii

a La chica come en el comedor
b El muchacho va a la escuela
c La reina viaja en el *Reina Isabel*
d El libro del autor es largo
e Lo interesante es que tiene una trama complicada
f Lo extraño es que no venga
g La cónsul habla con la presidenta
h Lo probable es que lo haga mañana
i Nació en El Cairo pero vive en La Coruña
j Se estropeó la central y se produjo un apagón
k Hice lo posible para arreglar el asunto
l Lo más fácil es escribir la carta

iii

a El batería se encontró la batería estropeada
b El defensa de hoy no suele jugar en la defensa
c El guardia formaba parte de la guardia
d El cabeza (but *La* in **M**) se hizo daño en la cabeza
e El cámara tomó la cámara
f El cura se interesa por la cura de las almas
g El Génesis se refiere a la génesis del hombre
h Entiendo la cólera del médico cuando contempla el cólera
i Es imposible poner una coma cuando has sido afectado por un coma
j Hubo un corte eléctrico durante una sesión de Las Cortes
k El fin de la final fue emocionante
l El sargento dio una orden para imponer el orden
m La panda fue al zoológico para ver al panda
n Se me cayó un pendiente y rodó por la pendiente

o No funcionaba un terminal en el circuito eléctrico y hubo un apagón en la terminal de autobuses

p El vocal no sabía pronunciar todas las vocales

q La facha del facha parecía amenazante

iv

a Usa esta pala para sacar ese palo del camino porque no nos deja pasar

b To lo advierto por última vez, si tú no me haces caso, entonces saldré corriendo hacia tu casa y te acusaré con tu mamá

c Cuando llueve mucho, y hace frío, nuestro seto se llena de hongos y setas

d En invierno, cuando esté nevando, saldré a llenar mi copa con copos de nieve

e Vivo cerca del puerto que es muy famoso por sus casitas con puertas de color rojo

f Un plato de plata es mucho más costoso que un plato de loza

g Un pato usualmente tiene dos patas, y si no, entonces ese pato que no tiene dos patas es cojo

h Mi libro pesa menos que medio kilo pero más que una libra

i Hace un rato que no veo una rata en el parque. ¿Será que se fueron de vacaciones?

j El accidente dejó una marca en la pintura; ahora tendremos que cambiar su marco

k Yo te aseguro que, aunque no sepa de música, un bombo no puede hacer tanto ruido como una bomba

l Las chicas de un harem podrían fabricar muchos velos con una vela

m El lugar donde comemos todos los días, que es una fonda, tiene un pasillo tan largo que es imposible ver que hay al fondo

n Me gusta ver la cara de mi amada a través de su velo, alumbrada sólo con una vela

v

a Da gusto tratar con él por su **ingenuidad** (*frankness*)

b Ese niño necesita hacer algunos ejercicios de **lectura** (*reading*). No lee bien.

c ¿En qué **librería** (*bookstore/shop*) compraste el libro aquel?

d Aquellas familias viven en la más absoluta **miseria** (*poverty*), no tienen nada para comer

e En los **muslos** (*thighs*) se le está acumulando mucha grasa

f Manuel tiene **pinta** (*appearance = looks*) de enfermo. Ha perdido mucho peso

g Soy mucho más **sensible** (*sensitive*) al frío que al calor

h Eva es una chamaca (**M**) muy **simpática** (*nice/pleasant*). Me cae muy bien

i Una **tabla** (*board*) de windsurf no tiene nada que ver con una mesa de cocina

j Esos **sucesos** (*events*) inquietantes alarman a todos los ciudadanos

k Me llegó la **confidencia** (*confidential remark*) de que te casaste en Acapulco

l El médico/doctor (**M**) americano se confundió cuando le dije que estaba **constipado** (*had a cold*). Me dio pastillas para el estreñimiento

m Tuvo la **desgracia** (*misfortune*) de perder a su hijo en un accidente

n Creo que está **embarazada** (*pregnant*) de cinco meses

o Finalizó sus estudios con **éxito** (*success*)

Unit 3 Level 1

i los/unos padres, las/unas madres, los/unos libros, los/unos estudiantes, las/unas paredes, los/unos árboles, los/unos ingleses, los/unos franceses, los/unos martes, las/unas primaveras, los/unos otoños, los/unos pies, las/unas tribus, los/unos matices, las/unas voces, los/unos atlas, las/unas caries, los/unos ratones, las/unas cárceles, los/unos bueyes, los/unos jerséis, los/unos alemanes, los/unos relojes

ii

Los niños están en las casas

Los árboles están en los parques

Los gatos están cerca de (*near*) las puertas

Los lápices están en las mesas

Las flores están en los floreros

Los jardines están detrás (*behind*) de los edificios

Las hoces están en las montañas

Las naciones están contentas

Las niñas están felices

Las tribus están en las selvas

iii

Hay un árbol en el jardín

El estudiante está en el aula

El cuadro está cerca de la ventana

El inglés está en el hotel

El alemán está en el salón

El rey está en el palacio

El convoy está en la carretera

La bicicleta está en la banqueta

Unit 3 Level 2

i

El gobierno pasa por una crisis económica, sobre todo el lunes. Yo creo que la crisis tiene su orígen en el virus de la computadora. Es casi cierto que el déficit del gobierno supera un billón de dólares y que rompe un récord. El déficit no tiene nada que ver con el régimen político. Espera que el superávit vuelva en el próximo mes. El elemento clave de esta situación reside en la fecha límite en que el gobierno, el lord y sobre todo el gángster, tendrán que devolver el billón prestado o robado. La alternativa es ingresar al granuja que es culpable en una cárcel modelo.

ii

Los jóvenes, con unos amigos israelíes y unas amigas hindúes, entraron en los almacenes con papel moneda. Querían comprar luces piloto pero no estaban en la zona euro y no hablaban español. Sólo sabían palabras clave(s), nada más, porque sus lenguas madre eran el árabe (y el hebreo). Los dueños les ofrecieron unas luces piloto de gran calidad. Salieron de los almacenes y, con sus amigos israelíes y sus amigas hindúes, entraron en unas bocacalles oscuras. Se encontraron en un café donde tomaron tés árabes de menta, y regresaron a la estación para ver a sus amigos yemeníes.

iii

a Tengo agujetas por haber hecho demasiado ejercicio

b El coche bomba saltó por los aires

c Una salva de aplausos acompañaba al líder de la carrera

d Los obreros rellenaron el hoyo con los escombros de la obra

e Dame tus datos personales para rellenar la ficha

f El estudiante hace muchos progresos en la universidad

g Me dan miedo las tinieblas cuando llega la noche

h Falta poco para que festejemos las bodas de plata

i Pon los cubiertos en la mesa, por favor
j Ganaron el Premio Nobel con sus investigaciones sobre el cáncer

Unit 4 Level 1

i Compro un carro, Buscas una flor, Necesita dinero, Toca el piano, Platicamos con un amigo, Habláis español, Rentan / Alquilan una casa

ii Estudio/estudias/estudia/estudiamos/estudiáis/estudian el portugués – Bebo/bebes/bebe/bebimos/bebéis/beben vino – Como/comes/come/ comemos/coméis/comen pan – Viajo/viajas/viaja/viajamos/viajáis/viajan mucho – Corro/corres/corre/corremos/corréis/corren los cien metros – Aprendo/aprendes/ aprende/aprendemos/aprendéis/aprenden la natación – Limpio/limpias/limpia/ limpiamos/limpiáis/limpian la cocina – Escribo/escribes/escribe/escribimos/ escribís/escriben una carta – Abro/abres/abre/abrimos/abrís/abren la puerta

iii (Yo) entro en la cocina y abro la ventana. Respiro el aire. Escribo una carta en la mesa. Coloco un sello/timbre en el sobre. No manejo un carro / No conduzco un coche. Camino/Ando hasta Correos. Meto la carta en el buzón. Los amigos viven en Estados Unidos. Mando la carta a Estados Unidos. Los amigos reciben la carta al día siguiente. Platico/hablo con el cartero. Bebimos tequila juntos en un café. Regreso a casa.

iv Yo bebo tequila, Tú comes tacos/tapas, Él compra una casa, Nosotros manejamos un carro, Vosotros mandáis/enviáis una carta, Ellas escriben una tarjeta, Uds. llegan mañana

Unit 4 Level 2

i (Yo) Aprendo a tocar el piano, Tengo ganas de tomar un vaso de agua, Tiene la suerte de aprobar el examen, (Ellos) No tienen los medios de/para pagar la cuenta, Tiene (la) intención de estudiar castellano, Tiene la bondad de comprar los boletos, (Nosotros) Tenemos la costumbre de trabajar por la mañana, Tengo el gusto de presentarte a mi novia, ¿Quiere Ud. abrir la ventana?, ¿Quieres (tú) tomar una copa de vino con nosotros?

ii Quiero/Quería enseñarle a leer, Deseamos/Deseábamos invitarlos a cenar, Necesitaba leer y escribir, Manda llamar al plomero/fontanero, por favor, Le aconsejé / Te aconsejo escribir la carta ahorita, Decidió / Ha decidido mandar apagar todas las luces

iii

Tengo (la) intención de visitar México. Deseo enterarme de la vida mexicana y de la cultura azteca. No tengo miedo de viajar solo/a, porque tengo la costumbre de viajar. Soy un/a trotamundos. Quiero tomar (**M**) / coger el avión mañana y llegar a la Ciudad de México a las cuatro. Necesito comprarme los boletos hoy. Tengo medios de comprar boletos de primera. Espero tener la oportunidad de encontrar a mis amigos/as en la capital. Lo cierto es que tengo la ventaja y el privilegio de hablar español, y tengo ganas de platicar con mis cuates (**M**) durante toda la semana. Me gusta la posibilidad de vivir en un ambiente auténticamente mexicano.

iv suelo, suelen, solemos, llevan, lleva, hace, hace

Unit 5 Level 1

i a He aprendido b Has copiado c Han comido d Han jugado e Ha
llovido f Ha pasado g No ha llegado h has comprado i Hemos vivido
j Habéis metido

ii a Sí, han llegado b Papá ha preparado la cena c No, no he entendido la
pregunta d No, no han vivido en Tejas / Texas e No, no he seguido todo el
curso f No, no he encontrado la cartera g Sí, Mamá ha planchado las camisas
h Sí, hemos comido muy bien i Sí, ha llovido todo el día j No, no he podido
terminar mi trabajo

iii

a He/has/ha/hemos/habéis/han empezado el libro hoy
b No . . . . vivido en San Francisco
c . . . . corrido en la maratón
d . . . . comido unas tapas
e No . . . . aprendido la lección
f . . . . ido al colegio hoy

Unit 5 Level 2

i

He llegado a la estación. He encontrado a mi amigo. Hemos hablado de política y fútbol. Hemos
comido en un excelente restaurante. Él ha regresado a su pueblecito. He permanecido en la
plaza. He encontrado a una amiga chilena. Hemos tomado juntos/as un café en una cafetería.
Hemos vivido momentos muy agradables. He despedido a mi amiga en la estación. He regresado
a casa muy contento/a.

ii

Deportes: ¿Ha jugado (Ud.) al fútbol? (no **al** in **M**). ¿Ha nadado (Ud.) en el mar? ¿Ha
corrido los diez mil metros? ¿Ha estudiado la esgrima? ¿Ha hecho esquí? ¿Ha estado
en el Polo Norte? ¿Ha subido al Himalaya o a las Montañas Rocosas? ¿Ha visto la
Copa del Mundo? ¿Ha querido batir el récord del mundo de cinco mil metros? ¿Ha
cazado rinocerontes? ¿Ha metido cinco goles en un partido de fútbol?

Finanzas: ¿Ha invertido veinte mil dólares? ¿Ha perdido una gran cantidad de dinero?
¿Ha ahorrado el cincuenta por ciento de su sueldo? ¿Ha preferido una cuenta corriente
a las otras cuentas? ¿Ha sabido distinguir entre varios tipos de acciones?

Capacidad imaginativa: ¿Ha pintado cuadros? ¿Ha tocado un instrumento de
música? ¿Ha cocido pan al horno? ¿Ha soñado con, y realizado, hazañas heroicas?
¿Ha remendado camisas?

Sensibilidad: ¿Ha oído mucha música clásica? ¿Ha visto películas de Luis Buñuel?
¿Ha leído *Los Hermanos Karamazov*? ¿Ha traducido una novela al inglés? ¿Ha escrito
poesía? ¿Ha compuesto sinfonías?

Personalidad y sentido práctico: ¿Se ha convertido al budismo? ¿Ha temido
grandes tentaciones? ¿Ha reñido a sus niños? ¿Se ha reído de un pobre desgraciado?
¿Ha puesto la mesa todos los días? ¿Ha huído de un peligro? ¿Ha fregado platos? ¿Ha
sufrido problemas psicológicos?

iii

Mamá: Oye, Pedro, ¿Qué has hecho esta tarde?

Niño/a: He trabajado como un condenado

M.:   ¿Qué has leído?

N.:   He leído un cuentecito llamado *Pulgarcito*

M.:   ¿Has hecho un poco de matemáticas?

N.:   Sí, he hecho una hora de matemáticas. Me he convertido en un pequeño
           Einstein

M.:   ¿Toda la clase ha cantado?

N.:   Sí, Mamá, todo el mundo ha cantado. He actuado como Plácido
           Domingo

M.:   ¿Habéis sacado buenas notas?

N.:   Hemos sacado todos muy buenas notas. Hemos sido alumnos ejemplares

iv

He llegado al rancho de un amigo. He abierto la barrera. He entrado en su casa. He platicado con el ranchero que me ha presentado a su familia. Me ha introducido en el salón y después hemos visitado el corral. He visto a los burros y otros animales. He subido a un caballo. Hemos recorrido juntos la hacienda. He ido a la pesca. Me he despedido del ranchero. Le he prometido regresar un día a verlos otra vez. He vuelto a casa muy feliz.

v

a He alquilado / Tengo alquilada / He rentado / Tengo rentada una casa

b Ha escrito / Tiene escritas cuatro cartas

c Han preparado / Tienen preparada la cena

d Hemos organizado / Tenemos organizada la visita

e ¿Habéis planeado / Tenéis planeada la táctica?

vi

a La mamá nos contó que el bebé había estado enfermo

b Adriana admitió que había habido muchos problemas

c Avisaron en el departamento que habían venido científicos franceses

d Me dijo que habían llegado ayer

e Supe esta mañana que el chico había comido cinco helados

f Me enteré esta tarde que las estudiantes se habían ido de vacaciones

g Me dijeron sus madres que las chicas habían aprobado todos sus exámenes

h Me avisó mi cuate que el carro se había descompuesto

i Me dijo mi padre que habían subido ochenta viajeros al camión

j Me informó una policía que había habido un accidente

k Me dijo mi padre que el coche se había averiado

Unit 6 Level 1

i

Les leeré el cuentito/cuentecito más tarde

El jefe estará en la oficina más tarde

La chica vendrá la semana que viene

Pagaré la factura en aquel banco

Recogeremos las manzanas mañana

Buscaré el vídeo este noche

Te llamaré después

Haré el trabajo en enero

ii darán, dirá, hará, pondrá, vivirán, durará, saldrá, vendrás, compraremos, vendremos, abriré, recibirán

iii cenarás, llegará, irán, mandaremos, aprenderán, sabrá, pondré, abrirá

Unit 6 Level 2

i a habrán llegado,   b habrán sido,   c habrá ganado,   d habrán tenido,   e habrá hecho,   f habrá tenido,   g habrá sabido,   h habrá puesto

ii

¿Quién será esta señora? Supongo que tocará un instrumento como el piano con los dedos tan finos. Parece muy inteligente, ejercerá entonces la profesión de abogada o contable. Trabajará con una empresa internacional. Será un piloto (haz investigaciones sobre el género de una pilota/o) y viajará mucho. Estará casada con un hombre muy comprensivo. Tiene pinta de mujer muy afectuosa. Les tendrá mucho cariño a los dos hijos porque todos los matrimonios listos se reproducen. Estará dotada de una inteligencia excepcional. Con un marido muy emprendedor, dispondrán de una gran cantidad de dinero. Tiene un aspecto muy atlético y habrá corrido los cinco mil metros en trece minutos. Con tanto dinero habrán comprado una casona magnífica / un departamento (**M**) magnífico. Con un vestido tan elegante, habrá podido pagarle un dineral a una costurera. Marido y mujer juntos habrán creado una vida que me daría envidia ¡Ojalà (*O that*) mis especulaciones se convirtieran (*were transformed*) en realidad!

RB/JPL

Unit 7 Level 1

i a guardábamos   b hablábamos   c salía   d veían   e iba   f corregíamos   g comía   h tenían   i lavaba
ii a Quería   b Pensaban   c Tenías   d Íbamos   e Queríamos   f Tenía   g Necesitaba   h Pensaban

Unit 7 Level 2

i a no había,   b no conseguían hacerlo,   c eran suecos,   d nunca les salía bien,   e esto no complacía a Mamá,   f nunca venías a la hora correcta,   g siempre llovía,   h yo no lo aceptaba

ii

Íbamos con frecuencia a un pueblito cerca de Chihuahua. Se llamaba Creel. Teníamos rentada (**M**) / alquilada una cabaña, y todos los días, salíamos en carro con un chofer o guía que nos conducía a El Divisadero que estaba en el corazón de Las Barrancas del Cobre que son muy parecidas al Gran Cañón. Bajábamos con frecuencia a un punto muy profundo. La vista era francamente impresionante. A medida que descendíamos al valle y que subía el sol en el cielo, subía la temperatura y aumentaba el calor. Yo sudaba como si estuviera (*were*) en un baño de vapor. En la zona más profunda hacía un calor inaguantable y allí se cultivaba una gran variedad de frutas. Cada día, queríamos hacer un poco de alpinismo, pero el guía nos advertía todo el tiempo que era muy peligroso lo que planeábamos hacer, y regresábamos decepcionados cada noche. Yo tenía ganas de cazar pero la caza estaba prohibida por la policía.

iii a llevábamos   b llevaba   c llevaban   d llevaba   e solía   f solían
  g solías   h solía   i desde hacía   j desde hacía

Unit 8 Level 1

i a Salimos   b Abrió   c Cerré   d comiste   e Perdí mi bolso   f Fueron
  g volviste   h pasó   i bebieron   j Estuvimos   k hizo   l vino

ii a compró   b Fui   c Cumplí   d regresaron   e estuvieron   f prepararon
  g salieron   h invitasteis   i Viviste   j Hizo

iii a Fui al campo   b Pasé casi todo el día allí   c Estuve con varios amigos
  d Todo el mundo disfrutó cantidad   e No, volvieron/regresaron a casa dos de los
  amigos   f Sí, comimos, o más bien, cenamos en un café   g Comimos pescado
  h Bebimos jugo (**M**) / zumo de naranja   i Volvimos/regresamos muy tarde
  j Sí, dormí como un lirón

Unit 8 Level 2

i a . . . llegó un cuate (**M**) que pidió una bebida   b . . . entró su hermano
  c . . . hubo un accidente   d . . . nos entregó una carta el cartero   e . . . me sentí
  mal   f . . . irrumpió mi hermana en el salón   g . . . vimos pasar una bandada de
  pájaros h . . . se oyó un ruido espantoso   i . . . se le descompuso (**M**) / estropeó el
  motor   j . . . mi di cuenta de haberlos chamuscado (*singed*)   k . . . alguien llamó a
  la puerta

ii fuimos, acompañaron, estudiaban, llevaba, tenía, Teníamos, era, funcionaba,
  llenamos, estuvimos, montamos, prepararon, dieron, subimos, Había, se veía, Nos
  asoleamos / Tomamos, Disfrutamos, gustaba, estuvimos, Regresamos/Volvimos,
  estuvo/estaba

iii
a Sí, lo he oído no sé cuantas veces
b Sí, la he leído varias veces
c Sí, la he visto tres veces
d Sí, las he perdido cuatro veces
e Sí, hemos ido allí dos veces
f Sí, lo hemos visitado cinco veces
g Sí, me he caído dos veces

Unit 9 Level 1

i a llegarían   b sería   c iría   d aprendería   e servirían   f podrían   g sería
  h cuidarían   i coincidiríamos   j comprarías

ii a Dijo/saldría   b Opinamos/vendrían   c Dijeron/habría   d creía/haría
  e avisó/vendría   f comentaste/rentarías   g Suponía/haría   h Creía/
  aprobaría   i Pensaba/pondrían . . . aquella noche   j Estaba seguro / nevaría
  aquella tarde

Unit 9 Level 2

i a dijo / habría acabado   b Estuvimos/estábamos / habrían arreglado   c Era / se habría descompuesto/averiado   d Nos advirtió / habría llovido   e prometió / habrían cargado   f Sugirió / se habría resuelto   g Contestó / habrían construido   h informó / habrían corregido   i Te garanticé/garantizaba / habría entregado   j insistió/insistía / habría terminado   k Estuve/Estaba / habrían hallado/ encontrado

Unit 10 Level 1

i a encontrándolos   b afeitándose   c apoyándolos   d prestándolas   e rasurándome   f vaciándolo   g dándoselos   h describiéndomelo   i trayéndolo   j entendiéndome   k llenándose   l reconociéndome

ii
a Estoy mirando los árboles
b Estamos pintando la casa
c Estamos lavando los platos porque están sucios
d Estamos fregando los platos porque están sucios
e Estoy comiendo en el comedor
f Estoy durmiendo en la cama (if it is possible to answer under these conditions)
g Juan está contestando al teléfono
h Papá está preparando la comida
i Estamos recogiendo los papeles en el jardín
j Estoy pidiendo dinero

iii
a Estoy trabajando ahorita
b Estoy leyendo ahorita
c Está viendo la televisión . . .
d Está pidiendo dinero . . .
e Estoy vendiendo fruta . . .
f Estoy enseñando la física . . .
g Está oyendo el radio / la radio . . .
h Está trayendo cartas . . .
i Están escribiendo tarjetas . . .
j Estamos corriendo . . .
k Están abriendo botellas de vino . . .
l Estáis abriendo la ventana . . .

iv
a Las estoy comprando / Estoy comprándolas
b Los está vendiendo / Está vendiéndolos
c Los estamos corrigiendo / Estamos corrigiéndolos
d Las están tirando / Están tirándolas
e ¿Por qué la estás pidiendo? / ¿Por qué estás pidiéndola?
f ¿Por qué lo estás pidiendo? / ¿Por qué estás pidiéndolo?
g ¿Dónde la estás sirviendo? / ¿Dónde estás sirviéndola?

h Los está trayendo / Está trayéndolos
i Los están escribiendo / Están escribiéndolos
j Lo estoy aprendiendo / Estoy aprendiéndolo

Unit 10 Level 2

i a El músico estaba tocando la guitarra cuando resbaló . . .   b Mi padre estaba durmiendo cuando empezó a llorar el bebé   c La familia estaba cenando cuando sonó el teléfono   d Carmen estaba telefoneando al momento que yo quise mandar . . .   e Carlos estaba limpiando la recámara/habitación mientras yo jugaba en el jardín   f Todo el grupo estaba bailando cuando la violinista empezó a toser   g El mesero estaba sirviendo el desayuno cuando rompió una copa   h El chofer/chófer preguntó por la dirección cuando llegó la policía

ii
a Las estudiantes venían corriendo porque era tarde
b Las tunas iban cantando por las calles
c Mi prima entró llorando en el salón
d Los amigos siguieron comentando la política
e El alumno pasó todo el día estudiando
f Ella volvió cojeando a la cocina
g El poeta Byron cruzó el río nadando
h El perro atravesó la calle corriendo

iii a estuvo   b estuvieron   c estuvo   d estaba   e estaba   f estábamos
g estaban   h estaban   i estuve   j estuvo

Unit 11 Level 1

i a Vende   b Ve   c Compra   d Abre   e Prepara   f Haz   g Sal
h Come   i Di   j Lee   k Ven   l Habla   m Pon   n Dale

ii a Compra   b Rompe   c Estaciona   d Aparca   e Manda   f Vende
g Coge   h Toma   i Aguanta   j Abre   k Bebe   l Haz

iii a Escribes   b Conduces   c Hablas   d Echas   e Pones   f Le das
g Metes   h Pagas   i Lees   j Reservas

Note. In most of these cases, it would be possible to use the infinitive, as in the exercise itself, if something else were added like: Escribir la carta ahora, Pagar la cuenta con visa, Reservar los boletos de avión con mucha antelación (*well in advance*)

Unit 11 Level 2

i a Hallen   b Manejen   c Platiquen   d Laven   e Jalen   f Pongan
g Tomen   h Hagan   i Empaquen   j Suban   k Prendan   l Limpien

ii a No agregues   b No escribas   c No corras   d No abras   e No le des
f No le digas   g No pongas   h No hagas   i No vengas   j No cojas / No

tomes (**M**) k No cuides l No prepares m No platiques n No laves
o No duermas p No aprendas

iii a No me esperes b No los invites . . . c No lo pongas . . . d No te levantes
e No te acuestes f No lo hagas . . . g No la ayudes h No la apagues i No
los llames j No las escuches k No le pidas . . . l No la cierres m No te
sientes n No las busques o No la pruebes p No los visites . . . q No te
despiertes (*Is this possible?*) r No me lo expliques

iv

Hermano mayor:	Oye, ¡Dame la pelota!
Hermano pequeño:	¡No me hables así!
Hermano mayor:	¡Hazme caso y dámela!
Hermano pequeño:	No te la doy si me sigues hablando así . . . pídemela por favor, y chance te la dé (*perhaps I'll give it to you*)
HM:	¡Que me la des, te digo!
HP:	¡Ya te dije que no me hables así! No quiero y no te la daré
HM:	¡No esperes que te ayude con tu tarea!
HP:	¡No me asustes!
HM:	¡Que me dejes jugar con la pelota!
HP:	¡Déjame en paz! ¡Entiende que no te la voy a dar!
HM:	Y tú, ¡obedece a tu hermano mayor!
HP:	¡Deja de fregar*! ¡Ve a molestar a alguien mas!
HM:	¡No seas tan respondón! ¡Cuida tu lengua** o se te va a caer!

Y regresaron abrazados a casa, amigos como siempre

* No es grosero, implica enojo . . .

** Expresión que se refiere a que no use palabras "fuertes" o agresivas

Unit 12 Level 1

i a cae b (Yo) hago c hace d voy e van f van g puedo h quieren
i tengo j venís k vienen l veo m dices n doy o quiere
p queremos

ii a tiene b volvemos c cierro d quieren e prefieren f dormimos
g devuelven h resuelvo i pensamos j empiezan k pierden
l encuentran m pedimos n enciendo o recuerdo p cuento

iii a sigo b repetimos c sirvo d siguen (**M**) (*and Spain if you don't know the people well*) / seguís e El profesor corrige f Te pido g dormimos h volamos
i Pensamos en las vacaciones j Piensan en la película k Uds. lavan vosotros
fregáis l invertimos / invierten (ellos) m os impedimos n recomiendo

Unit 12 Level 2

i a Oyó b cupe (allí) c supe d sonrió e olió f frió g irguió h dijo
i pude j hice k fue l quiso (en aquel momento)

ii a cuelgue b friegue c pleguemos d permanezca e establezcan
f merezcamos g se desplieguen h obedezca i agradezcas j escojan

iii a comuniqué   b eduqué   c cacé   d esforcé   e empecé   f castigué
   g marqué   h pagué   i acerqué   j reconocí

iv

Perdí cien dólares. Se lo comuniqué a mi hermano. Me acerqué al lugar donde los había perdido. Me esforcé por encontrarlos cerca de un árbol. Empecé a preocuparme, y enfadándome, volqué un vaso de cerveza. Cansado, desplegué una silla para sentarme. Después, relajado, me levanté y la plegué. Colgué mi americana en un árbol. Halagué a mi hermano para que me ayudara un poco más. Por fin, me marqué un punto al descubrir los billetes, los toqué con afecto, y marqué el número de teléfono de mi madre y le expliqué lo ocurrido. Y practiqué mi español al escribir este trozo.

Unit 13 Level 1

i a soy   b es   c está(s)   d está   e es   f estamos   g está   h está   i es
   j es   k están   l son   m es   n están   o está   p son (*could be* están)   q es
   r está   s son   t es

ii

Mamá:	Estás pálida, chica
Yo:	No estoy bien. Estoy mala. ¡Ay Mamá! ¿Qué será de mí?
Mamá:	Voy a llamar al médico Buenos días, doctor. Mi hija está enferma
Médico:	¿Está con gripe? ¿Está acatarrada/constipada?
Mamá:	No estoy segura. Y no está claro.
Médico:	Ya voy.
Mamá:	¿Está Ud. listo para venir ahora?
Médico:	Sí, estoy dispuesto a ir ahora mismo
Mamá:	Viene el médico. Es muy simpático, muy listo y muy chistoso.
Médico:	Buenas tardes, Sra Núñez. ¿Qué pasa?
Mamá:	Mi hija está constipada y está muy mala. Siempre es muy viva y muy feliz pero hoy está descontenta y está ahora de mal humor, lo que no es normal.
Médico:	¿Dónde está?
Mamá:	Está en aquel cuarto. Es un gran cuarto bien iluminado pero hoy está oscuro. Perdón.
	El médico examina a la paciente
Médico:	No es nada. No pasa nada. Estoy por recomendar mucha fruta. Y dentro de un par de días estará otra vez de buen humor. Es una chica muy entusiasta y entretenida, y ya está a punto de contar chistes otra vez.

Unit 13 Level 2

i a Es/fue   b estoy   c estaba   d estoy   e está   f es   g está   h estuviste
   i estuve   j estuviste   k estuvo   l estaban   m estaba   n estaba   o estaban
   p eran/son

ii a Una subida cansada produce cansancio y un caminante cansado tiene cansancio
El primero se usa con **ser** y el segundo con **estar**
b Un chico callado es un chico que habla poco y una plaza callada no tiene ruidos
El primero se usa con **ser** y el segundo con **estar**

c Un dolor molesto causa molestia o disgusto y una persona molesta tiene o siente molestia

El primero se usa con **ser** y el segundo con **estar**

d Un enfermo es una persona que padece una enfermedad y una persona enferma padece también una enfermedad, pero el primero se usa con **ser** y el segundo se usa con **estar**. Es la diferencia entre el nombre y el adjetivo

e Cuando se usa con el verbo **ser**, indica que la persona tiende a confiar en los demás = *trusting*

Cuando se usa con **estar**, muestra confianza o esperanza en algo preciso o concreto y aquí tiene el sentido de *confident* e.g. Estoy confiada en que llegarán hoy *I am confident they'll arrive today*

Unit 14 Level 1

i a transitive   b transitive   c transitive   d intransitive   e intr   f trans
  g intr   h intr   i intr   j intr   k intr   l trans   m trans   n trans

ii

a se levanta se levanta os levantáis se levantan

b se peina se peina os peináis

c me desayuno se desayuna se desayunan

d nos arreglamos se arreglan

e os ducháis se duchan

f se baña se baña se bañan

g se disfrazan se disfrazan

h me presento nos presentamos os presentáis

i te quejas nos quejamos se quejan

j se alegran/se alegran

iii

a Rosa y Luis no se entienden

b Nos escribimos Sara y yo

c Nos conocemos el doctor y yo

d Nos despedimos Juana y nosotros

e Nos ayudamos mutuamente / entre nosotros

f Carlos y Teresa se quieren

g Adriana y Jorge no se conocen

h No nos hablamos Roberto y yo

Unit 14 Level 2

i

a Debes despedirte inmediatamente

b Los muchachos están asoleándose

c Puedes caerte por las escaleras

d ¿Van a casarse pronto?

e Estoy ensuciándome la ropa

ii

a Nos pensamos ir a las dos de la tarde

b Se quieren quedar en el hotel

  c Se desean levantar temprano

  d Pedro se va a enojar mucho

  e Te tienes que levantar ahora

  f Me sigo divirtiendo

  g Nos continuamos paseando

  h Me estoy arreglando

  i Se están pintando los ojos

  j Te estás ensuciando la ropa

iii

  a Todo el mundo se está aburriendo con el profesor

  b Los niños se están acostando con Mamá

  c Los niños se están alegrando con la fiesta

  d Me canso con la lectura

  e La familia se está paseando conmigo

  f Se te está secando el pelo

  g El equipo se está entrenando con el técnico

  h Los novios se están casando con el cura

iv

(Yo) me levanto/levanté a las siete. Me lavo/lavé con un poquito de jabón. Me lavo/lavé con la manopla, froto/froté/tallo/tallé el cuerpo con esponja/zacate y me limpio/limpié la cara con agua calentita. Me acerco/acerqué al espejo. Me veo/ví en él. Me afeito/afeité/rasuro/rasuré de mala gana. Veo/Vi en el espejo a una persona que se arregla/arreglaba pero que no se pinta/pintaba como mi esposa. Se moja/mojó la cara con más agua. Esa persona que se muestra/mostró en el espejo se enoja/enojó/enfada/enfadó por la faena. Se cansa/cansó con tanto trabajo. Se corta/cortó el dedo con la navaja y se enoja/enojó otra vez. Se presenta/presentó después una mujer y ahora se ven/vieron dos personas en el espejo. Nos saludamos pero no nos reconocemos/reconocimos. No hablamos/platicamos porque no nos conocemos/conocíamos. Se ven/veían ahora dos personas que están/estaban dándose un toque agradable y que se están/estaban preparando para salir a la calle. Se están/estaban arreglando bien. La mujer se quita/quitó los rulos/tubos para ponerse guapa y para poder ponerse el sombrero. Los dos se están/estaban endomingando/puliendo porque quieren/querían presentarse perfectamente vestidos con sus amigos. Salen/Salieron sin hablarse el uno con el otro y sin dirigirse ni una palabra el uno al otro.

RB/JPL

Unit 15 Level 1

  i a Hace un tiempo (muy) agradable   b Hace (mucho) sol   c Hace (mucho) frío
    d Hace un tiempo muy suave   e Hace buen tiempo pero llueve   f Hace mucho
    viento y graniza   g Llueve mucho y hace sol   h Hace mucho calor   i Hace
    mucho frío   j Hace demasiado calor con temperaturas altísimas (*very high*)

  ii a llueve/nieva   b hace sol   c hace mucho viento   d el cielo está nublado
    e hay niebla   f el sol brilla   g está lloviendo / llueve   h llueve   i hace mal
    tiempo   j nieva   k hay luna   l hay neblina (*mist*)

  iii a ¿Qué hay en el estudio?   b ¿Qué hay en el dormitorio?   c ¿ . . . en la cocina?
    d ¿ . . . en la mesa?   e ¿ . . . en el salón?   f ¿ . . . en el paquete?   g ¿ . . . en el

techo? h ¿ . . . en el comedor? i ¿ . . . en el garage (**M**)/garaje? j ¿ . . . en el baño?

Unit 15 Level 2

i a amanece b anochece c apetece d conviene / convenga (**M**)
e gusta(ría)/encanta(ría) f gusta(ría) g importa h parece
i nevando/lloviendo/neviscando

ii

Es una pena ver a tanta gente sin dinero

Es (una) lástima malgastar tu dinero

Es importante comer correctamente

Es esencial cuidar el cuerpo

Es lógico dormir siete u ocho horas

Es natural tener hambre después de tanto tiempo sin comer

Es inevitable tener inundaciones con tanta lluvia

Es mejor comer ahora y salir después

¿Es posible darme un regaderazo (**M**) / darme una ducha?

Es imposible dar de comer a treinta personas

iii a quieres/puedes b debió/debe c he d caben e faltan f Sé/sabes/
sabe etc. g tienes h quedan i puedo/puedes, etc. j Sé/sabes, etc.
k sobran l bastan

Unit 16 Level 1

i a haga b vuelva c se retiren d acepte e vayas, f compre/compres/
compre/compremos/compréis/compren g descanse h estudien i se
acuesten

ii

a El profesor ordena que se **callen** los alumnos / ordena **callarse** a los alumnos

b El patrón exige que **trabajemos** más duro

c Urge que la **llevemos** al hospital / Urge llevarla . . .

d Decido hacer todos mis deberes ahora mismo

e Necesito que me **ayudes/ayudéis/ayuden** (**M** = *Uds.* = familiar form)

f La ley decreta que **hagamos** todos el servicio militar

g Siempre insisten en que **paguemos** nosotros los boletos (**M**) / billetes / las entradas
(*entradas* for movie/show in Spain)

iii

a Le pido que **venga**

b Le ruego a Ud. que **atienda** a mi petición / Le ruego **atender** a . . .

c (Yo) prefiero que (tú) **regreses** a casa ahora

d (Ella) siempre consigue que (yo) **maneje** el carro

e El profesor siempre logra que sus alumnos **aprueben** los exámenes

f Él logra **correr** los cien metros en diez segundos

g Consigo **esconder** mi intención

h Os suplico que no os **enfadéis** (not in **M** where the **Uds.** form is used, and, in any case, **enojarse** is by far the more common verb in Mexico for *to get angry*. So, a Mexican translation could be: Les suplico que no se **enojen**)

iv

a Siempre me anima **a trabajar / a que trabaje** más duro

b Invitamos a nuestros amigos / cuates (**M**) **a cenar / a que cenen** con nosostros

c ¿Me permites sugerir que **vayamos** todos juntos?

d A veces aconsejamos a nuestros clientes **tomar / que tomen** vacaciones en México

e Es mejor que **cortéis** la hierba / **corten** el pasto (**M**) ahora

f Nuestros padres / papás (**M**) siempre nos presionan para que **hagamos** mucho ejercicio físico

g Basta / Es suficiente que **leas** sólo estos tres libros

h Tengo que convencerte/os/les (**M**) que **comas / comáis / coman** (M) menos azúcar y grasa, y más fruta

v Te propongo que **compartamos** los gastos / Te propongo **compartir** los gastos. La empresa me propone que **cambie** de ciudad para el trabajo. Le propone a su novia que le **acompañe** al teatro. ¿Por qué me sugieres que me **compre** otro carro (**M**) / coche? La psicóloga me sugiere que no **trabaje** tanto / me sugiere no **trabajar** tanto. Mis tíos sugieren que **pasemos** todo el día en la playa

vi a veas   b salga   c jueguen   d hagan

vii (a suggestion)

El profesor permite que los alumnos dispongan de / tengan más tiempo para sus deberes, pero, por desgracia, les impide que aprovechen una chuleta. Lo cierto es que prohíbe que los alumnos se la coman, por muy sabrosa que sea. ¿Por qué el profesor no deja que los alumnos coman la chuleta, si es muy rica? (Una pista: **chuleta** tiene dos sentidos)

viii

a (Yo) lamento mucho que (él) **esté** tan triste

b (Yo) siento que (tu) no **puedas** venir

c Nos encanta que Uds. nos **acompañen** / vosotros nos **acompañéis**

d (Yo) tengo miedo de que (él) **diga** la verdad

e Me molesta (tanto) que los chicos **hagan** (tanto) ruido

f Me alegro de que **sea** así

g Celebro que todos **vengan** a la boda

h No me extraña que (ellos) no **vengan** para Navidades

i (Ella) desea que (nosotros) **vayamos** juntos

j Espero que no **llueva** este fin semana

k Ellos quieren jugar (al) fútbol esta tarde / Yo quiero que (ellos) **jueguen** (al) . . . / Ellos quieren que yo **juegue** (al) . . .

l Está previsto que **haga** sol toda esta semana

ix (a suggestion)

María:	¡Hola, Marta! Me alegro de que **estés** aquí en México
Marta:	Yo también y celebro que **podamos** pasar una semana juntas.
María:	Me extraña mucho que no **pueda** venir tu hermano
Marta:	Siento que no nos **acompañe**. Tiene previsto trabajar esta semana

María: Lamento yo también que no **pueda** venir, porque me encanta escuchar su conversación

Marta: No es importante que no **esté** con nosotras. A mi me encanta que **podamos** visitar juntas todos los museos

María: ¡Ojalá (que) **aprovechemos** estos pocos días! Me temo que **pase** el tiempo demasiado de prisa

Marta: Confío en que tu mamá te **deje** salir conmigo todos los días y que **haya** la posibilidad de visitar Cuernavaca

x

	E	C	H	E	N
D	E	I	S	S	A
I	S	E	A	T	D
G	T	R	L	A	E
A	I	R	G	L	M
N	R	E	A	L	O
	E	S	T	E	S

Horizontal: echen, deis, sea, estés
Vertical: digan, estire, cierres, salga, estalle, nademos
Infinitivos: echar, dar, ser, estar, decir, estirar, cerrar, salir, estallar, nadar

xi a Niego / No es verdad . . .   b ¿Crees . . .   c No ha dicho . . . / No es verdad . . . / No estoy seguro de . . . ,   d Va al cine cada noche sin . . .   e Excluyo/ descarto . . .   f No creo / Dudo . . .   g No creo / No estoy seguro de . . .

xii (a suggestion)

Yo: Quiero que **tomes** el mismo menú que yo.

Amigo/a: No estoy de acuerdo. Prefiero que **pidamos / elijamos / ordenemos** (**M**) dos menús diferentes

Yo: ¿Por qué?

Am.:   Dudo que el menú que **pidas / encargues / ordenes** (**M**) me **guste**.

Yo: Es raro que nuestros gustos no **sean** iguales. Te aconsejo que **pidas** al menos dos platos como los míos.

Am.:   ¿Por qué sugieres que yo **siga** tu opción?

Yo: Porque si no te gusta lo que **pidas**, me vas a pedir que yo te **dé** un pedacito de mi plato.

Am.:   Es una pena que no me **dejes** pedir / elegir / ordenar (**M**) un menú que me **guste**.

Yo: En ese caso, yo te propongo que **regresemos** a casa y comamos lo mismo

xiii a **Acaso / quizá / tal vez / posiblemente** se vayan todos
    b **Posiblemente / se puede que / puede ser que** sean hermanos

xiv

a Es mejor que te **quedes / se quede / os quedéis / se queden** (**M** = *familiar form*) aquí

b Está previsto que **suban** todas las acciones

c Pienso que es natural que los niños **hagan** mucho ruido

d Es increíble que se **diviertan**

e ¿Por qué dices que es lógico que no **quieran** venir?

f Siempre es importante que **hagas** lo posible en el examen

g (Ella) se ha hecho daño, entonces es importante que la **llevemos** al hospital

h Es imperativo que **aprendas** a manejar (**M**) / conducir correctamente

i Basta / Es suficiente que **trabajes** treinta y cinco horas a la semana

j Es triste que no **puedan** venir antes de la semana próxima

k No es normal **beber** litros y litros de agua

l Es de esperar que se **arregle** el asunto pronto

xv

a . . . **afin de que / para que podamos** ver la película

b . . . **a condición (de) que / con tal que** no lo **malgastes**

c . . . **aun cuando se enfade**

d . . . **como llegue** temprano (also **si llega** temprano)

e . . . **en caso de que necesites** más dinero

f . . . **siempre que sea** necesario

g . . . **supuesto que no tenga** tiempo para ir andando?

h . . . **sin que** yo lo/le **vea**

i . . . **a menos que / a no ser que** me pagues la entrada

j . . . **de manera que / de modo que pueda salir** cuando llueva

Unit 16 Level 2

i

a . . . **se caiga**

b . . . no **salga** bien del examen

c . . . **llegue** el domingo!

d . . . les **haya pasado** algo malo

e . . . **hayan tenido** un accidente de carretera

f . . . el avión se **haya estrellado** contra una montaña

g . . . no **quiera** enfrentarse con la verdad

h . . . se **haga** daño

ii

a Importa que **cerremos** el contrato pronto

b Es dudoso que **sea** el autor del crimen

c Es inevitable que un hombre tan generoso **pague** los boletos (**M**) / las entradas

d Es lástima que **tengan que** marcharse antes de la boda

e Es de esperar que los chicos **aprueben** todos los exámenes

f Es de temer que el equipo **pierda** su plaza en primera

g Es previsible que **acaben** separándose

h No está bien que **cobren / ganen (M)** tan poco

iii

a . . . **sea** más rápido

b . . . me **sepa** arreglar el (**M**) / la radio?

c . . . al primero que **corra** los cien metros en diez segundos (¿Hay un(a) campeon(a) olímpico(a) que lea esto?)

d . . . me **cuide** el auto (**M**) / coche

e . . . **resista/aguante** estas heladas tan fuertes

f . . . me **guste**

g . . . **estés** en Guanajuato

h . . . hasta que me **llames** para la comida

i . . . **al llegar** a casa

j . . . **al recibir** la invitación

k . . . **al volver** él mañana

l . . . **al terminar** yo mis deberes

m . . . medio de transporte que **elijas**

n . . . **nade** en esta alberca (**M**) / piscina

iv

a Quienquiera que sea (Ud.)

b Dondequiera que estén

c Hagan lo que hagan

d Comoquiera que lo arregles / Lo arregles como lo arregles

e Haga el tiempo que haga

f Cualquiera que pueda ser tu opinión

g Pase lo que pase

h Quienquiera que lo quiera

i Cualquiera interés que expreses

j Vaya o no vaya (ella)

k Piense lo que piense (ella)

l Vengas de donde vengas / vengáis de donde vengáis / vengan de donde vengan (**M**)

m Por muy fuerte que sea

n Por mucho que me pidas que lo haga

o Por más comida que compres

v

a Cuando hayan arreglado el camión iremos a Cuernavaca

b Cuando hayas llenado el depósito, vuelve a casa / Cuando hayas llenado el tanque, regresa a casa (**M**)

c En cuanto hayas telefoneado a Juan saldremos

vi

a Si yo **hubiera/hubiese sabido** que estabas allí, **hubiera/hubiese/habría venido**

b Si me **hubieras/hubieses dicho** que la película era tan buena la **hubiera/ hubiese/habría visto**

c Si yo **tuviera/tuviese** un carro (M) / un coche, **visitaría** España

d Si **fueras/fueses** millonario, ¿qué te **comprarías**?

e Le prometí que, cuando yo **regresara/regresase**, iríamos al teatro

f Si mi mamá (**M**) / madre **hacía** galletas, siempre **invitaba** a cuates (**M**) / amigos a casa

g Convenimos en que, cuando **mejorara** el tiempo, **iríamos** todos a la playa

h Yo tenía miedo de que se **despertara/despertase** cuando **volviera/volviese / regresara/regresase** (**M**) tarde

i Permitimos que los niños **jugaran/jugasen** todo el día de manera que **estuvieran/estuviesen** muy cansados y **quisieran/quisiesen** acostarse temprano

j Les aconsejamos que **sacaran/sacasen** / Les aconsejamos **sacar** cheques de viaje dado que las divisas del país eran inseguras

k Negué que el chofer del camión (**M**) / conductor del autobús **hubiera/hubiese provocado** el accidente

l Por si no **tuviéramos/tuviésemos** bastante dinero **cambié** un cheque de viaje

NB Ten en cuenta que la forma *-ase/-ese* se usa más bien en textos escritos en España y que se usa raramente en México

vii

Tú: Me interesaría comprar una casa en Las Lomas pero ¿cuánto costaría si yo pagara un depósito de cien mil pesos?

Agente: Sería mejor si pidiera un préstamo al cinco por ciento y no pagara un depósito

Tú: Si no pagara un depósito, me costaría mucho más

Agente: Si no diera un depósito no tendría necesariamente que pagar más. De todas formas, el precio total es de diez millones de pesos.

Tú: Pero, si yo hubiera comprado esta casa hace diez años, ¿cuánto habría ganado?

Agente: Bueno, esta casa hace diez años habría tenido un valor de cinco millones de pesos. Si la hubiese adquirido en aquel entonces, ¡habría ganado Ud. cinco millones!

Tú: Si yo comprara la casa ahora, ¿es casi seguro que valdría el doble dentro de diez años?

Agente: El mercado no funciona siempre así. Pero yo podría garantizar más o menos que subiría el valor en un cincuenta por ciento si hiciera Ud. la inversión hoy.

Tú: ¿Por cuánto la rentaría si yo encontrara un inquilino?

Agente: ¡Híjole! Si yo consiguiera una casa así nunca tendría ganas de rentarla

RB/JPL

viii

a Prepararé el almuerzo **antes de que hagas** las tareas domésticas

b Jugaremos/echaremos una partida de ajedrez **después de que se acueste** Pedro

c **Mientras que estés** en la cocina, leeré el periódico

d **Luego que te hayas dado** un regaderazo (**M**) / una ducha, iremos al partido de fútbol

e Llámanos **en cuanto llegues** a casa

f Espera **a que nos llamen**

g Esperaré aquí **hasta/a que (no) vengan**

h Limpiaremos el carro (**M**) / coche **antes de salir** para la sierra

i Iremos de vacaciones **a los pocos días de que termines** tu trabajo

Unit 17 Level 1

i a Lo hago   b Lo limpio   c Lo barren   d Lo cierro   e Lo compro   f Lo venden   g Lo oyen   h Lo tocamos   i Lo rompo   j Lo bebo

ii a La toco   b La pongo   c La doy   d La abren   e La hacen   f La estudiamos   g La aplico   h La queman   i La tomas   j Lo coméis

iii a Las abrimos   b Los lavan   c Los friegan   d Las arreglan   e Las aprendes   f ¿Los comes?   g Los prefiero   h Las traen   i Los necesitamos   j Los compran

iv a La vendo   b Las pago   c Las/los preparo   d La como   e Las estudio   f La visito   g Lo gasto   h Lo escribo   i Los aceptan   j Los aprenden

v a Le enseña el carro   b Le da el regalo   c Les llevan el paquete   d Le muestra la página   e Le trae los platos   f Les compran las tazas

vi a Lo compro para él   b Lo venden por ti   c Las arreglan sin mí   d La termino contigo   e Los acaba con ellos   f Lo hago sin ti   g Hablan de ti   h Los compran por ellas   i Las venden por vosotras   j Va por ti   k Está enfrente de ellos   l Se sienta encima de nosotros

Unit 17 Level 2

i a Te lo regalo   b Se la dio   c Me lo enseñaron   d Se lo devolví   e Te lo regresé ayer   f Te los llevaré   g Se lo he dado   h Se lo pedí   i Me las mandaron   j Se lo sugirió

ii a Voy a ayudarte   b Van a castigarles/los   c Van a decírselo   d Van a prohibírmelo   e Voy a garantizártelo   f Iba a recomendársela   g Quería proponérselo   h Evitó prometérmelo   i Impidieron hacérselo   j Logró mandármelo

iii a ¡Mándalo!   b ¡Escríbelo!   c ¡Escríbanselas!   d ¡Dámelo!   e ¡Devuélveselos!

iv a ¡No les preguntes!   b ¡No me ayuden!   c ¡No los llame!   d ¡No se los des!   e ¡No me esperen!   f ¡No se lo lleven!   g ¡No nos vayamos!   h ¡No los saluden!   i ¡No lo arregles!   j ¡No lo cantes!

Unit 18 Level 1

i a mi   b tu   c su   d sus   e vuestro   f mi   g tu   h mi   i nuestros   j sus   k mi   l nuestra

ii a Es mío   b Son mías   c Es mía   d Son mías   e Son míos   f Son mías

iii a el tuyo / el suyo / el nuestro / el vuestro   b los míos / los suyos / los nuestros / los vuestros   c las mías / las tuyas / las suyas / las vuestras   d la tuya / la suya / la vuestra   e los míos / los tuyos / los nuestros / los suyos   f las mías / las tuyas / las nuestras / las vuestras

iv a la tuya / la suya / la vuestra   b el tuyo / el suyo / el vuestro   c el tuyo / el suyo / el vuestro

v a Hago el trabajo que me dejas   b Veo los programas que ves   c Preparo la cena que comes   d Comen la cena que preparas   e Pintas las casas que compro

vi a La mujer que canta es guapa   b El chico que es alto es listo   c La mesa que es blanca es vieja   d El jardín que tienes es grande   e La ciudad que está cerca es pequeña   f La calle que es grande está concurrida   g Las gafas que uso son viejas

vii a qué   b cuál   c quién   d cuánto   e quién   f cuáles   g qué / a quién

Unit 18 Level 2

i a mía   b nuestra   c vuestros   d tuyos   e suyos   f suyas   g míos   h nuestra

ii a Con quién/quiénes   b Por/Para quién   c de quien   d con quienes   e a quienes   f Quienes   g Con quién/quiénes   h a quienes   i De quién   j a quién   k Con quién/quiénes   l de quien

iii

a Me extrañó lo que dijo tu hermano / Lo que dijo tu hermano me extrañó
b Estudié mucho, lo que me ayudó a aprobar el examen
c El chofer manejaba el camión como loco, lo que me dio mucho miedo
d Sé lo que está permitido
e Hice lo que me aconsejó
f Pregúntale lo que quiere

Unit 19 Level 1

i a No conocemos a ningún actor   b . . . ningún bolígrafo   c . . . ningún hijo   d . . . ningún estudiante   e . . . ningún bolso   f . . . ningún amigo   g . . . ningún cuadro   h . . . ningún libro

ii a No estudiamos nada de ruso   b No hablo nada de alemán   c No tenemos nada de sed   d No sé nada de química   e No tienen nada de prisa   f No necesito nada de pan

iii a No veo a nadie   b No van a comprar nada/ninguno   c ¿No quieres nada?   d No viene nadie / Nadie viene   e No quiero ningún libro   f ¿No necesitas a nadie?   g No estudio ninguna asignatura   h No sabemos nada de chino

iv a Esperamos a alguien   b Juan necesita algo   c Alguien pregunta por tu dirección   d Tienen algún libro de texto   e La muchacha pide algo   f Alguien viene   g Quieren algo   h Tiene algún libro

Unit 19 Level 2

i a La que b El que c los que d la que e El que f Las que g Las que
h la que i el que / la que j la que

ii a Cualquier b cualquiera c cualquier d cualquier/cualquier
e cualesquiera f cualquiera g Cualquier h Cualquiera i cualquiera
j cualquiera k Cualquiera l cualquier

Unit 20 Level 1

i a estos b estas c estos d Estos e Estas f Estos g esta h Estos
i Este j Estas

ii a esas b Esas c ese d Esa e ese f ese

iii a aquél b aquéllos c aquél d aquélla e aquél f aquéllas

iv a éste b ésta c éste d éstos e éstas f éstos

Unit 20 Level 2

i a Los libros esos b La cocina esta c El ordenador ese d Las sillas estas
e las plantas estas f los botes esos g La computadora esa h el plato ese

ii a el b los c el d la (*but* **el** *in* **M** *in which case it would be* **caros**) e la f el
g la h las

Unit 21 Level 1

i
a el poncho amarillo / las faldas amarillas / las bolsas amarillas / los bolsos amarillos /
los cuadernos amarillos / la chaqueta amarilla
b el camión chico / las guitarras chicas / el sarape chico / los niños chicos / la
alfombra chica
c la pluma larga / las calles largas / los sarapes largos / la regla larga / la pintura larga
/ los pasillos largos
d los coches grandes / las perlas grandes / los vestidos grandes / la sala grande / las
cómodas grandes / los árboles grandes
e el libro rectangular / la alfombra rectangular / las mesitas rectangulares / el radio
(**M**), la radio rectangular / los cuadernos rectangulares
f una pendiente suave / un pelo suave / colores suaves / carácter suave / garbanzos
suaves / temperaturas suaves
g una chica mexicana / una comida mexicana / bebidas mexicanas / muchachos
mexicanos
h las mejores notas / el mejor carro / las mejores vacaciones / la mejor computadora

ii a un buen carpintero b el tercer libro c un gran hombre d primer curso
e un mal albañil f un buen actor g una gran casa h el tercer curso i el
primer martes j un mal escritor

iii

a La raza negra tiene buenos atletas

b La novia lleva un vestido blanco

c La Calle Mayor no es necesariamente la mayor calle

d No me gustan los vinos fuertes

e ¿Te apetece un menú español o un menú italiano?

f Las hojas verdes caen de los árboles

g No puedo subir a los departamentos/pisos superiores

h Le gusta llevar tacones altos

i Un buen equipo argentino es el mejor del mundo

j Este país tiene un buen sistema financiero

Unit 21 Level 2

i El agua hirviendo . . .   b . . . rinocerontes macho/hembra   c . . . una rata hembra/macho   d Los pájaros hembra . . .   e Las soluciones modelo(s) . . . f cobijas/mantas naranja/rosa/violeta   g . . . una palabra tabú   h . . . telas rosa

ii

a cierta vergüenza / indicios ciertos

b diferentes soluciones / posibilidades completamente diferentes

c gran hombre / finca grande

d hombre medio / medio litro

e pobre chica / familia pobre

f único consejo / hija única

iii

a Sí, pero lo curioso es que no hay bastantes estudiantes

b Sí, pero lo malo es que en verano hace demasiado calor

c Sí, pero lo inaceptable es que fuma cuando trabaja

d Sí, pero lo molesto es que no son muy generosos

e Sí, pero lo absurdo es que no entiendo nada de sus novelas

f Sí, pero lo raro es que no sacan provecho de su inteligencia

g Sí, pero se me escapó el dinero demasiado rápidamente

h Sí, pero lo malo era que no me quedaba dinero para ir al cine

i Sí, pero lo extraño es que me daba vergüenza pedirte ayuda

j Sí, pero lo más agradable sería cenar después

Unit 22 Level 1

i

a a Luisa / a los señores / a Manuel / a la maestra / a las niñas / a los pajaritos

b a sus amigos / a la niña / a Carlos / a las muchachas

c al doctor / a mis amigas / al muchacho / a los alumnos

d a la muchacha / a Jorge / a mis cuates / al bebé / al gato

e a nuestros papás / a mi abuela / a tus primas / a los perritos

Unit 22 Level 2

i a Necesito a mis niños   b Ven a las chamacas (**M**)   c ¿Quieres a tu mamá?
d Oimos a los alumnos   e Están esperando a la familia   f Recibo al médico
g ¿Acoges a todos los chicos?   h Traigo a mis dos hijas   i ¿Oyes a las muchachas?
j No entiendo al profesor   k Llevo a todos los muchachos en mi carro
l Admiramos a estos músicos

ii
a El verbo sigue al pronombre / El pronombre sigue al verbo
b No hallamos un doctor que sepa curar a nuestro hijo
c Quería ver a su esposa y a sus hijos
d La cocinera peló el ganso
e Mataron dos/tres faisanes y dos/tres ciervos
f Yo quisiera comprar un caballo (*He doesn't know the horse*)
g Él quería vender a su caballo (*He knows his horse*)
h Presentaron su hija al director / el director a su hija
i La madre llevaba a los hijos al colegio
j El carro rápido rebasó al carro lento / El carro lento rebasó al carro rápido
k El gato persigue al perro / El perro persigue al gato / Al gato le persigue el perro /
   Al perro le persigue el gato
l El político no pudo sobornar al juez / Al juez no le pudo sobornar el político
m Quería saber a quién llamaba
n Yo no veía a nadie
o Le pregunté si conocía a alguien en el colegio

Unit 23 Level 1

i a a...de   b de   c de   d de   e en   f de   g de   h al   i a   j bajo
k al   l al   m a   n A   o ante   p con   q de   r contra   s de
t desde...hasta   u al

Unit 23 Level 2

i a además de   b debajo de   c delante de   d detrás de   e lejos de   f junto
a / cerca de   g dentro del   h encima de   i enfrente de / detrás de   j fuera de
k después de   l a través del   m a través de   n A pesar de

ii
a Se apresuró a acabar sus deberes
b No se atrevería a subir hasta la cumbre sin ayuda
c Se decidió a salir dado que se aburría en casa
d La niña se hizo daño en el tobillo y rompió a llorar
e Se puso a pintar un paisaje
f Echó a correr detrás del autobús
g Acababa de terminar su trabajo cuando regresé
h Había dejado de comer cuando entramos
i Su razonamiento no termina de convencerme
j Se paró a hablar con el vecino

Unit 24 Level 1

i a para b por c para d por e por f para g por h para i para
j por k por l por *and* para m por n para o para p por *and* para
q por r por

Unit 24 Level 2

i a para b por c por d por e por f *por *and* para (*but meaning is different*)
g para h Por i por j para k para l Por m por n para o por *and*
para p Para q por r Por s Para t Para u por v para w para
x por y Para z por aa por bb por cc para dd por ee por
ff por

*The meaning is different according to the preposition because the use of **por** suggests that the scientifist had accomplished great exploits and received money in recognition of this; the use of **para** suggests that money was given to him/her to help him/her to promote his/her research.

Unit 25 Level 1

i a felizmente b únicamente c afectuosamente d amablemente
e amablemente f cruelmente g respetuosamente/amablemente
h sumamente i altamente j afectuosamente k largamente
l ciegamente m afectuosamente n pacientemente o inmediatamente
p tranquilamente q fácilmente r posiblemente s totalmente
t directamente u constantemente v puntualmente w Nuevamente
x rápidamente y independientemente

ii a, b, d, e, g, i, j, k, all **recién** c correcta y cortésmente f constante y
lentamente h firme e insistentemente

iii a mal b mal c temprano . . . sólo/solamente d tarde e a tiempo
f siempre

Unit 25 Level 2

i
a Quizá(s) esté nevando
b Acaso/quizá(s) sienta/sintiera miedo
c Apenas si nos deja dormir
d Mira hacia atrás
e Échate para atrás, hay una culebra allí
f Págame al contado o con cheque, es igual
g Nos sorprendió la noche en la montaña y tuvimos que pasarla al raso
h De buena gana me pasearía por el río
i Siempre hace sus deberes de mala gana, no le gusta estudiar
j Saltó por encima de la tapia

ii a Atravesó/Cruzó   b entró/salió   c está   d Conozco   e hacerme
f nadar/bañarse (**bañarse** *not here in* **M**)   g Llegaré/Llamaré   h has dejado
i dispararon . . . murió   j encuentras

Unit 26 Level 1

i

a ¿A dónde va(s) este verano?

b ¿Cuándo / A qué hora vais / van (**M**) al cine?

c ¿Cuándo / A qué hora comen?

d ¿Cuándo van a jugar (al) fútbol?

e ¿Cómo escribe(s)?

f ¿Cuáles flores prefieren?

g ¿Cuánto cuesta este libro?

h ¿Por qué te acuestas ahora?

i ¿Quién es el alumno más listo?

j ¿Qué estás haciendo?

ii

a No veo a nadie

b No/nunca trabajan toda la semana / No trabajan nunca toda la semana

c No estoy leyendo un libro / No estoy leyendo ningún libro / No estoy leyendo libro
alguno (see level 2.5 for the last sentence)

d No entienden nada de lo que digo

e No vamos nunca / Nunca vamos a la alberca/piscina el viernes

f Nadie cena aquí esta noche

iii a Nadie ha venido   b Nunca he visto las B. del C.   c Nunca hemos estudiado el
japonés   d Nada me interesa   e Ningún banco me ha escrito

iv

a Van (**M**) / vais al teatro esta noche ¿verdad?

b Sale con toda la familia ¿verdad?

c Compran (**M**) / Compráis verduras hoy, ¿verdad?

d Te duele la espalda ¿verdad?

e Fueron (**M**) / Fuisteis a Albuquerque / Nuevo México el año pasado ¿verdad?

f Tu mamá vive en Las Vegas ¿verdad?

Unit 26 Level 2

i

a Llegó a la playa sin playeras/playera ni toalla

b Empezó a nadar sin gafas/visor ni aletas

c Se subió a la tabla de windsurf sin guantes, sin zapatillas ni arnés

d Salió del agua sin traje de baño ni zapatillas

e No protestó ni su madre/mamá ni su padre/papá

f No quiso ponerse ni traje de baño ni pantalón corto

g No sólo era mal educado sino también difícil de convencer

ii

a No entiendo ni el comportamiento del niño ni su modo de hablar

b Este chaval/jovencito no tiene nada para cubrirse

c Nunca he visto nada igual en la vida

d Ni yo tampoco

e ¿No le puedes prestar algo de ropa?

f Pero no acepta ni ayuda ni sugerencia

g No acabo de entender por que se comporta así

h No dejes de decirle que es un mal educado por no cubrirse

i No he podido nunca hacerle entrar en razón bajo ningún motivo

j ¿No sería posible llamar a un policía?

k Sí, pero el policía diría que "No es nada, y el chaval/jovencito no sabe nada de nada"

l Entonces en una democracia, ¿Las autoridades admiten tal conducta como si nada?

m Pero, hay que decirle al niño "¡Nada de tonterías!"

n Yo que tú, diría que nunca jamás permitiría eso

Unit 27 Level 1

i a tres hombres   b una clase   c ocho casas   d once alumnos
e quince carros   f veintiuna ideas   g once mesas   h veintiocho estudiantes
i treinta bebidas   j cuarenta y cinco árboles   k cien vehículos   l mil
espectadores   m quinientas tazas   n diez mil pesos   o ciento cincuenta mil
libras   p un millón de dólares

ii a cuatro y cinco son nueve   b cinco menos tres son dos   c dos y seis son ocho
d once menos siete son cuatro   e dieciséis y cuatro son veinte   f diecisiete
menos tres son catorce   g veinticinco y tres son veintiocho   h veintitrés menos
tres son veinte   i treinta menos once son diecinueve   j veintinueve menos quince
son catorce

iii cero cero treinta y cuatro novecientos cuarenta y tres veinte cuarenta y cinco treinta
y dos (*Spain*)
cero cero cincuenta y dos ochenta veintiuno setenta y uno noventa y tres (**M**)

iv a martes   b lunes   c viernes   d sábado

v a el sexto día de la semana   b el cuarto . . .   c el séptimo . . .   d el segundo . . .

vi a el undécimo mes del año   b el duodécimo mes . . .   c el séptimo mes . . .
d el cuarto mes . . .   e el segundo mes . . .   f el noveno mes . . .   g el primer
mes . . .   h el quinto mes . . .

vii

a Son las dos y cuarto

b Son las doce y diez

c Son las cinco menos veinte / Son cuarenta para las cinco (**M**)

d Es la una y veinte

e Son las doce menos seis minutos / Son cincuenta y cuatro minutos para las doce (**M**)

f Son las cuatro menos cuarto / Son/Es cuarto para las cuatro (**M**)

g Son las once menos diez / Son diez para las once (**M**)

h Es la una y cinco
i Son las diez menos cinco / Son cinco para las diez (**M**)
j Son las seis y cuarto

Unit 27 Level 2

i

a treinta más cincuenta son ochenta
b cuarenta y cinco más cuarenta y cinco son noventa
c treinta y dos más cincuenta y ocho son noventa
d setenta y siete más veintitrés son cien
e cien menos cuarenta son sesenta
f noventa y nueve menos cincuenta y nueve son cuarenta
g ochenta y cuatro menos treinta y cuatro son cincuenta
h setenta y ocho menos treinta y seis son cuarenta y dos
i ochenta y ocho menos veintiocho son sesenta
j veinte (multiplicado) por treinta son seiscientos
k veinte y siete por cuarenta son mil ochenta
l cincuenta por sesenta son tres mil
m setenta y tres por cuarenta y uno son dos mil novecientos noventa y tres
n cuarenta y cinco dividido por quince son tres
o sesenta dividido por veinte son tres
p doscientos dividido por cinco son cuarenta
q mil dividido por veinticinco son cuarenta
r diez mil dividido por mil son diez

ii

Fui a Cuernavaca la semana pasada, y la próxima voy a Guanajuato. A finales de año pasaré quince días en las Barrancas del Cobre, y el año que viene me gustaría ir al Gran Cañón. Quisiera pasar ahí quince días ya que ocho días no son suficientes. La mejor época del año para visitar estos dos cañones es junio.

Me gustaría mucho visitar el Gran Cañón porque tiene casi dos mil metros de profundidad y muchos kilómetros de ancho. Desde abajo, tiene dos mil metros de altura. Lo más impresionante es que es tan largo que cubre centenares de kilómetros. Yo quisiera visitar nuevamente las Barrancas del Cobre dentro de unos meses. Este cañón es tan largo, tan ancho y tan profundo como el Gran Cañón. El año pasado, bajé hasta el fondo de las Barrancas del Cobre con una veintena de cuates (**M**) / amigos. La mitad de ellos, o sea diez, se quedaron/quedó en el fondo, y los otros, o sea una decena, volvieron a subir. Hay trayectos del río que está en el fondo hasta con diez metros de profundidad, cincuenta de anchura/ancho, y varios kilómetros de largo.

Planeamos pasar ocho días en el fondo de las Barrancas. Estando abajo, el tiempo apremiaba, y pensamos que nos quedaba poco tiempo. Salimos rápidamente del cañón, y arriba, nos dimos cuenta de que habíamos calculado muy mal y que nos sobraban cuatro días. ¿Qué haríamos con estos cuatro días?

RB/JPL

Unit 28 Level 1

i

a Alicia se divierte más que Rosa. Rosa se divierte menos que Alicia. Rosa no se divierte tanto como Alicia

b Los muchachos descansan más que yo. Yo descanso menos que los muchachos. Yo no descanso tanto como los muchachos

c El doctor se cansa más que su hijo. Su hijo se cansa menos que el doctor. Su hijo no se cansa tanto como el doctor

d Los niños gritan más que Juanito. Juanito grita menos que los niños. Juanito no grita tanto como los niños

e Me preocupo más que tú. Tú te preocupas menos que yo. Tú no te preocupas tanto como yo

f La señora trabaja más que Marta. Marta trabaja menos que la señora. Marta no trabaja tanto como la señora

g Tus amigas platican/hablan más que tú. Tú platicas/hablas menos que tus amigas. Tú no platicas/hablas tanto como tus amigas

h Teresa gasta más que sus hijos. Sus hijos gastan menos que Teresa. Sus hijos no gastan tanto como Teresa.

i Ellos comen más que yo. Yo como menos que ellos. Yo no como tanto como ellos

j La niña se queja más que su hermano. Su hermano se queja menos que la niña. Su hermano no se queja tanto como la niña

ii

a No hay tantas montañas en tu país como en el mío

b Lupe no saltó tantos metros como Alicia

c En los pueblos no hay tanta niebla como en las ciudades

d Alicia no toma tanta leche como Luis

e Lucía no practica tantos deportes como nosotros

f Rosa no echó a perder tanto papel como yo

g Nosotros no tenemos tanto dinero como Jorge

h En tu coche no hay tanto lugar como en el mío

i Tere no recibió tantos regalos como Elena

j Tus sobrinos no comieron tantas aceitunas como los míos

Unit 28 Level 2

i

a Trabaja como un loco

b Me baño/nado en el mar más/menos veces que tú

c Recibió tantos regalos cuantos parientes tenía

d Envía tantas postales como envía su amigo

e Coge/Toma tantos cuantos / tantas cuantas puedas

f Coge/Toma tantas flores como puedas

g Estoy tanto más ronco que no dejé de hablar/platicar en toda la noche

h Llegó con mucho más/menos retraso de lo que solía llevar

i Es más/menos culto de lo que yo pensaba

j Tiene más dólares que yo, de suerte que me invita a cenar

k Le ofrecí un helado por que tenía menos dinero que yo

l Había más de mil espectadores y no cabían todos

m Había menos de veinte nadadores en la alberca/piscina y había mucho espacio

n Compré más/menos peras por que tenía más/menos dinero de lo que pensaba

o Aprobó todos sus exámenes, es más listo de lo que pensaba

Unit 29 Level 1

i

a El médico le recomienda tranquilidad / Le recomienda tranquilidad el médico / Le recomienda el médico tranquilidad / Tranquilidad, le recomienda el médico (*English does not have this flexibility*)

b Me gusta andar en bicicleta

c Me quedan dos semanas para las vacaciones

d Sobran tres metros de tela

e Pocos hablan bien dos idiomas

f La chica canta mal la canción

g El tiempo corre de prisa / Corre el tiempo de prisa

h La carretera corre junto al río / Corre la carretera junto al río

i El partido conservador se opone a los cambios / Se opone a los cambios el partido conservador / Se opone el partido conservador a los cambios

j La familia brasileña se queda en México / Se queda en México la familia brasileña

k Queda por barrer la salita y el despacho

l Los árboles verdes y las casas negras nos tapan la vista / Nos tapan la vista los árboles verdes y las casas negras

m Podemos alcanzar las altas cumbres de las montañas

n Dame otros doscientos euros

o Las diez primeras chicas ganaron premios / Ganaron premios las diez primeras chicas / Las primeras diez chicas ganaron premios / Ganaron premios las primeras diez chicas (See note to (a) above)

p Llegamos el sábado dos de octubre

Unit 29 Level 2

i

a Se les prohíbe a los soldados salir del campamento militar

b No se les deja a algunos de los policías regresar temprano / No se les deja regresar temprano a algunos de los policías

c No se les recomienda a la mayoría de los profesores trabajar más de cuarenta horas / No se les recomienda trabajar más de cuarenta horas a la mayoría de los profesores

d No se les prestan a los clientes más de diez mil euros

e Se les impidió a casi todos los conductores usar la autopista / Se les impidió usar la autopista a casi todos los conductores

f Se les avisará a todos los clientes sobre el valor de sus acciones

g Se le ayudó a toda la familia a pagar los gastos médicos / Se le ayudó a pagar los gastos médicos a toda la familia

h Se le animó al estudiante colombiano a estudiar más horas / Se le animó a estudiar más horas al estudiante colombiano

Unit 30 Level 1

i almohadilla, bajito, campanilla, chiquito/chiquillo, cigarrillo, copita, farolillo, florecita/florecilla, guerrilla, jardincito, jovencito, lugarete, mamaíta, nubecilla, papaíto, piedrecita, pobrecito/pobrecillo, poquito, pedacito, pastelito, relojito, saloncito, señorito, sillita, tacita, trocito, vasito

Unit 30 Level 2

i

Aquí tienes una adaptación bastante libre del trozo original

El domingo pasado, decidimos dar un paseo en el carrito y visitar nuestra casita de campo que está muy cerca de un hermoso pueblito llamado Tepoztlán. Llamé a los abuelitos a quienes siempre les gusta acompañarnos, sobre todo para ver a sus nietecitos. Saqué el carrito del garage. Dejamos en casa a los perritos y a los gatitos porque no cabían en la cajuelita del cochecito que tenemos. En el trayecto, por una carreterita muy angostita, nuestra hijita María preguntó a su Mamá: "¿Mamita, preparaste bocadillos, pastelitos y tenemos agüita de naranja también?" Mamá contestó: "Sí, mi amor, preparé panecillos con quesito y jamoncito."

Nos detuvimos un poquitito antes de llegar a nuestra casita porque queríamos visitar un bosquecito muy bonito a la entrada del pueblito. Nos gustaba mucho ese lugarcito porque estaba lleno de florecitas, y zumbaban todo tipo de bichitos, y los pajaritos piaban todo el tiempo. Nuestros niños, Mariquita, Carlitos y Juanito fueron a jugar cerca de un lago donde había patos con sus patitos. Un arroyito desembocaba en el lago, aunque por su tamaño mas bien parecía un laguito. Muy cerquita vimos caballitos, burritos y todo tipo de animalitos.

Después de comer, nuestros hijitos se acostaron y, en un ratito, estuvieron dormiditos. Después de una horita, se despertaron, y Carlitos se quejó, diciendo que le dolía la pancita. Le dimos una pastilla y se le quitó su dolorcito de barriguita. Por la tarde, caminamos por el pueblito, viendo las artesanías hasta que se nos hizo de noche. El cielo estaba lleno de estrellitas centelleantes. Regresamos a casa acompañados por montones de lucecitas bailarinas, ¡eran las luciérnagas! Después de cenar, nuestros hijitos les dieron las buenas noches a sus abuelitos. Los tres chamaquitos estaban muy cansados: "Mamita, Papito, estamos cansados. Queremos acostarnos." Les dijimos a los niños: "Antes de acostarse, denles un besito a sus abuelitos y sus papitos queridos." Y se fueron a la cama para dormir y soñar con los angelitos.

RB/JPL

Notes:
Strangely enough, in Mexico **paseo** does not have the diminutive **paseíto** which is common in Spain.

The following Mexican diminutives have these Peninsular equivalents:

M	**Spain**
poquitito>	*poquitín* (diminutive of **poquito** which is a diminutive of **poco**)
bosquecito>	*bosquecillo*
florecita>	*florecilla*
arroyito>	*arroyuelo*
pueblito>	*pueblecito*
Papito>	*Papaíto / Papi*
Mamita>	*Mamaíta / Mami*

The diminutives used in Spain sound odd, or old-fashioned, to a Mexican, while Spaniards would find these Mexican equivalents equally odd. Needless to say, there is no mistaking the meaning and no possibility of ambiguity.

Other Mexican diminutives in the text, which would not be used in Spain, and their non-diminutive Mexican and Peninsular equivalents:

agüita	*agua* (water)
angostita	*angosto* (literary in Spain, and little used = narrow = ***estrecho*** in Spain)
cajuelita	*cajuela* (in Spain ***maletero*** = trunk, boot of car)
dolorcito	*dolor* (pain)
barriguita	*barriga* (stomach = tummy)
hijito	*hijo* (son)
lugarcito	*lugar* (place, spot)
chamaquito	*chamaco* (***chico*** in Spain = boy)
laguito	*lago* (lake)

It should be repeated that many of these diminutives do not necessarily suggest "small." They can merely be an affectionate form of expressing yourself, often in a family situation.

Note. You have now reached the very end of the course. It is hoped that you will continue to build on what you have learnt, using the dictionary material suggested at the beginning of the book.

Index of grammar and vocabulary

References are to topics, not pages. All references to the Subjunctive are in the separate Subjunctive index.

a 23.1.2
a, adverbial idioms with 23.2.16
a, personal 22.1.1
a, personal, + animals 22.1.3
a, personal, + collective noun 22.1.2
a, personal, miscellaneous features 22.2.5
a, personal, more possible confusion 22.2.7
a, personal, omission of 22.2.3
a, personal, + proper names 21.1.4
a, personal, use and non-use of 22.2.1
a, personal, when **not** used 21.1.5
a, personal, with dir. and indir. object 22.2.4
a, personal, with *nadie, alguien, quien* 22.2.6
a, personal, with personification 22.2.2
a tiempo 25.1.3
a través de 23.2.14
a with infinitive 23.2.20
abad(esa) 2.2.1
abogado(a) 2.2.1
abrelatas 2.2.5
absolute superlatives of adjectives 28.2.5
absolute superlatives of adverbs 28.2.6
abstenerse 14.1.5
acaso 16.1.3.2
acento tónico 1.1.2
acera/o 2.2.6
acerca de 23.2.2
acercar 12.2.2
acercar(se) 14.1.2
achacar 12.2.2
acostar(se) 14.1.2
acta/o 2.2.6
actor 2.2.1
adjectives, invariable 21.2.1/21.2.3
adjectives, location of 21.2.5
adjectives, nouns functioning like 21.2.6
adjectives, variability of meaning 21.2.4
adjectives as adverbs 21.2.2
adjectives + nouns 29.1.4, 29.2.1
adverbial expressions 25.1.2
adverbial phrases 25.2.5
adverbs, formation of 25.1.1
adverbs, other 25.1.3
adverbs involving affirmation 25.2.11
adverbs involving doubt 25.2.10
adverbs involving negation 25.2.11

adverbs involving time and movement 25.2.12
adverbs of degree 25.2.9
adverbs of manner 25.2.8
adverbs of place 25.2.7
adverbs of time, place, degree 25.2.1
afable 2.2.7
afeitar(se) 14.1.2
age 27.2.4
agente 2.2.1
agilidad 2.1.3
agreement in number and verb 3.2.4
agreement of adjectives 21.1.1
agreement of verbs 4.2.1
agregar 12.2.2
agua 2.1.1
agujetas 3.2.2
ahogar 12.2.2
aires, por los 3.2.2
airplanes 2.1.2
alcalde(sa) 2.2.1
alemán 21.1.1
alfombra 2.2.7
algo 19.1.1
alguien 19.1.1
alguno 19.1.1
alhaja 2.1.1
Alhambra 2.1.1
alicate 3.2.3
almacén 3.1.1
almorzar 12.2.2
alphabet 1.1.1
altavoz 2.2.5
altura 27.2.3
alumno/a 2.1.3
alza 2.1.1
amanecer 15.2.1
ambición 2.1.1, 2.1.3
amigo/a 2.1.3
amo 2.1.1
amor 2.1.2
amplio 2.2.7
análisis 2.1.3, 3.1.1
ancho 2.2.7
anchura 27.2.3
ancla 2.1.1
andaluz 21.1.1

andamiaje 2.1.2
andas 3.2.2
anglicisms 3.1.2
anochecer 15.2.1
ansiedad 2.1.3
ante 2.2.4, 23.1.3
antes de / que 23.2.3
antiguo 21.2.4
apaciguar 12.2.2
apagar 12.2.2
aparecer(se) 14.2.2
apetecer 15.2.1
aplausos 3.2.2
apocalipsis 2.1.3
aprender + *a* + infinitive 4.2.1
aprendiz 2.2.4
aquel 20.1.1
aquél 20.1.2, 20.1.3
aquello 20.1.4
aquellos 20.1.1
árbitra 2.2.1
arca / o 2.2.6
Argentina 2.1.2
armazón 2.1.5
arpa 2.1.1
arrancar 12.2.2
arreglar(se) 14.1.2
arrepentirse 14.1.5
arte 2.1.5
artista 2.1.3
Asco 2.2.7
así 25.2.1
asma 2.1.3
aspirador(a) 2.2.4
atracar 12.2.2
auge 2.2.4
augmentatives 30.2.2
aún 25.2.1
ausentarse 14.1.5
Australia 2.1.2
autor 2.1.2
autor(a) 2.2.1
avance 2.2.4
avergonzar(se) 14.1.2
averiguar 12.2.2
aversión 2.2.7
avestruz 2.2.4
avión 2.1.3
azteca 21.1.1
azúcar 2.2.4

bajar 14.1.3
bajar(se) 14.2.2
bajo 23.1.4
banca / o 2.2.6
banco 2.1.2
barbas 3.2.2
base 2.2.4
basic distinction between *ser* and *estar* 13.1.1
bastar 15.2.5, 16.14.1
batería 2.2.3
batidor(a) 2.2.4
belga 21.1.1

bestia 2.2.3
biblioteca 2.2.7
bien 25.1.3
bien with verbs 29.1.3
bilis 2.2.4
blanco 21.1.1
bocacalles 2.2.5
bodas 3.2.2
Bolivia 2.1.2
bolsa / o 2.2.6
bomba trampa 2.2.5
bomba / o 2.2.6
braga 3.2.3
Brasil 2.1.2
bueno 21.1.1
¡Buenos días! 3.2.2
buscar 12.2.2

caballo 2.1.2
caber 12.2.1, 15.2.4
cabeza 2.2.3
caer 12.1.1
caer(se) 14.2.3
café concierto 2.2.5
café teatro 2.2.5
cal 2.2.4
calavera 2.2.3
cáliz 2.2.4, 3.1.1
calor 2.1.2
cama 2.1. 3.
cama nido 2.2.5
cámara 2.2.3
camión 2.1.3
camión cisterna 2.2.5
caña / o 2.2.6
Canadá 2.1.2
candidata 2.2.1
cañón 3.1.1
cansar(se) 14.1.2
capital 2.2.3
carácter 3.1.1
cárcel 2.2.4
cárcel modelo 2.2.5
cardenal 2.1.2
cardinal numbers 27.1.1
carga / o 2.2.6
carisma 2.1.3
carreras reina 3.2.1
cars 2.1.2
casa 2.1.3
casa / o 2.2.6
casar(se) 14.2.2
casete 2.1.5
casetes 3.2.2
caso 2.1.2
catástrofe 2.2.4
cauce 2.2.4
caza 2.1.3, 2.2.3
cazar 12.2.2
cegar 12.2.2
celos 3.2.2
célula madre 2.2.5, 3.2.1
cenar fuerte 21.2.2

centinela 2.1.2
central 2.2.3, 2.2.4
cereal 2.2.4
cerrar 12.1.2
certamen 2.1.2
certidumbre 2.1.3
Chile 2.1.2
China 2.1.2
cierto 21.2.4
cigarro 2.1.2
circular 2.2.4
cisma 2.1.3
cities + definite article 2.2.1
ciudad dormitorio 2.2.5
ciudades dormitorio 3.2.1
ciudades modelo 3.2.1
clase 2.2.7
clienta 2.2.1
clima 2.1.3
club 3.1.1
cocer 12.2.2
coche bomba 2.2.5
coche cama 2.2.5
coche patrulla 2.2.5
coches bomba 3.2.1
coches patrulla 3.2.1
cocinero/a 2.1.3
coger 12.2.2
cólera 2.2.3
colgar 12.2.2
collective numbers 27.2.5
Colombia 2.1.2
color 2.1.2
coma 2.2.3
comenzar 12.2.2
comer (perfect tense) 5.1.1
comer(se) 14.2.3
cometa 2.1.3, 2.2.3
comida 2.1.3
comparison of adjectives 28.1.1
comparison of adverbs 28.1.2
compasivo 2.2.7
cómplice 2.2.1
componente 2.2.4
compound nouns 3.2.1.
compound prepositions 23.2.1
comprar (imperfect) 7.1.1
comprar (perfect tense) 5.1.1
comprar (present indicative) 4.1.1
comprar (preterit) 8.1.1
comprensivo 2.2.7
comunicar 12.2.2
con 23.1.5, 23.2.17
concejal(a) 2.2.1
conditional perfect tense 9.2.1
conditional tense 9.1.1
conductor 2.1.2
conferencia 2.2.7
confianza 2.2.7
confuso 2.2.7
conocer 12.2.2, 15.2.3
conocido/a 2.1.3
conocimientos 3.2.2

consonants 1.2.2
constante 2.2.4
constar 15.2.1
cónsul 2.2.1
contar 12.1.2
contra 23.1.6
convenir 15.2.1
copa/o 2.2.6
corista 2.2.1
corregir 12.2.2
correos 3.2.2
corriente 2.2.3
corte 2.2.3
cortés 2.2.7, 21.1.1
cosquillas 3.2.2
costar 12.1.2
costumbre 2.1.3
countries + definite article 2.2.1
crecer 12.2.2
creces 3.2.2
creer 16.1.3.1
crema 2.1.3
criado/a 2.1.3
crin 2.2.4
crisis 2.1.3, 3.1.1.
cruz 3.1.1
¿cuál? 18.1.5
¿cuánto? 18.1.5
cuanto . . . tanto 28.2.3
cuartel 2.2.7
cubiertos 3.2.2
cuenta/o 2.2.6
cura 2.1.2, 2.1.3
cuyo 18.1.4

dama 2.1.3
dar and time 27.2.1
datos 3.2.2
days 27.1.4
de 23.1.7, 23.2.18, 23.2.21
debajo de 23.2.4
deber 15.2.3
deberes 3.2.2
declive 2.2.4
defender 12.1.2
defensa 2.2.3
déficit 3.1.1
definite article 2.1.1, 2.2.1
dejar 2.2.7
delante de 23.2.5
delta 2.1.3
demonstrative adjectives 20.1.1
demonstrative pronouns 20.1.2
dentro de 23.2.11
desahogar 12.2.2
desayunar(se) 14.2.2
desde 23.1.8
desliz 3.1.1
desnudo 2.2.1
despertar(se) 14.1.2
desplegar 12.2.2
después de 23.2.13
detrás de 23.2.6

devolver 12.1.2
día 2.1.3
diferente 21.2.4
different meaning according to gender 2.2.3
dignar 14.1.5
diluviar 15.2.1
dimensions 27.2.3
diminutives 30.1.1, 30.2.1
dínamo 2.1.2
diphthong 1.2.1
diputada 2.2.1
disjunctive pronouns 17.1.4, 17.2.3
disponer 16.1.1.1
distinto 21.2.4
division of time 27.2.2
dormir 12.1.2
dormir(se) 14.2.3
duda 16.2.1
dulce 21.1.1
durante 23.1.9

e 1.2.6
edil(a) 2.2.1
editorial 2.2.3
educar 12.2.2
efectivos 3.2.2
el 2.1.1
el + adjective 21.2.8
él 17.1.1
elision 1.2.3
ella 17.1.1
ellas 17.1.1
ellos 17.1.1
emblema 2.1.3
enhorabuena 2.2.5
empezar 12.1.2, 12.2.2
emprendedor 21.1.1
en 23.1.10, 23.2.19
en cuanto 16.2.9
enaguas 3.2.2
encantar 15.2.1
enchufe 2.2.4
encima de 23.2.7
encontrar 12.1.2
encontrar(se) 14.2.3
enfadar(se) 14.1.2
énfasis 2.1.3
enfermar(se) 14.2.2
enfermedad 2.1.3
enfrente de 23.2.8
engaño 2.2.7
enojar(se) 14.1.2
enseñar + *a* + infinitive 4.2.1
entre 23.1.11
entrenar(se) 14.2.2
época 27.2.2
equipaje 2.1.2
erguir 12.2.1
escalera 3.2.3
escándalo 2.2.7
escarlata 21.2.1
esclarecer 12.2.2
escocer 12.2.2

escocés 21.1.1
escoger 12.2.2
escolta 2.2.3
escombros 3.2.2
ese 20.1.1
ése 20.1.2
esforzarse 12.2.2
eso 20.1.1, 20.1.4
espada 2.2.3
España 2.1.2
espantapájaros 2.2.5
esparcir 12.2.2
espécimen 3.1.1
esperanza 16.2.1
espesor 27.2.3
espiral 2.2.4
esquí 3.1.1
estadística 3.2.3
Estados Unidos 2.1.2
estar 13
estar, various tenses of 13.2.1
estar + adjective 13.1.2, 13.2.5
estar and *ser* 13.1.1, 13.1.3
estar frío 15.1.1
estar + gerund 13.2.3
estar + passive voice 13.2.4
estar + preposition 13.1.4
estar used impersonally 15.2.2
estar with nouns and pronouns 13.2.2
este 20.1.1
éste 20.1.2, 20.1.3
esto 20.1.1, 20.1.4
estratagema 2.1.3
estrella 2.2.1
estreñido 2.2.7
etapa reina 2.2.5
eternidad 2.1.3
excepto 23.1.12
excepto que 16.1.6.1
éxito 2.2.7
expensas, a mis 3.2.2
éxtasis 2.1.3
extenso 2.2.7
exterior 21.1.1

facha 2.2.3
factor sorpresa 2.2.5
factores sorpresa 3.2.1
falsificar 12.2.2
faltar 15.2.5
faz 2.2.4
fecha tope 2.2.5
fechas tope 3.2.1
¡Felices Pascuas/Navidades! 3.2.2
feminine nouns 2.1.3
final 2.2.3
físico/a 2.2.1
flor 2.2.4
fonda/o 2.2.6
forma 2.1.3
forzar 12.2.2
fosa/foso 2.2.6
foto 2.1.2

fractions 27.2.6
francés 21.1.1
Francia 2.1.2
fraude 2.2.4
fregar 12.1.2, 12.2.2
freidora 2.2.4
freír 12.2.1
frente 2.2.3
frente a 23.2.8
fresco 21.1.1
fruta/o 2.2.6
fuera de 23.2.12
fuerzas 3.2.2
funerales 3.2.2
future perfect tense 6.2.1
future tense 6.1.1, 6.2.2

gallina 2.1.3
gán(g)ster 3.1.1
gas ciudad 2.2.5
gastar 15.2.1
gender 2.1.2, 2.1.4
gender of compound nouns 2.2.5
génesis/Génesis 2.2.3
gente 2.1.3, 3.2.3
gerund 10.1.1, 10.2.
gorrión 2.1.3
grande 21.1.2, 21.2.4
Grecia 2.1.2
gripe 2.2.4
guardia 2.1.3, 2.2.3
Guatemala 2.1.2
guía 2.2.3

haba 2.1.1
haber 15.1.2, 15.2.6
haber de 15.2.3
haber debido 15.2.7
habla 2.1.1
hablador 21.1.1
hablar alto/fuerte 21.2.2
hacer 4.2.1, 7.2.1, 12.1.1
hacer = ago 15.2.8
hacer calor 15.1.1
hacer frío 15.1.1
hacha 2.1.1
hacia 23.1.13
halagar 12.2.2
hamaca 2.1.1
hambre 2.1.1
harpa 2.1.1
hasta 23.1.14
hasta que 16.2.9
hay 13.1.6
hay que 15.1.2
haya 2.1.1
hazmerreír 2.2.5
helada/o 2.2.6
hembra 21.2.1
hereje 2.2.1
higiene 2.2.4
hincha 2.2.3
hirviendo 21.2.1

Holanda 2.1.2
holandés 21.1.1
holgazán 21.1.1
hombro 2.1.2
hora pico 2.2.5
hora punta 2.2.5
hoy 25.2.1
hoz 2.2.4
huele rico 21.2.2
huérfano 2.1.3

ideas clave 3.2.1
imagen 3.1.1
imperative mood 11.1.1, 11.2.1
imperfect tense 7.1.1
impersonal use of reflexive 14.2.1
importar 15.2.1
indagar 12.2.2
indefinite article 2.1.1, 2.2.1
indefinite pronouns 19.1.1
Indian 2.1.2
índole 2.2.4
inferior 21.1.1
ingenio 2.2.7
ingeniosidad 2.2.7
inglés 21.1.1
intemperie 2.1.3
interrogante 2.1.5
interrogative pronouns 18.1.5
interrogative sentences 26.1.1
intoxicar 12.2.2
intransitive verbs 14.1.2
intransitive verbs, differences between transitive
    and 14.1.4
intuición 2.1.3
investigaciones 3.2.2
invocar 12.2.2
irregular verbs 12.1.1, 12.2.1
irregular verbs in preterit 8.2.1
(ir)se 11.2.2, 11.2.3, 14.2.3
islands 2.1.3
Italian 2.1.2

jactarse 14.1.5
Japón 2.1.2
jardín 3.1.1
jefa 2.2.1
jesuita 2.1.3
joven 2.2.1, 3.1.1
juez 3.1.1
jugar 12.1.2
jugar limpio 21.2.2
junto a 23.2.9
justificar 12.2.2

la 2.1.1, 17.1.2
labor 2.1.2
languages 2.1.2
lápiz 3.1.1
las 3.1.1, 17.1.2
lavadora 2.2.4
le 17.1.2
leer(se) 14.2.3

lejos de 23.2.10
lengua madre 2.2.5
lente(s) 2.1.5
león 2.1.2
les 17.1.2
letters of alphabet 2.1.3
levantar(se) 14.1.2
libertad 2.1.3
líbido 2.2.4
libra/o 2.2.6
libro 2.1.2
líder 3.1.1
lima 2.1.3
límites tope 3.2.1
linde 2.1.5
llegar 12.2.2
llevarse 4.2.1, 7.2.1, 14.2.3
llover 12.1.2, 15.1.1
lloviznar 15.1.1
lluvias 3.2.2
lo 17.1.2
lo + adjective 21.2.7
lo que 18.2.3
localizar 12.2.2
lombriz 2.2.4
longitud 2.1.3, 27.2.3
los 3.1.1, 17.1.2
lucir 12.2.2
luego 25.1.3
lunes 3.1.1

macho 21.2.1
madre patria 2.2.5
madreselva 2.2.5
mal 25.1.3
mal with verbs 29.1.3
mala fama, de 2.2.7
malla 3.2.3
malo 21.1.1
malva 21.2.1
mañana 2.2.3, 25.2.1
manga/o 2.2.6
mano 2.1.2
mapa 2.1.3
mar 2.1.5
maratón 2.1.5
marca/o 2.2.6
marcar 12.2.2
margen 2.1.5, 3.1.1
marroquí 3.1.1
Martínez 3.1.1
mártir 2.2.1
más 25.1.3
más de 28.1.4
más . . . que 28.1.2
masculine nouns 2.1.2
mathematical expressions/signs 27.2.7
matiz 3.1.1
mayor 21.1.1, 28.1.1
me 17.1.2
mediante 23.1.15
médica/o 2.2.1

medio 21.2.4
medio litro 2.2.7
mejor 21.1.1, 25.1.3, 28.1.1
menor 21.1.1, 28.1.1
menos 25.1.3
menos de 28.1.4
menos . . . que 28.1.2
mente 2.2.4
mentir 12.1.2
mesa 2.2.7
meta 2.2.3
metals 2.1.2
metamorfosis 2.1.3
metrópoli 2.2.4
Mexican imperative 11.2.1
México 2.1.2
mi 18.1.1
mía/o 18.1.2
mías/os 18.1.2
miel 2.2.4
miembro 2.1.2, 2.2.1
ministra/o 2.2.1
mis 18.1.1
míster 3.1.1
moda/o 2.2.6
model auxiliary verbs 15.1.1
model verbs 4.1.1
modelo 2.1.2, 21.2.1
modista/o 2.2.1
mojar(se) 14.1.2
mole 2.2.4
monarca 2.1.2
monja/e 2.2.1
months 2.1.2, 27.1.4
moral 2.2.3
morir(se) 14.2.3
moto 2.1.2
mountains 2.1.2
muchacho 2.1.3
muchedumbre 2.1.3
mucho 25.1.3
multinacional 2.2.4
muñeca/o 2.2.6
municiones 3.2.2
muslo 2.2.7
muy 25.1.3

nación 2.1.3
nada 19.1.1, 19.2.4
nadie 19.1.1, 19.2.4
naranja 21.2.1
naufragar 12.2.2
negar 12.2.2
negation 26.1.3
negative prefixes 26.2.7
negro 21.1.1
neuter gender 2.2.2
neuter pronouns 20.1.4
nevar 15.1.1
ni siquiera 26.2.3
nieves 3.2.2
ninguno 19.1.1

no . . . ni . . . ni 26.2.1
no sólo 26.2.2
nos 17.1.2
nosotras/os 17.1.1
notificar 12.2.2
noun + *ser* + noun 3.2.5
nouns 2.1.2, 2.1.3
nuestro 18.1.1, 18.1.2
Nueva Zelanda 2.1.2
nuevo 21.2.4
number 3
numbers + *otros* 29.1.6
nunca 25.1.3

o 1.2.6
obedecer 12.2.2
oceans 2.1.2
ocurrir(se) 14.2.3
oír 12.2.1
ojo 2.1.2
orden 2.2.3
ordenanza 2.2.3
order of pronouns 17.2.1
ordinal numbers 27.1.3
origen 2.1.2, 3.1.1
os 17.1.2

paciente 2.2.4
pacificar 12.2.2
padres 3.1.1
pagar 12.2.2
paisaje 2.1.2
Países Bajos 2.1.2
pala/o 2.2.6
palabra clave 2.2.5
palo 2.1.2
Panamá 2.1.2
panda 2.2.3
pantalón 3.2.3
papás 3.1.1
papel moneda 2.2.5
papelera/o 2.2.6
para 24.1.1, 24.1.2, 24.2.1
paraguas 2.2.5
parar(se) 14.2.2
pararrayos 2.2.5
parecer 12.2.2, 15.2.1
pareja 2.2.3
paréntesis 2.1.3
parte 2.2.3
pasar(se) 14.2.3
pasatiempo 2.2.5
pasear(se) 14.1.2
pasión 2.1.3
passive perfect tense 5.1.1
past anterior 5.2.3
past definite 8.1.1
pata/o 2.2.6
patente 2.2.4
pedir 12.1.2
pegar fuerte 21.2.2
pena 2.2.7

pendiente 2.2.3, 2.2.4
pensar 12.1.2
peor 21.1.1, 25.1.3, 28.1.1
perder 12.1.2
perdiz 2.2.4
perecer 12.2.2
personal pronouns 17
personal pronouns as direct object 17.1.2
personal pronouns as indirect object 17.1.3
personal pronouns as subject 17.1.1
pertrechos 3.2.2
Perú 2.1.2
pez 2.2.4
pianista 2.2.1
pijama 2.1.3, 3.2.3
pimienta/o 2.2.6
pinta/o 2.2.6
pinza 3.2.3
pirámide 2.2.4
piso piloto 2.2.5
piyama 2.1.3, 3.2.3
planeta 2.1.3
planicie 2.1.3
plata/o 2.2.6
plazo 27.2.2
plegar 12.2.2
pluperfect tense 5.2.2
plural of nouns 3.1.1
pobre 21.2.4
poco 25.1.3
poder 12.1.2, 15.1.1, 15.2.3
policía 2.2.1, 2.2.3
poner 12.1.1
por 24.1.1, 24.1.3, 24.2.2
portavoz 2.2.5
possessive adjectives 18.1.1
possessive pronouns 18.1.2, 18.2.1
postal 2.2.4
posterior 21.1.1
preguntón 21.1.1
prepositions, basic 23.1.1
prepositions, other compound 23.2.15
present indicative 4.1.1
present participle 10.1.1
presidenta/e 2.2.1
preterit 8.1.1
preterit and imperfect, differences between 8.2.2
preterit and perfect, differences between 8.2.2
preterit and perfect in **M** 8.2.3
primero 21.1.1
princesa 2.1.3
príncipe 2.1.2
problem genders 2.2.4
problema 2.1.3
profeta 2.2.1
profetisa 2.2.1
profundidad 27.2.3
pronouns, imperative with 11.2.4, 11.2.5

pronouns with reflexive verbs 14.1.5
pronto 25.1.3
pronunciation 1.1.1, 1.2.1
próximo 27.2.2
prudente 2.2.7
prueba reina 2.2.5
puerta 2.1.3
puerta/o 2.2.6
puntilloso 2.2.7
purasangre 2.2.5

que 18.1.4
¿qué? 18.1.5, 18.2.4
quedar 15.2.5
quedar(se) 14.2.3
quedirán 2.2.5
quehaceres 2.2.5
quejarse 14.1.5
querer 16.1.2.2
¿quién? 18.1.5
quince días 27.2.2
quincena 27.2.2
quisquilloso 2.2.7

radical changing verbs 12.1.2
radio 2.1.2, 2.2.3, 2.2.4
radioreceptor 2.2.5
raíz 3.1.1
rasurar(se) 14.1.2
rata/o 2.2.6
rato 27.2.2
real 2.2.7
recluta 2.2.3
recomendar 12.1.2
reconocer 12.2.2
récord 3.1.1
recordar 12.1.2
redundant pronouns 17.2.2
reflexive pronouns, variations in
    14.1.8
reflexive verbs 14.1.3, 14.1.6
reflexive verbs, impersonal 14.2.1
reflexive verbs with parts of the body
    14.1.7
reflexives as intensifiers 14.2.3
regaliz 2.2.4
regar 12.1.2
régimen 2.1.2, 3.2.1
región 2.1.3
regresar(se) 14.2.2
reina 2.1.3
reírse 12.2.1
relampaguear 15.1.1
relative pronouns 18.1.4, 18.2.2
remordimientos 3.2.2
reo 2.2.1
reportera 2.2.1
resolver 12.1.2
respondón 21.1.1
retrato robot 2.2.5
retratos robot 3.2.1
rivers 2.1.2

rogar 12.2.2
rompecabezas 2.2.5
rosa 21.2.1
rubí 3.1.1
rules for verbs 4.2.1
rules for written accents 1.2.4

saber 12.2.1, 15.2.3
sal 2.2.4
salida 2.2.7
salir de 2.2.7
salir(se) 14.2.3
salvo 23.1.16
sangre 2.2.4
santo 21.1.1
sarampión 2.1.3
sartén 2.2.4
se 17.2.1
seas 2.1.2
seasons 27.1.4
secador(a) 2.2.4
sectores clave 3.2.1
sede 2.2.4
segar 12.2.2
según 23.1.17
senadora 2.2.1
señal 2.2.4
sensación 2.1.3
sensato 2.2.7
sentir 12.1.2
ser 13
ser + adjective 13.1.2, 13.2.5
ser and *estar*, basic differences 13.1.1,
    13.1.3
ser in passive voice 13.2.4
ser, imperfect tense 7.1.1
ser + preposition 13.1.4
ser used impersonally 15.2.2
ser, various tenses 13.2.1
serie 2.1.3
seta/o 2.2.6
severidad 2.1.3
ships 2.1.2
siempre 25.1.3
sien 2.2.4
simiente 2.2.4
sin 23.1.18
sinalefa 1.2.3
síndrome 2.2.4
sino 26.2.2
sinrazón 2.2.5
síntesis 2.1.3
sobrar 15.2.5
sobre 23.1.19
soccer teams 2.1.5
soler 4.2.1, 7.2.1, 12.1.2, 15.2.4
sólo 25.1.3
soplar fuerte 21.2.2
soprano 2.1.2
Spanish plural = English singular 3.2.2
Spanish singular = English plural 3.2.3
spelling 1.1.1

spelling changes of verbs 12.2.2
spelling traps 1.2.5
stress 1.1.2
su(s) 18.1.1
suave 21.1.1
subir 14.1.3, 14.2.2
subject + verb + object 29.1.1
sucursal 2.2.4
sufrimiento 2.2.7
sumergir 12.2.2
superávit 3.1.1
superior 21.1.1
superlatives 28.1.3
suyo 18.1.2

tabú 3.1.1, 21.2.1
táctica 3.2.3
tampoco 26.2.2
tan . . . como 28.1.1, 28.1.2, 28.1.4
tanto más/menos . . . cuanto que 28.2.3
tarde 25.1.3
te 17.1.2
telephone numbers 27.1.2
temprano 25.1.3
tener 12.1.2
tener calor 15.1.1
tener frío 15.1.1
tener que 15.2.3
tener + noun + *de* + infinitive 4.1.1
tercero 21.1.1
terminal 2.2.3
terremoto 2.2.5
tesis 2.1.3
testigo 2.1.2, 2.2.1
tez 2.2.4
tía/o 2.2.1, 3.1.1
tiempo récord 2.2.5
tigre 2.1.2
timbre 2.2.4
time, division of 27.2.2
time and clock 27.1.5
tinieblas 3.2.2
tomar(se) 14.2.3
tormenta/o 2.2.6
tos 2.2.4
tostador(a) 2.2.4
tostar 12.1.2
towns 2.1.5
trabaja duro 21.2.2
traducir 12.2.2
trama 2.1.3
trama/o 2.2.6
transitive and intransitive verbs, differences between
    14.1.4
transitive verbs 14.1.1
transportes (públicos) 3.2.2
tranvía 2.1.3
tras 23.1.20
trees 2.1.2
tribu 2.2.4
triphthong 1.2.1
tronar 15.1.1

tropa 3.2.3
tú 17.1.1
tuyo/a 18.1.2

u 1.2.6
Ud./Uds. 17.1.1
ulterior 21.1.1
ultimatum 3.1.1
un(a) 2.1.1
único 21.2.2
útil 21.1.1

vaca 2.1.3
various tenses of *ser* and *estar* 13.2.1
varying gender 2.1.5
vehículo todo terreno 2.2.5
vela/o 2.2.6
vencer 12.2.2
vender
    present indicative 4.1.1
    preterit 8.1.1
Venezuela 2.1.2
venir(se) 14.2.3
ventiscar 15.2.1
ver 12.1.1
verb followed by subject 29.1.2, 29.2.3
verbs 4
verbs, imperfect tense 7.1.1
verbs, impersonal 15.1.1
verbs, intransitive 14.1.2
verbs, irregular 12.1.1
verbs, modal auxiliary 15.1.1
verbs, radical changing 12.1.2
verbs, reflexive 14.1.4
verbs, reflexive > different meaning
    14.2.2
verbs, spelling changes 12.2.2
verbs, transitive 14.1.1
verbs with no English equivalent 7.2.1
verdad 2.1.3
¿verdad? 26.1.2
verdadero 2.2.7
vergüenza 2.2.7
verter 12.1.2
viaje 2.1.2
víctima 2.2.4
vigía 2.2.3
violento 2.2.7
violeta 21.2.1
violinista 2.2.1
virgen 3.1.1
virtud 2.1.3
virus 3.1.1
vísperas de, en 3.2.2
vivir
    perfect tense 5.1.1
    present indicative 4.1.1
    preterit 8.1.1
vocal 2.2.3
volar 12.1.2
volcar 12.2.2
volumen 2.1.2

volver 12.1.2
vos 17. 2. 4
vosotras/os 17.1.1
vowels 1.1.2
voz 3.1.1
vuestra/o 18.1.1

watches 2.1.2
weeks 27.1.4
word order 29

word order with reflexive *se* 29.2.6
written accents 1.2.4

y 1.2.6
yema 2.1.3
yemení 3.1.1
yo 17.1.1

zarzal 2.2.4
zona euro 2.2.5

Subjunctive index

a condición de que 16.1.6.1
a fin de que 16.1.6.1
a las pocas horas de que 16.1.6.1
a los pocos días de que 16.1.6.1
a medida que 16.1.6.1
a menos que 16.1.6.1
a no ser que 16.1.6.1
aconsejar 16.1.1.3
agradecer 16.1.1.3
aguardar 16.2.9
alegrarse 16.1.2.1
animar 16.1.1.3
antes de que 16.1.6.1
aun cuando 16.1.6.1
aunque 16.1.6.1

bastar 16.1.1.3, 16.1.4.1
bien que 16.1.6.1

causation 16.1.1
celebrar 16.1.2.1
command 16.1.1.1
como 16.1.6.1
como si 16.1.6.1
comoquiera 16.2.4
con tal que 16.1.6.1
confiar 16.1.2.1
conjunctive expressions 16.1.6.1
conseguir 16.1.1.2
consentir 16.1.1.4
convencer 16.1.1.3
convenir 16.1.4.1
cualquiera 16.2.4
cuando 16.2.9
cuandoquiera 16.2.4

danger 16.1.3.2
dar miedo 16.1.2.1
de manera que 16.1.6.1
de modo que 16.1.6.1
decidir 16.1.1.1
decir 16.1.1.1
decretar 16.1.1.1
dejar 16.1.1.4
denial 16.1.3.1
descartar 16.1.3.1
desde que 16.2.9
desear 16.1.2.2

deseo 16.2.1
desmentir 16.1.3.1
después de que 16.2.9
disponer 16.1.1.1
dondequiera 16.2.4
doubt 16.1.3
duda 16.2.1
dudar 16.1.3.1

emotion 16.1.2
en caso de que 16.1.6.1
en cuanto 16.2.9
encantar 16.1.2.1
es *dudoso / imperativo / importante / increíble /*
    inevitable / inútil / justo / lástima / lógico / mejor /
    natural / necesario / normal / preciso / previsible raro / triste
    16.1.5.1
es posible 16.1.3.2
es probable 16.1.3.2
es una pena 16.1.4.1
esperanza 61.2.1
esperar 16.1.2.2, 16.2.9
está previsto 16.1.5.1
establecer 16.1.1.1
excepto que 16.1.6.1
exigir 16.1.1.1
extrañar 16.1.2.1

feeling 16.1.2.1
figurarse 16.1.2.2

gustar 16.1.2.1

hacer falta 16.1.4.1
hasta que 16.2.9
hindrance 16.1.1.4

imaginarse 16.1.2.2
imagining 16.1.2.2
impedir 16.1.1.4
imperfect subjunctive 16.2.7
impersonal verbs 16.1.4
importar 16.1.4.1
incertidumbre 16.2.1
independientemente de lo que 16.2.3
influence 16.1.1
insistir 16.1.1.1
invitar 16.1.1.3

lograr 16.1.1.2
luego que 16.2.9

mandar 16.1.1.1
más vale 16.1.1.3
mientras que 16.2.9
molestar 16.1.2.1

necesidad 16.2.1
necesitar 16.1.1.1, 16.1.1.2
negar 16.1.3.1
negation 16.1.3.1
no creer 16.1.3.1
no decir 16.3.1
no es cierto/seguro 16.1.3.1
no estar bien 16.1.5.1
no querer decir 16.1.3.1
no ser 16.1.3.1
noun clauses 16.2.1

¡ojalá! 16.1.2.2
oponerse 16.1.1.4
ordenar 16.1.1.1

pedir 16.1.1.2
perfect subjunctive 16.2.6
permission 16.1.1.4
permitir 16.1.1.4
pluperfect subjunctive 16.2.7
por (muy) que 16.2.5
posibilidad 16.2.1
posiblemente 16.1.3.2
possibility 16.1.3.2
preferir 16.1.1.2
presionar 16.1.1.1
prever 16.1.2.2
probability 16.1.3.2

probablemente 16.1.3.2
prohibir 16.1.1.4
prohibition 16.1.1.4
proposal 16.1.1.3
puede ser 16.1.3.2

querer 16.1.2.2
quienquiera 16.2.4
quizá(s) 16.1.3.2

reclamar 16.1.1.1
request 16.1.1.2
risk 16.1.3.2
rogar 16.1.1.2

sentir 16.1.2.1
ser + de + infinitive + que 16.2.2
siempre que 16.1.6.1
sin que 16.1.6.1
sugerir 16.1.1.3
suggestion 16.1.1.3
suplicar 16.1.1.2
supuesto que 16.1.6.1

tal vez 16.1.3.2
temer(se) 16.1.2.1
tener miedo 16.1.2.1

una vez que 16.2.9
urgir 16.1.1.1

velar 16.1.1.1

wishing 16.1.2 2

ya que 16.2.9